"Transpersonal Ecology is a pioneering work that brings together two of the most important disciplines of our time, transpersonal psychology and ecology. Warwick Fox's wide reading, thoughtfulness, and subtle distinctions will give readers much to think about."

—ROGER WALSH, author of
Staying Alive: The Psychology of Human Survival

"A beautifully organized, coherent, and lucid book that will facilitate healing ourselves, our communities, and our relationships with Nature."

—ALAN R. DRENGSON,
author of *Beyond Environmental Crisis*
and editor of *The Trumpeter: Journal of Ecosophy*

"Warwick Fox demonstrates a comprehensive grasp of the fundamental role played by human psychology in our ecological situation."

—MILES A. VICH, editor of
The Journal of Transpersonal Psychology

"Toward a Transpersonal Ecology ought to be read not only by supporters of the deep ecology movement but also by its critics. It is destined to be a classic in the field."

—EUGENE C. HARGROVE,
editor of *Environmental Ethics*

"As a leading deep ecology scholar, Warwick Fox provides the most comprehensive and detailed examination of the development of philosophical deep ecology yet in print."

—GEORGE SESSIONS,
co-author of *Deep Ecology*

Warwick Fox

TOWARD A TRANSPERSONAL ECOLOGY

Developing New Foundations for Environmentalism

SHAMBHALA
BOSTON & LONDON
1990

SHAMBHALA PUBLICATIONS, INC.
Horticultural Hall
300 Massachusetts Avenue
Boston, Massachusetts 02115
SHAMBHALA PUBLICATIONS, INC.
Random Century House
20 Vauxhall Bridge Road
London SW1V 2SA

9 8 7 6 5 4 3 2 1

First Edition
Printed in the United States of America on acid-free paper
Distributed in the United States by Random House, Inc.
in Canada by Random House of Canada Ltd., and in the United Kingdom by Random Century Group.

Library of Congress Cataloging-in-Publication Data
Fox, Warwick.
    Toward a transpersonal ecology/Warwick Fox.—1st ed.
        p.   cm.
    Originally presented as the author's thesis (Murdoch University).
    Includes bibliographical references.
    ISBN 0-87773-533-6 (alk. paper)
    1. Human ecology—Philosophy.   2. Man—Influence on nature.
    I. Title
    GF21.F68   1990   89-43315
304.2—dc20   CIP

*To my colleagues, for their inspiration.
Long live Earth and the myriad entities
with which we coexist!*

Contents

Preface

IN THIS BOOK I advance an argument concerning the nature of
the deep ecology approach to ecophilosophy. In order to advance
this argument in as thorough a manner as possible, I present it
within the context of a comprehensive overview of the writings
on deep ecology. This means that I provide an almost exhaustive
guide to the significant primary and secondary literature that has
been published on deep ecology from its inception in the early
1970s until the end of the 1980s. Further, where it is appropriate
to my argument, I also draw upon a considerable number of
unpublished manuscripts that have been circulated informally
within the ecophilosophy community. The upshot of this com-
prehensiveness, however, is that I cite what some readers may
experience as a somewhat daunting number of references—
particularly in the first few chapters. It goes without saying, of
course, that those readers who are not interested in these sources
are free to skip over them. However, those who wish to follow
up any aspect of deep ecology—and many aspects of ecophilosophy generally—in greater detail should find this close to exhaustive listing invaluable. Moreover, given the rate at which the
volume of literature on deep ecology is growing, it seems unlikely
that there will in future be available such a nearly exhaustive
listing of the literature—at least not one short of a book-length
annotated bibliography.

I hope that this book will serve to interest the reader not only
in ecophilosophical issues in general but also in the kinds of
lifestyles and political actions that flow from the adoption of an
ecocentric orientation toward the world. Transpersonal ecology
represents the particular approach to a more ecocentric orientation toward the world that has most inspired me. I would like to
invite you to see if it also inspires you.

Acknowledgments

I DO NOT SEE how anyone can write about ideas and not develop at least some degree of ecological consciousness. Such writing inevitably leads one to realize just how much one's "own" ideas are a complex interactive function of the ideas that one has absorbed from others—others whose "own" ideas are, in turn, a complex interactive function of the ideas that *they* have absorbed, and so on. This book is therefore dedicated to my colleagues, with the greatest of appreciation and respect.

Although there are many people who have contributed to the ecology of ideas in which I find myself at home, I hope I will be forgiven for singling out two people for special mention: Patsy Hallen and Robyn Eckersley.

When I first approached Dr. Patsy Hallen, back in late 1982, about the possibility of writing a Ph.D. dissertation under her supervision on the deep ecology approach to ecophilosophy, she understood exactly what I wanted to do and encouraged me to do it. Since then she has offered nothing but insightful and careful criticism of my work, as well as encouragement, encouragement, and more encouragement. I cannot believe my good fortune! It continues to be a source of great joy to know Patsy as a close friend and colleague.

Although a number of people have offered general comments on the entire manuscript or detailed comments on aspects of it, Robyn Eckersley is the only person besides Patsy Hallen to have offered detailed comments on the entire manuscript. I am profoundly grateful to Robyn for the many improvements that have resulted from her comments. I am also deeply grateful to Robyn for our many wonderful discussions throughout the course of writing this book and for her help in a thousand and one other ways, which made the writing process much easier than it would otherwise have been.

This book has also benefited immensely from my conversations and correspondence with the following people: Charles Birch, J. Baird Callicott, Bill Devall, Alan Drengson, Neil Evernden, Arne Naess, John Seed, George Sessions, and Michael Zimmerman.

Conversations and correspondence with the following people have also contributed to the development of the ideas advanced herein: Robin Attfield, John Cobb, Anne and Paul Ehrlich, Joseph Grange, William Grey, David Griffin, Peter Hay, J. Donald Hughes, Hwa Yol Jung, Dolores LaChapelle, John Livingston, John Martin, Freya Mathews, Andrew McLaughlin, Jeff McMahan, Arthur Peacocke, Jonathon Porritt, (the late) Peter Reed, David Rothenberg, David Seamon, Rupert Sheldrake, Richard Sylvan, and Len Webb.

I am also grateful to many of the people whose names I have noted for providing me with papers and/or books that have been of direct relevance to this work. Many of these materials would have been difficult or, in some cases, impossible to obtain by other means.

I also want to express my appreciation to three institutions, and their relevant members, for supporting my research in various ways. First, my thanks to Murdoch University, Western Australia, for financial support by way of a Murdoch University Research Studentship over the period 1984–87. Second, my thanks to Cambridge University, England, for use of the University Library, the History and Philosophy of Science Library, and the Philosophy Library during the first eight months of 1984. And finally, my thanks to my colleagues at the Centre for Environmental Studies of the University of Tasmania's Department of Geography and Environmental Studies—in particular, Peter Hay, (the late) Dick Jones, John Todd, Jane Parker, and David Sommerville—for their ideological, administrative, library, and technical support, all of which contributed to providing me with an excellent working environment since the beginning of 1986.

The process of transforming what began as a Ph.D. dissertation into the book you are now reading was supported by an Australian government-funded National Research Fellowship, for which I am truly thankful.

Earlier versions of a few paragraphs scattered throughout this book appeared in papers of mine published in *Environmental Ethics* and *The Trumpeter*. I am grateful to the editors of these journals for their willingness to allow me to draw on these papers.

Finally, my thanks to Jeremy Hayward and the other good people at Shambhala Publications, with whom it has been an unalloyed pleasure to work.

PART ONE

CONTEXT: ENVIRONMENTALISM, ECOPHILOSOPHY, AND ANTHROPOCENTRISM

It is very necessary these days to apologize for being concerned with philosophy in any form whatever. . . . In my opinion, the greatest scandal of philosophy is that, while all around us the world of nature perishes—and not the world of nature alone— philosophers continue to talk, sometimes cleverly and sometimes not, about the question of whether this world exists.

—Karl R. Popper

1

Moving Away from Human-Centeredness: From *Silent Spring* to Deep Ecology

THE EMERGENCE OF THE ENVIRONMENTAL MOVEMENT AND ECOPHILOSOPHY

IN TODAY'S WORLD, environmental problems have become part of everyday existence. Pick up almost any newspaper or general scientific magazine and you will be confronted by such environmental issues as terrestrial pollution; the pollution of freshwater and marine environments; atmospheric pollution (ranging from local effects to such global concerns as acid rain, the greenhouse effect, and the depletion of the ozone layer); the unintended consequences of the widespread use of biocides (ranging from damage to human health to the emergence of biocide-resistant varieties of pests); the long-term containment of highly toxic chemical and nuclear wastes; the hazards associated with nuclear testing and nuclear power generation; the immediate, mid-term, and long-term devastation that would be caused by nuclear war and the nuclear winter that would follow such a war; the hazards associated with releasing genetically engineered organisms into the environment; the degradation and depletion of fisheries, forests, croplands, and grazing lands and the related issues of topsoil erosion, desertification, and urban expansion or citification; the destruction of wilderness; the destruction of nonhuman habitat (whether wilderness or not); the extinction or threatened extinction of particular plant and animal species and, more generally, the astonishing rate of these extinctions; the cruelties inflicted upon nonhuman animals in the course of factory farming and scientific study; the degradation and extinction of aboriginal human cultures; and, finally, the plethora of problems associated with exponential human population growth.[1]

Increasing awareness of these worldwide problems has given rise to a variety of popularly based responses that are collectively referred to as the environmental movement. This movement has increasingly become a significant minority force in contemporary social and political life at whatever level one wishes to consider— local, national, or international. The birth of the environmental movement as a vigorous, temporally continuous, geographically widespread, and increasingly well-organized social and political phenomenon is typically dated to the virtual explosion of interest that attended the 1962 publication of Rachel Carson's *Silent Spring*.[2] Carson indicted modern humanity for its headlong and unthinking rush down the technological "quick fix" path of employing synthetic chemicals to control insects. She referred to these pesticides, themselves initially a by-product of Second World War research into chemical warfare, as "elixirs of death," and she warned that they invited the prospect of a dying world, a world in which springtime might no longer bring forth new life, only a chilling silence. Carson's forceful statement had an enormous impact at the time: her book generated both widespread concern and fierce controversy, remained on the *New York Times* best-seller list for thirty-one weeks, sold half a million copies in hardcover before being brought out in paperback, aroused attempts at the character assassination of Carson as well as the intimidation of her publishing company, and went on to win a string of awards.[3] Given the way in which *Silent Spring* served to raise and galvanize public concern over environmental issues, and given the continuing and likely future importance of these issues to society at large, it can be seen why Robert B. Downs included Carson's book, along with the Bible and works by such figures as Plato, Aristotle, Copernicus, Newton, Darwin, Marx, and Freud, as the most recent of the twenty-seven entries in his *Books That Changed the World*.[4]

Although *Silent Spring* was primarily concerned with the biological damage we were doing to the world and, particularly, to ourselves, it was clear that, at another level, Carson's book was also an indictment of our arrogant conception of our place in the larger scheme of things. For Carson, our ecological thoughtlessness was matched only by our lack of philosophical maturity. In the last paragraph of her book, Carson concluded that "the 'control of nature' is a phrase conceived in arrogance, born of the Neanderthal age of biology and philosophy, when it was supposed that nature exists for the convenience of man." The effect of Carson's critique was to suggest to many people that what was needed first and foremost in regard to ecological problems was not bigger and better technical solutions but rather a thorough rethinking of our most fundamental attitudes concerning our place in the larger scheme of things.

This view was powerfully reinforced just a few years later in a now-famous paper by the medieval historian Lynn White, Jr., presented to a meeting of the American Association for the Advancement of Science held in December 1966. This paper was published the following March in *Science* under the title "The Historical Roots of Our Ecologic Crisis" and has since been reprinted in numerous places.[5]

White struck an extremely sensitive nerve in the body of Western culture in arguing that "especially in its Western form, Christianity is the most anthropocentric [i.e., human-centered] religion the world has seen" and that, accordingly, "Christianity bears a huge burden of guilt" for the ecological problems that have attended the "Occidental, voluntarist realization of the Christian dogma of man's transcendence of, and rightful mastery over, nature." White was implying a distinction between the Christian tradition that developed in the Latin West and that which developed in the Greek East. As White explained in his paper, Western Christianity developed in the direction of seeking to "understand God's mind by discovering how his creation operates," whereas Eastern Christianity continued to conceive of nature "primarily as a symbolic system through which God speaks to men: the ant is a sermon to sluggards, rising flames are the symbol of the soul's aspiration."[6] The Latin West, in other words, adopted an active, voluntarist approach to nature whereas the Greek East maintained a contemplative-intellectualist approach.

In concluding his analysis, White urged that the solution to our ecological problems lay not in the abandonment of religion per se, but rather in the abandonment of anthropocentrism:

What we do about ecology depends on our ideas of the man-nature relationship. More science and more technology are not going to get us out of the present ecologic crisis until we find a new religion, or rethink our old one. . . . We shall continue to have a worsening ecologic crisis until we reject the Christian axiom that nature has no reason for existence save to serve man. . . . Since the roots of our trouble are so largely religious, the remedy must also be essentially religious, whether we call it that or not. We must rethink and refeel our destiny.[7]

In White's view, the remedy for our ecological problems lay in the direction of the alternative Christian view of the human-nonhuman relationship provided by St. Francis of Assisi: "St. Francis proposed what he thought was an alternative Christian view of nature and man's relation to it: He tried to substitute the idea of the equality of all creatures, including man, for the idea of man's limitless rule of creation." St. Francis's attempt "to depose man from his monarchy over creation and set up a democracy of all God's creatures" makes him, for White, "the greatest spiritual revolutionary in Western history." Accordingly, White concluded his analysis by proposing St. Francis as "a patron saint for ecologists."[8]

For his heretical indictment of Western Christianity for its anthropocentic nature, White's paper has probably generated more controversy than any other paper—as distinct from book—in the history of modern environmental thought. Moreover, this straightforward but erudite paper is *still* compulsory reading for anyone interested in ecophilosophy or the development of science and technology. And for those who have previously read White's paper, rereading it remains a rewarding experience.

White's critics have generally attempted to show that the Bible is best interpreted as advocating an attitude of benign stewardship on the part of humans toward the nonhuman world. However, White does not doubt that the resources exist within the Christian tradition for a less anthropocentric approach to the nonhuman world (indeed, as we have just seen, he proposes St. Francis as "a patron saint for ecologists"). Rather, as a historian, White is more concerned with how the Bible *has* been interpreted. And even here, he accepts that these interpretations have not always been employed in such a way as to encourage and legitimate the technological domination of the nonhuman world; this is the point of his contrast between the voluntarist Latin West and the contemplative-intellectualist Greek East.

White reiterated his rejection of anthropocentrism a few years later in a strong and insightful (but far less well-known) defense of his controversial "Historical Roots" paper:

> I have not discovered anyone who publicly advocates pollution. Everybody says that he is against it. Yet the crisis deepens because all specific measures to remedy it are either undercut by "legitimate" interest groups, or demand kinds of regional cooperation for which our political system does not provide. We deserve our increasing pollution because, according to our structure of values, so many other things have priority over achieving a viable ecology. [The problem with] our structure of values [is that] a man-nature dualism is deep-rooted in us. . . . Until it is eradicated not only from our minds but also from our emotions, we shall doubtless be unable to make fundamental changes in our attitudes and actions affecting ecology.[9]

This rejection of the assumption of human self-importance in the larger scheme of things is, of course, hardly original with Carson and White. It can be traced right back through the rich, albeit minority, philosophical and religious tradition that informs the modern environmental movement. One thinks, for example, of the pre-Socratics, of St. Francis, Spinoza, Thoreau, John Muir, Santayana, Robinson Jeffers, Aldo Leopold, and the later Heidegger.[10] What is of interest here, however, is the fact that although *Silent Spring* effectively laid down a nonanthropocentric challenge to philosophers at what is typically considered the birth of the modern environmental movement, it can be generally said that philosophers did not seriously begin to address the question of our anthropocentric attitudes toward the nonhuman world until the early 1970s. The few papers and books that addressed this issue in anything more than a passing fashion prior to the mid-1970s are thus now considered as "early" work in this area of inquiry—an area that has since come to be referred to as *ecophilosophy, environmental philosophy,* or *environmental ethics.*

A note on terminology is warranted at this point. I will employ the term *ecophilosophy* in preference to *environmental philosophy* or *environmental ethics* herein for two reasons. First, the term *environment* refers to the *external* conditions or surroundings of organisms, whereas *ecology* refers to the *relationships* between organisms and their external conditions or surroundings, that is, their environment. The prefix *eco-* (for "ecology") is therefore more appropriate for my purposes than the adjective *environmental* because the kind of approach that I will be developing herein is one that attempts to break down the rigid distinctions that we tend to draw between ourselves and our environment. Instead of seeking to maintain these distinctions, this approach attempts to foster a greater awareness of the intimate and manifold relationships that exist between what we conventionally designate as *self* and what we conventionally designate as *environment.* It attempts, in other words, to foster the development of an *ecological* rather than *environmental* consciousness. Second, my approach (in common with other ecophilosophical approaches) is one that includes considerations that would generally be conceived of as belonging not only to the sphere of ethics but also to the spheres of metaphysics, epistemology, and social and political philosophy. *Philosophy* is therefore a better covering term than *ethics.* Thus, my strong preference for the term *ecophilosophy.*

Ecophilosophical thought proceeded to develop quite vigorously during the mid- to late 1970s and can be considered as having attained the status of an institutionalized force in contemporary philosophy—to have come of age, we could say—in 1979, with the publication of the consistently interesting and high-quality journal *Environmental Ethics.* This was the first professional, academic journal exclusively devoted to the *philosophical* aspects of environmental problems broadly conceived.[11]

Many in the wider environmental movement might well consider that ecophilosophy's coming of age was in fact too long in coming. After all, it followed some seven years after the first major international conference on environmental problems (the "United Nations Conference on the Human Environment," Stockholm, May–June 1972); some seven years also after the 1972 publication of such landmarks in environmental awareness as *The Limits to Growth* (a report commissioned by the Club of Rome) and *A Blueprint for Survival* (written by the editors of *The Ecologist*); and some seventeen years after the 1962 publication of Rachel Carson's *Silent Spring*.[12] But this late development itself simply further illustrates the human-centeredness that Carson and White identified as pervading our culture—as does the fact that ecophilosophy is still very much a marginal rather than a mainstream pursuit in contemporary academic philosophy. For the truth is that the assumption of human self-importance in the larger scheme of things has, to all intents and purposes, been the single deepest and most persistent assumption of (at least) all the *dominant* Western philosophical, social, and political traditions since the time of the classical Greeks.

Before moving on to illustrate this last claim, it is important to note two significant qualifications that are built into it. First, I say "to all intents and purposes" because where these dominant traditions have supposedly been primarily theocentric rather than anthropocentric, it has of course still been humans who have, by divine decree, had "dominion . . . over all the earth [which they are enjoined to] fill and subdue . . . and over every living thing that moves upon the earth" (Gen. 1:26, 28). Moveover, from a nonanthropocentric perspective, personalistic kinds of theocentrism, such as the dominant form of Christianity where humans are made in the image of a god to whom they have a privileged personal relationship, are in any case simply anthropocentric *projections* upon the cosmos. The second qualification is in the phrase "since the time of the *classical* Greeks" (i.e., the Sophists, Socrates, Plato, and Aristotle) as distinct from the *early* Greeks, who initiated Western philosophy (i.e., the early and later Ionians, the Pythagoreans, the Eleatics, and the Atomists—often collectively referred to as the pre-Socratics), because, as Bertrand Russell has pointed out, "What is amiss, even in the best philosophy after Democritus [i.e., after the pre-Socratics], is an undue emphasis on man as compared with the universe."[13]

Moving on to illustrate the assumption of human self-importance in the larger scheme of things, we can see that this assumption shows through, for example, in those prescientific views that saw humans as dwelling at the center of the universe, as made in the image of God, and as occupying a position well above the "beasts" and just a little lower than the angels on the Great Chain of Being. And while the development of modern science, especially the Copernican and Darwinian revolutions, served to sweep these views aside—or at least those aspects that were open to empirical refutation—it did no such thing to the human-centered assumptions that underlay these views. Francis Bacon, for example, saw science as "enlarging the bounds of Human Empire"; Descartes likewise saw it as rendering us the "masters and possessors of nature."[14] Approximately three and a half centuries later, Neil Armstrong's moon walk—the culmination of a massive, politically directed, scientific and technological development effort—epitomized both the literal acting out of this vision of "enlarging the bounds of Human Empire" and the literal expression of its anthropocentric spirit: Armstrong's moon walk was, in his own words at the time, a "small step" for him, but a "giant leap for Mankind." Back here on earth, we find that even those philosophical, social, and political movements of modern times most concerned with exposing discriminatory assumptions have typically confined their interests to the human realm, that is, to issues to do with imperialism, race, socioeconomic class, and gender.

When attention is finally turned to the exploitation by humans of the nonhuman world, our arguments for the conservation and preservation of the nonhuman world continue to betray anthropocentric assumptions. We argue that the nonhuman world should be conserved or preserved because of its use value to humans (e.g., its scientific, recreational, or aesthetic value) rather than for its own sake or for its use value to *nonhuman* beings. It cannot be emphasized enough that the vast majority of environmental discussion—whether in the context of public meetings, newspapers, popular magazines, reports by international conservation organizations, reports by government instrumentalities, or even reports by environmental groups—is couched within these anthropocentric terms of reference. Thus, even many of those who deal most directly with environmental issues continue to perpetuate, however unwittingly, the arrogant assumption that we humans are central to the cosmic drama; that, essentially, the world is made for us. John Seed, a prominent *non*anthropocentric ecological activist, sums up the situation quite simply when he writes, "The idea that humans are the crown of creation, the source of all value, the measure of all things, is deeply embedded in our culture and consciousness."[15]

For the large majority of philosophers, however, anthropocentrism is simply not an issue. It is "where they live," and they have no desire to demolish such a secure and comfortable home. Descartes, the acknowledged father of modern philosophy, provides what can be seen as an archetypical image here: in the first of his six *Meditations* he describes how he has cut himself off from the world—"Today I have expressly rid my mind of all worries and arranged for myself a clear stretch of free time. I am here quite alone . . . sitting by the fire, wearing a winter dressing-gown"—in preparation for a sweeping review of his beliefs, in which he manages to doubt the existence of everything but his own existence.[16] William Barrett accurately sums up the legacy of this tradition when he writes, "The idea of nature has played a small part in contemporary philosophy. Bergson once remarked that most philosophers seem to philosophize as if they were sealed in the privacy of their study and did not live on a planet surrounded by the vast organic world of animals, plants, insects, and protozoa, *with whom their own life is linked in a single history*" (emphasis added).[17] Of course, ecophilosophers also need clear stretches of uninterrupted time to think their views through and set them down, but the point of the image provided by Descartes is, as Barrett's quotation suggests, that the social, psychological, and ecological circumstances of his thinking—a solitary, thinking being cut off from the world—so perfectly match the content of his thinking, which gives priority to the reality of his own existence qua a thinking being at the expense of everything else.

The dominance of this anthropocentric philosophical tradition is such that those philosophers who find its atmosphere too stifling are likely to find themselves professionally locked out in various ways if they should venture too far afield. A public but by no means isolated example of this possibility is provided by the editor of *Environmental Ethics,* Eugene Hargrove. In a Fall 1987 editorial, Hargrove explained to his journal's readers why he was refused tenure in his university's philosophy department and, consequently, why the question of the continued publication of *Environmental Ethics,* the journal he had founded, had reached a crisis point:

> This state of affairs [i.e., refusal of tenure] was not entirely unexpected. The journal and I came to the university [of Georgia] expecting to participate in a planned master's program in philosophy and ecology, which was turned down by the philosophy faculty three weeks before I arrived on campus. Soon thereafter some members of the department unofficially indicated to me that the negative vote on the master's program implicitly defined environmental ethics outside of philosophy, and that, as a result, I needed to discontinue or greatly reduce my emphasis on research work in environmental ethics if I wanted to have any chance at getting tenure—work in an area that was no longer "real" philosophy could not count as quality professional work. From then on I frequently received similar advice both formally and informally. My last annual evaluation before the tenure vote, given over the objections of the chairman, reported the majority view that *my work as the editor of this journal did not count as significant scholarly and professional activity* and that *none* of my published research work was of sufficient quality to meet the standards of the department (first emphasis added).[18]

Although everybody working in the area of ecophilosophy is familiar with this sort of thing it is particularly depressing when it occurs to the editor of the central journal in one's field. For all this, however, a growing number of philosophers have, as it were, been leaving the respectable, anthropocentric home they were brought up in and turning feral. In challenging the anthropocentric assumptions that have dominated our culture, these ecophilosophers have been vigorously addressing problems that, by and large, are still struggling for a hearing in such ecologically relevant disciplines as geography, sociology, political theory, and economics. In their own way, ecophilosophers—especially those who have gone "far out"—are now howling in the moonlight for others (including their more domesticated professional colleagues) to join them. The question now is, how many will respond to this call of the wild? It is interesting to note here that the *Collins English Dictionary* defines *the wild* as referring not only to wilderness but also to "a free natural state of living."

A CLOSER LOOK AT THE ISSUE OF ANTHROPOCENTRISM

But why *should* anyone respond to this philosophical call of the wild? In other words, what's wrong with being anthropocentric? This is a massive question, and the answers to it can be elaborated upon to fill whatever space one wishes to devote to it—indeed, virtually every paper and book that ecophilosophers have written either implicitly or explicitly develops some kind of answer to this question. However, since my primary concern herein is with the positive exposition and development of a particular approach to ecophilosophy rather than with the critique of anthropocentrism per se, I intend to summarize the general kinds of arguments that can be employed against anthropocentrism quite briefly. Reflection upon the significance of these arguments and upon the extent to which they could be elaborated should be enough to show, however, that anthropocentrism represents not only a deluded but also a dangerous orientation toward the world.

There is a prima facie reason why we should at least be on our guard with respect to anthropocentric assumptions. This is because anthropocentric assumptions—assumptions that magnify our sense of self-importance in the larger scheme of things—are obviously *self-serving* assumptions. And everybody knows the temptation that is involved in accepting self-serving views of any kind; we are generally all too prepared to accept such views on the basis of less than rigorous scrutiny. We are, for example, much less likely to question a favorable assessment of ourselves than an unfavorable assessment. When was the last time any of us tried to convince our teacher or professor that they had given us too *high* a mark for an assignment; or our employer that they were paying us too *much* relative to the skills of those around us? Favorable assessments are "obviously" correct assessments; poor assessments are "obviously" suspect assessments. Of course, the fact that a view happens to be self-serving does not, in itself, represent a decisive argument against the view. A favorable assessment *can* also be a correct assessment: someone may not only believe that they are just about the fastest sprinter on earth; they may also *be* just about the fastest sprinter on earth. All that is being highlighted here is the point that we need to subject self-serving views to considerable critical scrutiny if we are interested in establishing the most genuine truths possible, rather than simply settling for "truths" of convenience.

In addition to this prima facie reason for at least being on our guard with respect to anthropocentric assumptions, there are at least five general kinds of arguments *against* anthropocentrism. First, in those instances where we have been able to check our anthropocentric assumptions against reality, we have discovered again and again that these views—views that have been of the first importance in determining our thinking about our place in the larger scheme of things—have been empirically incorrect and, hence, disastrous for the development of our theoretical understanding of the world. We do not live at the center of the universe and we are not biologically unrelated to other creatures. And yet, although "everybody knows" these truths, it is still worth reminding ourselves of the perhaps subtler points that we are not even psychologically, socially, or culturally different *in kind* from all other animals and that we are not the "end point" of evolution.

In regard to the question of human uniqueness, Peter Farb neatly summarizes the situation at the beginning of his book *Humankind*: "Scientists now know that the chasm separating humans from animals is not so wide as it once appeared. Some animal species have evolved a rich communication system, while others make and use tools, solve difficult problems, educate their young, live in complex social organizations, and apparently possess an aesthetic sense. . . . So any definition of human uniqueness obviously would have to be based on differences in degree."[19] And before we get carried away with emphasizing the "differences in degree" between humans and other animals (differences that Farb is, of course, entirely willing to emphasize), we need to remember that such differences *cut both ways* (a point that Farb does not emphasize): just as there are lots of things that humans have more of or do much better than many other animals, so the reverse is also true. What we need to bear in mind, then, is that, as John Rodman points out, the attempt to assimilate other animals to the status of inferior *humans* makes as little sense as "regarding women as defective men who lack penises, or humans as defective sea mammals who lack sonar capability and have to be rescued by dolphins." As Rodman argues, assimilations of this kind succeed only in degrading other beings by failing "to respect them for having their own existence, their own character and potentialities, their own forms of excellence, their own integrity, their own grandeur."[20]

As for the view that humans effectively represent the end point of evolution, every evolutionary theorist who is taken seriously in the scientific community rejects such a claim outright: evolution is a luxuriously branching bush, not a linear scale of increasing developmental perfection. Recently, however, some speculations in physics that go under the name of the *anthropic cosmological principle* have, for some people, rekindled the "end-point" line of thinking. All I will say about such speculations here is that it is a safe bet that any strong, genuinely anthropocentric version of the anthropic cosmological principle will go the same way as the pre-Copernican, pre-Darwinian, pre-comparative psychology, and pre-ethological anthropocentric assumptions to which I have

already alluded. John Earman's critical examination of the strong
version of the anthropic principle provides a guide to the smart
money: "And insofar as anthropic principles are directed at
promoting Man or Consciousness to a starring role in the
functioning of the universe, they fail; for either the promotion
turns out to be an empty tease or else it rests on woolly and ill-
founded speculations."[21]

The second general kind of argument against anthropocentrism is that our anthropocentric attitudes have proved disastrous
in practice. This line of argument has already constituted an
important theme of the first part of this chapter. It was the *point*
of the critiques authored by Rachel Carson and Lynn White, Jr.,
and it is a point now routinely made by other thinkers who
ponder the roots of our human-caused ecological ills.

The third general kind of argument against anthropocentrism
is that anthropocentrism is not even a logically consistent position: it is not possible to specify any reasonably clearly discernible, morally relevant characteristic that includes all humans but
excludes all nonhumans. Popular examples of reasonably clearly
discernible characteristics that are often held to be morally
relevant and to refer only to humans include such traits as
rationality, self-awareness, free will, the capacity for symbolic
communication, and the capacity to enter into arrangements
involving reciprocal duties and obligations. However, accepting
any of these characteristics as a criterion of moral considerability
means that one excludes not only all nonhumans from the domain
of moral considerability (or let us at least say this for the sake of
the argument) but also some or all of the following classes of
humans: members of "primitive" cultures, imbeciles, infants,
the senile, human "vegetables," and people who are temporarily
or irreversibly comatose. Conversely, any reasonably clearly discernible, morally relevant characteristic that includes *all* humans
(e.g., being alive) will include many nonhumans as well.

It is possible, of course, to specify vague and entirely contentious characteristics that are held to be morally relevant and to
refer only to humans; for example, the claim that all humans and
no nonhumans have a special relationship to God or the claim

that all humans and no nonhumans possess a soul. However, claims of this kind work against themselves as much as they work for themselves since it can just as easily be charged that they represent nothing more than self-serving anthropocentric *projections* upon the cosmos. The upshot is that vague and entirely contentious claims of this kind represent impotent contributions to rational debate.

The fourth general kind of argument against anthropocentrism comes from the increasing number of moral philosophers who have been coming to the conclusion that anthropocentric attitudes are morally objectionable. It is important to realize that this kind of objection is distinct from the previous charge of logical inconsistency. This is because the moral philosophers to whom I am referring are effectively arguing that, even if it *were* possible to specify some kind of clearly discernible, morally relevant characteristic that included all humans but excluded all nonhumans, the kinds of criteria that *ought* to be accepted as deeming an entity worthy of moral consideration are such as to include not only humans but many other kinds of entities as well.

I will not attempt at this point to summarize the main kinds of arguments that have been developed for a nonanthropocentric ethics. To do justice to these revolutionary arguments requires considerably greater exposition than is appropriate in the context of this brief summary of the general kinds of arguments against anthropocentrism. However, these arguments are outlined in some detail and critically examined in chapter 6.

Finally, a number of apparently highly perceptive people have claimed, independently of any obvious reference to the foregoing kinds of arguments, that anthropocentrism simply does not accord with a genuinely open approach to experience. (A much greater number of other apparently highly perceptive people have claimed that anthropocentrism does accord with their experience of the world, of course, but the extent to which these experientially based claims really are perceptive is called into question by the other four general kinds of arguments against anthropocentrism that I have cited here.) It is possible to offer many eloquent examples of the point that a genuine openness to the world leads one away from anthropocentrism rather than toward it. The following three brief expressions of this point should, however, be sufficient to convey something of the flavor of this general kind of argument against anthropocentrism. First, in an address delivered at the University of California in 1911, the American-European philosopher George Santayana claimed that the philosophical systems handed down since the time of Socrates could be characterized as "egotistical . . . anthropocentric, and inspired by the conceited notion that man, or human reason, or the human distinction between good and evil, is the center and the pivot of the universe." But, Santayana told his audience, things would have been very different "if the philosophers had lived among your mountains, . . . [for] the mountain and the woods . . . suspend your forced sense of your own importance not merely as individuals [i.e., your egotism], but even as men [i.e., your anthropocentrism]."[22] Another example of this kind of argument is provided by the American existentialist-oriented philosopher William Barrett, who concludes in his significant book *The Illusion of Technique* that the "first lesson [of trees and rocks] is to draw us outside the narrow and presumptuous horizons of our humanism."[23] Finally, the Taoist- and Zen-inspired writer Alan Watts argues in *Nature, Man, and Woman* that a genuine openness to nonhuman nature leads us to see "all the weirdly abstract and pompous pursuits of men . . . [as] natural marvels of the same order as the immense beaks of the toucans and hornbills, the fabulous tails of the birds of paradise, the towering necks of the giraffes, and the vividly polychromed posteriors of the baboons. Seen thus, neither as something to be condemned nor in its accustomed aspect of serious worth, the self-importance of man dissolves in laughter."[24]

This brief summary of the general kinds of arguments against anthropocentrism should be enough to show that anthropocentrism can be trenchantly criticized on the grounds that it is empirically bankrupt and theoretically disastrous, practically disastrous, logically inconsistent, morally objectionable, and incongruent with a genuinely open approach to experience. That doesn't leave much to recommend it!

To place the above arguments in the general context of this book, it will be seen that the arguments in chapter 6 draw mainly upon the logical and, especially, moral arguments against anthropocentrism, while the arguments in chapters 7 and 8 draw mainly upon the scientific (or cosmological) and experiential (or psychological) arguments against anthropocentrism. The argument that anthropocentrism is practically disastrous has been an important theme in the first part of this chapter.

The fact that anthropocentric assumptions are convenient, self-serving assumptions that have become, to repeat John Seed's phrase, "deeply embedded in our culture and consciousness," means that criticisms of anthropocentrism, in any form, naturally meet with various kinds of reactions. These reactions range from considered counter-criticisms to outright attacks which can easily justify the label hysterical. The most obvious ill-considered, knee-jerk sort of reaction to such criticisms is the charge of misanthropy. The extent to which people in general are ready to equate being opposed to human-centeredness with being opposed to humans per se is itself a function of the dominance of the anthropocentric frame of reference in our society. Just as those who criticize capitalism, for example, are liable to be labeled as communists and, by implication, the enemy, when in reality they may be concerned with such commendable aspirations as a more equitable distribution of wealth in society, so too those who criticize anthropocentrism are liable to be labeled *mis*anthropists when, in reality, they may be (and, in the context of environmentalism, generally are) concerned with advancing a more impartial, ecosphere-centered (or *ecocentric*) view of the world and of advocating behaviors appropriate to such a view. In failing to notice the fact that being opposed to human-*centeredness* is logically distinct from being opposed to humans per se (or, in other words, that being opposed to anthropo*centrism* is logically distinct from being *mis*anthropic), and in equating the former with the latter, these critics commit what I refer to as *the fallacy of misplaced misanthropy*.[25] Criticizing nonanthropocentrists on the basis of such fallacious reasoning involves not just a crucial misreading of their negative or critical task (i.e., opposing anthropo*centrism*) but also the oversight of two other considerations that simply contradict such a misreading. First is the positive or constructive task urged by ecocentrically oriented nonanthropocentrists of encouraging an egalitarian attitude on the part of humans toward all entities in the ecosphere—*including* humans. And second is the fact that ecocentrically oriented nonanthropocentrists are among the first to highlight and draw inspiration from the fact that some humans have not been human-centered, both within the Western tradition and outside it. Far from being misanthropic, ecocentrically oriented nonanthropo-centrists celebrate the existence of these human beings.

There is also a more considered and subtle kind of objection that is regularly directed at the charge of anthropocentrism. This is the objection that it is in any case impossible to escape anthropocentrism since all our views are, necessarily, human views. However, critics who put forth this argument fail to distinguish between the weak, trivial, tautological sense of anthropocentrism and the strong, informative, substantive sense of the term. Such a criticism is weak in that it does not allow us to make any distinctions between statements (i.e., it suggests that all human statements are *equally* human statements); trivial in that it simply states the obvious; and tautological in that it is true by definition.

Consider the following. The tautological fact that everything I think and do will be thought and done by a male with white skin does not mean that my thoughts and actions need be sexist or racist in the strong, informative, substantive sense, that is, in the sense of exhibiting unwarranted differential treatment of other people on the basis of their sex or race—which is the sense that really matters. Similarly, the tautological fact that everything I think and do will be thought and done by a human (the weak, trivial, tautological sense of anthropocentrism) does not mean that my thoughts and actions need be anthropocentric in the strong, informative, substantive sense, that is, in the sense of exhibiting unwarranted differential treatment of other beings on the basis of the fact that they are not human—which, again, is the sense that really matters. Note that in both cases "unwarranted differential treatment" can be understood in both an aggressive sense and a passive sense. In the aggressive sense it refers to acts of commission—that is, to overt acts of discrimination—whereas in the passive sense it refers to acts of omission—that is, to actions and decisions that "innocently" overlook certain beings or entities by virtue of the fact these beings or entities simply do not figure in one's awareness.

To imply that the views of nonanthropocentrists are anthropocentric in some informative, significant sense thus repesents a logical sleight of hand that can only be accomplished by conflating the trivial and significant senses of anthropocentrism. It confuses the inescapable fact of our human *identity,* the trivial sense of anthropocentrism, with the entirely avoidable possibility of human chauvinism or human imperialism, the significant sense of anthropocentrism. (The terms *human chauvinism* and *human imperialism* might for convenience be taken as emphasizing, respectively, the passive and aggressive faces of this significant sense of anthropocentrism.) Such a confusion amounts to the same as implying that a male who argues for equal opportunity or affirmative action for women is being "sexist" simply on account of the fact that his view is androcentric (i.e., male-centered) in the weak, trivial, tautological sense that it is a view put forward by a male. If this is granted, then all male views (and all female views for that matter) are equally sexist and the significant function of the word *sexism* is lost.

The conflation of different senses of a term in order to enable a conclusion that would not otherwise be possible commits what philosophers technically refer to as the *fallacy of equivocation.* However, since this practice is so common in ecophilosophical discussion, I have previously proposed that we identify this particular form of the fallacy of equivocation by referring to it as *the anthropocentric fallacy* or, more generally (to cover the same fallacy in regard to issues of race, class, age, and sex, as well as species), *the perspectival fallacy,* since it conflates obvious and inescapable facts about a speaker's perspective with the substance of the speaker's view.[26] Whenever the anthropocentric fallacy occurs in ecophilosophical discussion, or whenever moves are made in that direction, it should be pointed out immediately that while all human views are equally anthropocentric in the trivial sense of the term ("all our views are human views"), they are stunningly different in the significant (chauvinistic, imperialistic) sense of the term, that is, in the extent to which they see humans as all-important or at least as morally superior to other beings and, hence, in the extent to which they advocate or at least legitimate the relentless exploitation of the nonhuman world by humans.

To make my own position perfectly clear, then, I employ the term *anthropocentrism* throughout in what I have here characterized as its significant sense—a sense that, as I have noted, can also usefully be subdivided into a passive sense and an aggressive sense. This is, of course, in accordance with the normal usage of the term by nonanthropocentrists (for example, Lynn White's usage, above) and would have gone without saying were it not for critics who have insisted on conflating the trivial and significant senses of this valuable term.

THE VARIETIES OF ECOLOGY AND ENVIRONMENTALISM

In the course of examining the emergence of the environmental movement and ecophilosophy in the first section of this chapter, something of the extent to which anthropocentrism pervades Western thinking in general has been illuminated. The present section will now focus on the pervasiveness of anthropocentrism in a much more specific way by drawing attention to the fact that anthropocentrism is widely regarded as pervading even those *particular* kinds of thinking that have been characterized as *ecological* or *environmentalist*.

In contemplating the sheer range of contemporary environmental problems, their intractability, and their degree of causal interconnectedness, it would seem to be the case that more and more people have been coming to agree with Lynn White's conclusion, if not always with his analysis, that, at base, these problems must be considered as requiring a reorientation in human beings of the most fundamental kind—a reorientation that is philosophical, psychological, or religious in nature. From this viewpoint, the continued application of technical solutions while "we"—and especially wealthy, male humans in the financial capitals of the world—essentially carry on with "business as usual" is simply not good enough. What is instead required is a reorientation toward a nonanthropocentric—or, in more positive terms, toward an ecocentric—way of being in the world. However, analysts of ecological and environmentalist thought have recognized that it is a mistake to regard the class of people with ecological or environmentalist interests as homogeneously constituted by those who seek such a reorientation. Rather, these analysts have generally recognized that the strength and pervasiveness of anthropocentrism in (at least) Western culture is such that it even permeates many of the ideas that have been subsumed under the labels of ecology and environmentalism. This lack of ideological homogeneity has therefore led these analysts to attempt to characterize ecological and environmentalist thought in terms of essential *types* (usually just two types).

I propose to provide the most extensive survey of these typologies of ecological and environmentalist thought that has appeared in ecophilosophical literature so far. There are two reasons for doing this. First, this survey ought to clearly demonstrate that anthropocentric assumptions have been *widely* perceived as pervading ecological and environmentalist thought and that this perception has been deemed to be of considerable analytical importance. Second, drawing this degree of attention to the variety of attempts that have been made to characterize the essential types of ecological and environmentalist thought *compels* the asking of a question that has basically been overlooked in ecophilosophical discussion: why is it that one of these typologies—the shallow/deep ecology typology—should have become extremely well known and widely used in the ecophilosophical literature, as well as increasingly well known and used beyond the confines of that literature, while almost all of its potential competitors now rarely rate a mention in the ecophilosophy literature (if, indeed, they were ever really registered by the ecophilosophy community in the first place) and are, in general, unknown outside this literature? We will examine the influence of the shallow/deep ecology typology and the reasons for its success in chapters 2 and 3 respectively.

I now confront the task of showing that anthropocentrism is widely regarded as pervading even those *particular* kinds of thinking that have been characterized as *ecological* or *environmentalist*. While it is difficult to draw precise boundaries around these terms of reference, it should be noted that I have excluded at least five related categories of typologies from the survey that follows. The first three categories include typologies that distinguish along anthropocentric/nonanthropocentric lines but that are not *specifically* concerned with ecological or environmentalist thought; the last two categories include typologies that *are* specifically concerned with ecological or environmentalist thought but that do not distinguish along anthropocentric/nonanthropocentric lines. The excluded categories are as follows:

1. Typologies that have been developed by thinkers concerned with the broader, historical question of characterizing *attitudes toward nature* in general, as opposed to characterizing those attitudes that are revealed specifically in the context of ecological or environmentalist thought—which are essentially quite modern forms of thought when considered under those names. Examples of broad, historically informed typologies of general attitudes toward nature are provided by Walter O'Briant's *man apart from nature/man a part of nature* typology; Ian Barbour's *domination over nature/stewardship of nature/unity with nature* typology; and John Passmore's *man as despot/stewardship of nature/co-operation with nature* (in order to "perfect" it)/*nature mysticism* typology.[27]

2. Typologies of the range of *possible* positions that humans generally, rather than that class of people with specifically ecological or environmentalist interests, can adopt in regard to their treatment of the nonhuman world. These overviews of

attitudes toward nature are derived more on the basis of philosophical than historical considerations.[28]

3. Related distinctions that have been made in regard to other disciplines or areas of study. For example, with respect to the discipline of philosophy, Henryk Skolimowski contrasts a cluster of views that he characterizes as *eco-philosophy* with a cluster of views that he characterizes as *contemporary philosophy;* with respect to the discipline of sociology, William Catton, Jr., and Riley Dunlap identify the broadest unit of consensus within their discipline as the *human exemptionalism* (or the *human exceptionalism*) *paradigm* (HEP) and contrast it with what they call the *new ecological paradigm* (NEP).[29]

4. Typologies that, in contrast to the three preceding categories, relate specifically to ecological and environmentalist thought, but that distinguish between this thought on the basis of methodological or structural considerations rather than in terms of its content (such as the extent to which it is anthropocentric or nonanthropocentric). Thus, for example, Otis Duncan distinguishes between a systematic, empirical, scientific approach and a holistic, social, philosophical approach to human ecology in his *Encyclopaedia Britannica* overview of this emerging discipline.[30]

5. Typologies that relate specifically to ecological and environmentalist thought and that *are* based on considerations relating to content as opposed to method or structure, but that do not run along anthropocentric/nonanthropocentric lines. These typologies can virtually all be traced to the work of political scientists and sociologists—people whose disciplinary backgrounds, as Catton and Dunlap have argued, mean that they have been thoroughly immersed in the anthropocentric human exceptionalism paradigm. Thus, for example, Grant McConnell distinguishes between a conservative and a more radical form of environmentalism in terms of the relative importance that is placed on economic growth and material values generally; Frederick H. Buttell and Oscar Larson III consider that "the possible forms of environmentalism can be adequately described in terms of the notions of 'left,' 'right,' and 'center' "; and Stephen

Cotgrove, in his book *Catastrophe or Cornucopia,* distinguishes between a *traditional* and a *radical* form of environmentalism. Cotgrove holds that both forms of environmentalism share an attraction to small-scale decentralized communities, a skeptical attitude toward scientific modes of thought, and an opposition to industrialism. Where they differ, he says, is in regard to the relative importance that is placed on socially sanctioned authority versus personal autonomy and inequality (*differentiation*) versus equality. These differences seem to approximate the traditional political distinction between conservative and liberal on these issues.[31]

What should be noted about this last group of typologies is that it is not as if the authors concerned consider the issue of anthropocentrism versus nonanthropocentrism as a possible basis for a typology of environmentalism and then argue against the usefulness or validity of this distinction; rather, they simply either do not address this issue at all or else do not address it in anything more than a passing fashion. Thus, for example, Cotgrove refers in passing to quantitatively based American research by Riley Dunlap and Kent Van Liere that demonstrates significantly higher levels of support for nonanthropocentric views among members of a state-wide Washington environmental organization than among members of that state's general public.[32] Yet despite the existence of this evidence (the general trend of which is clear to Cotgrove despite the fact that he misreports the details), Cotgrove frankly admits that his own empirical research on environmentalism "did not include questions on relations with the natural environment"! This omission can be confirmed by examining the questionnaire used by Cotgrove, which is contained in an appendix to his book.[33]

Having indicated the five related categories of typologies that are excluded by my terms of reference, we can now proceed with the survey of anthropocentric/nonanthropocentric based typologies of ecology and environmentalism.

One of the earliest of these typologies was presented by the literary critic Leo Marx. Writing in *Science* in 1970, Marx distinguished between the *conservationist viewpoint,* in which "nature is a world that exists apart from, and for the benefit of, mankind," and the *ecological perspective*, in which "man (including his works—the secondary, or man-made, environment) is wholly and ineluctably embedded in the tissue of natural processes." For Marx, "conservationist thought is pragmatic and meliorist in tenor, whereas ecology is, in the purest meaning of the word, radical." Referring to the latter perspective, Marx added that "if this organic (or holistic) view of nature has not been popular, it is partly because it calls into question many of the presuppositions of our culture."[34]

In a 1977 book *Nature's Economy*, a highly regarded study of the history of ecological ideas from the eighteenth century to the present, the historian Donald Worster shows that the tension between the two perspectives that Marx refers to has long been at work in competing conceptions of how the idea of ecology should be understood. In Worster's words, ecology has suffered from "a persistent identity problem." Is it primarily a science of manipulation and control of the nonhuman world or is it "a philosophy of interrelatedness"? Worster refers to the ecological traditions that inform this tension as the *imperial* tradition and the *arcadian* tradition respectively. The arcadian tradition urges "a simple rural life in close harmony with nature . . . coexistence rather than domination; humility rather than self-assertion; man as part of, rather than superior to, nature." In contrast, the imperial tradition urges the employment of science to extend humanity's power over the nonhuman world as far as possible. For Worster, "the split in ecology between this organic, communal ideal and a more pragmatic utilitarianism remains unresolved," and "our fundamental task . . . in the current 'Age of Ecology' " is choosing between these two "moral courses."[35]

The cultural historian Theodore Roszak, in his deservedly influential 1972 book *Where the Wasteland Ends*, identifies essentially the same tension in ecological thinking as Worster, but gives particular emphasis to the spiritual dimension inherent in this tension:

> Ecology stands at a critical cross-roads. Is it, too, to become another anthropocentric technique of more efficient manipulation, a matter

of enlightened self-interest and expert, long-range resource budgeting? Or will it meet the nature mystics on their own terms and so recognize that we are to embrace nature as if indeed it were a beloved person in whom, as in ourselves, something sacred dwells? . . . The question remains open: which will ecology be, the last of the old sciences or the first of the new?[36]

In his controversial 1983 book entitled *Algeny* (*algeny* being a neologistic splicing together of *alchemy* and *gene* to capture the alchemical ideal underlying the technology of splicing genes themselves), the social issues researcher and activist Jeremy Rifkin cautions that, unless we debate biotechnology issues right now, ecology and evolution as we have known them in the post-Darwinian context are about to be superseded by the advent of genetic engineering, whether we like it or not. Rifkin concludes his analysis with a challenge similar to that posed by Roszak: "Two futures beckon us. We can choose to engineer the life of the planet, creating a second nature in our image, or we can choose to participate with the rest of the living kingdom. Two futures, two choices. An engineering approach to the age of biotechnology or an ecological approach. The battle between [them] is a battle of values. . . . Our choice, in the final analysis, depends on what we value most in life."[37]

For Rifkin, the engineering and ecological approaches to ecology and evolution correspond to two forms of knowledge, which he refers to as *technological knowledge* and *empathetic knowledge* respectively.

Today we are well versed in how to pursue technological knowledge but virtually untutored when it comes to pursuing empathetic knowledge. Technological knowledge gives us foresight so that we can better appropriate the life around us. Empathetic knowledge gives us foresight so we can better cooperate with the community of life. With technological foresight, security comes in exercising power over nature. With empathetic foresight, security comes from belonging to a community.[38]

The theorist of environmentalism Timothy O'Riordan captures the general thrust of the foregoing distinctions in his comprehensive 1976 overview, *Environmentalism.* In outlining these contrasting approaches to environmental concerns, O'Riordan distinguishes between *technocentric* and *ecocentric* approaches:

> The technocratic ideology . . . is almost arrogant in its assumption that man is supremely able to understand and control events to suit his purposes. This assurance extends even to the application of theories and models to manipulate and predict changes in value systems and behaviour, while the exercise of science to "manage" nature has been assumed for some time. . . . Ecocentrism preaches the virtues of reverence, humility, responsibility, and care; it argues for low impact technology (but is not antitechnological); it decries bigness and impersonality in all forms (but especially in the city); and demands a code of behaviour that seeks permanence and stability based on ecological principles of diversity and homeostasis. Until recently ecocentrism was more of a moral or spiritual crusade, its proponents generally preferring to shun the political arena in favour of the world of rhetoric and contemplation. . . . Ecocentrism is concerned with *ends* and the proper kind of means, whereas technocentrism focuses more on *means per se,* particularly the utilisation of managerial principles, since its optimism about the continued improvement of the human condition allows it to be rather less troubled about the evaluative significance of its achievements.[39]

The philosopher Alan Drengson draws a distinction in similar terms between what he calls *technocratic paradigms* and *person-planetary* or *pernetarian paradigms* (from per[son]/[pla]net; this terminology draws upon that employed by Roszak in his exceptional book *Person/Planet.*)[40] In the technocratic paradigm the world is understood, manipulated, and controlled for human benefit by breaking it down into replaceable, interchangeable parts as if it were a machine. In the person-planetary paradigm, the world is approached with respectfulness and humility. It is understood that "individuals do not exist in isolation, but in relationship"[41] and that individual existents are unique (and irreplaceable in the future) by virtue of the special set of relationships in which only they are (and can remain) embedded. The world is therefore seen in organismic terms rather than mechanical ones, in terms of interacting processes and fields rather than isolated things, and, socially, in terms of an extended ecological *community* rather than in terms of essentially separate, competing individuals.

Yet another distinction of this kind is implied by Joseph Meeker, who distinguishes between an approach to environmentalism that is informed by "the long-standing tradition of humanistic philosophy" and an emerging approach that is being informed by the development of "a new natural philosophy."[42] Meeker refers to the former approach as *homocentric environmentalism* but offers no name for the latter approach other than the label he gives to the philosophical orientation that he sees as informing it (i.e., "the new natural philosophy"). We could perhaps refer to this latter approach as *holistic environmentalism* since it is an approach that seeks "wholeness for humanity in a whole world."

In urging that it is in humanity's own best interests to take care of the earth, homocentric environmentalism, according to Meeker,

> provides a rationale for environmental responsibility consistent with what most people habitually prefer to believe about themselves (i.e., that they are central to creation), so no new thinking about humanity's place in natural environments has seemed necessary. Unfortunately, the same rationale has historically been used to support the thoughtless exploitation that has brought about drastic environmental imbalances. From the origins of agriculture to the destructive technologies of the modern industrial system, the highest humanistic goal has been to use the natural world in the service of human interests.[43]

In contrast, the newly emerging natural philosophy that Meeker sees as informing a nonhomocentric, holistic approach to environmentalism

> will use the human mind to probe the world for understanding and it will respect the human species for the interesting and remarkable one that it is, but it will not seek to rank it first in a hierarchy of species. More interesting is the question of the relative functions of species as they interact with one another in complex systems. The

well-being and integrity of such systems is the primary concern of the new natural philosophy.[44]

Rather than distinguishing between different kinds or senses *of* ecology or environmentalism, the ecopolitical theorist Murray Bookchin has, since the early 1970s, put forward a typology that distinguishes between *environmentalism* on the one hand and *ecology* or *social ecology* on the other hand.[45] "Ecology, in my view," he says, "has always meant *social* ecology."[46] But while Bookchin employs the terms *environmentalism* and *ecology* in highly restrictive senses, the substance of his distinction is similar to that of the other typologies of ecology and environmentalism presented here. Specifically, environmentalism, for Bookchin, refers to "a mechanistic, instrumental outlook that sees nature as a passive habitat composed of 'objects' such as animals, plants, minerals, and the like that must merely be rendered more serviceable for human use."[47] Environmentalism, in other words, "does not bring into question the underlying notion of the present society that man must dominate nature; rather, it seeks to facilitate that domination by developing techniques for diminishing the hazards caused by domination."[48] In contrast, ecology or social ecology refers to an approach that rests on "the ecological principles of unity in diversity, spontaneity, and the nonhierarchial nature of ecological communities," and that attempts "to overcome the splits between society and nature, mind and body, thought and reality that mark Western images of the world."[49]

Bookchin's attempt to give the word *ecology* a specific, normative sense illustrates a common tactic that is employed in ideological battles over significant concepts: winning the semantic battle puts you well on the way to winning your particular war—and not just at a theoretical level. With this in mind, other writers have drawn on certain attractive semantic implications of the etymological meaning of the word *ecology* in elaborating their own typologies of ecology and environmentalism. As is often pointed out, the word *ecology*, coined by the German biologist and philosopher Ernst Haeckel (initially as *oecology*) in 1866, derives from the Greek *oikos*, "referring originally to the family household and its daily operations and maintenance."[50] The term *ecology* is therefore intended to refer to the study of the conditions of existence that pertain to, and the interactions between, all the entities that make up our larger, cosmic household here upon earth.

Given this etymological indebtedness of the term *ecology* to the image of the home, and the appealing nature of this image, it is only to be expected that some writers should have been drawn to the image of the home in outlining similar distinctions to those that I have already mentioned. Thus, for example, Stephen Toulmin, who is well known in philosophical circles generally for his work in philosophy of science and for his contributions to mainstream ethical discussion, makes good use of the possibilities offered by this image in the conclusion of his 1982 book *The Return to Cosmology*: "To be at home in the world of nature does not just mean finding out how to utilize nature economically and efficiently—home is not a hotel! It means making sense of the relations that human beings and other living things have toward the overall patterns of nature in ways that give us some sense of their proper relations to one another, to ourselves, and to the whole."[51] These images of nature as hotel and home underlie the split that Toulmin sees in the ecological movement:

> At the present time, the ecological movement is itself divided into two groups. . . . In the one group there are those whose support for enlightened ecological policies rests ultimately on an appeal to our own longer-term interests as human beings; . . . its supporters still have basically anthropocentric, even utilitarian attitudes. . . . In the other group there are those whose view of our place in nature is more genuinely cosmological: who find themselves compelled to set utilitarian, anthropocentric arguments aside and extend to other forms of life an honorary (though nonvoting) citizenship in Kant's Kingdom of Ends, together with the dignity and respect appropriate to that citizenship. . . . For [them] Nature itself has become once again an "overall scheme" or cosmos, and so a target for genuine piety."[52]

In a rarely cited 1977 paper, the philosopher Joseph Grange explores what might be called the *phenomenology of home* in articulating "two fundamentally opposed ways of understanding ecology," which he refers to as *dividend ecology* and *foundational ecology*:

> "Dividend ecology" . . . regards the interaction of humankind and nature solely from the perspective of investments and returns. . . . Dividend ecology has a simple message: if we continue to destroy our environment, we will perish. Its motive force is fear, being largely a negative movement that seeks to restrain our greed and diminish the aggression with which we attack nature. This way of understanding ecology can do little in the long run, for it only serves to reinforce the basic mode of consciousness that brought on our environmental disaster. . . . The second way of understanding ecology has yet to be structured, organized and given a name. Still: its birth pains as well as its first feeble steps can be recognized in a growing number of psychological, philosophic, scientific and poetic works. I shall call it "foundational ecology" since this discipline seeks the ground of our relation with nature as well as its corresponding depths in the human psyche.[53]

Drawing primarily on the ideas and language of Heidegger (particularly the later Heidegger), Grange presents foundational ecology as concerned with "human homecoming," which he explicates as follows:

> Homecoming is not merely the act of returning to a specific place that we call "home." Home is not a spatial location. Home is the region of nearness within which our relationship to nature is characterized by [what Heidegger refers to as] sparing and preserving. . . . Human homecoming is a matter of learning how to dwell intimately with that which resists our attempts to control, shape, manipulate and exploit it. . . . [Foundational] ecology is therefore the effort to structure our modes of dwelling so that they reflect an essential and authentic way of being human. That way is an existence that opens itself to nature rather than aggressively reconstructing it according to personal ends [as in dividend ecology].[54]

Finally, the philosopher John Rodman has presented an insightful four-part typology of environmentalism that also distinguishes along anthropocentric/nonanthropocentric lines. Rodman describes and evaluates "four currents of thought discernible in the history of the contemporary environmental movement," referring to them as *resource conservation, wilderness preservation, moral extensionism,* and *ecological sensibility.*[55] Although these forms of consciousness can all be mapped on to present environmental constituencies, Rodman presents them as representing a historical progression dating from the turn-of-the-century debate between Gifford Pinchot (first head of the U.S Forest Service) and John Muir (founder of the Sierra Club). For Rodman, the resource conservation approach, exemplified by Pinchot, attempts to restrain reckless resource exploitation but does so on the basis of considerations concerning what is in the enlightened self-inter-est—particularly the enlightened economic self-interest—of some particular human population. Thus, when all is said and done, the resource conservation approach amounts to "simply a more prudent form of resource exploitation." In contrast, the wilderness preservation approach, which Rodman sees as exem-plified by Muir, rejects the hegemony of the utilitarian, economic frame of reference in favor of a religious/aesthetic frame of reference. The upshot of this is that actions judged as "wise use" of resources within the economic frame of reference may be judged as "desecration" within the religious/aesthetic frame of reference.

In contrast to both these approaches, says Rodman, a number of more recent environmental thinkers have wanted to move beyond what they have seen, on the one hand, as the untenable anthropocentrism of the resource conservation approach and, on the other hand, as the unconvincing theology or unsatisfactory subjectivism of the religiously/aesthetically based wilderness preservation approach. According to Rodman, "what has hap-pened is that, after both the prudential and reverential stages of ideological adaptation represented by resource conservation and wilderness preservation came to seem inadequate, a more radical claim that nature had value 'in its own right' seemed in order."[56] However, this emphasis on justice rather than prudence or reverence has, in Rodman's view, too often led to the attribution of intrinsic value to members of the nonhuman world by way of the simple extension of existing, human-centered ethical thinking. The problem with this moral extensionism approach, as Rodman has done much to show in his earlier work, is that those members of the nonhuman world that are considered to be of value in their own right tend to be assimilated to "inappropriate models, without rethinking very thoroughly either the assumptions of conventional ethics or the ways in which we perceive and interpret the natural world."[57] Although this comment no doubt sounds rather cryptic at this stage of the discussion, it will be clarified in chapter 6, in the section entitled "Objections to Intrinsic Value Theory Approaches." What is important for present purposes is the conclusion that Rodman's comment leads to: "It is probably a safe maxim," he says, "that there will be no revolution in ethics without a revolution in perception." Thus, for Rodman, dissatisfaction with the moral extensionism approach is leading to the (still emerging) advocacy of an *ecological sensibility*. By this, Rodman means to refer to the cultivation of "a complex pattern of perceptions, attitudes, and judgments which, if fully developed, would constitute a disposition to appropriate conduct [including ecologically appropriate conduct] that would make talk of rights and duties unnecessary under normal conditions."[58]

ENTER THE SHALLOW/DEEP ECOLOGY TYPOLOGY

We have now seen that a considerable number of anthropocentric/ nonanthropocentric based typologies of ecology and environmentalism have been suggested. These include contrasts between perspectives that have been described by Marx as conservationist versus ecological; by Worster as imperial versus arcadian; by Roszak as expedient versus sacramental (labels I suggest for convenience, since Roszak does not provide any short labels for the perspectives that he describes); by Rifkin as engineering/ technological versus ecological/empathetic; by O'Riordan as technocentric versus ecocentric; by Drengson as technocratic versus person-planetary (or pernetarian); by Meeker as homocen-

tric versus (what I have for convenience labeled) holistic; by
Bookchin as environmentalism versus social ecology; by Toulmin
as anthropocentric versus cosmological; by Grange as dividend
versus foundational; and by Rodman as resource conservation
versus wilderness preservation versus moral extensionism versus
ecological sensibility.

Yet despite the labor that has gone into the construction of
these typologies, as well as into the often difficult task of coining
labels to describe such generalized clusters of views, only a few
of these typologies have been taken up by other writers, and then
typically only in isolated instances. For example, David Pepper
employs O'Riordan's technocentrism/ecocentrism typology
throughout his 1984 book *The Roots of Modern Environmentalism;*
Grange's dividend/foundational typology is briefly taken up by
both David Seamon in his 1982 overview of "The Phenomenological Contribution to Environmental Psychology" and by Neil
Evernden in his 1985 book *The Natural Alien;* and George
Sessions discusses Rodman's fourfold typology in his *Ecophilosophy*
newsletter and in a lengthy review of the ecophilosophical literature.[59]

The only terminology presented in any of the foregoing
typologies that can in some sense be said to have caught on is
Bookchin's term *social ecology.* However, even this claim needs to
be qualified in at least four respects. First, the environmentalism
half of Bookchin's distinction is rarely mentioned by other
writers, let alone seriously taken up. This can perhaps be
explained partly in terms of the fact that it is the social ecology
aspect of Bookchin's distinction that constitutes its challenging,
radical, and, hence, most interesting aspect, and partly in terms
of the fact that Bookchin's own energies have been overwhelmingly directed to this aspect of his distinction. However, it also
seems likely that the environmentalism aspect of Bookchin's
distinction has not been taken up because his particular, highly
restrictive use of the term flies in the face of its conventional
range of meanings and so serves to confuse rather than illuminate
discussions of environmentalism. Second, the number of writers
who have taken up the social ecology half of Bookchin's distinc-

tion in a positive way (as distinct from people who have simply heard of this term) is still quite limited.[60] Third, in common with each of the other typologies presented here, Bookchin's elaboration of what he calls social ecology has had minimal impact on mainstream ecophilosophical discussion. (However marginal ecophilosophy may be in the context of mainstream philosophy in general, one can still talk about the mainstream of ecophilosophical discussion considered in its own right.) An illustration of this third point is the fact that the *first* paper to be published in *Environmental Ethics,* the central journal in ecophilosophy, that discussed Bookchin's ideas in any degree of detail— a paper by Robyn Eckersley entitled "Divining Evolution: The Ecological Ethics of Murray Bookchin"—did not appear until mid-1989.[61] Moreover, Eckersley, despite her sympathetic exposition of Bookchin's ideas, essentially concluded that the promise of Bookchin's ideas could best be fulfilled not by Bookchin's own ecological ethics but rather by the ideas being developed under the banner of deep ecology—Bookchin's bête noire. Finally, to the extent that the social ecology half of Bookchin's typology has caught on, it needs to be borne in mind that this term has become considerably more widely known since 1987 precisely *because* of a vitriolic attack—there is no more adequate description for it—that Bookchin launched upon an ideological competitor that was receiving, and that continues to receive, much greater attention from the ecophilosophical community than Bookchin's own ideas.[62]

This brings us to the only anthropocentric/nonanthropocentric based typology of ecology and environmentalism that has been taken up in mainstream ecophilosophical discussion to the point where it now not only pervades such discussion but also spills over into much of the popularly based discussion of environmentalism. This typology is one that contrasts *shallow ecology* with *deep ecology*. It was formulated by the distinguished Norwegian philosopher Arne Naess in 1972 and published the following year in the journal *Inquiry*.[63]

Having established in this chapter something of the background against which such typologies of ecology and environmentalism can be viewed, the main task with which we will be concerned in the following chapters is that of exploring Naess's widely used but often poorly understood typology in considerable detail. More precisely, we will especially be concerned with exploring the positive, challenging aspect of Naess's typology (i.e., deep ecology), since this is the aspect into which Naess's hopes and main energies, as well as those of his colleagues, have been directed—and, by the same token, the aspect with which critics of Naess and his colleagues have also been most concerned. In line with this focus of interest, I will usually just speak in terms of *deep ecology* from now on, instead of always referring to *Naess's distinction,* the *shallow/deep ecology distinction,* or the *shallow/ deep ecology typology.* The fact that *deep ecology* refers to one aspect of a typology and so implies a particular contrast or contrasts ought to be implicit in what follows and will in any case be taken up explicitly in chapter 5.

In pointing out that deep ecology is far and away the main *focus* of interest for those who have been influenced by Naess's typology—supporters and critics alike—it should nevertheless be noted (as we will see in chapter 2) that the term *shallow ecology* is also widely known and employed in the ecophilosophy literature, as also is a now well-known alternative for this term: *reform ecology.* There is therefore no comparison between the fate of Naess's term *shallow ecology* and that of Bookchin's comparable term, *environmentalism,* which, as I have already noted, is rarely even mentioned by other writers, and which has been totally ignored in the ecophilosophy literature.

In order to provide an adequate appreciation of deep ecology, I intend, for present purposes, to adopt the adage that "a little knowledge is a dangerous thing" and deliberately refrain from defining Naess's distinction—or deep ecology in particular—any more precisely than saying that this distinction can be understood as making a point similar to the largely overlapping typologies of ecology and environmentalism that have already been presented (i.e., as drawing a contrast between anthropocentric and nonanthropocentric—or ecocentric—approaches to ecology and environmentalism). There are two reasons for my reluctance to be more specific at this stage. First, to provide *a* simplified (but more specific) definition at this stage might prejudice receptivity to the *variety* of meanings that I wish to show are bound up in Naess's understanding of deep ecology (three basic meanings, in fact). And second, even if one accepts in advance that there are several basic meanings of deep ecology, it would be unprofitable, possibly even misleading, to provide several short definitions of deep ecology at this stage because the ideas that constitute the context of, and are embodied in, these meanings of deep ecology are complex and require detailed explication. The proper place for such short definitions is, therefore, after this explication has taken place, not before.

I will explicate the basic meanings of deep ecology in chapter 4. But before proceeding to do this, it is important to do two things. The first is to take a fairly close look at just how influential Naess's distinction—and particularly his understanding of deep ecology—has become in the context of ecophilosophical, ecopolitical, and environmentalist thinking and activism. This should provide some sense of the burden that has been placed upon Naess's distinction and, consequently, a sense of the significance that attaches to further clarification of his distinction—particularly to further clarification of deep ecology, which represents the distinction's positive focus of interest. Second, in the light of these considerations, it is important to consider why Naess's distinction, and particularly his understanding of deep ecology, has met with such success while apparently similar distinctions either have not been taken up at all or else have not been taken up to anywhere near the same extent. The importance of this question for understanding deep ecology lies in the fact that it leads us to consider what it is, if anything, that is distinctive about the deep ecology approach to ecophilosophy. As I observed earlier, the question of what is distinctive about deep ecology has tended to be overlooked in ecophilosophical discussion.

I therefore propose to examine the influence of Naess's distinction and the reasons for its success in chapters 2 and 3 respectively. Those readers who are not especially interested in the question of how influential deep ecology has become or the question of why it has become so influential may wish to proceed directly to chapter 4: "Arne Naess and the Meanings of *Deep Ecology*." Those readers who choose the longer route, however, will benefit in two main ways. First, they will gain a comprehensive overview of both the main primary literature on deep ecology and the main critical literature that has emerged in reaction to it. And second, they will avail themselves of a richer context in which to evaluate both the significance and the validity of the argument that follows.

PART TWO
THE INFLUENCE
OF DEEP ECOLOGY

*The main hope for changing humanity's present course may lie
. . . in the development of a world view drawn partly from
ecological principles—in the so-called deep ecology movement.*
—Paul Ehrlich

2
Deep Ecology: A Focus
within Ecophilosophy—and Beyond

THE INFLUENCE OF DEEP ECOLOGY
UPON ACADEMIC ECOPHILOSOPHY

THE TERM *deep ecology* and the ideas associated with it are now continually being referred to—whether with approval or otherwise—in academic ecophilosophical discussion. This applies whether one considers papers published in *Environmental Ethics,* ecophilosophical papers published in other academic philosophical journals, recent books on ecophilosophy, recent overviews of the ecophilosophical literature, or talks delivered at ecophilosophical or ecophilosophically related conferences.[1]

It is possible to refer to a large number of authors who could be said to pursue deep ecological *themes* in their papers and books but who, for one reason or another, do not specifically refer to *deep ecology.* My primary concern in this and the following chapters is with the work of those authors who have self-consciously devoted themselves to the development of deep ecology *under that name.* Moreover, I am not primarily concerned herein with deep ecology as a broadly based social movement— the so-called deep ecology movement—nor with deep ecology as an approach to ecopolitics. Rather, I am primarily concerned with deep ecology as an approach to *ecophilosophy.* I trust, however, that my primarily philosophical level of analysis will stimulate considerable thought at both the sociological level (in regard to the characterization of the deep ecology movement) and the political level (in regard to the development of an ecopolitics inspired by deep ecology).

Deep ecology constitutes the central focus of interest for the two most influential newsletters/journals in ecophilosophy other than *Environmental Ethics,* namely, *Ecophilosophy* and *The Trumpeter.* The reason for this is straightforward: the editors of these publications are in both cases personally committed to deep ecology. This itself suggests something about the motivational power of these ideas and the attraction that deep ecology holds for at least some of those thinkers who are most committed to the development of ecophilosophy. George Sessions (sometimes with assistance from Bill Devall) wrote and published the brilliant series of six, often quite lengthy, *Ecophilosophy* newsletters that were put out on an informal basis between 1976 (three years prior to the publication of *Environmental Ethics*) and 1984.[2] As the philosopher John Passmore correctly noted in 1980, at the time of the second edition of his study *Man's Responsibility for Nature,* "For a general survey of the ecological literature from the standpoint of 'deep' ecology there is nothing to compare with the newsletter *Ecophilosophy* issued by George Sessions."[3] Alan Drengson has edited and published the excellent quarterly journal *The Trumpeter* since the end of 1983, and it has gone from strength to strength during that time.[4] *The Trumpeter* now constitutes not only the main forum for the regular exchange of ecophilosophical views that are devoted to the articulation, analysis, and further elaboration of deep ecology, but also the most influential ecophilosophy journal of any kind apart from *Environmental Ethics.*

The influence of deep ecology upon ecophilosophical discussion has been such that it has now become common for ecophilosophical thinkers to employ the ideas associated with deep ecology (or at least what they *take* to be the ideas associated with deep ecology) as a sort of standard reference point against which to proceed in presenting their own preferred solutions to ecophilosophical problems. In addition to many individual writers, one important group one could point to in this regard consists of those thinkers who are informed by feminist theory and practice.[5]

Another indication of the fact that deep ecology has become something of a standard reference point in ecophilosophical discussion is the fact that authors of ecophilosophically relevant books published prior to the widespread adoption of the notion of deep ecology have made a point of contrasting their own position with deep ecology in the prefaces to new editions of their books.[6]

While one can point to many ecophilosophers who have referred to deep ecology here and there in the course of developing their own approaches to ecophilosophical questions, perhaps the best indication of the influence of deep ecology upon ecophilosophical thinking is to be found in the critiques that deep ecology has attracted. There are two reasons for saying this. First, the influence of deep ecology upon ecophilosophical thinking is indicated simply by the number of writings that have been more or less *devoted* to critizing deep ecology as compared with the number of critiques that have been more or less devoted to criticizing other ecophilosophical approaches. And second, in view of the fact that there is no need to react heavy-handedly to views that have attracted little or no interest (indeed, to do so in these cases can be counter-productive), the influence of deep ecology upon ecophilosophical thinking is also suggested by the tone of a number of these critiques. In reviewing a number of the main critiques of deep ecology in this *particular* context, then, we will not be concerned so much with their specific arguments as with gaining some idea of their general tone. (As indicated in the notes relating to these critiques, supporters of deep ecology, including myself, have responded to the arguments of these critiques in other places.)[7]

In what must be the most moderate critique of deep ecology to date, William Grey (formerly William Godfrey-Smith) provides a cautiously worded analysis of what he is content to refer to as some "internal tensions" in deep ecology theorizing.[8] The "internal tensions" that Grey refers to center on the role and place of science in the cultivation of an ecological world-view. However, Grey misunderstands the attitude of deep ecologists to modern science. The fact that deep ecologists object to science that is oriented toward ever greater manipulation and exploitation of the world does not mean that they also object to science that is oriented toward increasing our understanding of the nature of the cosmos and our place in it. Thus, despite the title of his paper, many deep ecologists, including myself, would *agree* with almost everything that Grey has to say in regard to the role and place of science in the cultivation of an ecological world-view. I am at one with Grey when he says:

> Scientific investigations have provided us with a marvellous conception of our unity and interdependence with the natural world which is, I suggest, as rich and profound as any which has been provided by an animistic or pantheistic world view. . . . It is very puzzling to me how anyone can find a science based view of the world to be shallow and disappointing. Eric Ashby has suggested that whereas other cultures have identified with their environment through animism, our culture has enabled us to identify through scientific understanding.[9]

The only qualification I would add to this suggestion is that scientific understanding and animism are not necessarily mutually exclusive. Recent work in physics, chemistry, biology, and ecology on complex, self-organizing systems suggests the possibility that the scientific world-picture may be heading away from one that is based on mechanism and toward one that might plausibly be described as a kind of scientifically formulated animism (or *hylozoism,* which is the philosophical term given to the view that life is one of the properties of matter; from the combining form *hylo-,* "matter," and the Greek root *zoe,* "life"). My agreement with Grey's general remarks is, however, not contingent on any particular outcome in this regard.

Other critics of deep ecology are far less restrained in their criticisms than Grey. Far from being content with suggesting modifications to "internal tensions" in deep ecological theorizing, Richard Watson, for example, goes so far as to claim in one of his critiques that the "internal contradictions" of deep ecology are so serious that "the position must be *abandoned*" (emphasis added).[10] In a brief, subsequent critique, Watson adopts a somewhat different and apparently more moderate line of criticism in stating that he does not object to the ideals of deep ecology per se but rather to the fact that they are based on an unrealistic, utopian view of human nature.[11] However, in a still more recent critique, Watson changes tack again—as well as tone—in objecting to deep ecology not so much on the basis of its internal consistency or its view of human nature as on the basis that its implications would lead to the curtailment of human freedom— particularly his freedom, it seems (he does not state whether he also opposes gun control laws and drunk driving laws on the basis of this same great liberal ideal). Fearing that he has in the past "greatly underestimated . . . the extent to which deep ecologists and eco-philosophers believe that they know what is right for earth and humankind," Watson makes it clear that he is "disturbed, even horrified" over what he considers these "eco-nuts" to have in mind. "It is bad enough," he complains, "to have to watch out for parents who know what the family wants me to do, businessmen who know what the economy wants me to do, presidents who know what the country wants me to do, and popes who know what the church wants me to do; now I have to watch out also for deep ecologists who know what the ecosystem wants me to do."[12]

Watson says, for example, that "if deep ecologists gained political power, they would [among other things] enforce vast birth control programs." He does not seem to recognize, however, that many people who have nothing to do with the group of people that he is referring to as "deep ecologists" also believe that such programs should be implemented. One can point to examples as diverse as the Chinese government, which has for some years now been attempting to enforce a policy of one child per family, and the polymath Isaac Asimov, who, in the light of a concise overview of the human population explosion and its consequences, contained in his encyclopedic *Asimov's New Guide to Science,* concludes that "if we are to avoid catastrophe, motherhood [and, Asimov should add, fatherhood] must become a privilege sparingly doled out. Our views on sex and on its connection with childbirth must be changed."[13]

Whereas Watson is concerned about what he sees as deep ecologists' advocacy of interference with human freedoms (such as the freedoms to breed and to technologize, citify, and otherwise domesticate the planet), Alston Chase bases his critique of deep ecology, contained in his book *Playing God in Yellowstone,* on what he sees as deep ecologists' *failure* to advocate interference when it comes to the preservation of wildlife. In his view, "the major insight of the deep ecologists, . . . the principle of noninterference [in the course of nonhuman affairs, has provided] a rationale for doing nothing" with respect to the preservation of wildlife in Yellowstone National Park. According to Chase, the Park Service has, in its uncritical acceptance of "the religious, scientific, and political insights that emerged from the redwood think tanks of California during the last two decades," fallen prey to "the bewitching power of a false idea [i.e., the principle of noninterference]." The upshot of this analysis is that Chase lays the ultimate blame for "the destruction of America's first national park" not at the door of the Park Service, outside pressures, or public indifference, but rather at the door of the deep ecologists, whom he dubs "the California Cosmologists." For Chase, Yellowstone is "a casualty of the environmental crisis that the California Cosmologists had sought to resolve."[14]

Although Chase's book is important and thought provoking, it must also be said that it is particularly frustrating. As Doug Peacock correctly notes in his *Earth First!* response, "This is a slippery book; despite the symmetry of his arguments and his unrelenting critism of the Park Service, it's hard to tell what is being advocated."[15] Barry S. Allen expresses a similar kind of frustration at the conclusion of his review: "Chase's urge to criticize everyone and everything outside a very narrow range of what he considers 'real ecology' may leave the reader angrier with Chase than with the National Park Service."[16] What does appear to be clear, as George Sessions notes in his *Earth First!* response to Chase, is that, contrary to what seems to be implied by the title of Chase's book, Chase's "main complaint about 'playing God' in Yellowstone seems to be that we have done a bad job of it to the detriment of wildlife (in our attempts at managing), not that we ought to stop trying to 'play God' "—which *is* the *long-term* wish of deep ecologists.[17]

However serious Watson's and Chase's accusations concerning

the political and environmental policy implications of deep ecology may be, they are nevertheless expressed in positively mild terms when compared with the accusations made by other critics in regard to the politics of deep ecology. For example, Henryk Skolimowski, who, like Watson, has also written a number of critiques of deep ecology, sees deep ecologists as having a "party line" (as opposed, say, to displaying a rare degree of commonality in regard to the profoundly difficult problems with which ecophilosophy is concerned) and as treating deviants from that line "in the way party apparatchicks treat their opponents" (i.e., "deviate from it [the party line], and we shall shoot you"). [18] But by far the most objectionable and vitriolic claims in regard to the presumed political/policy evils of deep ecology have come from Murray Bookchin. He actually sees the ghost of Nazism "begin to grimace with satisfaction" from the center of deep ecological theorizing! It is not surprising, then, that Bookchin concludes his critique with the stern warning that unless we "let 'deep ecology' sink into the pit it has created for us, the ecology movement will become another ugly wart on the skin of society." [19]

In line with the tone suggested by these last comments, Bookchin's critique of deep ecology wins the prize, hands down, for rhetorical overkill. For example, his references to deep ecology alone include, among other things: "a vague, formless, often self-contradictory and invertebrate thing"; "a 'black hole' of half-digested, ill-formed, and half-baked ideas"; "a deluge of 'Eco-la-la' "; "muck"; "a goulash of notions and moods"; "the fast food of quasi-radical environmentalists"; and, what is perhaps his best effort, if one can call it that, "a bottomless pit in which vague notions and moods of all kinds can be sucked into the depths of an ideological toxic dump." "With so much absurdity [in deep ecology] to unscramble," says Bookchin, "one can indeed get heady, almost dizzy, with a sense of polemical intoxication." Indeed. [20]

The final critique of deep ecology that I want to mention here comes from Richard Sylvan (formerly Richard Routley) and represents the most comprehensive philosophical critique of deep ecology that has been written to date. Although the (toned down) final vision of Sylvan's critique concludes, in contrast to earlier versions, that deep ecology should, on balance, be recommended for "restoration" rather than "abandonment," Sylvan nevertheless employs metaphors of disease, decay, darkness, and rubbish disposal throughout his critique in describing deep ecology. In his first two pages, for example, he speaks of deep ecology as "a conceptual bog" and "an afflicted notion," and notes that "many notions no more afflicted than deep ecology . . . have been assigned to the historical scrap-heap"; we read of the "conceptual murkiness and degeneration" of deep ecology and of the "degenerative spread of deep ecology." Later we are told that deep ecological theorizing is "symptomatic of other old-consciousness malignancies"; and that a particular view that I endorsed in an earlier paper on deep ecology "is garbage and can mostly be assigned to the deep ecology rubbish basket (for which, as we'll see, a sizable one is needed)"; and so on.[21]

Clearly, deep ecology has exerted an extraordinary influence upon academic ecophilosophy—in terms of its ability both to attract and to repel.[22]

THE INFLUENCE BEYOND ACADEMIC ECOPHILOSOPHY

Academic ecophilosophy is the place where one must begin in discussing deep ecology, since it is there that the ideas associated with deep ecology were first articulated under that name. However, moving beyond a consideration of academic ecophilosophy, it can be seen that a number of professional ecologists have also been inspired by the ideas associated with deep ecology. For example, the influential ecologist Paul Ehrlich thoroughly endorses deep ecology in the introduction to his book *The Machinery of Nature:*

> The main hope for changing humanity's present course may lie . . .
> in the development of a world view drawn partly from ecological
> principles—in the so-called deep ecology movement. The term

"deep ecology" was coined in 1972 by Arne Naess of the University of Oslo to contrast with the fight against pollution and resource depletion in developed countries, which he called "shallow ecology." The deep ecology movement thinks today's human thought patterns and social organization are inadequate to deal with the population-resource-environmental crisis—a view with which I tend to agree. Within the movement disagreement abounds, but most of its adherents favor a much less anthropocentric, more egalitarian world, with greater emphasis on empathy and less on scientific rationality.

I am convinced that such a quasi-religious movement, one concerned with the need to change the values that now govern much of human activity, is essential to the persistence of our civilization.[23]

To ensure that the context of the remarks I have quoted here is preserved, it should be noted that Ehrlich is not remotely concerned with endorsing any kind of *anti*-scientific approach. As he correctly proceeds to point out: "But agreeing that science, even the science of ecology, cannot answer all questions—that there are 'other ways of knowing'—does not diminish the absolutely crucial role that good science must play if our overextended civilization is to save itself. Values must not be based on scientific nonsense."[24]

Yet another group of thinkers who have reached essentially the same conclusion as Ehrlich is to be found among those writers who are concerned with analyzing the fundamental assumptions of our modern, global, urban-industrial-informational culture (i.e., our high population density, high physical resource throughput, high information throughput culture) and who attempt not simply to characterize the contradictions, destructiveness, and dissatisfactions that attend this culture but also to address these problems in a hopeful and constructive way. Significant analyses of our fundamental cultural assumptions such as those presented by Theodore Roszak, Morris Berman, and Fritjof Capra have all argued toward an essentially deep ecological position—whether under that name or some other.[25] In his analysis of "science, society, and the rising culture," Fritjof Capra, for example, explicitly endorses a deep ecology position in the final pages of his impressive best-selling book *The Turning Point:*

> The new vision of reality is an ecological vision in a sense which goes far beyond the immediate concerns with environmental protection. To emphasize this deeper meaning of ecology, philosophers and scientists have begun to make a distinction between "deep ecology" and "shallow environmentalism." Whereas shallow environmentalism is concerned with more efficient control and management of the natural environment for the benefit of "man," the deep ecology movement recognizes that ecological balance will require profound changes in our perception of the role of human beings in the planetary ecosystem. In short, it will require a new philosophical and religious basis.
>
> Deep ecology is supported by modern science, and in particular by the new systems approach, but it is rooted in a perception of reality that goes beyond the scientific framework to an intuitive awareness of the oneness of all life, the interdependence of its multiple manifestations and its cycles of change and transformation. When the concept of the human spirit is understood in this sense, as the mode of consciousness in which the individual feels connected to the cosmos as a whole, it becomes clear that ecological awareness is truly spiritual. Indeed, the idea of the individual being linked to the cosmos is expressed in the Latin root of the word religion, *religare* ("to bind strongly"), as well as in the Sanskrit *yoga,* which means union.[26]

Like Capra and Ehrlich, Roszak, Berman, and Alwyn Jones also see the cultivation of ecological consciousness in "spiritual" (Capra) or "quasi-religious" (Ehrlich) terms. This reminds us of Lynn White's conclusion that "the remedy [for our present ecological predicament] must also be essentially religious, whether we call it that or not."[27] However, since these kinds of terms are often associated with other-worldliness and quietism, it needs to be emphasized that, for each of these writers, the cultivation of ecological consciousness is thoroughly grounded in this world and has significant political implications.

The influence of deep ecology is again obvious when one turns from ecophilosophical, ecological, and cultural analyses (all of which *imply* certain political courses) to works that are *primarily* engaged in the task of articulating an ecologically oriented politics. Of particular note in this regard are the widely available and influential articulations of Green politics presented by Charlene Spretnak and Fritjof Capra: deep ecology is repeatedly referred to as providing the philosophical underpinning for the ecological and spiritual basis of Green politics.[28]

Although the literature to which I have been referring so far is largely theoretically oriented in nature, it would be a mistake to think that the influence of deep ecology is limited to the stylistic confines and readership of such literature. Rather, the influence of deep ecology now extends not only into the wider environmental movement but also into popular culture in general. With respect to the wider environmental movement, this influence is illustrated by examples such as (1) the controversial activist-oriented U.S. publication *Earth First!*, founded by Dave Foreman, which regularly carries articles and reviews that discuss deep ecology or that are written by prominent deep ecology writers; (2) the Australian-based newsletter *The Deep Ecologist*, founded by John Martin, which is a grassroots-level, exchange-of-views-cum-networking newsletter for people in the environmental movement who identify with the ideas associated with deep ecology; and (3) articles that appear from time to time in a variety of spiritual growth/peace/environmentally oriented journals and magazines. These latter publications include, from the U.S.: *Awakening in the Nuclear Age Journal* (published by Interhelp), *ReVision: The Journal of Consciousness and Change*, *The Amicus Journal* (published by the Natural Resources Defense Council), and *The Ten Directions* (published by the Zen Center of Los Angeles); from Britain: *Resurgence* (founded and edited by Satish Kumar) and *The Ecologist* (founded and edited by Edward Goldsmith and his colleagues); from Australia: *Habitat Australia*, the color magazine of the Australian Conservation Foundation; and from India: *Holistic Human Concern for World Welfare*, the silver jubilee publication of the Indian Theosophical Science Study Group.[29]

With respect to the influence of deep ecology on popular

culture in general, articles discussing deep ecology have appeared in such popular, often glossy, newsstand publications as *New Age Journal, Whole Earth Review, Yoga Journal, Mother Jones, Simply Living, The Nation, Mother Earth News, Omni, Arete,* and even that standard-bearer of pop-culture journalism *Rolling Stone.*[30] Indeed, by the very end of the 1980s, discussion of deep ecology had even made the pages of that prestigious forum for mainstream critical discourse *The New York Review of Books.*[31]

Deep ecology, then, has clearly become an influential label within ecophilosophy—and beyond. Given the number and recency of popular and semi-popular expositions and discussions of deep ecology, it can be seen why R. Wills Flowers began his November 1987 response to Bookchin's critique of deep ecology with the observation that "the deep ecology movement has *in the last three years* caught the *public* attention with amazing speed" (emphases added).[32] Prior to this, however, deep ecology had caught the attention of the ecophilosophical community with equal speed—once it had begun to catch on. Thus, although deep ecology was (despite its introduction in 1973) rarely mentioned in the ecophilosophy literature until 1980, by February 1983, John Passmore, the well-known Australian philosopher and author of the influential 1974 book *Man's Responsibility for Nature* could justifiably write that "it is now *customary* to divide the family of 'ecophilosophers'—that limited class of philosophers who take environmental problems seriously—into two genera, the 'shallow' and the 'deep' " (emphasis added).[33] Since then, as we have seen, deep ecology (however it is understood) has become a sort of standard reference point in ecophilosophical discussion as well as a source of inspiration not only to environmental activists but also to ecologically oriented thinkers across a range of areas that includes ecological science, broad cultural analyses, sociology, and politics.

3
Why So Influential?

THE QUESTION IS unavoidable: Why has *deep ecology* become such an influential term in ecophilosophy—and beyond—while comparable terms, deriving from distinctions apparently comparable to the shallow/deep ecology distinction, have met with minor or no success? As noted in chapter 1, this is not a question that ecophilosophers have tended to ask. The reason for this is, perhaps, that the two most obvious possible answers to this question have seemed *so* obvious that there has not appeared to be much point in considering the question in any formal sort of way. These answers may be termed *the historical answer* and *the advocacy answer*. In formally considering this question here, we will explore these answers, and I shall argue that the historical answer is wrong while the advocacy answer is correct as far as it goes, but that it does not go far enough. There is a deeper, third kind of answer to the question that ecophilosophers have tended to overlook—an answer that may be termed *the substantive answer*.

THE HISTORICAL ANSWER

There seem to be two main versions of the historical answer, which may be thought of in terms of *colonization* and *conventionalism*. The colonization version holds that the success of Naess's 1973 typology is due to the fact that it was the first typology of modern environmentalism to have been set forth in an international publication and that it simply caught on before any of the other typologies had a chance to become established. The conventionalist version accepts the historical precedence of Naess's typology but rejects the view that this typology effectively colonized a particular theoretical niche before closely related species of ideas could establish themselves. Instead, it argues that as the number of alternatively formulated typologies grew, the ecophilosophy community found it convenient to settle on a single typology and so tended increasingly toward the use of Naess's typology, in recognition of its historical precedence.

But both the colonization and the conventionalism versions of this "early bird gets the worm" kind of explanation appear to be wrong on every count. First, in regard to the question of historical precedence, which underlies both versions, we have already seen in chapter 1 that Naess's typology is *not* the first to have been set forth in an international publication. Leo Marx's conservationist/ecological distinction, for example, was published in 1970 in *Science,* which is not only a far more widely read journal than *Inquiry* but also one that in the late 1960s and early 1970s was well-known for its stimulus to (what would come to be known as) ecophilosophical thinking.[1] Another distinction that preceded Naess's and that was also presented in a widely noted publication was that posited by Theodore Roszak in his influential 1972 book *Where the Wasteland Ends,* between what I have for convenience referred to as expedient and sacramental approaches.[2] Thus, although Naess's 1973 typology of ecology and environmentalism was *one* of the earliest to have been presented in an international publication, it was by no means *the* first.

Second, the colonization version of the historical answer is contradicted by the fact that, as I mentioned at the end of chapter 2, Naess's 1973 typology was rarely mentioned in the ecophilosophy literature until around 1980 (after which its use did spread rapidly). This effectively means that *any* of the typologies referred to in chapter 1 that were put forward by 1980 might be considered to have had a fair chance of filling the theoretical niche that came to be occupied by the shallow/deep ecology typology. Thus, not only does the colonization version of the historical answer overlook the existence of Marx's and Roszak's distinctions but, in erroneously assuming that Naess's typology became widely adopted almost as soon as it appeared on the scene, it also overlooks the fact that by 1980 there was a range of comparable distinctions in existence, any one of which could possibly have been taken up and pushed by a few writers to the point where the distinction that *they* favored might have become accepted as standard by the wider ecophilosophy community. As we have seen in chapter 1, by 1980 the range of candidates available to fill the theoretical niche that came to be occupied by the shallow/deep ecology typology included not only Marx's conservationist/ecological distinction (1970) and Roszak's distinction between what I have referred to as expedient and sacramental approaches (1972) but also the following: Bookchin's environmentalism/social ecology distinction (1974), Timothy O'Riordan's technocentric/ecocentric distinction (1976), Joseph Grange's dividend/foundational distinction (1977), Donald Worster's imperial/arcadian distinction (1977), John Rodman's resource conservation/wilderness preservation/nature moralism ecological resistance distinction (1978; Rodman did not replace the latter two terms with *moral extensionism* and *ecological sensibility* until 1983), and, if we include contributions as late as 1980, Alan Drengson's technocratic/person-planetary distinction and Joseph Meeker's distinction between a homocentric approach and what I have for convenience labeled a holistic approach.[3]

With respect to Drengson's distinction, it should be noted that Drengson makes it clear in both the 1980 introduction of his distinction, "Shifting Paradigms," and its 1983 book-length elaboration, published under the same title, that he considers himself to be expressing his own formulation *of* deep ecology rather than setting up a rival formulation.[4] His distinction therefore serves as much to reinforce the usefulness of Naess's shallow/deep ecology terminology as to suggest an alternative terminology. However, this does not mean that others may not have found Drengson's terminology more appealing than Naess's and thus adopted it in preference.

The list of distinctions given above includes all but two of the distinctions considered in chapter 1: Toulmin's anthropocentric/cosmological distinction (1982) and Rifkin's engineering/ecological or technological/empathic distinction (1983). One might therefore speculate that the success of the shallow/deep ecology distinction has meant that the steady flow of similar distinctions that were suggested between 1970 and 1980 has slowed to a trickle as ecologically sympathetic writers have realized that the anthropocentric/nonanthropocentric point has been made and is now widely being referred to in terms of Naess's typology. In this regard, it is interesting to note that Toulmin's and Rifkin's post-1980 distinctions both come from thinkers whose work, while ecologically sympathetic, does not demonstrate any particular familiarity with mainstream ecophilosophical literature.

Having seen that the historical sequence of events does not substantiate the colonization version of the historical answer, let us turn now to the conventionalism version. This view is contradicted by the fact that there is simply no evidence in the ecophilosophy literature to justify the contention that the ecophilosophy community *has* demonstrated any kind of collective desire to settle on a single typology of ecology and environmentalism—let alone to do so on the basis of the particular criterion of historical precedence. As we shall see below, the ecophilosophy community's acceptance of the shallow/deep ecology distinction is due far more to the powerful advocacy that the distinction received from a couple of writers from 1979–80 on, rather than to any kind of collective decision on the part of the ecophilosophy community. In other words, as with so many ideas, the shallow/deep ecology distinction was effectively thrust upon its relevant intellectual community rather than "elected to office." It should also be pointed out that if the conventionalist version of the historical answer *were* an adequate one then at least some ecophilosophers would have noted the existence of Marx's or Roszak's earlier distinctions, with the result that the shallow/deep ecology distinction would have been dropped in favor of one of these, or perhaps of some even earlier typology of which I am not aware.

On this last point, it is of particular interest to note that George Sessions—one of the influential advocates of the shallow/deep ecology distinction to whom I have just alluded—referred in the first (1976) issue of his influential *Ecophilosophy* newsletter not only to the papers in which Marx and Naess presented their respective distinctions but also to the specific five-page section of Roszak's *Where the Wasteland Ends,* entitled "Ecology and the Uses of Mysticism," in which Roszak presented his particular distinction.[5] Sessions was thus well aware of all three sets of distinctions by at least the mid-1970s. Why, then, did he become such a strong advocate of Naess's distinction from the *late* 1970s on? Clearly, the historical answer to this question is bankrupt. The reason for the success of Naess's typology has to be looked for in some other direction than that of historical precedence.

THE ADVOCACY ANSWER AND A LOOK BEHIND THE SCENES

If the unsatisfactory historical explanation for the success of Naess's shallow/deep ecology typology is nevertheless one that seems obvious to some ecophilosophers, the satisfactory-as-far-as-it-goes advocacy explanation is one that is obvious to all ecophilosophers. Moreover, the fact that ecophilosophers do not consider it necessary to explicitly examine the question of why it is that Naess's shallow/deep ecology typology has been so successful says something not only about the obviousness of this advocacy explanation but also something about the extent to which it has implicitly been regarded as *adequately* accounting for the success of Naess's typology (i.e., as providing an answer that is entirely satisfactory as opposed to satisfactory-as-far-as-it-goes).

As everyone in the ecophilosophy community will tell you, the success of Naess's shallow/deep ecology typology is due to the fact that it found a couple of persuasive, committed, industrious, and eloquent supporters where the other typologies did not. The widely accepted principle here is that you can keep pushing your own distinction and remain an isolated voice, but as soon as your ideas and terminology find even one or two vigorous advocates you have the beginnings of an identifiable intellectual movement/ grouping/school. Even if detractors should disagree with my choice of adjectives to describe these advocates of Naess's distinction, they would nevertheless agree on the identities of the writers to whom I am referring: Bill Devall and George Sessions. These two thinkers are generally, and rightly, acknowledged by ecophilosophers, first, as being almost wholly responsible for having introduced Naess's distinction to the ecophilosophical community (in about 1979–80); second, as being very largely responsible, along with Naess, for having influenced the ecophilosophical community in general to the point where reference to Naess's typology became accepted as standard within the space of a few years (by around 1983–84); and, third, as being very largely responsible—again, along with Naess—for having influenced a number of individual ecophilosophers to the point where these individuals now identify themselves and/or are identified by other ecophilosophers as *deep ecologists*—or, at least, as close relatives.

I refer to this explanation for the success of Naess's distinction as the *advocacy answer* because it attempts to account for the success of this distinction primarily in terms of the advocacy it received per se, rather than in terms of anything *intrinsic* to Naess's ideas that made his distinction more likely than the other distinctions to attract and then sustain vigorous support. However, despite the fact that everyone in the ecophilosophy community knows that Devall's and Sessions's work was decisive in bringing widespread attention to bear on Naess's distinction, the background to Devall's and Sessions's successful advocacy of Naess's work—"the story behind the headlines," as it were—has received little attention. I therefore propose, in the rest of this section, to outline the background to Devall's and Sessions's successful advocacy of Naess's distinction.[6] In the course of doing this I will also provide an introduction to the group of ecophilosophical thinkers who have been influenced by Devall, Sessions, and Naess to the point where they now identify themselves and/ or are identified by other ecophilosophers as deep ecologists, or as close relatives.

Devall and Sessions met in 1968 when they shared an office at Humboldt State University in Arcata in northern California. Both were thirty. Sessions had just completed graduate school at the University of Chicago (1964–68), where, he says, he had been "intensely involved in analytic philosophy and philosophy of science," and had come to Humboldt to take up his first teaching job. Devall had begun his teaching career in 1966 as a sociologist at the University of Alberta, where he taught for the two years prior to his arrival at Humboldt. In between his teaching duties at Humboldt, Devall would fly down to San Francisco to do research for his doctorate (from the University of Oregon, 1970) on "The Governing of a Voluntary Organization: Oligarchy and Democracy in the Sierra Club." Despite the sober title of his thesis, Devall was studying the Sierra Club—established in 1892 under the leadership of John Muir, one of its cofounders—at a fascinating and turbulent time in its history, for this was the period in which internal frictions led to the ousting/resignation of David Brower, the Club's executive director from 1952 to 1969. This event, in turn, led to Brower's establishing Friends of the Earth, a little over two months after his resignation. Sessions was also very interested in these events. Having shared John Muir's and David Brower's passion for rock climbing and mountaineering in the Yosemite area since his middle teens, Sessions had adopted these figures as early heroes and had joined the Sierra Club when he was fifteen. He was subsequently appointed to the Mountaineering Committee of the Sierra Club in 1962, at age twenty-four.

Sessions left Humboldt at the end of the 1968–69 academic year to take up a teaching job at Sierra College in Rocklin, California—considerably closer to Yosemite. He has continued to work at Sierra College since then, while Devall has continued to work at Humboldt. The next few paragraphs will focus on Sessions's work during the early to mid-1970s, because, as would be expected from considering Devall's and Sessions's differing kinds of Ph.D. training (sociology/politics and philosophy respectively), it was Sessions's work that was most relevant to the development of ecophilosophy during the early years of their professional careers. Devall's crucial contributions to the advocacy and development of deep ecology entered the picture in the later 1970s.

By the time Sessions moved to Sierra College he had been strongly affected by Lynn White's 1967 article on the historical roots of ecological destruction, as well as by Paul Ehrlich's ecological work on the implications of exponential human population growth. In consequence, he began to think seriously about the philosophical foundations of ecological problems. The initial result was a sixty-page paper—completed in 1973 but never published in its original form—entitled "The Metaphysics of Ecology." However, when Devall invited Sessions to contribute to a special issue of the *Humboldt Journal of Social Relations* that he was editing on environmentalism, Sessions pared this paper down, and the result was published in the Fall/Winter 1974 issue of HJSR under the title "Anthropocentrism and the Environmental Crisis."[7] This erudite paper, which deserves far wider notice among philosophers than its publication in HJSR has been able to bring, effectively provides in just a few pages an overview of Western philosophy from an anti-anthropocentric point of view.

In 1973 Sessions met Joseph Meeker, who was teaching at UC Santa Barbara and was environment editor of the *North American Review*. Meeker told Sessions about an invitational conference on The Rights of Nonhuman Nature that was being coordinated by John Rodman and that was to be held at Pitzer College, Claremont, California, in April 1974. Sessions sent a copy of his "Metaphysics of Ecology" paper to Rodman and asked if he could participate in the conference. He received an encouraging response and was invited to the conference to comment on the papers that were to be delivered by the Whiteheadian process philosophy oriented thinkers Charles Birch, John Cobb, and Charles Hartshorne (other paper presenters included, along with Meeker and Rodman, Garrett Hardin, William Leiss, John Lilly, John Livingston, Roderick Nash, and Paul Shepard). Sessions's commentary—another lengthy and erudite paper—was entitled "Panpsychism versus Modern Materialism: Some Implications for an Ecological Ethics."[8] An anthology that was supposed to have come out of the conference never eventuated. The result was that Sessions's paper was never published. (Meeker saw to the publication of a number of papers from the conference in the *North American Review*; however, Sessions's paper was obviously too lengthy and heavily footnoted for this kind of publication and, as a detailed commentary, properly required publication along with the conference papers with which it was concerned.) Sessions responded to this situation by putting out the first of his *Ecophilosophy* newsletters in 1976, "to keep the ideas going." As he stated in the opening paragraph of that first newsletter: "This newsletter is intended to serve as a postscript to my recent papers on ecophilosophy—'Anthropocentrism and the Environmental Crisis' and 'Panpsychism versus Modern Materialism'—and to provide an updated bibliography for those reading and writing in ecophilosophy. I would be happy to supply an initial mailing list for anyone interested in continuing the 'informal newsletter' tradition. But perhaps the time is ripe for an ecophilosophy journal. Any prospective editors?" At this stage, there was no established ecophilosophical forum such as *Environmental Ethics* or *The Trumpeter*.

Meeker also told Sessions in 1973 about the Norwegian philosopher Arne Naess, whom Meeker knew personally. One of the things that initially interested Sessions about Naess was Naess's strong interest in, and innovative approach to, the work of Spinoza. Sessions says that he had himself "arrived at Spinoza as the answer in the process of teaching history of philosophy by about 1972 and independently of being in contact with Naess." Sessions therefore wrote to Naess at this time, and their association has continued ever since.

Naess invited Sessions to the Scandinavian Spinoza Symposium held in 1977—the three hundredth anniversary of Spinoza's death—but Sessions could not attend.[9] However, at Naess's urging, Sessions submitted his paper on "Spinoza and Jeffers on Man in Nature"—yet another lengthy and erudite affair—to that year's edition of *Inquiry*, and it was promptly published.[10] In one of the many footnotes to his paper (a mine of information in themselves), Sessions referenced a number of Naess's ecophilosophically relevant books and papers, including the 1973 paper in which Naess introduced the shallow/deep ecology distinction.

As far as I am aware, this is the earliest reference to Naess's 1973 paper, by an author other than Naess, in a mainstream philosophy journal.[11] Sessions also commented in this footnote: "Naess has been the most outspoken advocate of an ecological interpretation of Spinozism and I have profited considerably from his writings."[12] Sessions finally got to meet Naess for the first time in the spring of the following year (1978) when Naess, as a visiting professor at UC Santa Cruz, called together a group of Spinoza scholars from California and beyond "to discuss teaching Spinoza as deep ecology and as a 'way of life.' "[13]

During this period, Devall had been engaged in sociological and political science research on environmental issues rather than specifically philosophically oriented research.[14] In addition, he had been devoting much time and energy to environmental activism, which he continues to do. As Sessions wrote of Devall in his second (1979) *Ecophilosophy* newsletter:

> Bill has put his deep ecology commitment into practice. He practices "living in place" with a very low-entropy, low consumption life style. For the last ten years, Bill has worked relentlessly with environmental organizations and individually to save the Siskiyous, redwoods, Humboldt Bay and seacoast, and the entire North Coast area from further environmental degradation from the US Forest Service, the timbering companies, developers, and others. He was largely instrumental in setting up the Northcoast Environmental Center, a coalition of environmental groups (Sierra Club, Audubon, Friends of Earth, Friends of the River, etc.) and a model of its kind. Bill is a frequent contributor to *Econews* (Newsletter of the Northeast Environmental Center).[15]

Devall's combination of intellectual and activist engagement in environmentally related matters during the 1970s had led him to grow increasingly disenchanted with the dominant approaches to environmentalism, approaches that he felt were too reformist, too concerned with symptoms rather than underlying causes. "My intuition," he says, "said something was needed that was not being addressed by the Sierra Club and other such groups." This sense of disenchantment had been progressively leading him to extend his reading and professional concerns beyond sociology and politics to take in history and philosophy as well. When Devall read Naess's 1973 paper in 1977 he felt that he had found the touchstone he had been looking for. In Devall's opinion, "Naess said what needed to be said." Inspired by Naess's paper, Devall wrote a short article on the shallow and deep ecology movements entitled "Currents in the River of Environmentalism" for the April 1977 issue of *Econews*.[16] Sessions correctly notes in regard to this article that "Until that time virtually no one had paid much attention (except perhaps in Scandinavia) to Naess's paper." (Sessions's references to Naess's paper in his 1976 *Ecophilosophy* newsletter and his 1977 "Spinoza and Jeffers" paper simply noted the publication details of Naess's paper, without elaborating upon its content. Devall's *Econews* article, on the other hand, elaborated the shallow/deep ecology distinction but, appearing as it did in an activist oriented magazine, did not reference Naess's paper.)

The sense of enthusiastic discovery that Devall and Sessions experienced in the course of further developing Naess's distinction clearly comes across in Sessions's review of these events. Sessions says he "picked up on Devall's short piece and encouraged him to turn it into something longer." Inspired by the implications that he saw in Naess's distinction, Devall had accelerated the development of his already growing interests in the philosophical and historical aspects of environmentalism. So Devall, with encouragement and suggestions from Sessions, lengthened his original piece. "By this time," says Sessions, "we were both getting excited about it. Then it became a question of what to classify where. I finally decided that animal liberation was a shallow position." Devall continued to work on the paper, with input from Sessions, until it reached its final, monograph-length version under the title of "Streams of Environmentalism" in 1979. Sessions described this paper at the time (accurately, in my view) as making "an immense contribution to sorting out the different contemporary environmental movements."[17] However, when it came to journal submission, "Streams" ran into the same problem as some of Sessions's earlier papers: it proved to be too long for acceptance as a single journal article. Devall therefore wrote it up as two separate papers, leaving out large chunks of the original in the process and reworking much of what he retained. These papers were published as "Reformist Environmentalism" in a 1979 issue of the *Humboldt Journal of Social Relations* and "The Deep Ecology Movement" in a 1980 issue of the *Natural Resources Journal* devoted to the topic of environmentalism.[18]

The latter paper constituted the first full-length elaboration of deep ecology to be published in an academic journal. The five-and-a-half page 1973 paper in which Naess introduced the term *deep ecology* consisted essentially of a series of seven suggestive points that made no attempt to survey the existing ecophilosophically relevant literature in terms of the typology that was being suggested. Moreover, as we will see in the next section of this chapter, even though Naess continued to develop the *ideas* associated with deep ecology in a number of publications between 1973 and 1980, he did so with only passing reference to the term *deep ecology* itself and continued to be relatively unconcerned with surveying the ecophilosophically relevant literature from the point of view of his distinction. In contrast, Devall's paper both elaborated the basic ideas of deep ecology at greater length *under the name of deep ecology* and surveyed and classified much of the existing literature in terms of its points of contact with these ideas.

"By this time," says Sessions, "I was all fired up and went to work on *Ecophilosophy II* (1979)" (this was Sessions's first ecophilosophy newsletter since *Ecophilosophy I* in 1976). In this second newsletter, Sessions continued the process begun in Devall's monograph of employing Naess's shallow/deep ecology typology to classify the various sources of ecophilosophically relevant ideas. Under shallow ecology he classified the resource conservation and development position and the future generations of humans position; the philosophy of humanism; and the animal rights or "animal liberation" movement. Under deep ecology he classified Christian Franciscanism (as opposed to Benedictine resource stewardship); the philosophy of Spinoza; the later philosophy of

WHY SO INFLUENTIAL? o 67

Martin Heidegger; the pantheistic ecophilosophy of Robinson
Jeffers; Aldo Leopold's ecosystem-oriented ethics; John Rodman's
ecological resistance/ecological sensibility position; Eastern process philosophy (Taoism and Buddhism); Western process philosophy (Heraclitus, Whitehead, and, for Sessions, Spinoza as well);
and the ecological wisdom of various tribal cultures. In regard to
this last category, Sessions says that he "spent time with Gary
Snyder [a Pulitzer prize winning ecopoet, Zen Buddhist, reinha-
bitant, and student of "the old ways," i.e., of primal peoples]
who gave me a great deal of anthropological and bioregional
information which I incorporated into that [second] issue of the
[Ecophilosophy] newsletter."

Sessions also completed two other significant papers during
this 1979–80 period, both for conferences. The first was in
response to an invitation to participate in the Reminding national
conference, held in San Raphael, California, in mid-1979. For
this conference, Sessions again combined his interests in Spinoza
and ecology but, this time, in the light of his and Devall's
current work, drew on Naess's work far more extensively and
explicitly than in his 1977 "Spinoza and Jeffers" paper. The
result was a paper entitled "Spinoza, Perennial Philosophy and
Deep Ecology."[19] Sessions was pleased to meet thinkers such as
Gregory Bateson, David Bohm, Jacob Needleman, and Theodore
Roszak at this conference but notes that he "wasn't impressed
with talk of implicate order and holograms, although it was all
the rage."[20] Once again, an anthology that was supposed to have
come out of the conference never eventuated and, once again,
Sessions did not publish his paper elsewhere but rather simply
distributed it among interested members of the ecophilosophy
community.

The other paper that Sessions wrote during this period was in
response to an invitation from the enviromental historian Donald
Hughes to write the bibliographical essay for the Earthday X
Colloquium to be held at the University of Denver in April
1980. This conference was to be the most significant ecophilosophy conference held in the United States since the 1974 Rights
of Nonhuman Nature conference. Hughes's invitation followed

in response to Sessions's shallow/deep ecology based overview of the philosophical literature in *Ecophilosophy II*, which had been circulated to about 150 scholars and others. Sessions researched his essay, which drew on "Streams of Environmentalism" and his *Ecophilosophy II* work, throughout the fall of 1979 and up to the time of the conference. The result, published the following year in the proceedings of the conference, was an authoritative, broad-ranging, and bibliographically detailed review of the ecophilo-sophical literature from the perspective of deep ecology.[21]

Taken together, then, the following combination of events meant that by 1980 deep ecology had "arrived": Devall's privately distributed paper on "Streams of Environmentalism" (1979), the publication of his two papers on "Reformist Environmentalism" (1979) and "The Deep Ecology Movement" (1980), the publicity given to these papers in Sessions's privately distributed *Ecophilosophy II* newsletter (1979), Sessions's privately distributed paper on "Spinoza, Perennial Philosophy and Deep Ecology" (as well as the distribution of his earlier papers— "Anthropocentrism and the Environmental Crisis," "Panpsychism versus Modern Materialism," and "Spinoza and Jeffers on Man in Nature"—which, by 1979–80, were being distributed by Sessions in the spirit of them being articulations of deep ecology written prior to his employment of that particular term), and Sessions's deep ecology based overviews of the ecophilosophical literature in *Ecophilosophy II* (1979) and for the Earthday X Colloquium (1980). In reviewing these events at my request, Sessions is absolutely correct to conclude: "So, I suppose you could say that these events, from 1978–80, more or less lifted Naess's distinction and paper out of relative obscurity and into the center of the ecophilosophical debate."

The first papers drawing on deep ecology by writers other than Devall, Sessions, and Naess began to appear in 1980.[22] As we will see below, this trickle has swelled to a steady flow—perhaps at times a torrent—as others have also joined in the task of articulating deep ecology in a positive way. The upshot, as already noted in chapter 2, was that by as early as February 1983 John Passmore felt confident in writing that "it is now customary to divide the family of 'ecophilosophers' . . . into two genera, the 'shallow' and the 'deep' " (and this observation in an article written for a general rather than an academic audience).[23] Looking back from the vantage point of 1987, Alston Chase, writing on deep ecology in *Rolling Stone* magazine (which itself says much about the spread of deep ecology), considers that "it took the environmental community by storm."[24]

From 1980 to 1983–84, the papers that appeared on deep ecology were virtually all essentially positive in their approach (although the vast majority of these were still being written by Devall, Sessions, and Naess). However, while the positive articulation of deep ecology has continued apace since 1983–84, we have seen in chapter 2 that, since 1983–84, deep ecology has also attracted a range of critiques. Thus, the development of deep ecology since Naess's proposal of his distinction in 1973 can be divided into three general periods: first, a latency period, which corresponds to the period up to and including Devall's and Sessions's work on Naess's distinction prior to its "arrival" on the ecophilosophical scene in 1980; second, a honeymoon period, which corresponds to the period from 1980 to 1983–84, during which deep ecology began to attract widespread positive attention but little in the way of published criticism; and third, a post-honeymoon, or maturing period, which corresponds to the period since 1983–84, during which many critiques of deep ecology have appeared at the same time as a growing number of writers have been drawn to the task of helping to develop deep ecology ideas in a positive way.

Devall and Sessions have continued to be extremely active in promoting deep ecology in its post-1980 phases through *Ecophilosophy* newsletters III (1981)–VI (1984), individually written papers, a joint paper published in *Environmental Ethics,* their joint book entitled *Deep Ecology*, participation in open conferences in both the U.S. and (for Devall) Australia, and participation in in-house gatherings. Through these writings and personal interactions, Devall and Sessions have, along with Naess, played a leading role not just in elaborating the ideas of deep ecology but also in encouraging a number of other ecologically concerned thinkers to join with them in this task. The upshot is that there now exists a group of ecophilosophical thinkers who both identify themselves and are identified by other ecophilosophers as being devoted to the elaboration of deep ecology.

In addition to Devall, Sessions, and Naess, the main writers who have been committed to developing the ideas of deep ecology and defending them against criticism over the last few years include Alan Drengson (University of Victoria, B.C.), Michael Zimmerman (Tulane University, New Orleans), and myself (University of Tasmania). But many other people have also been making significant contributions to deep ecology theorizing. They include those who are sympathetic to deep ecology but who tend to refer to deep ecology in their writings only occasionally or in passing rather than making its elaboration the focus of *most* of their work; those who do tend to focus specifically on deep ecology in their writings but whose primary profession or interest means that they are not engaged in writing on a regular basis (e.g., those whose primary profession involves either experientially as opposed to theoretically oriented teaching or hands-on activism as opposed to theoretically oriented activism, which is what I consider committed ecophilosophy to be); those who may be devoted to the development of the ideas of deep ecology but who have only recently begun to write on deep ecology; and those who are primarily dedicated to the elaboration of an ecophilosophical approach that is essentially similar to the deep ecology approach but which is not elaborated under that name (an obvious example is Rodman's work on *ecological resistance* and *ecological sensibility*). These (by no means exclusive) categories of writers include such people as: Dolores LaChapelle, a ritualist and experientially oriented teacher who directs the Way of the Mountain Learning Center in Silverton, Colorado; the Zen Buddhist teacher Robert Aitken; the Zen Buddhist practitioner, student of primal cultures, and distinguished ecologically inspired poet Gary Snyder; John Seed, who runs the Rainforest Information Centre from Lismore in New South Wales, Australia; Joanna Macy, a Buddhist scholar and social/ecological activist who focuses on experiential approaches to personal and community empowerment; Jeremy Hayward, a scholar of science and spirituality, Buddhist practitioner, and founding trustee of the Naropa Institute; and the following ecophilosophers: Neil Evernden and John Livingston (both at York University, Downsview, Ontario), Andrew McLaughlin (Lehman College, New York), Freya Mathews (Murdoch University, Western Australia), John Rodman (Pitzer College, Claremont, California), David Rothenberg (Boston University), and Alan Wittbecker (Marsh Institute, Viola, Indiana). New writers are also beginning to emerge and to add their voices to the positive articulation and defense of the field of deep ecology.[25]

A guide to the work of all of these authors is provided in appendix A: "A Guide to the Primary Sources on Deep Ecology Published During the 1980s."

We have now seen the decisive role that Devall's and Sessions's work has played in bringing deep ecology to the attention of ecologically concerned thinkers in general and in inspiring others to join with them in this task. But it now becomes apparent that the advocacy answer to the question, Why has deep ecology been so influential? still leaves us with the question of how to account for Devall's and Sessions's initial attraction to Naess's ideas. Moreover, and perhaps even more significantly, we are left with the question of how to account for the fact that these ideas have *continued* to be of interest to Devall and Sessions—and, increasingly, to other writers as well. More generally, we are led to ask: What is it about Naess's ideas that has *sustained* a relatively united and vigorous commitment from a variety of ecophilosophically oriented thinkers; why haven't they, like so many other ideas, come and gone in a "flavor-of-the-month" fashion?

One possible response to these questions is to refuse to go beyond the advocacy answer; that is, to say that there is nothing of particular note about Naess's ideas per se; that Devall and Sessions "just happened" to come across Naess's distinction (as opposed to one of the other distinctions I have noted) at a time when they were receptive to the usefulness of such a distinction, and that the success of Naess's distinction is more or less solely due to Devall's and Sessions's vigorous advocacy and elaboration of this distinction. The implication here would be that Devall and Sessions might just as easily have taken up some other comparable distinction to Naess's with similar results. However, any familiarity with the work of Devall, Sessions, and Naess will show that this view is empty. The question of why deep ecology has become so influential requires an additional, and deeper, answer.

THE SUBSTANTIVE ANSWER

A close examination of Devall's and Sessions's work shows that they have not simply borrowed Naess's distinction; they have drawn upon Naess's ecophilosophical ideas in general, to the point where one can say that the essential ideas to be found in Devall's and Sessions's work on deep ecology can all be traced back to Naess. This is, of course, not to take anything away from the skillful and influential elaboration of these ideas by Devall and Sessions, but it is to say that there is something about Naess's ideas per se that has defined and sustained the approach to ecophilosophy that goes under the name of deep ecology.

A single but significant illustration of this general point can be seen by turning to chapter 5 of Devall and Sessions's *Deep Ecology*, in which the central ideas of deep ecology are presented. Following a brief introduction, this chapter essentially consists of three parts: the first explicates the "ultimate norms" that Naess has proposed as the basis of his own system of *ecosophy* (i.e., "ecological wisdom");[26] the second centers on a list of eight "basic principles of deep ecology" that were drawn up by Naess and Sessions while camping together in Death Valley, California, in April 1984, and which have since been presented by Naess and Sessions in a variety of contexts; and the third consists of excerpts from an interview with Naess on deep ecology that was conducted at the Zen Center of Los Angeles in April 1982 and published in the Center's journal *The Ten Directions* (see the list of Naess's publications in appendix A for precise publication details). Thus, Devall and Sessions's explication of the philosophical heart of deep ecology in *Deep Ecology* literally consists of Naess, Naess (together with Sessions), and more Naess. It is not for nothing, then, that Devall and Sessions dedicated their book to Naess (along with Gary Snyder).

As a way of amplifying this point, let me also say that the more I have immersed myself not just in the writings of Devall and Sessions but in the writings of all those people that I have included within the deep ecology fold (*fold* in the sense of "any group or community sharing a way of life or holding the same values"), the more I have come to the conclusion that the *essential* ideas of deep ecology either derive from Naess's work or, at the least, find their most explicit and detailed articulation in his work. Thus, even if other deep ecology writers have not drawn upon Naess's ideas as consciously as have Devall and Sessions, it is the similarity of their ideas and sensibility to those of Naess that, in my view, has led them to be perceived as deep ecologists—or as close relatives.

What I am suggesting, then, is that there is something *distinctive* about the substance of Naess's ideas and sensibility that resonated strongly with Devall and Sessions in the first place and that has continued to interest them and, increasingly, other writers as well. Another way of putting this is to say that there is a legitimate answer to the question, Why has deep ecology been so influential? in addition to the advocacy answer. This additional answer is an answer of a deeper kind than the advocacy answer because it helps to explain *why* Naess's ideas have received and continue to receive such advocacy. We can refer to this deeper answer as the *substantive answer* because it refers to the *substance* of Naess's ideas and sensibility.

This substantive answer carries two noteworthy implications. First, the fact that it points to the centrality of the ideas of a Norwegian thinker means that it flies in the face of those critics who find it convenient to imply that deep ecology is some kind of quintessentially Californian fad—something dreamt up by "the California Cosmologists" in their "redwood think tanks"; something that has "parachuted into our midst quite recently from the Sunbelt's bizarre mix of Hollywood and Disneyland."[27]

Indeed, in this regard one can point not only to the fact that the fundamental ideas of deep ecology have been inspired by the work of a Norwegian thinker but also to the fact that these ideas have received strong support in a number of places besides California, such as Australia and Canada. Peter Hay and Marcus Haward provide a likely explanation for this international pattern of interest in deep ecology in their paper "Comparative Green Politics: Beyond the European Context?" They argue that wilderness issues necessitate the raising of fundamental questions about the validity of anthropocentric modes of thinking and acting in a way that other kinds of environmental issues do not. Thus, for them, "the cutting edge of environmentalism" (by which they mean environmentalism that is ecocentrically as opposed to anthropocentrically based) is to be found "in those countries where wilderness rather than nuclear power has provided the main impetus to national green movements, and where left radical political traditions have not been exclusively industrial-Marxist" (since orthodox Marxism both embraces industrialism and reinforces anthropocentrism).[28] Hence, the stronger ecocentric emphasis (and, for our purposes, the stronger interest in deep ecology) in such countries as Australia, Canada, Norway, and the U.S. as compared with, say, England, France, and Germany (notwithstanding the various electoral successes of a number of the European Green parties).

The second, and more significant, implication of the substantive answer to the question of the influence of deep ecology is this: to say that there is something *distinctive* about Naess's ideas is to say that deep ecology does not *simply* refer to a nonanthropocentric, or ecocentric, approach to the world since comparable terms in other similar distinctions all share this meaning, as we have seen. Moreover, if shallow and deep ecology could simply be equated with anthropocentric and nonanthropocentric approaches to environmentalism respectively then it would be necessary to include within the deep ecology fold *all* those thinkers who are concerned with the development of a point of view that is (at least to a reasonable degree) nonanthropocentric. This would mean the inclusion of most ecophilosophers. However, even though the term *deep ecology* is often used in such a way as would warrant this inclusion (i.e., as effectively referring to *any* kind of nonanthropocentric approach), it is nevertheless the case that most ecophilosophers see "the deep ecologists" as a more or less distinctive subset of their number—a subset whose membership is constituted along the lines of the group of thinkers already mentioned. Neither can there be any doubt that this particular subset of ecophilosophical thinkers also see themselves as having far more in common with each other's ideas than with the ideas of the ecophilosophical mainstream. Thus, there is at least an implicit acceptance within both the larger ecophilosophical community and the deep ecology fold itself that while the term *deep ecology* can and does refer to a nonanthropocentric approach to environmentalism, it also stands for a particular *kind* (or, perhaps, particular kinds) of nonanthropocentric approach.

This line of reasoning runs down the middle of what appear to be the two main ways of thinking about deep ecology. The first is that of considering deep ecology to stand for a *single* basic idea, namely, the idea of nonanthropocentrism or ecocentrism. The other main way of thinking about deep ecology—one that appeals especially to critics who either fail to or do not wish to acquaint themselves with the deep ecology literature in anything more than a superficial manner—is that of considering deep ecology to be a catch-all for any number of ideas that are more or less vaguely related to ecology and environmentalism. For these commentators, deep ecology is an ideological hodgepodge which, in the words of Alston Chase, "has more interpretations than the Bible."[29] On this view, deep ecology does not constitute a coherent enough body of ideas to warrant anyone seriously talking about it as offering any distinct—let alone distinctive— kind of approach to anything.

In contrast to these views, I intend to show that a close analysis of Naess's work reveals that Naess has employed the term *deep ecology* to subsume precisely *three* related but analytically distinct meanings or fundamental ideas. Moreover, while one of these meanings refers to the idea of nonanthropocentrism or ecocentrism in general (this being the sense in which I have been referring to deep ecology up until now and the sense in which deep ecology is popularly understood), another of these meanings defines a particular kind of nonanthropocentric approach that is distinctive to deep ecology. I will be arguing that the third sense of deep ecology that is to be found in Naess's work is largely confined to his work, and that it is, in any case, untenable.

The term *deep ecology* can therefore be seen as one that does double duty, referring on the one hand to a whole class of approaches (i.e., all nonanthropocentric approaches) and on the other hand to a particular kind of approach within this class. This, I think, accounts for the vaguely defined sense that many people have of deep ecology as offering an ecumenical face while at the same time possessing a distinctive esoteric core. Indeed, the use of such a spiritual/religious metaphor is appropriate here in that, as we will see in later chapters, the "esoteric core" of deep ecology is bound up with the psychological-spiritual-metaphysical idea of what Naess refers to as *Self-realization*.

Having indicated this much about the various meanings associated with Naess's conception of deep ecology, it is important to note two things in regard to the claim of this section that Devall and Sessions took up Naess's distinction not simply because it offered a catchy pair of labels to use in distinguishing between anthropocentric and nonanthropocentric approaches but also, and more particularly, because it offered a distinctive kind of approach to nonanthropocentrism. The first is that Naess was developing the idea of *Self-realization,* usually, but not always, linking it to his term *deep ecology,* in *numerous* publications prior to and during the time that Devall and Sessions were beginning to present his shallow/deep distinction to a wider audience (i.e., up to and including 1980).[30] And, second, on the other side of the coin as it were, one can trace Devall's and Sessions's attraction to the metaphysical-spiritual basis of deep ecology, their cognizance and referencing of Naess's Self-realization work, and their employment of Naess's term *Self-realization* (as well as terms of their own that do similar work) from 1978–80 on.[31]

I will show in part four that it is Devall's and Sessions's commitment to the substance of Naess's Self-realization approach (even if they sometimes employ different terms) that constitutes the distinguishing feature of their own, and their deep ecology colleagues', approach to ecophilosophy. First, we will turn, in part three, to a presentation and critical consideration of Naess's three senses of deep ecology.

PART THREE

THE LABEL *DEEP ECOLOGY*: ITS MEANINGS AND SHORTCOMINGS

There is nothing in "ecosophy," or in any other more fragmentary work, which I would regard as established. On the contrary, I feel that all I have published has been "on the way.". . . When I leave a subject and proceed to something new, it is always because I am impelled to do so by the movement of my own thought and actions, not because what I leave seems well enough worked out and accomplished. With greater talents, the works would have been better rounded off, but basically I think humans are something essentially "on the way," destination unknown, and they are justified in expressing themselves, talented or not, when moving along.

—Arne Naess

4

Arne Naess and the Meanings
of *Deep Ecology*

ARNE NAESS

ARNE NAESS'S ecophilosophical work follows upon an already long and distinguished academic career in which he made substantial contributions not only to a variety of specific areas in philosophy but also to the international philosophy community in general; for example, he founded and for many years edited *Inquiry,* an innovative and internationally respected journal of philosophy and the social sciences.

Naess was born in 1912 and appointed to the chair of philosophy at the University of Oslo at the age of twenty-seven. Prior to taking up this chair, Naess had, in his early to mid-twenties, already attended meetings of the Vienna Circle, the members of which "received [him] with touching cordiality, and for some years treated [him] as a new comet on the philosophical firmament"; he had subjected himself to an intense, fourteen-month, six-days-a-week psychoanalysis with Edward Hitchmann, a personal colleague of Freud's (also in Vienna); and he had worked at Berkeley with the brilliant psychologist and learning theorist E. C. Tolman, a name that should be familiar to every psychology undergraduate.[1] Naess occupied the chair of philosophy at the University of Oslo until 1969. Although Naess could have held this position until 1982, his basic reason for resigning was, he told me, because he "wanted to live rather than to function."

Naess's ecophilosophical work corresponds roughly to the period since his resignation in 1969 and therefore constitutes the most recent phase of his professional work (professional work as distinct from personal interests, since the latter have included a fascination with and love for the nonhuman world for as long as he can remember). This is not to say that Naess has stopped working in other areas of interest since 1969; however, it is to say that there has been a definite emphasis in his other work on subjects that, for Naess, are intimately related to his ecophilosophical work (e.g., normative systems and the philosophies of Spinoza and Gandhi—all of which I will discuss in later sections of this chapter).

Since so much of the rest of this book is concerned with Naess's ideas and influence, and since most non–Norwegian speaking ecophilosophers do not have much of an idea about the nature of Naess's pre-ecophilosophical work or the extent of his influence outside ecophilosophy, I will provide in this section some further introductory remarks on the work and character of Arne Naess. What follows is, however, only an introduction. The idea of attempting to provide a general intellectual biography of Arne Naess is very *tempting,* since Naess's ideas have been developed in the context of an exceptionally rich personal and professional life, but it is not, and cannot be, the task of *this* book to provide such a biography. The following comments and follow-up references should, however, suffice to convey at least a general sense of the inspiring and influential person that is Arne Naess.

The entry for Scandinavian Philosophy in *The Encyclopedia of Philosophy* informs the reader that

> the philosophical milieu in Norway today [i.e., circa 1967] is determined by an internationally known and original philosopher (who is also a famous mountain climber), Arne Naess (born 1912). Naess, who became a professor at Oslo in 1939, is the originator of a radical type of empirical semantics and the leader of the so-called Oslo group. . . . If it is correct that Norwegian philosophy has had a dead period, it is equally correct to assert that, primarily because of Arne Naess, Norwegian philosophy is now in the middle of a period of life and growth.[2]

Some annotations to this entry may be helpful. First, with regard to mountain climbing, Naess is known, among other

ARNE NAESS AND DEEP ECOLOGY ∘ 83

things, for having made the first ascent of Tirich Mir (7,690 meters; 25,230 feet), the highest peak in the Hindu Kush, in 1950. He was climbing in the Himalayas as recently as 1985. Anyone who knows Naess can testify to the fact that he is extraordinarily energetic. For example, having spent time with Naess at his treasured cabin in the mountains of Norway as well as in Oslo (1984), Perth (in Western Australia, 1986), and Hobart (in Tasmania, 1986), I know that discussions with Naess are always punctuated by periods of physical activity—skiing and rock climbing in Norway, for example, and bushwalking and tennis in Australia. Naess would suddenly rise from the table in his isolated cabin and say: "Enough talking for now! Time to do some skiing!" For the record, I can also testify that I have played the most vigorous two hours of tennis of my life with Naess. I was thirty-two at the time, and he was seventy-four. Needless to say, this was not an ordinary game of tennis. We played "Arne's rules," which are exhausting (but lots of fun) *and* noncompetitive.

Second, Naess's work on empirical semantics, which he developed primarily during the 1940s and 1950s, has, as the term suggests, been concerned with exploring the ways in which language is *actually* used in particular contexts. This work needs to be understood largely as a reaction against the emphasis that was placed by the logical atomists (the early Wittgenstein and Russell) and the logical empiricists or logical positivists (the Vienna Circle) upon the logical demarcation of sensical statements from nonsensical statements or, in other words, upon delimiting the ways in which language may *legitimately* be used.[3]

Finally, the so-called dead period in Norwegian philosophy corresponded roughly to the last seventy years of the nineteenth century—a period dominated by Hegelianism—and is so named because hardly anything was published. While there may be no correlation between Hegelianism and a lack of publishing in philosophy, it is nevertheless interesting to note that Naess's Spinozist leanings recall those of Niels Treschow, Norway's first professor of philosophy (University of Oslo, 1813–14), rather than those of Treschow's nineteenth-century Hegelian successors

84 ∘ THE LABEL *DEEP ECOLOGY*

(especially Marcus Jacob Monrad, who held Treschow's chair from 1845 to 1897). Naess's philosophical productivity also recalls that of Treschow, who continued to publish almost until his death in 1833.

In a detailed overview, "Philosophy in Norway since 1936," published in the Polish-based philosophy journal *Ruch Filozoficzny*, the Norwegian philosopher Ingemund Gullvag makes a similar assessment of the significance of Naess's impact upon contemporary Norwegian philosophy to that made in *The Encyclopedia of Philosophy*:

> The philosophical milieu in Norway after the war is to a great extent created and—by agreement or disagreement—for a long time influenced by one man, Arne Naess (1912–). The social science that has developed in this country after the war was also, from the beginning, in no small degree inspired by him. . . . His works and personal influence created a new climate of philosophy as well as social research. . . . [Indeed, Naess's work] became influential not only in philosophy and social research, but in wider circles. It belongs to the intellectual heritage of a whole generation of university trained people, because of the Norwegian system of *examen philosophicum*, requiring all students to pass introductory examinations in logic and methodology and the history of philosophy, regardless of their choice of specialized study. From 1939 till 1954, Naess was the only professor of philosophy in Norway, and in charge of organizing the courses for the *examen philosophicum* [by 1980 Norway had 33 permanent positions in philosophy spread across its four universities]. His paradigm of inquiry . . . soon dominated not only the courses in "logic" . . . but also the courses in the history of philosophy, because of his approach to the subject. . . . This gave rise to an "academic culture" whose influence may be difficult to appreciate for outsiders not trained in it.

Since the fifties, philosophy in Norway has developed towards increasing pluralism. There is now quite a broad spectrum of approaches: analytic and formal methods, ordinary language philosophy, phenomenology, hermeneutics, Marxism, existentialism, transcendental philosophy, historical studies, etc. The pluralism as well as the interest in the history of philosophy are to a great extent due to Naess. Openmindedness in relation to different approaches and positions marks all his writings about other philosophers, and his attitude has influenced many of the philosophers now active in Norway.[4]

Naess has authored a prodigious volume of work in a broad range of areas, and in a number of languages, including Norwegian, Danish, Swedish, German, and English. The most complete published bibliography of his work is contained in the *Philosophers on Their Own Work* series.[5] Although this bibliography only runs up to January 1982 (and Naess has continued to be very productive since then), it records that Naess has authored 28 books; 18 monographs and articles in the University of Oslo's *Philosophical Problems* series; 143 articles in specialized, academic journals and collections (even here, the 143rd entry, for example, actually consist of *nine* replies to articles in a particular book); 45 articles in nonspecialized, general interest journals; 29 articles in newspapers; and 17 mimeographed monographs and other miscellaneous technical articles. It also records that Naess has coauthored another 6 books and monographs and offers 12 examples of "other literary activity (on mountaineering and the like)."

In regard to the broad range of Naess's work, even a casual inspection of the contents of the bibliography in *Philosophers on Their Own Work* reveals that Naess's work covers general philosophical topics, including the history and problems of philosophy; various significant philosophers, such as Kierkegaard, Carnap, Wittgenstein, Heidegger, and Sartre; as well as much work in or on philosophy of science, philosophy of language and communication, logic, skepticism, ethics and (what Naess refers to as) *normative systems,* Spinoza, Gandhi, and *ecosophy* (a term which Naess prefers to the far more widely accepted *ecophilosophy*).

The extent of Naess's philosophical influence is attributable to a number of factors. First, as has just been indicated, there is the sheer volume, substantive range, and typically innovative quality of his work. Second, Naess's work has had an international reach for reasons above and beyond the foregoing. Special note must be made in this regard of *Inquiry,* the well-known interdisciplinary journal of philosophy and the social sciences which Naess founded in 1958 and edited until 1975. Note should also be made here of Naess's visiting professorships, "lecturing in many places, most of them beautiful and preferably near mountains or deserts (some places: Berkeley, Santa Cruz, Reykjavik, Hangzhou, Helsinki, Tromso, Peking, Canton, Hong Kong, Chengdu, Jerusalem. . . .)," as well as his willingness to present his ideas in a variety of popular or semi-popular as opposed to purely academic contexts (examples here include Naess's debate with A. J. Ayer on Dutch television in the early 1970s; his interview for the journal of the Zen Center of Los Angeles in 1982; and his 1987 Schumacher Lecture in Britain).[6] But above and beyond these reasons it is also clear that the extent of his influence is also very much a function of a certain spirit of genuine inquiry that pervades his life and work. In their preface to *In Sceptical Wonder*, the delightfully titled collection of "inquiries into the philosophy of Arne Naess on the occasion of his 70th birthday," Naess's colleagues Ingemund Gullvag and Jon Wetlesen comment on Naess's spirit of inquiry in the course of explaining the relevance of the *festschrift's* title:

> According to an old saying by Aristotle, philosophy starts from a sense of wonder. It seems, however, that many philosophers stop wondering pretty soon, and become more preoccupied with certain answers than with the questions that gave rise to them. Some philosophers, on the other hand, manage to keep their wonder alive, to question old answers and raise new ones. This would apply to those who have a sceptical bent of mind, especially to the Pyrrhonian sceptics, or the *zetetai* as they preferred to call themselves, that is, the seekers or inquirers.
>
> Arne Naess appears to be a philosopher of this kind. When he started an interdisciplinary journal of philosophy and the social sciences in 1958, he first wanted to call it *Zetetikos*. It was, however, named *Inquiry*. Over the years Naess has opened up many fields of research and inspired others to follow suit. At the age of 70 he continues to be a vigorous and unconventional inquirer and a major source of inspiration in Scandinavian philosophy and social science. In the eyes of many he encourages not only professional research, but also a search at a deeper level connected with what was called wisdom in the ancient traditions.[7]

As this assessment implies, Naess's personality has itself been a factor in the attention that his work has received. Fons Elders makes some interesting observations about the personalities of the eight philosophers who took part in the series of four debates he organized for Dutch television (as I have noted, Naess debated Ayer; participants in some of the other debates included Karl Popper, Noam Chomsky, and Michel Foucault). In regard to Naess, Elders writes, in part:

> Arne Naess skiing, Arne Naess sitting in the bath, Arne Naess climbing mountains, Arne Naess boxing, Arne Naess living alone in his mountain home, Arne Naess playing the comic, Arne Naess writing about scepticism. . . .
>
> Arne Naess is a radical pluralist. . . . I have sometimes wondered how Arne Naess would have reacted to all the philosophers of *Reflexive Water*. His philosophy would have prepared him to meet each of them on his own terms, but without accepting a final "truth" in any of their systems. . . . I got the impression that Naess approaches everyone, from the beginning, on the assumption that they are going to be both right *and* wrong.
>
> I told him of my plan to write about each of the eight philosophers in a postscript, giving my impressions of their philosophies and their personalities. I also expressed my fear that to do so might create some misunderstandings at a personal level, and that I might lose the friendship or trust of some of them. He predicted that this would happen; that probably none of the eight would like what I was writing, but that I should go ahead, if I felt it to be right. I liked Naess's answer because it is at the heart of his philosophy to approach situations in a radical pluralist way.[8]

What, then, is Elders's impression of the relationship between Naess's philosophy and Naess's personality? Although he refers to Naess as "an extraordinary thinker in Western philosophy," Elders notes that "Naess is not as integrated [psychologically], and probably cannot be as integrated as his philosophy demands that he should be. How can one take seriously every different kind of philosophy without ending up like a king looking down from the top of a mountain?" Contrasting Ayer and Naess in regard to the relative integration of their philosophies and personalities, Elders reiterates this view of Naess:

> Both Ayer and Naess are, in my opinion, classic examples of this paradoxical relationship [in which "often a philosophy is quite at variance with the psychology of its proponent"]: the integration which Naess defends philosophically is not matched by an equal integration at the emotional level, while the emotional integration shown by Ayer does not correspond to an equally integrated philosophy. Many philosophers seem to develop a philosophy to counteract their psychological make-up rather than as an elaboration, justification, or coherent cosmology based on and expressive of their whole life-style.[9]

Elders has also drawn attention to the way in which Naess's radical pluralism informs his character, and vice versa, in the opening essay of the *festschrift* for Naess's seventieth birthday: "Arne Naess laughs a lot too, sometimes with a poker face, sometimes without, then suddenly he looks very serious. He is an actor, because he is the bearer of many perspectives, which all have certain aspects of truth for him."[10] Nor is Elders the only commentator to have made this kind of observation about Naess. For example, the final essay in the same *festschrift, In Sceptical Wonder,* is a humorous but nevertheless instructive treatment by Geir Hestmark of the many faces of Arne Naess. Hestmark provides an account of a meeting of "The Loch Naess Monster Research Society," which is constituted by nine, jokingly named fictitious characters who represent different aspects of Arne Naess: the scientific behaviorist, the Pyrrhonian sceptic, the Gandhian, the Spinozist, the empirical semanticist, the ecosopher, and so on. Hestmark warns us in mock seriousness at the outset that "none of the participants were deemed capable of giving an accurate account of the proceedings of the meeting."[11]

Naess is "the bearer of many perspectives" not only with respect to specific philosophical views, but even with respect to the subject of philosophical *style.* For example, in one paper he will say that "while deep ecology need not be a finished philosophical system, this does not mean that its philosophers should not try to be as clear as possible"¹²; yet elsewhere he will sing the praises of vagueness:

> If something is vague and open to many interpretations and precisations, it leads to discussion. And that is the most we can hope for any honest philosophy in today's world. It can become well known, and may have an influence. Within existentialism, Zapffe [a significant Norwegian existentialist] is not so well known because he is *too precise*. His ideas are so disturbing, humorous and tough, *but they are clear*. But Sartre is so vague, many people want to talk about him. . . . Now "Self-realization" [which, as we will see, is the central term in Naess's own ecophilosophical approach] like "non-violence," is a vague term. . . . It is tantalizing for our culture, this seeming lack of explanation. . . . Being more precise does not necessarily create something that is more inspiring (emphases added).¹³

It is at least arguable then that Naess is the bearer of so many perspectives that it would simply be impossible for him to be able to maintain them all at the same time without cutting the odd logical corner or engaging in a bit of plain bluffing here and there. Moreover, anyone who knows Naess knows that he will sometimes adopt fairly extreme positions (or do certain things!) not because he considers that his view has any privileged status vis-à-vis other views but rather in order both to provoke others to think through their own position and to encourage openness to a diversity of views. As Naess would be the first to point out, for him to seriously maintain that whatever position he had adopted was the "correct" one would, in any case, be incompatible with his Pyrrhonian skepticism.

Although it is true that Naess's character is nothing if not complex (which can lead to frustration but never to boredom!), one also realizes, over time, that Naess demonstrates a stance toward the world that is consistently open, playful, inquiring, supportive, and generous in spirit. And that kind of consistency is tremendously impressive. None of this is to say that Naess does not oppose certain things, but it is to say that in situations of conflict, including ecological conflict, Naess is as open to, cheerful with, interested in, supportive of, and generous to those whose views he is attempting to change as the circumstances will allow. Taken together with his many and diverse achievements, this disposition adds up to a person who employs a light touch in the service of a profound intelligence and a remarkably strong will.

Finally, as this last observation no doubt suggests, Naess's work has also been influential because it has not been restricted to theory. Thus, for example, Erik Dammann, the Norwegian founder of the Future in Our Hands movement, comments on the significance of Naess's engagement in ecologically oriented nonviolent action as follows:

> As we have seen, a number of academics in several countries have already given up their elite positions in order to make their knowledge available to [grassroots] movements and to use their analytical faculties in investigating the possibilities for action on the movements' premises. A Norwegian example is the philosopher Arne Naess who gave up his professorship and emerged from academic isolation in order to be freer to participate in the multitude of popular campaigns for ecology and social change. His fearless action has added weight to these campaigns, and the well-known picture of the internationally renowned professor calmly being carried away by the police from the protest camp at Mardola has certainly given many good citizens a new understanding that activists are not only "hysterical extremists." His books, perhaps especially *Ecology, Society and Lifestyle,* have without doubt strengthened many of the more intellectually oriented campaigners in their understanding of such things as the importance of a holistic approach and of value priorities.[14]

As we will see in the section on "Naess's Philosophical Sense of Deep Ecology," Naess's interest in Gandhi's philosophy of nonviolent direct action dates to 1930. Naess's experiences in actions of nonviolent resistance include involvement in the Norwegian nonviolent resistance movement to Nazi occupation during World War II and, subsequently, involvement in the peace movement (especially during the postwar years to 1955) and the ecology movement (especially since 1970). In view of this, it is perhaps surprising to realize that Naess has a practical as opposed to armchair interest in boxing! (As I have said, Naess's character is nothing if not complex.) Naess claims that such experience aids in developing fearlessness for actions of nonviolent resistance. I suppose that is true, but would suggest that aikido is the martial art that is most suited to the philosophy of nonviolent participation in conflict situations. To my mind, boxing is the antithesis of aikido. (It is interesting to note in this regard that Bill Devall and Alan Drengson are both experienced practitioners of aikido.) That said, it is probably true to say that Naess has an aikido-like attitude to boxing (if that is not a contradiction in terms!).

In a paper entitled "Intellectuals and Popular Movements: The Alta Confrontation in Norway," Ron Eyerman describes another protest in which Naess was involved. The Alta confrontation took place on 14 January 1981 when "about 1,000 people, primarily members of a regional Lapp community but including a significant number of college professors, lawyers, and scientists, chained themselves together in a final effort to prevent the construction of a power-plant and dam project in the far north of Norway. During the next 24 hours, they were forceably cut from their chains and carried off by 600 policemen in the biggest police action in Norway's history."[15] Naess was one of those chained among the demonstrators and Eyerman devotes the second half of his paper to an examination entitled "The Politicized Professional: Arne Naess and the Norwegian Ecology Movement."

How, then, does an internationally distinguished professor of philosophy—the epitome of an armchair discipline in the eyes of many—articulate the philosophy that underlies what he refers to as his "participation in environmental conflicts (sometimes being arrested)"?[16] The rest of this chapter is concerned with answering this question.

NAESS'S FORMAL SENSE
OF DEEP ECOLOGY

The best way of approaching the three senses of deep ecology that I consider need to be distinguished in Naess's work is through what I will refer to as Naess's formal sense of deep ecology. This sense of deep ecology is predicated upon the idea of asking progressively deeper questions about the ecological relationships of which we are a part. Naess holds that this deep questioning process ultimately reveals bedrock or end-of-the-line assumptions, which he refers to as *fundamentals,* and that deep ecological views are derived from such fundamentals while shallow ecological views are not.

This asking-deeper-questions/derivation-from-fundamentals sense of deep ecology underpins all of Naess's writings on deep ecology; however, it is only explicitly referred to in some of his published papers, and then often only in passing, which means that one has to know what to look for. What is in many ways the most straightforward and detailed exposition of this sense of deep ecology is contained in an unpublished (and virtually unknown) paper written by Naess in 1982, entitled "Deepness of Questions."[17] I shall therefore concentrate on this paper initially and, since it is virtually unknown, also quote several significant paragraphs from it.

In "Deepness of Questions," Naess argues that "questions are roughly divided into everyday, technical, scientific and philosophical" and that asking progressively deeper questions—asking strings of *why* and/or *how* questions—eventually takes one beyond the realm of the everyday, the technical, and the scientific and into the realm of the philosophical. In Naess's view: "Persistent why's and how's lead to philosophy. . . . *Every why- and how-string leads to philosophy.*" This strikes me as an elegant and simple way of answering the question What is philosophy?—a question to which many philosophers seem unable or unwilling to provide any kind of simple, easily communicated answer.

Naess recognizes that questions can be qualitatively distinguished by criteria other than that of depth and cites "relevance" and "fruitfulness" as examples. On the one hand, deeper questions are often less relevant ones from the point of view of action and, on the other hand, deeper questions are often less fruitful ones from the point of view of scientific research, which is why "the scientist 'jumps off' the [question/answer] string well before landing in philosophy—provided he does not belong to the pioneers working along the borderline between science and philosophy." Moreover, science, in Naess's view, is not the only area of intellectual inquiry in which the participants jump off well before the end of question/answer strings. Naess also thinks that much of modern philosophy "manifests less abhorrence at lack of depth than lack of clarity." In contrast, Naess suggests that "*within* philosophy . . . comparisons of deepness [of questions] may have consequences for decisions about priorities of work."

Against this background, Naess provides a formal definition of deepness of questioning that is theoretically clear (and, hence, helpful at the level of discussion) even if it raises a host of questions at the operational level: "Given a dialogue, or 'question/answer string' of the kind 'Why A?, because B, why B?, because C . . . [or of the kind 'How A?, like this, B; how B?, like this, C; . . .],' a question P is deeper than a question Q, if and only if there is at least one answer which P questions which Q does not question, and there is no answer which Q questions which P does not question."

When Naess turns to consider "the deepness of the deep ecology movement," he explicitly invokes this concept of deepness of questioning:

> Some authors use the term "the deep ecological movement" slightly differently from that originally intended. [Although Naess only says "slightly differently" here, it should be noted that he *typically* states his case in the gentlest possible terms.] This motivated the criterion of deepness of questions [outlined above].
>
> In the movement instigated largely through the effort of Rachel Carson and her friends, the "unecological" policies of industrial nations were sharply criticized. The *foundation* of the criticism was *not* pollution, waste of resources and disharmony between population and production rate in non-industrialized nations. The foundation rested on answers to deeper questions of "why?" and "how?". Consequently the recommended policies also touched fundamentals such as man's attitude towards nature, industrial man's attitude

towards non-industrial cultures, and the ecological aspect of widely different economic systems.

The difference between the shallow and the deep movement is one of deepness of argumentation, and of differences in conclusions. In the shallow movement in favour of decreasing pollution and economy of resources, positions are tacitly assumed valid which are questioned in the deeper movement. But the differences in conclusions are largely due to certain questions, especially of value-priorities, not being seriously discussed and answered in the shallower movement.

I subscribe to the hypothesis that when the deeper issues are introduced in a debate, the conclusions tend towards those of the deeper movement, even among those who at the start of the discussion favoured shallow policies or who did not hold any definite view. . . .

[Nevertheless] because "going deep" is the essential point, I recommend that a point of view might be characterized as "deep" even if it defended some of the most wasteful and socially destructive policies, namely, if it were derived from a coherent philosophy answering deep questions. I wish only to add that I cannot see any philosophy that would be suitable for such a derivation. Whatever philosophy, whether Western or Eastern, we take as a starting point, it will not be compatible with, or at least not suitable for a defense of, present unecological policies.

The mainly technical recommendations of the shallow movement reflect absence of philosophy rather than an unecological philosophy.

According to this view, then, deep ecology is defined in purely formal terms ("asking deeper questions") rather than by reference to its content (i.e., the nature of the answers to these questions). Two consequences and a startling corollary follow immediately. First, whatever its content, a *deep* ecological position is, in contrast to a shallow ecological position, necessarily a philosophical position. This is because a deep ecological position is derived in response to questions that go *deeper* (as that term is formally defined by Naess) than the realm of the everyday, the technical, and the scientific. Second, since the purely formal requirement of "asking deeper questions" cannot by itself guarantee what the answers to such questions will be, there may be many different deep ecological philosophies. Naess therefore refers to his particular articulation of deep ecology, which I will introduce in the next section, as *Ecosophy T: ecosophy* from the combining form *eco-* and the Greek *sophos,* "wisdom" (i.e., "ecological wisdom"), and *T* to emphasize that this particular version of ecosophy is just one possible formulation. The startling corollary to this second consequence of defining deep ecology in a purely formal way is that even an environmentally destructive view must be characterized as a deep ecological philosophy if it is derived from fundamentals. In this regard, I have already quoted Naess as saying "because 'going deep' is the essential point, I recommend that a point of view might be characterized as 'deep' even if it defended some of the most wasteful and socially destructive policies, namely, if it were derived from a coherent philosophy answering deep questions." Naess claims that no deep ecological philosophy (in his formal sense of *deep*) can be derived that would issue in "unecological" practices. However, it should be recognized that if an environmentally destructive point of view should be derived that satisfies Naess's formal requirement of depth then it is not a matter for "recommendation" as to whether it should be characterized as deep, but rather a logical consequence of this definition of deep ecology.

Naess has proposed a four-level derivational model in order to illustrate his view that there can be (and, indeed, are) a multitude of deep ecological philosophies that nevertheless all share certain ecologically relevant features when viewed at a certain level of generality. In order to provide an example of this model rather than simply to describe it in general terms, it is first necessary to introduce the basic ideas and terminology associated with Naess's work on what he refers to as *normative systems.* Naess divides the kinds of formulations that are used in describing any complex view into two classes: evaluative statements, which he refers to as norms, and descriptive statements, which he refers to as hypotheses. (The term *hypotheses* is not meant to indicate uncertainty but rather to suggest at least the possibility of testability and revisability.) Naess distinguishes norms from hypotheses by writing norms with an exclamation mark: for example, Knowledge! (read: "Love/Value Knowledge!"), Communication! (read:

"Love/Value Communication!"), or, Don't Pollute! Naess notes in this regard that "it has been objected that the term 'norm' and the sign of exclamation make the norm-sentences seem absolutistic and rigid. Actually their *main function* is that of proposing tentative guidelines. Little is gained by more complicated, relativistic terminology. Decisions—the aim of normative thinking—are absolutistic in the sense of being either carried out or sabotaged."[18]

With these simple tools, it is possible to specify the basic logical structure of any view that involves both evaluative and descriptive elements. This is done by beginning with evaluative and descriptive assumptions (i.e., norms and hypotheses that are fundamental to a system in the sense that they are not themselves logically derived from any other norms and hypotheses within the system) and then adding defensible hypotheses to logically derive further norms. Here is a simple example of such a normative system:

NORMATIVE SYSTEM K (FOR "KNOWLEDGE")

N1 (read: "norm 1"): Knowledge!
  Comment: This is the most fundamental norm or the top norm in this *particular* normative system in the sense that it is not logically derived from any other norm but rather is itself employed, together with hypotheses that are specified below, to logically derive the other norms in the system. It is also possible, of course, to construct normative systems that proceed from more than one assumed or fundamental norm.

H1 (read: "hypothesis 1"): Knowledge is gained and transmitted most readily by means of clear communication.

H2 (i.e., the second hypothesis in this normative system): Clarity in communication is aided by distinguishing one's evaluative views (norms) from one's descriptive views (hypotheses).

H3: Normative systems of the kind suggested by Naess (and of which this is an example) provide a useful way of attempting to distinguish norms and hypotheses.

N2 (i.e., the second norm in this normative system): Normative systems!

Comment: this is logically derived from N1, H1, H2, and H3.

H4: A good way to learn about normative systems is to read Arne Naess's "Notes on the Methodology of Normative Systems," *Methodology and Science* 10 (1977): 64–79.

N3: Read Naess's paper on normative systems!

Comment: From N2 and H4.

H5: A good way to learn about normative systems is to put some thought into the beginning norms and hypotheses of one's own approach to a specific issue or, more ambitiously, into one's own world-view or one's own approach to the question of what kind of relationship we should have with the nonhuman world.

> *Comment:* My hand-out to students on normative systems carries the following advice at this point: "Don't be surprised if you find yourself having to think quite hard to articulate your own norms and hypotheses—it is always difficult to articulate one's own most fundamental views and assumptions. And don't worry if what you come up with doesn't seem very 'profound' to you—it's a beginning and you can elaborate over time."

N4: Think about how to express one's own approach to a specific issue/one's own world-view/one's own ecophilosophy in the format of a normative system!

Comment: From N2 and H5.

In a hand-out to environmental studies students on normative systems I also add the *hypothesis*:

H6: A good way to learn about normative systems is to arrive at Warwick's lecture/workshop prepared to work on and discuss your own ecophilosophical normative system. [19]

This hypothesis is still being tested; however, it does allow us to derive the logically compelling conclusion(!):

N5: Arrive at Warwick's lecture/workshop prepared to work on and discuss your own ecophilosophical normative system!

This simple example illustrates two general observations that can be made in regard to any normative system. First, normative

systems proceed from very general kinds of norms and hypotheses
(e.g., N1: "Knowledge!"; H1: "Knowledge is gained and transmitted most readily by means of clear communication") to more
and more specific kinds of norms and hypotheses (e.g., N3:
"Read Naess's paper on normative systems!"; N5: "Arrive at
Warwick's lecture/workshop prepared to work on and discuss
your own ecophilosophical normative system!"). Second, the fact
that normative systems proceed from the general to the particular
means that one can unfold the potential meanings of higher level
norms (such as, N1: "Knowledge!") in quite different directions
depending upon the hypotheses that one adds to the system
(e.g., if H1 in the above example were replaced with the
hypothesis "The only true knowledge is direct knowledge of God;
all other forms of knowledge are illusory," then the system would
proceed in an entirely different direction to the one that it
presently takes).

This brief introduction to the basic ideas and terminology
associated with Naess's work on normative systems means that I
am now in a position not only to outline the general structure of
Naess's four-level derivational model of deep ecological philosophies but also to provide a concrete example of this model as we
proceed. Following is a summary of Naess's model.

LEVEL ONE

Level one contains formulations of the most fundamental philosophical and/or religious ideas and intuitions of supporters of the
deep ecology movement. These can be many and varied, for
example, Buddhist, Christian, philosophical (e.g., Spinozist),
and so on. Indeed, these fundamental views can exhibit diversity
to the point of incompatibility or, at least, incomparability. (A
note on terminology here: in presenting his four-level model,
Naess describes fundamentals as being philosophical and/or religious in nature whereas in his "Deepness of Questions" paper he
only describes fundamentals as being philosophical in nature.
However, nothing of consequence is intended by this variation in
terminology [e.g., is Buddhism a philosophy or a religion?]. By

the terms *philosophical* and *religious* Naess is simply meaning to refer to points of view that "go deeper" than the realms of the everyday, the technical, and the scientific.)

A simple example of fundamental (or highest level) philosophical and/or religious norms and hypotheses would be:

ECOPHILOSOPHY P (FOR "PANTHEISM")

N1: God! (i.e., Love/Value God!)

H1: God is identical with the universe (i.e., God is Nature).

N2: Nature! (i.e., Love/Value Nature!)

LEVEL TWO

Level two contains formulations of the *most general views that are considered to be common to supporters of the deep ecology movement*. Thus, while the variety of views held at level one represent the fundamental assumptions of *individuals* (or groups of individuals) who support the deep ecology movement, the views derived from level one that are *shared* at level two can be said to represent the basic principles of the deep ecology *movement*. Continuing with the construction of Ecophilosophy P, then, examples of level two views would be:

H2: To truly love or value something is to love or value it for its own sake/in its own right rather than because of its use value to oneself.

N3: Value Nature (inclusive of humans, of course) for its own sake/ in its own right!

Comment: Note that there may be many steps involved in getting from a level one norm to a level two norm, i.e., many more hypotheses may be needed than I have used in this example and many intermediate norms may be derived in the process.

H3: If we value something for its own sake/in its own right then we seek to allow it to unfold in its own way. (This aim can simply be referred to as that of *preservation.*)

N4: Preserve Nature!

H4: If we wish to preserve Nature then it is necessary to preserve the richness and diversity of life forms (including human cultures).

N5: Preserve richness and diversity of life forms (including human cultures)!

H5: Preserving richness and diversity of nonhuman life forms means minimizing those forms of human interference in Nature that go beyond what is necessary for the satisfaction of significant (i.e., nontrivial) human needs.

N6: Minimize inessential human interference in the nonhuman world!

H6: The preservation of richness and diversity of nonhuman life forms requires a substantial decrease in human population.

H7: The preservation of richness and diversity of human cultures is compatible with a substantial decrease in human population by means of the widespread application of birth control methods.

H8: The preservation of richness and diversity of human cultures is not compatible with a considerable decrease in human population by means of war, pestilence, famine, and so on.

N7: Substantial human population reduction by means of the widespread application of birth control methods!

LEVEL THREE

Level three contains formulations of the more or less general consequences—political and lifestyle policies—derived from level two, that is, derived from the shared views that constitute the platform of the deep ecology movement. As with level two, additional hypotheses are needed to carry through with the derivations. In terms of the above example, hypotheses at this level would refer to such things as which forms of food, shelter, clothing, transport, and energy usage most support the kinds of views outlined at level two; which forms of family planning, employment, leisure, and activism most support these views; and which political parties, voluntary organizations, and ideologies most support these views. From these hypotheses one would then derive such level three norms as: "Organic farming!"; "Low-impact, energy-efficient housing!"; "Recycling!"; "More walk-

ing, cycling, and use of public rather than private transport!";
"Widespread education on birth control!"; "Government subsi-
dization of birth control methods!"; "Join the Wilderness Society!"; and "Support political party A!"

LEVEL FOUR

Level four contains formulations of the particular decisions that
are or would be made in concrete situations. These decisions are,
of course, derived from the policies contained in level three by
the addition of further hypotheses (such as descriptions of the
concrete situation). In terms of the above example, the addition
of these further hypotheses would result in specific norms of the
kind: "Cycle over to John's today!"; "Recycle this piece of office
paper!"; "Participate in the Wilderness Society's protest this
Saturday!"; and "Donate $X to this particular environmental
cause!"

In the context of this four-level model, then, Naess's formal
sense of deep ecology may be summarized by saying that it refers
to any ecologically relevant view (no matter how "unecological"
it might in fact be) that is derived from assumptions or premises
located at level one, which is to say from philosophical or
religious fundamentals. These fundamentals are themselves arrived at by a process of asking progressively deeper questions,
(and Naess provides a formal definition for deciding whether one
question is deeper than another).

If this characterization of Naess's formal sense of deep ecology
seems somewhat vague when it comes down to operational
specifics (such as what can count as a fundamental, i.e, an end of
a question/answer string), one can only say that Naess's various
expositions of this sense of deep ecology do not allow for any
more precision than this. But whatever the shortcomings of
Naess's formal characterization of deep ecology (an issue we will
take up in the next chapter), Naess is strongly committed to this
sense of deep ecology. For example, Bill Devall notes, "In a letter
to me written in 1980, Professor Naess says he prefers to reserve

the term 'deep ecology' to mean 'primarily the level of questioning, not the content of the answer.' "[20] Naess reiterates this point of view in various papers in addition to the "Deepness of Questions" paper, already considered. For example:

> The essence of deep ecology is to ask deeper questions. The adjective "deep" stresses that we ask why and how, where others do not.[21]
>
> The term "deep" refers to the depth of questioning.[22]
>
> I cannot give up [the view] that adequate articulation of a *deep* ecology position must *by definition* include fundamental views—basic [or, in terms of the above model, level one] assumptions or premisses corresponding to vigorous basic attitudes of supporters of the movement.[23]
>
> The term *deep* is supposed to suggest explication of fundamental presuppositions of valuation as well as of facts and hypotheses.[24]
>
> Why use the adjective "deep"? . . . The decisive difference [between shallow and deep ecology] concerns willingness to question and to appreciate the importance of questioning every economic and political policy in public. [In deep ecology] The questioning is "deep" and public. It asks "why" more insistently and consistently, taking nothing for granted. . . . The deep ecological movement tries to clarify the fundamental presuppositions underlying our economic approach in terms of value priorities, philosophy, and religion. In the shallow movement, argument comes to a halt long before this. The deep ecology movement is therefore "the ecology movement which questions deeper."[25]
>
> The main theoretical complaint against shallow ecology is not that it is based on a well-articulated but incorrect philosophical or religious foundation. It is, rather, that there is a lack of depth—or complete absence—of guiding philosophical or religious foundations. . . . The shallow movement has not offered examples of total views comprising the four levels. I am tempted to say that there will be no examples. Serious attempts to find a deep justification of the way life on the planet is treated today . . . are doomed to failure. What I say is meant as a challenge: is there a philosopher somewhere who would like to try?[26]

Naess's formal sense of deep ecology is the key sense in linking together his other two senses of deep ecology, since it provides the four-level structure within which the content of these other two senses can be located. The first of these other two senses refers, of course, to the philosophical basis (i.e., to level one or the fundamental norm[s]) from which Naess's own approach to ecophilosophy—Ecosophy T—proceeds. This sense may therefore be referred to as Naess's philosophical sense of deep ecology. The second refers to the general orientation that, in Naess's view, characterizes the most general kinds of views that his own approach to ecophilosophy has in common with the approaches adopted by other supporters of the deep (questioning) ecology movement. That is, this sense of deep ecology refers to level two views or to the most general kinds of ecologically relevant views that are popularly shared by those who derive their views from philosophical or religious fundamentals. This sense of deep ecology may therefore be referred to as Naess's popular sense of deep ecology.

We will consider each of these two senses, in turn, in the next two sections.

NAESS'S PHILOSOPHICAL SENSE
OF DEEP ECOLOGY

In its most recent version, Naess's own ecologically inspired normative system—Ecosophy T—runs like this:

ECOSOPHY T

N1: Self-realization!

H1: The higher the Self-realization attained by anyone, the broader and deeper the identification with others.

H2: The higher the level of Self-realization attained by anyone, the more its further increase depends upon the Self-realization of others.

H3: Complete Self-realization of anyone depends on that of all.

N2: Self-realization for all living beings!

H4: Diversity of life increases Self-realization potentials.

N3: Diversity of life!

H5: Complexity of life increases Self-realization potentials.

N4: Complexity!

H6: Life resources of the Earth are limited.

H7: Symbiosis maximizes Self-realization potentials under conditions of limited resources.

N5: Symbiosis!

Naess then proceeds to add other hypotheses in order to derive such norms as: "Local self-sufficiency and cooperation!"; "Local autonomy!"; "No centralization!"; "No exploitation!"; "No subjection!"; "All have equal rights to Self-realization!"; "No class societies!"; and "Self-determination!"[27]

Although Naess varies the precise formulation of some of the norms and hypotheses of Ecosophy T in different presentations, these presentations are all more or less, as Naess would say, "cognitively equivalent."[28] Most importantly, all presentations of Ecosophy T proceed from the fundamental norm of "Self-realization!"—and from that fundamental norm alone.[29] How, then, should we understand what is meant by "Self-realization!"? How, in other words, should we understand the philosophical basis of Naess's own approach to ecophilosophy? The answer is to look to the two people whom Naess most admires and whose work has most influenced the content of his approach to ecophilosophy: Spinoza (1632–77) and Gandhi (1869–1948). We will consider these influences in turn.

Naess's thinking has been profoundly influenced by the thinking of Spinoza ever since he read Spinoza's *Ethics* in Latin at school at the age of seventeen (1929). Indeed, even the *form* of Naess's approach to ecophilosophy has been strongly influenced by Spinoza. This can readily be seen by comparing the form of Spinoza's presentation in the *Ethics,* which was explicitly modeled on the "geometric (i.e., deductive) method," with that employed by Naess in his normative systems. Referring to his ideas on normative systems in a letter to me, Naess notes, "Of course, Spinoza was my 'hero' in system-making."[30]

Naess explains the origin of his interest in Spinoza in another letter to me: "A member of the Norwegian Supreme Court I met in the mountains said that there was a philosopher, Spinoza, whose views suited the mountains. Spinoza hooked me immediately. [Later] as a professor I could [in studying Spinoza] combine professionalism with something uplifting."[31]

The best way to approach Naess's interpretation of Spinoza is through Spinoza's concept of *conatus*, which constitutes the central motivational factor in Spinoza's approach to psychology. For Spinoza, *conatus* (from the Latin *conari*, meaning "to try" or "to strive") refers to the basic motivation that is considered to constitute the essence of all things, namely, the endeavor to persist in their own being.[32] *Conatus* is therefore typically rendered into English as "self-preservation," which, at first glance, might seem to imply nothing more than an urge toward self-preservation in a narrow, atomistic sense; indeed, even in a Hobbesian "war-of-all-against-all" sense. However, as Bertrand Russell argues in relation to Spinoza's concept of *conatus*, "self-preservation alters its character when we realize that what is real and positive in us is what unites us to the whole, and not what preserves the appearance of separateness"—and, of course, in Spinoza's metaphysics, we are united to the whole since there is ultimately only one *substance*; reality is a unity, which we may refer to as God or Nature.[33]

When we realize that we are united to the whole, alienation drops away and we identify more widely with the world of which we are a part. Another way of expressing this is to say that we realize a larger sense of self; our own unfolding becomes more and more bound up with the unfolding of other entities (or, in Spinoza's terminology, with the unfolding of the other *modes* of the single *substance* of which we are ourselves a mode). Thus, in a close textual and logically formulated study of Spinoza, Naess suggests that "a term that is somewhat more capable of carrying the burden Spinoza places upon 'self-preservation' is 'self-realization.' The self 'is to be realized.' If the term self refers to something capable of development to an expansion, self-realization is more than preservation and conservation."[34]

This is the key to Naess's interpretation of Spinoza. For Naess, Spinoza's philosophy points us toward the realization of as expansive a sense of self as possible. Moreover, it points us toward the *this-worldly* realization of as expansive a sense of self as possible since the world of which we are a part is the sum-total of reality (e.g., there is no *transcendent* God). And this is precisely what Naess means to point to when he employs the term "Self-realization!" as his fundamental norm in Ecosophy T: the this-worldly realization of as expansive a sense of self as possible.

In regard to Naess's terminology, it should be noted that he generally employs the terms *self*, written with a lowercase *s*, and *Self*, written with a capital *S*, to distinguish between a narrow, atomistic, particle-like, or egoic sense of self and a wide, expansive, field-like, or nonegoic sense of self respectively. Thus, for Naess, the term *self-realization* refers to realization of the narrow self, which is consistent with self-aggrandizement and "ego-trips," whereas the term *Self-realization* refers to the realization of as expansive a sense of self as possible. Using this terminology, we could therefore formulate the essence of Naess's interpretation of Spinoza as the view that self-realization leads to Self-realization. This is because, for humans at least, *self*-realization (our *conatus*) leads us to seek, among other things, and under suitable conditions, to understand the world and our place in it, and understanding the world and our place in it (i.e., understanding that reality is a unity, that all entities are *modes* of a single *substance*) leads us to identify more widely with the world of which we are a part; it leads, in other words, to the realization of a more and more expansive sense of self (i.e., *Self*-realization).

In line with the equation that is implied here between wider identification and the realization of a more and more expansive sense of self, we can see that the first hypothesis in the version of Naess's Ecosophy T that is quoted at the beginning of this section states: H1: "The higher the Self-realization attained by anyone, the broader and deeper the identification with others." Also consistent with this equation, we can see that Naess notes in his major logically formulated study of Spinoza that "the opposite of the process of self-realization we give . . . the name 'alienation' "

(Naess does not employ his capitalizing convention in this early [1975] context; however, he is meaning to refer to the opposite of what he would now call "the process of Self-realization").[35]

I will have much more to say about the significance of the process of identification to deep ecological thought and about the various possible kinds of identification in chapters 7 and 8 respectively.

The other main influence upon Naess's concept of Self-realization is Gandhi. Despite the fact that Spinoza has influenced Naess just as profoundly as Gandhi, and despite the fact that, for Naess, the upshot of Spinoza's and Gandhi's ideas is much the same, I shall nevertheless concentrate on Gandhi at somewhat greater length than Spinoza for several reasons. First, as we will see, Naess takes the term *self-realization* from Gandhi. Accordingly, when Naess applies this term to Spinoza's concept of *conatus* in his detailed logical study of Spinoza, he explicitly provides a general Indian metaphysical context and a specifically Gandhian context for the interpretation of this term.[36] Second, the precise *formulation* of Ecosophy T has been profoundly influenced by Gandhi's thought in particular. This can be seen from the fact that Naess's earliest work on Ecosophy T (done in the early 1970s) is formulated (at least at the level of its highest norms and hypotheses) in terms that are virtually *identical* to those used by Naess when he attempted to formulate Gandhi's views in the form of a normative system in the 1950s.[37] More recent versions of Ecosophy T are formulated in slightly different terms to those used by Naess in his systematization of Gandhi's views; however, these more recent versions are more or less "cognitively equivalent" to Naess's earliest work on Ecosophy T—as I have pointed out in an earlier note—and so clearly have their origins in Naess's systematization of Gandhi's views. Third, despite the fact that Spinoza's own (relatively short) life was notable for a number of noble acts and that his temperament appeared to be generally consistent with the integrity, rationality, and breadth of vision to which his philosophy aspired, when Naess looks for an exemplar of Spinoza's ideals he nevertheless looks, first and foremost, to Gandhi. For example, in response to a colleague's interpretation of Spinoza, Naess argues:

> Whereas Wetlesen's Spinoza in the last analysis markedly is other-worldly and tenderminded (in the sense of William James), as I see him, [Spinoza] combines marked this-worldly and toughminded aspects with obvious tenderminded traits. . . .
>
> Does Spinoza think of the sage as a meditative rather than socially and otherwise active person? The interpretation of Wetlesen goes in the first direction. I shall argue for the latter. . . .
>
> My main argument is, paradoxically enough, inspired by the same variety of Mahayana Buddhism as is Wetlesen's: The teaching that the further along the path to supreme levels of freedom a human being proceeds, the greater the identification and compassion and therefore the greater the effort to help others along the same path. This implies activity of social and political relevance. Gandhi, considering Buddhism to be a reformed Hinduism, furnishes a good example. His mistakes were many, but he tried through meditation of sorts (combined with fasting) to improve the quality of his action, especially the consistency in maintaining a broad and lofty perspective. He deplored the followers in his ashrams who spurned outward action and concentrated on metaphysics, meditation, and fasting. He conceived that as a kind of spiritual egotism. He did not recognize yoga, the meditation and prayer as an *adequate* way to insight, perfection and freedom. Advance towards the highest levels requires interaction with the terrifying complexities of social life.[38]

As with Naess's early discovery of Spinoza, he discovered Gandhi at a young age—at eighteen (1930). Naess has been powerfully influenced by Gandhi ever since. Naess writes:

> As a student and admirer since 1930 of Gandhi's non-violent direct actions in bloody conflicts, I am inevitably influenced by his metaphysics which to him personally furnished tremendously powerful motivation and which contributed to keeping him going until his death. His supreme aim was not India's *political* liberation. He led a crusade against extreme poverty, caste suppression, and against terror in the name of religion. This crusade was necessary, but the liberation of the individual human being was his supreme aim. It is strange for many to listen to what he himself said about this ultimate goal:

What I want to achieve—what I have been striving and pining to achieve these thirty years—is self-realization, to see God face to face, to attain *Moksha* (Liberation). I live and move and have my being in pursuit of that goal. All that I do by way of speaking and writing, and all my ventures in the political field, are directed to this same end.[39]

Gandhi describes the purpose of life as self-realization in various contexts. For example, in the English weekly journal *Young India,* Gandhi writes: "Life is an aspiration. Its mission is to strive after perfection, which is self-realization"; and in a commentary on his beloved *Bhagavad Gita,* he writes: "Man is not at peace with himself till he has become like unto God. The endeavour to reach this state is the supreme, the only ambition worth having. And this is self-realization. This self-realization is the subject of the *Gita,* as it is of all scriptures . . . to be a real devotee is to realize oneself. Self-realization is not something apart."[40] It is also true that Gandhi speaks with equal fervor of realizing God and realizing Truth, however, as Naess points out, for Gandhi, " 'To realize God,' 'to realize the Self' and 'to realize Truth' are three expressions of the same development."[41]

In choosing Gandhi as his exemplar of the philosophy of self-realization, Naess is referring to someone who located himself within his native Indian religious tradition—yet another example of Gandhi's commitment to local self-sufficiency—but who nevertheless went against the grain of that tradition in the extent to which he endorsed the reality of the phenomenal or empirical world. This can be explained as follows. Following the great Indian philosopher Shankara (788–820), the dominant traditional Indian metaphysics of Advaita (i.e., nondualistic) Vedanta impugns the reality status of the empirical world. Specifically, it reduces the empirical world to a realm of mere appearance since reality is ultimately considered to be pure, undifferentiated consciousness. And since this view is nondualistic, the individual's real or basic self (*atman*) is considered to be identical with this ultimate reality (*Brahman*).[42]

The enormous practical consequences that this view can have

are neatly illustrated in an anecdote presented by the anthropologist Agehananda Bharati in an article entitled "The Self in Hindu Thought and Action":

A Belgian Jesuit missionary who had spent the better part of his life proselytizing Hindus and keeping them to the faith, complained to me: "When you commiserate with Hindus, about their poverty and the general lack of positive events in their lives, they tell me, don't bother, God is eternal! How can I contradict? But why on earth is God's eternity marshalled when misery and poverty are pointed out?" What this man did not realize was that modern Hindu parlance, in English or in an Indian vernacular, *assumes* familiarity with the monistic axiom, and thus the implied ellipsis, "God [Brahman] is eternal, you [as atman] are really God, hence these tribulations are not really yours."[43]

But this was not Gandhi's idea of self-realization. Gandhi expressed his variant of Advaita Vedanta this way:

I am an *Advaitist* and yet I can support *Dvaitism* (dualism). The world is changing every moment, and is therefore unreal, it has no permanent existence. But though it is constantly changing, it has something about it which persists and it is therefore to that extent real. . . . Joy or what men call happiness may be, as it really is, a dream in a fleeting and transitory world. . . . But we cannot dismiss the suffering of our fellow creatures as unreal and thereby provide a moral alibi for ourselves [which the example quoted from Bharati, above, presents as the practical upshot of the dominant Indian religious tradition]. Even dreams are true while they last and to the sufferer his suffering is a grim reality."[44]

It is clear, then, that while Gandhi's thought is rooted in his native Indian religious tradition, he also, as Ramashray Roy points out in his illuminating study of Gandhi's thought, "effects certain radical changes" to the thrust of Indian thought; specifically, "While Indian thought emphasizes repelling and overcoming the forces of life, [Gandhi] accepts the reality of this world and, proceeding on this basis, insists on remaining in this world and seeking salvation through serving the world."[45] This means that, as we saw in regard to the Spinozist context for Naess's fundamental norm of "Self-realization!," the Gandhian context for this norm is also a this-worldly one. Moreover, when we move on to Naess's own metaphysical views, we see that Naess, unencumbered by subscription to the metaphysics of Advaita Vedanta (but nevertheless sympathetic to this metaphysics), defends the ontological validity of the empirical world—or "the world of concrete contents," as he calls it—more vigorously than Gandhi, and, indeed, more radically than the vast majority of empirical scientists would be prepared to do.[46] Consequently, Naess's sense of "Self-realization!" has to be understood in even more this-worldly terms than Gandhi's—although this is not to detract from the Gandhian inspiration for Naess's sense of the term.

In choosing Gandhi as his exemplar of the philosophy of self-realization, it also needs to be pointed out that Naess could be said to be looking, in philosophical terms, even further to the East than India. This is because the path of seeking self-realization through serving the world—the upshot of Gandhi's version of Indian thought—is most readily associated with the Bodhisattva ideal, which is the ideal of Mahayana (or Northern) Buddhism, rather than with the more Hindu-inspired ideal, which is also strongly associated with Hinayana (or Southern) Buddhism, of seeking one's own salvation first and foremost, and even withdrawing from the world to do so. As Naess notes in this regard: "Gandhi sides with *mahayana* Buddhism rather than *hinayana* . . . the latter asserting the possibility of *individual* salvation, the former denying it. Gandhi's Hinduism is heavily influenced by Buddhism. Indeed he seems simply to regard reformed Hinduism as embracing the teachings of Buddha. . . . [Gandhi] treat[ed] Buddha as the great, inestimable reformer of Hinduism."[47]

For their part, modern-day Buddhist teachers look to Gandhi as an exemplar of their own Bodhisattva ideal. For example, the respected American Zen teacher Robert Aitken writes: "Although the Bodhisattva ideal has been a doctrinal development in Northern Buddhism, in fact, the life of devotion to the welfare of others has not been a sectarian phenomenon in world history.

Mother Teresa, Mahatma Gandhi, A. T. Ariyaratne—Bodhisatt-vas emerge in all religious and cultural lines."[48]

As reflection on these names suggests, the Bodhisattva ideal involves both outer *and* inner work. That is, an aspirant to this ideal does more than simply help others since this can still be done with an egoistic intent; one can help others while still continuing to add up one's karmic merit points in the expectation of some kind of spiritual reward. For Gandhi and other Bodhi-sattvas, self-realization is not found through egoic attachment to the fruits of one's actions but rather through the path of selfless (i.e., nonegoic) action. Thus, as Roy recognizes, the spiritual quest that proceeds "in the world of here and now through service to the distressed" requires not only the cultivation of a particular lifestyle but also "the cultivation of the *self* in a particular manner" (emphasis added).[49]

The manner in which the self of the Bodhisattva is culti-vated—the manner in which one sheds egoic attachment to the fruits of one's actions—is nicely illustrated in a (superficially paradoxical) story that Robert Aitken relates about Gandhi: "A friend once inquired if Gandhi's aim in settling in the village and serving the villagers as best he could were purely humanitar-ian. Gandhi replied . . . 'I am here to serve no one else but myself, to find my own self-realization through the service of these village folk.' "[50]

Instead of defending himself against the implied charge of egoic self-interest, Gandhi responds, as Robert Aitken notes, like an exponent of judo (or, better, aikido) in that he makes his profound point by flowing with, and even exaggerating, the movement that is (however subtly) directed against him. In doing this, Gandhi shows that his own interests have become so identified with those of the villagers that he finds that his own self-realization cannot be separated from the self-realization of those around him.

From these considerations, then, it can be seen that the Gandhian inspiration for Naess's fundamental norm of "Self-realization!" leads us—as did my examination of the Spinozist inspiration for this norm—to understand Naess's fundamental norm as embodying at least two essential aspects. First, Naess's fundamental norm refers to self-realization in a this-worldly sense rather than an other-worldly sense. And second, this norm refers to self-realzation in the sense that one's own self-realization is intimately bound up with the self-realization of others rather than to self-realization in an egoic, narrowly self-centered, or "ego-trip" sense.

A third defining aspect of Naess's fundamental norm emerges if we follow the implication of Naess's interest in Gandhi through and consider this norm in the context of Buddhism rather than Hinduism. In an interesting unpublished paper entitled "Gestalt Thinking and Buddhism," Naess writes:

> Discontinuity and universal impermanence characterize the world of gestalts [by which Naess means the world as spontaneously experienced, prior to analysis into structural ingredients such as self and object; primary, secondary, and tertiary qualities; and so on]. Perhaps not quite in the sense of Buddhism, but in a closely related sense. . . .
>
> The "doctrine of no (permanent) self" is essential in both Buddhism and gestalt thinking.
>
> In my outline of a philosophy (Ecosophy T) "Self-realization!" is the logically (derivationally) supreme norm, but it is not an eternal or permanent Self that is postulated. . . . [As in Buddhism, there are] no entities which do not have the character of processes.
>
> To "realize oneself" as I use the word corresponds to some degree to the Buddhist expression "to follow the path" [which is, of course, a process conception, one that emphasizes becoming rather than being]. . . . It does not correspond to a Hindu idea of realizing the absolute atman. . . . The idea of a universal, absolute atman is foreign to Buddhism.[51]

If we take this process conception of "Self-realization!" into account along with the two other defining characteristics that emerge from an examination of the Spinozist and Gandhian inspiration for Naess's fundamental norm, we can summarize the philosophical basis of Naess's approach to ecophilosophy as follows: Naess's fundamental—or level one—norm of "Self-realization!" refers to the this-worldly realization of as expansive a sense of self as possible in a world in which selves and things-in-the-world are conceived as processes.

NAESS'S POPULAR SENSE
OF DEEP ECOLOGY

As I stated at the end of the section on Naess's formal sense of deep ecology, Naess's popular sense of deep ecology refers to the general orientation that, in Naess's view, characterizes the most general kinds of views that his own approach to ecophilosophy has in common with the approaches adopted by other supporters of the deep (questioning) ecology movement. That is, this sense of deep ecology refers to level two views or to the most general kinds of ecologically relevant views that are popularly shared by those who derive their views from philosophical or religious fundamentals.

Naess is adamant that level two formulations are supposed to *describe* the most general views that are popularly shared by supporters of the deep ecology movement, not to *prescribe* what these views ought to be. The representativeness of any set of formulations of the views shared at level two is thus an empirical question. Accordingly, Naess has invited people to work on the formulation of the most general kinds of ecologically relevant views that are popularly shared by those who derive their views from philosophical or religious fundamentals. Naess's own attempt to formulate these views during the 1970s consisted of an eighteen-point characterization of the deep ecology movement.[52] More recently, Naess has joined together with George Sessions to present a simpler and clearer eight-point characterization, which they refer to as a *platform* or list of *basic principles* of the deep ecology movement.[53] Naess and Sessions's list of level two points runs as follows:

1. The well-being and flourishing of human and nonhuman life on Earth have value in themselves (synonyms: intrinsic

value, inherent value). These values are independent of the usefulness of the nonhuman world for human purposes.

2. Richness and diversity of life forms contribute to the realization of these values and are also values in themselves.

3. Humans have no right to reduce this richness and diversity except to satisfy *vital* needs.

4. The flourishing of human life and cultures is compatible with a substantial decrease of the human population. The flourishing of nonhuman life requires such a decrease.

5. Present human interference with the nonhuman world is excessive, and the situation is rapidly worsening. (Note that the examples of level two norms and hypotheses used in my construction of Ecophilosophy P in the section on Naess's formal sense of deep ecology have much in common with these first five points of Naess and Sessions's platform.)

6. Policies must therefore be changed. These policies affect basic economic, technological, and ideological structures. The resulting state of affairs will be deeply different from the present.

7. The ideological change is mainly that of appreciating *life quality* (dwelling in situations of inherent value) rather than adhering to an increasingly higher standard of living. There will be a profound awareness of the difference between big and great.

8. Those who subscribe to the foregoing points have an obligation directly or indirectly to try to implement the necessary changes.

Naess and Sessions stress that these points are intended to be expressed in a general, nontechnical way in order to be understandable and acceptable to people coming from a wide variety of philosophical and religious backgrounds. This means that Naess and Sessions do not intend any particular *philosophical* significance to be attached to terms like *intrinsic value* and *life*. For them, the legitimate, nontechnical usages of such terms (or their cognitive equivalents) are extremely wide (e.g., "Value the Antarctic for its own sake!" or "Let the river live!").

In view of Naess and Sessions's extremely broad sense of the term *life,* it is clear that the general orientation that they advocate is concerned with encouraging a supportive, live-and-let-live, or symbiotic attitude on the part of humans not only toward all *members* of the ecosphere but even toward all identifiable *entities* or *forms* in the ecosphere. This orientation is intended to extend, in other words, to such entities/forms as rivers, landscapes, and even species and social systems. Ultimately, then, it is of little consequence to Naess whether one considers the kind of orientation that he advocates as one that extends only toward living entities (in an extremely broad sense of the term) or as one that extends toward both living and nonliving entities (in which case the ecocentric attitude of live-and-let-live can be reformulated more broadly in terms of be-and-let-be). Either way, the kind of orientation that Naess advocates is one that, within obvious kinds of practical limits, allows all entities (including humans) *the freedom to unfold in their own way unhindered by the various forms of human domination.*

There are, of course, all sorts of problems involved in defining such things as how far these practical limits should extend or, in many cases, even where one entity ends and another begins. But, against this, it must be remembered that Naess is not *intending* to advocate a specific set of guidelines for action; he is only intending to advocate a *general orientation.* Naess not only accepts but welcomes cultural diversity when it comes to effecting the specifics of this general orientation. After all, "the freedom to unfold in their own way unhindered by the various forms of human domination" applies to the unfolding of human cultures too. As Naess says, where we draw the limit between justifiable and unjustifiable interference with respect to this general orientation is "a question that must be related to local, regional, and national circumstances and cultural differences. And even then, certain areas of disagreement must be taken as normal."[54] For Naess, the only overriding consideration is that such limits should always be worked out *in the light of* the general orientation that he advocates. Naess captures the sense of this general orientation while also conveying a sense of the cultural (and personal) diversity it allows for when he says that "a rich variety of acceptable motives can be formulated for being *more reluctant* to injure or kill a living being of kind A than a being of kind B. The cultural setting is different for each being in each culture" (emphasis added).[55] It is this general attitude of being reluctant, prima facie, to interfere with the unfolding of A *or* B—indeed, to desire that both should flourish—that characterizes the general orientation that Naess advocates.

Naess and other deep ecologists have referred to this general orientation or attitude as one of *biospherical egalitarianism* or, more often (in order to suggest the intended comparison with an anthropo*centric* perspective more directly), *biocentric egalitarianism*. However, because the prefix *bio-* refers, etymologically, to life or living organisms, it has sometimes been assumed that deep ecology's concerns *are* restricted to entities that are (in some sense) biologically alive. To correct this impression, Naess and Sessions have, as I have already indicated, often pointed out that their sense of the term *life* is an extremely broad one of the kind implied in expressions such as "Let the river live!"—a sense so broad, in other words, that it takes in "individuals, species, populations, habitat, as well as human and nonhuman cultures."[56] To avoid the possibility of confusion in the first place, however, I prefer to describe the kind of egalitarian attitude that Naess and other deep ecologists subscribe to as *ecocentric* rather than *biocentric*. While there seems to be little reason for choosing between these terms on the basis of their ecological connotations, there are other grounds for preferring the term *ecocentric*.[57] First, *ecocentric*, with its etymological meaning of *oikos-*, "home-" or, by implication, "earth-centered," is more immediately informative than *biocentric*, which, with its etymological meaning of "life-centeredness," requires an appended explanation of the wide sense in which the term *life* should be understood. And second, *ecocentric* seems closer to the spirit of deep ecology than *biocentric*. This is because, notwithstanding their broad usage of the term *life*, the motivation of deep ecologists depends more upon a profound sense that the earth or ecosphere is *home* than it does upon a sense that the earth or ecosphere is necessarily alive. To be a supporter of deep ecology you don't have to subscribe to some ecological form of *hylozoism* (a philosophical term given to the view that life is one of the properties of matter; from the combining form *hylo-*, "matter," and the Greek root *zoe*, "life").

Of the three senses of deep ecology that I have distinguished in Naess's work, this last, very general, ecocentric sense is, of course, the one by which the term *deep ecology* is by far the most widely known. Moreover, this sense of deep ecology is an extremely useful one, as is attested to by the fact that almost all ecophilosophers consider the anthropocentric/ecocentric distinction to be central to their thinking. However, it is also clear that there is nothing distinctive about this distinction. Not only have a number of other thinkers proposed similar distinctions (as we saw in chapter 1), but, as pointed out in chapter 3, the fact that virtually all ecophilosophers are concerned with the development of a point of view that is (at least to a reasonable degree) nonanthropocentric—or, more positively, ecocentric—means that this sense of deep ecology fails to distinguish the approach that is adopted by ecophilosophers who are recognized as deep ecologists from the approaches that are adopted by ecophilosophers in general. The distinctive nature of the deep ecology approach to ecophilosophy must therefore lie in one of Naess's other two senses of deep ecology—either Naess's formal (asking-deeper-questions/derivation-from-fundamentals) sense of deep ecology or Naess's philosophical ("Self-realization!") sense of deep ecology.

In the next chapter, I will argue that Naess's formal sense of deep ecology is untenable. Following that, in part four, I intend to show that Naess's philosophical sense of deep ecology constitutes the essence of what is tenable and distinctive about the deep ecology approach to ecophilosphy. In doing this, I also hope to develop this exciting approach further.

5

The Problem with the Label *Deep Ecology*

THE PERCEIVED PROBLEM

HAVING EXPLICATED Naess's three senses of deep ecology, we can move on to certain matters of criticism and evaluation. This analysis will clear the way for us to take up the claims, made in the last section of chapter 3 and reiterated in the last section of chapter 4, that one of Naess's senses of deep ecology (namely, the philosophical sense) constitutes a distinctive approach to ecophilosophy and that it is a commitment to this approach that distinguishes deep ecologists from other ecophilosophers.

The best way to lead into the main focus of my critical comments, which center on Naess's formal sense of deep ecology, is to consider the term *deep ecology* itself. Although this name has clearly captured both the ecophilosophical and popular imaginations, it has also been found to mystify rather than enlighten and to alienate potential supporters—even among environmental activists—rather than enlist their support. Criticisms of the name *deep ecology* are only occasionally expanded upon in print, but they are often expressed in verbal discussions—and particularly at conferences. A brief article by Gary Suttle (a supporter of deep ecology) entitled "Deep Ecology by Any Other Name" provides the most explicit written discussion I have come across of the kinds of criticisms that the name *deep ecology* tends to attract—some would say invite. Suttle writes:

> I like the ideas behind "deep ecology," but the term itself bothers me. In fact it leaves me as cold as the waters of a Norwegian fjord. . . . With "deep ecology," I've encountered resistance from both academic people and environmentalists put off by the term and hence less receptive than they otherwise would be to the ideas we're

trying to spread [I can certainly endorse Suttle's experience in this regard]. I eschew the term for this reason, and for the reasons that follow. . . . [It] sounds like the study of benthic sea life or lake bottom flora, . . . [and therefore] it's misleading. . . . The fusion of two simple words, "deep" and "ecology," to stand for a raft of philosophical ideas produces . . . [a] term that fails to communicate its meaning to the uninitiated. . . . On another level, "deep ecology" seems redundant, like saying "wet water." The concepts of ecology are perforce deep and quintessential. . . . Additionally, the phrase sounds stilted. This becomes apparent when you add the intensifier "deep" to disciplines other than ecology [such as] deep biology, deep philosophy, etc. . . . For me, the biggest problem with "deep ecology" lies in its ponderous and pretentious ring. The term has a smug, self-congratulatory tone. . . . [It] alienates some fellow environmentalists (who don't pass the "deep" dogmas litmus test) and leads to unnecessary divisiveness within the larger environmental movement. It also reduces sympathetic response from the population at large because of its "holier-than-thou" overtones.[1]

It is this last point (rather than the charges of being misleading, obscure, redundant, or stilted) that also seems to bother professional philosophers the most when they take the time to comment upon the term *deep ecology* in their written work. For example, in introducing the shallow/deep ecology distinction, John Passmore implies that the two terms are pejorative and self-congratulatory respectively when he comments: "I need hardly add that this terminology was invented by the self-styled 'deep' ecophilosophers."[2] This observation no doubt contributes to Passmore's perception, expressed elsewhere, that " 'deep' ecologists . . . are not always enamoured of close reasoning."[3] Hwa Yol Jung seems to imply much the same when he says: "I shun Naess's use in a dichotomous way of 'deep' and 'shallow' ecology for their obvious semantic implications."[4] William Godfrey-Smith (now William Grey) is more explicit, referring to "a number of thinkers who (perhaps a little smugly and self-righteously) call themselves 'deep ecologists.' " He goes on to note that "the labels 'shallow' and 'deep' can themselves be viewed as a gratuitous put-down of reformists [i.e., those who

attempt to address environmental problems in a reformist way],
who are, after all, at least much of the time on the same side of
the fence." Thus, for Godfrey-Smith, labeling the reformist
position *shallow* demonstrates a "deliberate pejorative intent" and
underscores "some of the sanctimonious remarks which deep
ecologists sometimes level against 'reform.' "[5] When Tom Regan
introduces the shallow/deep ecology distinction, he likewise notes
that these labels were "initially introduced by those who favour
the latter view, which accounts for the pejorative element in the
name given to the former." Yet Regan, like many other writers,
nevertheless finds these terms sufficiently useful to proceed to use
them "despite the pejorative element of [the 'shallow'] label, and
the laudatory tone of 'deep ecology.' " Regan's way of taking his
own criticisms of these terms into account is simply to assert his
intention to use the terms in "a neutral way."[6]

For others, Regan's no-harm-intended approach is inadequate;
one does not neutralize the flavor of distasteful terms by fiat.
Even Bill Devall and George Sessions have come to eschew the
contrasting *shallow* label in favor of the (apparently) more neutral
and descriptive *reformist* (or *reform*) label.[7] But this solution, in
addition to abandoning the logical symmetry inherent in the
shallow/deep contrast, represents a rather unsatisfactory compromise whichever way it is considered. On the one hand, the
reformist (or *reform*) label implies that its contrast must be *radical*
or *revolutionary*, yet Devall specifically rejects the terms *radical
ecology* and *revolutionary ecology* in his first major published paper
on deep ecology because he considers them to "have such a
burden of emotive associations that many people would not hear
what is being said about deep ecology."[8] The only *positive* reason
that Devall offers in this context for using the term *deep ecology*,
however, is that he favors it in comparison to "several other
phrases that some writers are using for the perspective I am
describing in this paper"—terms such as *eco-philosophy, foundational ecology*, and *the new natural philosophy*—because *deep ecology*
is "the shortest label."[9] On the other hand, the *deep* label is
almost inevitably seen as implying that its contrast must in some
sense represent a shallow approach—whatever the "official" label

given to that contrast. Thus, Devall's and Sessions's use of the *reformist* (or *reform*) label is not sufficient to free the term *deep ecology* from the objection that it is alienating and divisive by virtue of being, on the one hand, pejorative by implication (and, hence, *ad hominem*) and, on the other hand, smug, self-congratu-latory, self-righteous, or holier-than-thou when considered in its own right.

Naess's approach to this problem seems even less satisfactory. As a way of preserving his original, logically symmetrical shallow/deep contrast, he attempts to separate the descriptive content of this contrast from its (apparent) *ad hominem* content by selectively retaining the terms *shallow ecology* and *deep ecology* while eschewing the terms *shallow ecologist* and *deep ecologist*. In particular, Naess has referred to *shallow ecologist* as "a useless term" and stated that it should be avoided for the same sorts of reasons that one should avoid speaking of a "shallow friend" or "shallow people."[10] Naess has never explicitly set this practice down as a *rule* for the usage of his shallow/deep terminology, but it is clear from his writings that he tends to treat it as such. Moreover, in conversation and in correspondence, he has also encouraged other sympathetic writers (including myself) to follow this practice, with the result that it now assumes at least something of the status of a "house rule" in much deep ecology writing. However, where deep ecology ecophilosophers use phrases like "supporters of deep ecology" or "students of deep ecology" where it would seem natural—and simpler—to write "deep ecologists," the linguistic awkwardness only serves to highlight, and thereby return us to, the original problem. If it is perfectly reasonable to refer to an educated student of scientific ecology as a "scientific ecologist," then, to most people, it is also perfectly reasonable to refer to an educated student of deep ecology (whatever that term might in fact be taken to mean) as a "deep ecologist." The vast majority of writers who comment upon the main deep ecology writers therefore refer to this group and their supporters as "deep ecologists," and this practice, which encourages the pejorative-by-implication/holier-than-thou objection I have been discuss-ing, simply cannot be expected to change so long as the name *deep ecology* is retained.

THE PROBLEM WITH *DEEP ECOLOGY* ∘ 123

When one also takes into account other objections to the term *deep ecology* (such as those made by Suttle that it is misleading, obscure, redundant, and stilted), it is easy to see why the suggestion is often made (again, typically in verbal discussion— whether formal or informal) that there must be a better name than *deep ecology* for the ideas that this term is taken to represent. Suttle himself, for example, wishing to avoid the "patronizing connotations of 'deep ecology,' " suggests that we "supplant the term 'deep ecology' with *panecology* (from the Greek *pan*, 'all,' plus *ecology*). Panecologists aver that all of our attitudes and actions should be based upon ecological values and the ecological realities of life. 'Panecology' connotes breadth as well as depth of commitment, without the negative undercurrents of 'deep ecology.' "[11] But Suttle also notes that his term has "drawbacks of its own. . . . It sounds like the study of microorganisms on poorly washed dishpans, is unfamiliar etc." In this connection, Suttle, a Californian, might not realize that his term could fare even worse on the other side of the Atlantic: in Britain *pan* is commonly used as an abbreviation of *lavatory pan* to refer to "the bowl of a lavatory" *(Collins English Dictionary)*. "Still," he concludes, "it evokes nicely the overarching role that ecological consciousness plays—or should play—in our lives."[12]

Now if Suttle's term were, on closer analysis, to turn out to be an appropriate replacement for *deep ecology* (a matter I will address below), this would be due more to Suttle having a reasonable "general feeling" for the ideas of deep ecology than to his discussion being grounded in any sort of thoroughgoing under- standing of the detailed formulation given to these ideas by their originator (i.e., Naess). While Suttle would probably not wish to claim any more than this himself, whatever the merits of Suttle's own suggestion might be, his discussion nevertheless suffers from two major, although not unrelated, inadequacies. In saying this, however, I also hasten to add that I am simply employing Suttle's discussion as a convenient *example* here and that, as I shall note, the inadequacies to which I am referring apply, in varying degrees, to the vast majority of discussions of deep ecology in the ecophilosophical literature.

The first inadequacy in Suttle's discussion is that, in common with the vast majority of discussions of deep ecology in the ecophilosophical literature, Suttle fails to distinguish between different senses of deep ecology. Thus, whereas Suttle considers himself to be offering a replacement name for deep ecology in general, considered in the context of the three senses of deep ecology that I have distinguished in Naess's ecophilosophical work, it should immediately be clear that his suggestion captures only one sense of deep ecology. That sense, not surprisingly of course, is the sense that I have referred to as Naess's popular sense of deep ecology, so named precisely because it refers to the ideas that most people who have heard of, or who support, the deep ecology movement associate with that movement. In employing the term *panecology* to refer to the view that "all of our attitudes and actions should be based upon ecological values and the ecological realities of life" and to evoke "the overarching role that ecological consciousness plays—or should play—in our lives," Suttle is attempting to capture Naess's popular sense of deep ecology, that is, an *ecocentric* (or ecology-centered as opposed to human-centered) orientation to ecology/living-in-the-world. In contrast, Suttle says nothing about deep ecology being concerned with asking deeper questions/deriving one's ecologically related views from fundamentals (i.e., Naess's formal sense of deep ecology) nor about deep ecology being concerned with the this-worldly realization of as expansive a sense of self as possible (i.e., Naess's philosophical sense of deep ecology).

It should be noted here that the terms *ecocentric* and *ecocentric ecology* have several advantages over the term suggested by Suttle. First, *ecocentric* is already accepted and widely used in the ecophilosophical literature to suggest precisely the kind of meaning that Suttle has in mind for his own neologism. Second, the fact that the *eco-* prefix has wider currency than the *pan* prefix in modern English usage in general, and even more so among people interested in *eco*logy and environmentalism, means that the term *ecocentric* is more immediately comprehensible than Suttle's term. Third, the terms *ecocentric ecology* and *ecocentric ecologist* are far less corruptible than the potentially comic *panecol-*

ogy and *panecologist.* Finally, it seems reasonable to argue that *ecocentric ecology* implies its intended contrast more directly than does *panecology.* The long-standing and deep-seated conceptual distinction between *humans* and *nature* that informs (at least) Western culture, taken together with the ready association that we now make between the terms *nature* and *ecology* (which was in earlier times referred to as *natural history*), means that most people are quick to see that the contrast intended by *ecocentric ecology* (i.e., an ecology- or nature-centered approach to ecology) is expressed in the term *anthropocentric ecology* (i.e., a human-centered approach). However, whereas this same contrast is also intended by *panecology* (literally "all ecology"), this term could, on a literal reading, be taken to imply that its intended contrast is with *none ecology,* whatever that might be construed to mean, rather than with *anthropocentric ecology.*

The second inadequacy in Suttle's discussion is that he fails to convey any understanding of what the term *deep ecology* is intended to mean. We have seen in chapter 4 that although Naess employs *deep ecology* to subsume three related but analytically distinct meanings or fundamental ideas, this term actually derives its name from just *one* of these meanings, namely, Naess's formal sense of deep ecology. As we have seen, Naess says that by the term *deep ecology* he means to refer "primarily to the level of questioning, not the content of the answer";[13] that "the difference between the shallow and deep movement is one of . . . deepness of questions";[14] that "the essence of deep ecology is to ask deeper questions. The adjective 'deep' stresses that we ask why and how, where others do not";[15] that "the term 'deep' refers to the depth of questioning";[16] that he "cannot give up [the view] that adequate articulation of a *deep* ecology position must *by definition* include fundamental views";[17] that "the term *deep* is supposed to suggest explication of fundamental presuppositions of valuation as well as of facts and hypotheses";[18] and that, in answer to his own question, "Why use the adjective 'deep'?" Naess responds, "The *decisive* difference [between shallow and deep ecology] concerns willingness to question and to appreciate the importance of questioning every economic and political policy in public. [In deep ecology] the questioning is 'deep' and public. It asks 'why' more insistently and consistently, taking nothing for granted. . . . The deep ecological movement tries to clarify the fundamental presuppositions underlying our economic approach in terms of value priorities, philosophy, and religion. In the shallow movement, argument comes to a halt long before this. The deep ecology movement is therefore '*the ecology movement which questions deeper*' " (emphases added). [19] Thus, as we have seen in chapter 4, Naess employs the adjective *deep* in *deep ecology* in order to refer to the idea that deep ecological views, in contrast to shallow ecological views, are derived from *fundamental* valuations and hypotheses that are arrived at by a process of asking progressively deeper questions.

As soon as one understands Naess's reason for employing the adjective *deep* in this context, the term *deep ecology* loses such mystery as it often seems to possess. It is at once revealed as having a quite specific rather than simply evocative meaning. Moreover, one also sees that the nature of this specific meaning is such that *deep ecology* is intended as a straightforwardly descriptive label (i.e., as describing an actual state of affairs) rather than as an evaluative or rhetorical label. Indeed, on this understanding, *deep ecology* should be understood as being just as descriptive, nonevaluative, and nonrhetorical a term as, say, *human ecology*. This is because it makes just as much sense to describe a deep questioning approach to our ecological interrelationships as *deep questioning ecology* or, for convenience, *deep ecology* as it does to describe a scientific approach to our ecological interrelationships as *scientific human ecology* or, for convenience, *human ecology*. Thus, a correct understanding of the *intended* meaning of the term *deep ecology* reveals that there is no substance to the pejorative-by-implication/holier-than-thou objection that I have been discussing. For this reason, I have abandoned Naess's "house rule" herein and employ the terms *shallow ecologist* and *deep ecologist* wherever it seems appropriate to do so.

The fact that Suttle conveys no appreciation of the intended meaning of the term *deep ecology* means that his discussion effectively proceeds in the dark. However, this hardly detracts from the value of his discussion vis-à-vis discussions by other writers who are critical of the term *deep ecology* since this criticism applies to these discussions as well. For example, this criticism applies to those critical comments already referred to, from authors such as Godfrey-Smith, Jung, Passmore, and Regan. Although these authors could say that their critical comments were "only made in passing," the fact of the matter is that this applies to most of the criticisms of the term *deep ecology* that one comes across in print. Suttle's brief article represents a rare exception to this observation in that it is explicitly devoted to a discussion of the merits of the term *deep ecology*. Moreover, whether one criticizes a term in detail or in passing, the general rule applies, particularly in philosophy, that if you are prepared to criticize a term then you are expected to know what the term is intended to mean.

For anyone who understands the intended meaning of the term *deep ecology,* it is clear that the only valid *theoretical* reason for rejecting this term is if its intended meaning is untenable, that is, if deep ecological views cannot clearly be shown to be arrived at by a process of asking deeper questions than those that are asked in formulating shallow ecological views. Of course, it is possible for someone to understand the intended meaning of the term *deep ecology* but still claim that this term is too open to *misinterpretation* as being pejorative by implication—not that any of the critics to whom I have referred *have* done this—and that it should therefore still be rejected on these grounds. However, this argument simply represents a pragmatic rather than a theoretical reason for rejecting the term. It does not speak to the central issue of whether or not deep ecological views can clearly be shown to be arrived at by a process of asking deeper questions than those that are asked in formulating shallow ecological views. Moreover, there is a perfectly adequate response to this pragmatic argument for rejecting the term *deep ecology* that does not involve abandoning this term. This response is that of embarking upon a concerted educational campaign in the ecophilosophical literature to explain what *is* meant by Naess's use of the adjective *deep* in this context. Thus, in the face of this response to the pragmatic argument, the above conclusion stands, namely, that the only circumstances under which the term *must* be rejected is if it can be shown to be theoretically flawed in a fundamental way, that is, if deep ecological views cannot clearly be shown to be arrived at by a process of asking deeper questions than those that are asked in formulating shallow ecological views.

THE FAILURE OF DEEP ECOLOGISTS TO FORESTALL THE PERCEIVED PROBLEM

Having criticized the critics of Naess's term *deep ecology* for their failure to understand its intended meaning, it is only fair to point out that the main writers on deep ecology must share the responsibility for the fact that the intended meaning of this term is so poorly understood. There are two reasons for saying this. First, the references that Naess, Devall, and Sessions have made to Naess's reason for employing the adjective *deep* in *deep ecology* have simply not been presented often enough, prominently enough, or in sufficient detail to get the message across. Although Naess does present his reason for using this adjective in the literature (as I have shown in chapter 4 and reiterated in the previous section), he does so occasionally rather than consistently. Moreover, these occasional expositions generally tend to be brief and mixed in with his discussions of the other senses of deep ecology that I have distinguished, rather than being given a prominence of their own.

When one moves on to consider the other main writers on deep ecology, one finds, first, that presentations of the intended meaning of the term *deep ecology* tend to be limited to the work of Devall and Sessions and, second, that Devall's and Sessions's presentations are, in any case, never elaborated and defended but only mentioned in passing. Indeed, Devall's and Sessions's presentations are so low-key as almost to suggest a lack of serious interest in the intended meaning of Naess's term (a point to which I will return). Thus, for example, even though Devall notes in his original "Streams of Environmentalism" manuscript that "Professor Naess says he prefers to reserve the term 'deep ecology' to mean 'primarily the level of questioning, not the content of the answer,' " this comment is confined to a footnote, and the point of the note plays no role whatsoever in Devall's main, textual explication of deep ecology, in either that paper or the revised, published paper on deep ecology that was derived from it (i.e., Devall's "The Deep Ecology Movement," published in the *Natural Resources Journal* in 1980). Moreover, Naess's point is not even footnoted in the latter paper, which means that this influential introductory paper on deep ecology contains no explanation for the use of the adjective *deep* in *deep ecology*. As we have already seen, the only positive reason that Devall offers in this paper for using the term *deep ecology* is that it is "the shortest label" when compared to "several other phrases that some writers are using for the perspective I am describing in this paper." It is clear, however, that this was hardly the only—let alone the primary—reason for Devall's use of Naess's term. We have seen in chapter 3 that Devall and Sessions had been highly influenced by Naess's ideas *in general* and had adopted his terminology for that reason, not because it happened to be shorter than some other labels.

Devall and Sessions are also very low-key about the intended meaning of the term *deep ecology* in their book *Deep Ecology*. For example, in chapter 5 of *Deep Ecology*, in which the central ideas of deep ecology are presented, their main comments alluding to what I have referred to as Naess's formal sense of deep ecology consist of a few sentences in which they state that "the essence of deep ecology is to keep asking more searching questions about human life, society, and Nature as in the Western philosophical tradition of Socrates. . . . [As] Naess points out . . . 'we ask why and how, where others do not.' "[20] However, although this may be taken to imply that the adjective *deep* is meant to refer to the idea of asking progressively deeper questions about the ecological relationships of which we are a part, Devall and Sessions do not actually say so in as many words (i.e., they do not explicitly say that this is why deep ecology is *deep*), and the point could easily be lost. Moreover, Devall and Sessions quickly move on from these comments in order to elaborate upon Naess's "ultimate norm" of "Self-realization!" (i.e., what I have referred to as Naess's philosophical sense of deep ecology) and Naess and Sessions's eight-point presentation of the "basic principles" of ecocentrism (i.e., what I have referred to as Naess's popular sense of deep ecology).

Thus, although the reason for referring to deep ecology as *deep* is occasionally presented in the literature, it generally tends to be mentioned in passing and mixed together with (as opposed to differentiated from) the other senses of deep ecology that I have distinguished. The upshot is that it is possible for one to have read a sizable amount of the deep ecology literature and still not know or at least not be clear about the reason for the use of the adjective *deep* in *deep ecology*. This state of affairs could legitimately be appealed to by critics of the term *deep ecology* in order to mitigate the charge that they have not understood the intended meaning of the term they are criticizing. Instead these critics were prepared to *assume* that the term *deep ecology* implied a pejorative contrast, when the appropriate thing to do would have been to point out that the meaning of this term was not at all clear to them and to call upon Naess and his colleagues to remedy the situation.

The second reason why the main writers on deep ecology must share more than a little of the responsibility for the fact that the intended meaning of Naess's term *deep ecology* is so poorly understood is that Naess, Devall, and Sessions have actually worked against their own attempts—such as these have been—to convey Naess's intention. This is because they have seen fit to alter their own terminology in response to the charge that the terms *deep ecology* and *deep ecologist* imply a pejorative contrast and that *shallow ecology* and *shallow ecologist* are directly pejorative. The fact that Naess has shunned the terms *shallow ecologist* and *deep ecologist* in favor of the expressions *supporter of the shallow ecology movement* and *supporter of the deep ecology movement* and that Devall and Sessions have abandoned the *shallow* label in favor of the *reformist* (or *reform*) label means that these authors have at least partially capitulated in the face of the criticisms that have been made of the shallow/deep terminology. The result has obviously been to add to the confusion surrounding the intended meaning of these terms rather than to detract from it. Why, then, we might ask, did these authors adopt this course of action rather than that of standing their ground and embarking upon a concerted educational campaign in the ecophilosophical literature to explain what is meant by Naess's use of the adjective *deep*?

This question leads us into interesting territory. It is my contention, which I propose to substantiate below, that Naess's intended meaning, that is, Naess's formal sense of deep ecology, does not constitute a defensible sense of deep ecology. If this is so, then it raises the interesting possibility that the reason for Devall's and Sessions's limited explication of Naess's intended meaning and the reason for their relative unpreparedness to defend this meaning against criticism is that, whether consciously or otherwise, they have also considered this meaning not to be particulary defensible.

Whatever it may be that distinguishes deep ecologists from other ecophilosophers, then, it clearly does not consist in adherence to Naess's formal sense of deep ecology. I have already noted that writers on deep ecology other than Naess, Devall, and Sessions rarely touch upon Naess's intended meaning of the term *deep ecology* at all—and certainly never in any detail. It is only Naess who reiterates and repeatedly expands upon what I have referred to as his formal sense of deep ecology.

THE "FUNDAMENTAL" PROBLEM

There is an obvious colloquial appeal in the idea of using the criterion of depth of questioning to distinguish reformist, anthropocentric approaches to environmentalism from more radical, ecocentric approaches. This can be illustrated by considering situations of the kind where decision-making authorities decide that the way to deal with preservation/development conflicts is to reach a "compromise" by simply preserving the most scenic aspects of the region concerned (i.e., where these authorities give priority to human aesthetic and recreational interests over the vital needs of the life forms that inhabit the region concerned); or where these authorities decide that the way to deal with certain forms of pollution is to build higher smokestacks or dump the pollutants further out to sea; or where they decide that the way to deal with perceived energy shortages is to develop nuclear power. In these kinds of situations it is easy to see why people who share a certain set of values will colloquially say (i.e., say in an informal or nontechnical sense) that these authorities have ignored the "deeper issues" involved. However, the key phrase here is *"people who share a certain set of values."* What such a judgment overlooks is the fact that people who share a different set of values may well feel that it is *their* analysis that has taken better account of the complexity of the situation and that has addressed the deeper issues. Thus, the important question in assessing Naess's formal sense of deep ecology is whether it can be sustained in anything other than a colloquial sense. Can it be sustained at the more formal or technical level of analysis that Naess clearly intends? Can it, in other words, be shown that asking deeper questions or deriving policies from fundamentals will always lead to ecocentric answers and policies?

When we move on to consider Naess's formal sense of deep ecology in the technical (formal) sense that he intends rather than simply at a colloquial (informal) level, we can see that there are grounds for suspicion right from the outset. These stem from the fact that Naess is contrasting views that are overwhelmingly dominant (i.e., anthropocentric views) with views that are located very much within a minority tradition (i.e., ecocentric views). The reason why a contrast of this general kind must raise certain suspicions about the validity of Naess's formal criterion for distinguishing the views of shallow and deep ecology can be explained as follows. The views of any group that offers a radical challenge to a dominant tradition appear distinctly odd, to say the least, from the perspective of the dominant tradition. The consequence of this is that, if a minority group wants the views that they advocate to become dominant, then they are more or less *forced* to argue their case from the level of basic assumptions (i.e., from what Naess refers to as *fundamentals*) in order to demonstrate to members of the dominant tradition that the minority group's more specific views are actually quite sensible when viewed within this alternative (and, the minority group hopes, more appealing) context. In contrast, however, members of a dominant tradition are not forced to do this. The very fact that their tradition is the dominant one means that almost everyone in that society (whether supporters of this dominant tradition or not) will have at least a tacit understanding of the basic assumptions that underlie the more specific views that are expressed by members of that society's dominant tradition. There is, in other words, simply no *need* for members of a tradition whose basic assumptions are commonly known to have to argue their more specific views from first principles. Moreover, just as a political candidate whose popularity is running extremely high may feel that there is nothing to *gain* (and perhaps much to lose) in agreeing to debate an opponent whose popularity is running extremely low, so members of a dominant tradition may feel much the same about debating their basic principles with members of a minority tradition: why bother when you think you're well in front? But the fact that members of a dominant tradition do not need to or may not wish to debate their basic principles with members of a minority tradition does not mean that they *cannot* argue their more specific views from first principles—or that they have not had to do so in the past (in order to establish their tradition as the dominant tradition, for example).

These observations should lead us to approach Naess's formal sense of deep ecology with considerable caution. This is because Naess is all too ready to jump from his personal view that "the [dominant] shallow ecology movement *has* not offered examples of total views comprising the four levels" (i.e., views that proceed from fundamentals) to the conclusion that nonecocentric views *cannot* be argued for from fundamentals: "I am tempted to say," says Naess, "that there will be no examples [of nonecocentric views being derived from fundamentals]. Serious attempts to find a deep justification of the way life on the planet is treated today . . . are doomed to failure. *What I say is meant as a challenge: is there a philosopher somewhere who would like to try?"* (emphases added.)[21]

This challenge leads us to the heart of the matter. Is it possible to derive nonecocentric views from fundamentals? If it is, then Naess's formal sense of deep ecology must be rejected as untenable so long as we hold deep ecology to be concerned with an ecocentric approach to ecology and living-in-the-world. Now, as a student and teacher of Naess's ideas on normative systems, I consider that it is a simple matter to derive nonecocentric views from fundamentals. I would also add that, much to my despair, some of my students have been known to derive quite anthropocentric views from fundamentals of their own. I will give just two examples here of the derivation of nonecocentric views from fundamentals in order to show how easy it is to derive such views from fundamentals. For the sake of example, I will adopt a plainly religious fundamental in one case ("Obey God!") and a more secular (or at least nontheocentric) fundamental in the other case ("Evolution!").

ECOPHILOSOPHY O (FOR "OBEDIENCE TO THE WILL/WAYS OF GOD")

N1: Obey God!
Comment: Naess gives no firm rule for establishing what can count as a fundamental above and beyond saying that fundamentals are those bedrock or end-of-the-line assumptions that one arrives at in response to repeated "why?" or "how?" questions. Thus, fundamentals may be as diverse as personal idiosyncrasies (and, of course, Naess sees this as a very good thing). For example, in regard to his own fundamental of "Self-realization!" Naess says that he "needed nothing more than intuition to choose it. I held to it. After twenty years, it is clear that it was worthwhile. Intuitions need not be precise. They are the basis of visions. And we do not criticize visions. They excite people. They are what stimulates people."[22] With this much latitude available in the selection of fundamentals, it is clear that a norm like "Obey God!" certainly qualifies as a fundamental. For some people—

indeed for many people—their "last word" in response to persistent "why?" questions will be something like, "Because you should obey God/do God's will/do as God commands." It is pointless to go on asking "why?" to an answer like this because this answer represents a bedrock or end-of-the-line assumption. From the point of view of a person who holds such a fundamental, the answer to the question "But *why* should you obey God?" can only be of the kind "Because you should!"—or "Because God says so!" which amounts to the same thing.

H1: The Bible is God's word.

Comment: It is in the nature of hypotheses (propositions that one tentatively considers to be true) that they are disputable. People with one set of views (such as ecocentric views) will wish to dispute many of the hypotheses that are put forward by people with a competing set of views (such as anthropocentric views), and vice versa. However, whether one personally accepts the hypotheses that are put forward in a normative system is irrelevant to the question of whether it is *possible* to derive certain views (e.g., anthropocentric views) from fundamentals by the addition of hypotheses. Thus, as Naess says, "The main theoretical complaint against shallow ecology is *not* that it is based on a well-articulated but *incorrect* philosophical or religious foundation. It is, rather, that there is a lack of depth—or complete absence—of guiding philosophical or religious foundations" (emphases added).[23] Note also that, as was explained in chapter 4, basic hypotheses are simply inserted into a normative system. They are not themselves logical consequences of one's fundamental norm. Later hypotheses may also be inserted into the system or they may be derived from earlier norms and hypotheses; norms other than fundamental norms are always derived from the combination of previous norms and particular hypotheses, as we shall see immediately below.

N2: Act in accordance with what is said in the Bible!
Comment: From N1 and H1.

H2: God has given humans *dominion* over the earth.
Comment: See Genesis 1:26–28.

H3: Having *dominion* over something means having authority to rule over and control (i.e., to govern) that thing as one sees fit.

H4: God has given humans the authority to govern the earth as they see fit (provided, of course, that they obey God in all other respects). *Comment:* From H2 and H3 (understood in the light of N1, as indicated in the parenthetical qualification to H4). It should again be noted that the fact that there are numerous competing interpretations of the Bible in respect of our attitudes toward the nonhuman world (indeed, even of Genesis 1:26–28, and even of the word *dominion*) is neither here nor there with respect to the question of whether it is *possible* to derive nonecocentric views from Judeo-Christian fundamentals by the addition of hypotheses.[24] Expressed more pointedly, the fact that it may *also* be possible to derive environmentally benign and perhaps even ecocentric views from the Bible (e.g., one might begin with a norm like "Glorify God!" and add quite different hypotheses to those employed above) is simply irrelevant to the question of whether or not it is *possible* to derive thoroughly anthropocentric and exploitative views from Judeo-Christian fundamentals.

Having arrived at H4, it is easy to see how one could proceed to develop a range of more specific views that, *depending upon which further hypotheses were added,* could vary from an anthropocentric conservation position ("stewardship") to the most outrageous exploitation position—one that would pursue the biblical injunction to "fill the earth and subdue it" (Genesis 1:28) with the utmost anthropocentric zeal. It is worth noting in this regard that *subdue* is defined in the *Collins English Dictionary* as "1. to establish ascendency over by force; 2. to overcome and bring under control, as by intimidation or persuasion; 3. to hold in check or repress." I take it that it is therefore unnecessary to pursue the development of this normative system in an anthropocentric direction any further.

If the derivation of anthropocentric views in the above example seems somewhat abstract, consider the following concrete example. However common it may be—and may have been—for many Jews and Christians to at least implicitly adopt the kind of interpretation of the Bible developed here, it is, of course, rare for any Jew or Christian to argue explicitly for such an interpretation in an *ecophilosophical* forum. This is because an elective

THE PROBLEM WITH *DEEP ECOLOGY* ∘ 137

affinity operates in such forums where almost all contributors would classify themselves as environmentalists or as environmentally sympathetic to at least some degree. To argue against environmentalist sympathies in these forums is therefore analogous to an out-and-out capitalist choosing to argue their case in a socialist magazine. However, a remarkable exception to this general trend comes from the philosopher and Judaic scholar Steven Schwarzschild in his erudite paper "The Unnatural Jew," which was published in *Environmental Ethics* in 1984. Rather than attempting to interpret Judaism in an environmentally benign or environmentally supportive way, Schwarzschild makes it quite clear that "from a traditional Jewish standpoint nature remains subject to humanly enacted ends." Moreover, he makes absolutely no apology for this view. His paper opens, in all seriousness, as follows:

> In my philosophy department the graduate students organize an annual picnic. For some time past quasi-formal invitations have explicitly excluded me on the ground that I am known to be at odds with nature. So I am. My dislike of nature goes deep: nonhuman nature, mountain ranges, wildernesses, tundra, even beautiful but unsettled landscapes strike me as *opponents,* which, as the Bible *commands* (Gen. 1:28–30), I am to fill and conquer. I really do not like the world, and I think it foolish to tell me that I had better. Like Dryden, "I condemn the world when I think on it" (emphases added). [25]

Schwarzschild then devotes the rest of his highly scholarly paper to showing that this view does not represent a personal idiosyncrasy but has to do with the fact that Judaism (in which culture and religion he is immersed) and nature are fundamentally "at odds." The point in this context, of course, is that even if one strongly disagrees with Schwarzschild's *interpretation* of Judaism (i.e., even if one disagrees with Schwarzschild's *hypotheses concerning the nature of* Judaism), the fact remains that, from a Naessian point of view, one must accept that Schwarzschild nevertheless derives his anthropocentric views from fundamentals. [26]

Now to my second example.

ECOPHILOSOPHY E (FOR "EVOLUTION")

N1: Evolution!

Comment: This norm can be understood as: "Value evolution (both the process and its products)!"; "Further evolution (both the process and its products)!"; and so on. If one asks people who hold this norm "But why should we value evolution/seek to further evolution?" and they reply with a throwing-up-their-hands sort of answer like "Because that's what it's all about!" or "What else is there?," then this norm can be taken as being a fundamental norm for them (i.e., as representative of their deepest intuitions). Of course, other people (e.g., many New Age/traditional wisdom adherents who adopt a kind of Gnosticized Darwinism) might reply with a substantive answer to this question like "Because we are God-in-the-process-of-becoming and evolution is the means by which all things are led toward the state or condition of God." Henryk Skolimowski, for example, gives precisely this sort of answer (at least for the case of human evolution) in his book *Eco-Philosophy*: "The new theology underlying Ecological Humanism is that we are God-in-the-process-of-becoming. We are fragments of grace and spirituality *in status nascendi*. We give testimony to our extraordinary (divine) potential by actualizing these fragments in us. . . . As the result of certain propensies of unfolding evolution, we possess the potential for making ourselves into spiritual beings, and thereby to bring to fruition some of the seeds of God in the process of self-making."[27]

The fundamental norm for people who reply in this way would then be something like "Realize God!," since if one were to ask them "But why should we aspire to the state or condition of God?" *they* would then be likely to give an answer such as "Because that's what it's all about!" or "What else is there?" In this latter case "Evolution!" would be a derived norm rather than an ultimate or fundamental norm. But that is not to say that "Evolution!" cannot be a fundamental norm for others, as pointed out above. Moreover, even if one began a different normative system with "Realize God!" and then derived the norm of "Evolution!," one could then proceed from that derived norm precisely as I do below if one wanted to add the same hypotheses.

H1: The process of evolution has a tendency to generate increasingly complex living systems.

THE PROBLEM WITH *DEEP ECOLOGY* ∘ 139

H2: The tendency referred to in H1 is not accidental but represents a directionality that is inherent in the process of evolution.

Comment: Whatever evolutionary theorists may think of H2, it is still a hypothesis that many people feel entitled—even compelled—to adopt. Again, it should be emphasized that the correctness or otherwise of this or any other hypothesis is neither here nor there with respect to the question of whether it is *possible* to derive certain views (e.g., nonecocentric views) from fundamentals by the addition of hypotheses.

H3: The more advanced an organism is in the evolutionary direction referred to in H2, the more valuable it is.

Comment: From N1 (understood as implying the proposition that evolution is valuable) and H2.

H4: Humans are the most advanced organisms (in the evolutionary direction referred to in H2) of which we are aware.

N2: Humans!

Comment: From N1, H3, and H4. This (derived) norm can be understood as: "Value humans!"; "Further human evolution!"; "Further humans and their ends!"; and so on.

H5: Humans are capable of accelerating the processes of evolution in the direction of increasing complexity by means of genetic engineering.

N3: Genetic engineering!

Comment: From N1, H3, and H5.

In view of N1 and H3, this last norm can be interpreted as calling for the genetic engineering of all organisms (human and nonhuman) in the general direction referred to in H2. Moreover, in combination with N2, this last norm can be interpreted as suggesting that humans are entitled to—indeed that they *ought* to—perform whatever kinds of genetic engineering experiments upon other organisms they think might be useful in helping our species to "speed up" its own evolution in the direction referred to in H2. From the fundamental norm of "Evolution!," then, it is possible to derive, by the addition of hypotheses that seem to have considerable popular currency, norms that would not simply sanction but actually recommend human interference in the biology of all organisms to a degree and on a scale that exceeds most environmentalists' worst nightmares.

The two examples I have just given of the derivation of nonecocentric views from fundamentals—Ecophilosophy O and Ecophilosophy E—both proceed from fundamental valuations that many people hold and incorporate hypotheses with which many people agree. It would therefore be a simple matter to go on providing examples of the derivation of nonecocentric views from fundamentals that proceed from more idiosyncratic fundamental valuations and that incorporate more idiosyncratic kinds of hypotheses. This discussion should have been enough, however, to establish the following points. First, there are very good reasons why the members of a dominant tradition—such as the anthropocentric tradition taken in general—do not *need* to or may not *wish* to argue their more specific views from the level of basic assumptions (fundamentals). Second, this is not to say that the members of a dominant tradition *do* not, *have* not, or *cannot* argue their more specific views from fundamentals. Third, it is in fact a simple matter to derive anthropocentric views from fundamentals. And fourth, notwithstanding the first point, the fact that Ecophilosophy O and Ecophilosophy E both proceed from fundamental valuations that many people hold and incorporate hypotheses with which many people agree suggests that it is at least as plausible to believe that anthropocentrists do in fact derive their views from fundamentals as it is to believe that ecocentrists derive their views in this way. Indeed, as noted in chapter 1, writers opposed to anthropocentrism such as Lynn White, Jr., George Sessions, and myself have made a point of emphasizing the extent to which fundamental philosophical and religious assumptions have underpinned *and been drawn upon* to justify anthropocentric views and practices. (Schwarzschild's argument to the effect that his anthropocentric views are a direct consequence of his Judaic philosophical and religious beliefs is merely one case in point here.) It also seems necessary to accept the fact that anthropocentric views have deep philosophical and religious roots in order to account for the strength of the resistance that one meets in attempting to change these views. The overall conclusion to be drawn from these points is clear: insofar as we hold deep ecology to be concerned with an ecocentric approach to ecology/living-in-the-world, Naess's formal, asking-deeper-questions/derivation-from-fundamentals sense of deep ecology is not a *tenable* sense of deep ecology. It fails to distinguish ecocentric views (or those who hold these views) from anthropocentric views (or those who hold these views).

FAREWELL TO *DEEP ECOLOGY*

A powerful motivational reason for Naess's attachment to his formal sense of deep ecology may have to do with the fact that, while he obviously *does* believe at some level that the views he associates with deep ecology are superior to those he associates with shallow ecology, it goes against his nature/philosophical orientation to say so in an outright manner. Naess's "lack of incentive to judge [one thing] . . . as unquestionably higher, nobler, more right, than any other" and his "enthusiasm for diversity" mean that he strives for a philosophical framework that will enable as large a range of views as possible to coexist.[28] Considered in this light, then, it can be seen that Naess's idea of deepness of questioning provides a philosophical way for him to "have his cake and eat it too." Naess's idea that different views correspond to different levels of derivation/questioning means that he does not have to reject anthropocentric views or to argue that ecocentric views are necessarily "higher, nobler, [or] more right" than anthropocentric views. Instead, he can simply claim that ecocentric views go "deeper" than anthropocentric views and that if supporters of anthropocentric views were to deepen their analyses then they, too, would end up endorsing ecocentric views.

But whatever Naess's personal motivations for his attachment to his formal sense of deep ecology, the fact that one can derive both ecocentric *and* anthropocentric views from fundamentals—

and the abundance of evidence to suggest that people do in fact draw upon basic philosophical and religious assumptions to justify both ecocentric *and* anthropocentric views—means that "the game is up" for this sense of deep ecology. Of course Naess can retain his formal sense of deep ecology and the term *deep ecology* if he is prepared to accept, as he claims he is, that a point of view can be "characterized as 'deep' even if it defended some of the most wasteful and socially destructive policies . . . [so long as it is] derived from a coherent philosophy answering the deep questions."[29]

However, it is clear that there would be no *ecophilosophical* point in retaining the shallow/deep ecology distinction in this circumstance since it would have nothing at all to do with distinguishing between anthropocentric and ecocentric views. The usefulness of the shallow/deep distinction would instead be restricted to logicians and others who want analytical tools for talking about world-views in a somewhat formal or structural sort of way (i.e., independently of the content of these world-views).

Since the intended meaning of the term *deep ecology* refers to what I have characterized as Naess's formal sense of deep ecology, and since this sense is ecophilosophically untenable (i.e., untenable as a way of distinguishing between anthropocentric and ecocentric views), it hardly makes sense to continue to refer to Naess's other two senses of deep ecology—both of which refer to distinctly ecocentric as opposed to anthropocentric viewpoints—as Naess's popular sense *of deep ecology* and Naess's philosophical sense *of deep ecology*. Alternative names are therefore required for the ideas to which these senses of deep ecology refer.

Before suggesting alternative names for these senses, however, I want to make it quite clear that I have not come to this conclusion lightly. I have thus far written all of my own ecophilosopical work under the banner of deep ecology and obviously feel closest to the ideas of other ecophilosophers who have also been writing under this banner. The necessity for rejecting Naess's term *deep ecology* has therefore only dawned upon me gradually as my study of the philosophical foundations of deep

ecology has . . . well, deepened. I certainly had no original intention, desire, or reason to believe that I would reach such a conclusion when I decided to analyze Naess's central ecophilosophical ideas in greater detail. However, with the exception of Naess's formal sense of deep ecology, which is more or less limited to Naess's work and which I *have* rejected, what is at issue here is the matter of a *name* for the ideas associated with deep ecology, not the ideas themselves (i.e., not the ideas that I have referred to as Naess's popular and philosophical senses of deep ecology, both of which *are* shared by other deep ecologists). It would, therefore, be fundamentally mistaken to see my rejection of the name *deep ecology* as putting me at odds with the *content* of the ideas expressed by my deep ecology colleagues.

As should be obvious from chapter 2, the use of the term *deep ecology* has gained such a momentum that it may well be a futile exercise to suggest that it be set aside in favor of other terms that more accurately describe Naess's popular and philosophical senses of deep ecology. On the other hand, the fact that ecophilosophy is a young and rapidly evolving field—one in which there is plenty of room for both innovative conceptual work and the clarification of established concepts—could lead one to surmise that, at least so far as eco*philosophical* discourse is concerned, the *considered* suggestion of alternative names for the ideas associated with Naess's popular and philosophical senses of deep ecology may not be a futile exercise. And if this is so, then the fact that popular acceptance of the term *deep ecology* followed upon its ecophilosophical usage, rather than the other way around, could lead one to think that even this popular acceptance of the term could change with a change in the terms that are employed in ecophilosophical discourse. But, whatever one's view of such a contingent, sociology of knowledge sort of matter, the concern here must lie with the logic of the argument, which requires that alternative names be given to Naess's popular and philosophical senses of deep ecology. It is then up to others to accept or reject these suggestions for greater conceptual clarity as they find them to be helpful or otherwise.

How, then, should we refer to Naess's popular and philosophical senses of deep ecology? As already indicated, my own preferred choice for Naess's popular sense of deep ecology is the term *ecocentric ecology,* meaning an ecocentric approach to ecology and living-in-the-world. The advantages of *ecocentric* over *biocentric,* which is often used in connection with this sense of deep ecology, were outlined in chapter 4 ("Naess's Popular Sense of Deep Ecology"). And the advantages of *ecocentric ecology* vis-à-vis Suttle's suggestion were discussed in the first section of this chapter. Most or all of the advantages listed in that context also apply when one compares *ecocentric ecology* with other possible terms. Since the obvious contrast for ecocentric ecology is anthropocentric ecology, this means that instead of talking about the *shallow ecology movement* and the *deep ecology movement* when one means to refer to those popular social movements that stress anthropocentrically based views on conservation and preservation and ecocentrically based views on conservation and preservation respectively, it would be clearer and far more accurate to distinguish between the *anthropocentric ecology movement* and the *ecocentric ecology movement.* Members of these movements would then be described as anthropocentric ecologists or anthropocentric environmentalists and ecocentric ecologists or ecocentric environmentalists.

This suggestion means that Naess and Sessions's eight-point list of the "common platform" of the deep ecology movement should be thought of as an eight-point characterization of the general views of the *ecocentric* ecology movement. To maintain instead that these general views represent the common platform of a specifically *deep* (i.e., deep-questioning) ecology movement is to maintain that these eight points are derived from fundamentals *and that a corresponding list of the general views of the anthropocentric ecology movement cannot be so derived.* As I have shown, however, such a claim is untenable. It is a simple matter to derive even the most outrageous kinds of anthropocentric views from fundamentals—let alone anthropocentric views that are relatively mild in comparison (such as conservation-oriented "stewardship" views)—and there is ample evidence to suggest that people do in fact do this.

This brings us, finally, to the question of how to refer to Naess's philosophical sense of deep ecology. However, the discussion of this sense of deep ecology deserves a separate and far more extended treatment than can be offered in this chapter. This is because Naess's philosophical sense of deep ecology constitutes the most interesting and significant of his three senses of deep ecology by virtue of the fact that it is both tenable *and* distinctive. By *tenable* I mean that this sense of deep ecology is, at a minimum, neither demonstrably false (like Naess's formal sense of deep ecology) nor logically inconsistent. Indeed, expressed more positively, this sense of deep ecology actually offers the most exciting and appropriate way of approaching the question of how we should live in the world. And by *distinctive* I mean that this sense of deep ecology constitutes a distinctive approach to ecophilosophy and that it is a commitment to this distinctive approach that distinguishes deep ecologists from other ecophilosophers. This distinctiveness criterion thus differentiates this sense of deep ecology from Naess's popular, ecocentric sense since the latter has been formulated under a range of labels by a variety of authors (as we have seen in chapter 1) and embraces every kind of approach to ecophilosophy that is (at least to a reasonable degree) nonanthropocentric.

In order to be able to see what is distinctive about the approach to ecophilosophy that is exemplified by Naess's philosophical sense of deep ecology, however, it is first necessary to know something about the most widely recognized approaches to ecophilosophy. We will therefore turn our attention to an overview of these approaches in chapter 6. We will then proceed to see, in chapter 7, that Naess's philosophical sense of deep ecology constitutes a distinctive approach to ecophilosophy (vis-à-vis the approaches to ecophilosophy discussed in chapter 6) and that it is a commitment to this approach that distinguishes deep ecologists from other ecophilosophers. I will also suggest an appropriate name for this distinctive approach to ecophilosophy in this context.

PART FOUR

TOWARD A TRANSPERSONAL
ECOLOGY: DRAWING OUT
WHAT IS TENABLE AND
DISTINCTIVE ABOUT THE
DEEP ECOLOGY APPROACH
TO ECOPHILOSOPHY

*Care flows naturally if the "self" is widened and deepened so
that protection of free Nature is felt and conceived as protection of
ourselves. . . . Just as we need not morals to make us breathe
. . . {so} if your "self" in the wide sense embraces another being,
you need no moral exhortation to show care. . . . You care for
yourself without feeling any moral pressure to do it—provided you
have not succumbed to a neurosis of some kind, developing self-
destructive tendencies, or hating yourself.*

—Arne Naess

6
The Most Widely Recognized Approaches to Ecophilosophy

THE VAST MAJORITY of ecophilosophers are primarily concerned with developing a theory of value in regard to the nonhuman world. Such a theory is more formally referred to as an *environmental axiology* (*axiology* derives from the Greek *axios,* meaning "worthy"). Ecophilosophers generally divide all value theory (or axiological) approaches into two major classes. However, as we will see in the next chapter, neither of these classes includes the approach that is exemplified by Naess's philosophical sense of deep ecology. That is, ecophilosophers generally do not seem to recognize even the *existence* of this approach—let alone its distinctiveness vis-à-vis the two major classes of approaches that they do recognize.

The first major class of approaches that ecophilosophers recognize consists of all those approaches that adopt the view that humans are valuable in and of themselves but that the nonhuman world is valuable only insofar as it is of value *to* humans. This class of approaches is therefore based on the view that humans have an *intrinsic value,* but that the only kind of value the nonhuman world can have is an *instrumental value.* The latter term derives, of course, from the fact that the nonhuman world is considered to be valuable only insofar as it can serve as a means— or insofar as it is *instrumental*—to human ends. Instrumental value may also be referred to as *use value* or *resource value,* but *instrumental value* is the term that is generally employed by ecophilosophers. This first class of ecophilosophical approaches may therefore be referred to as *instrumental nonhuman value theory.* However, many people, including many ecophilosophers, would probably prefer the term *instrumental environmental value theory* since they are used to referring to the nonhuman world by employing the term *environment* in the anthropocentric sense of "all that is external to or that surrounds the *human* world."[1] Either way, we may refer to this first class of ecophilosophical approaches simply as *instrumental value theory* as long as we bear in mind that what is being referred to is the value of the nonhuman world.

The second major class of approaches that ecophilosophers recognize consists of all those approaches that adopt the view that, in addition to humans, at least some members or aspects of the nonhuman world are also valuable in and of themselves. This class of ecophilosophical approaches may therefore be referred to, in turn, as *intrinsic nonhuman value theory, intrinsic environmental value theory,* or, more simply, as *intrinsic value theory* (as long as we again bear in mind that what is being referred to is the value of the nonhuman world).

It is appropriate initially to divide the variety of ecophilosophical approaches into these two major classes because the distinction between instrumental value and intrinsic value is central to most ecophilosophical theorizing. However, a variety of more specific approaches can, of course, be distinguished within each of these two major classes. I will therefore provide an overview of these more specific approaches by considering instrumental value theory and intrinsic value theory in turn.

INSTRUMENTAL VALUE THEORY

It is possible to distinguish many specific kinds of approaches that fall within the scope of instrumental value theory. However, for the purposes of an overview such as this, it is useful to distinguish three specific kinds of approaches in (what sociologists would refer to as) an ideal typical way. That is to say, my characterizations of these three instrumental value theory approaches are intended as heuristic constructions that illuminate "real world" approaches without necessarily corresponding to any particular "real world" situation precisely. The complexities of "real world" behavior are such that the instrumentalist approaches that people adopt in regard to ecological issues will often represent variations on or combinations of these three instrumental value theory approaches. Moreover, in practice, the conceptual scheme that is presented here is further complicated by the fact that one can end up adopting approaches that are much the same as those outlined below on the basis of views that also attribute *intrinsic value* to at least some members or aspects of the nonhuman world. This can occur when the intrinsic value attributed to humans so far outstrips the intrinsic value attributed to the nonhuman world that considerations relating to humans always trump considerations relating to the nonhuman world. In such situations, the attribution of some nominal degree of intrinsic value to members or aspects of the nonhuman world is cold comfort for the entities concerned. For all practical purposes, these entities might as well have been valued purely for their instrumental value in the first place.

The three instrumental value theory approaches that I will distinguish may be referred to as:

1. *unrestrained exploitation and expansionism;*

2. *resource conservation and development;* and

3. *resource preservation.*

Before outlining these approaches individually, it should be noted that one can attempt to argue for, justify, or legitimate any of these approaches on the basis of any view that restricts intrinsic value to humans (or that consistently bestows far greater intrinsic value upon humans than upon the nonhuman world). There is a wide range of possibilities here. For example, the kinds of criteria that have been held to confer intrinsic value exclusively upon humans (or upon humans by an overwhelming margin) include such things as a special relationship with God, the possession of a soul, rationality, self-awareness, free will, the capacity for symbolic communication, the capacity to enter into arrangements involving reciprocal duties and obligations, and

152 TOWARD A TRANSPERSONAL ECOLOGY

the capacity to anticipate and symbolically represent the future (and thereby to have knowledge of one's own mortality).

Now to the individual details of these three instrumental value theory approaches.

Unrestrained Exploitation and Expansionism

The unrestrained exploitation and expansionism approach may be characterized as follows:

1. It emphasizes the value to humans that can be acquired by physically transforming the nonhuman world (e.g., by farming, damming, mining, pulping, slaughtering, and so on). It emphasizes, in other words, the *physical transformation value* of the nonhuman world.

2. It not only *measures* the physical transformation value of the nonhuman world in terms of *economic* value, but also tends to *equate* the physical transformation of "resources" with economic growth. Economic growth is then equated, in turn, with "progress."

3. In order to legitimate the continuous expansion of resource exploitation (physical transformation) activity, this approach relies on the *myth of superabundance,* that is, on the idea that there is "always more where that came from." In view of this feature in particular, some writers have characterized this approach as *frontier* or *cowboy ethics.*[2] Unrestrained exploitation and expansionism—frontier or cowboy ethics—is "how the West was won."

4. It is totally anthropocentric; the nonhuman world is considered to be valuable only insofar as it is of economic value to humans.

5. It is characterized by short-term thinking, that is, its anthropocentrism does not even extend to consideration of the interests of future generations of humans. This can itself be viewed as an expression of the radical anthropocentrism of this approach since one can afford to ignore the possibility of future problems if one has an unquestioning faith in the capacity of

human ingenuity to meet these problems as they arise—which anticipates the next point.

6. When *forced* to consider the longer-term deleterious effects of continued unrestrained exploitation and expansionism—or continued "business as usual"—this approach falls back on technological optimism (i.e., on a faith that "technological fixes" will always be able to deliver us from possible harm).[3]

There is nothing that is remotely environmentalist about this approach. However, it represents a way of thinking about the environment in terms of its instrumental value that has been of the first importance for the situation in which we find ourselves today. Indeed, the influence of this approach has been and still is so pervasive that many people will start to claim that they are thinking "environmentally" as soon as they begin to acknowledge *any* kind of restraint upon this free-for-all, frontier ethic approach. Thus, for some people, *environmental awareness* or an *environmental ethic* (if not exactly a commitment to environmentali*sm*) amounts to the resource conservation and development approach or the resource preservation approach.

Resource Conservation and Development

The resource conservation and development approach may be characterized as follows:

1. Although this approach is also concerned with the physical transformation, "development," or exploitation of resources, it at least recognizes that there are limits to material growth— that there is *not* "always more where that came from."

2. It is thoroughly anthropocentric but has a longer-term focus than the unrestrained exploitation and expansionism approach. This is because if one combines anthropocentrism with the recognition that there are limits to material growth then one is obliged to take the interests of future generations of *humans* into account in deciding upon present courses of action.

3. As John Rodman points out, the dual (conservation/devel-

opment) nature of this approach means that there are two ways of "wasting resources"—both of which are considered tantamount to sin.[4] The first is to use resources inefficiently (this flows from the conservation aspect of this approach); the second is not to use potential resources at all, for example, not to "harness" the power of a "wild" river for electricity generation (this flows from the development aspect of this approach). Another way of expressing these concerns is to say that this approach emphasizes the idea of *maximum sustainable yield* (the emphasis on *maximum* yield flows from the development aspect of this approach while the emphasis on *sustainable* yield flows from its conservation aspect).

4. It can therefore be thought of as the unrestrained exploitation and expansionism approach (which urges maximum yield) modified by considerations of "enlightened (human) self-interest," which, it is held, ought to suggest the rationality of sustainable yield.

With respect to the last point, it must constantly be borne in mind that the reality of the operations of transnational capital is such that it can actually be economically "rational" to use a resource in a thoroughly unsustainable way in order to maximize economic profit in the here and now and then to move that capital on to another country and/or the exploitation of another kind of resource. The extent to which a policy of sustainable yield is economically "rational" is therefore very much a function of whether the operations in question are locally based or, ultimately, transnationally based.

RESOURCE PRESERVATION

The difference between the resource conservation and development approach and the resource preservation approach is purely one of emphasis. As its name implies, the resource *preservation* approach tends to stress the instrumental values that can be enjoyed by humans if they allow presently existing members or aspects of the nonhuman world to follow their own characteristic patterns of existence. The emphasis in the resource conservation and development position, on the other hand, is on the values that can be realized by dramatically altering (physically transforming) the characteristic patterns of existence of presently existing members or aspects of the nonhuman world (e.g., by farming, damming, mining, pulping, slaughtering, and so on)—albeit in a way that is presumed to be reasonably sustainable.

It is useful to relate this difference in emphasis to the etymological meanings of the terms *preservation* and *conservation*. The prefix *pre-* derives from the Latin for "before," "beforehand," or "in front," whereas the prefix *con-* derives from the Latin for "together" or "with." *Serve* derives from the Latin for "a slave." Thus, *preserve* carries the sense of "before slavery," which in turn carries the suggestion of preventing something from becoming a slave. *Conserve,* on the other hand, carries the sense of "together with a slave," which in turn carries the suggestion not of preventing something from becoming a slave but of working together with something that already is a slave. My use of the words *preservation* and *conservation* clearly draws on this etymologically based distinction.

William Godfrey-Smith (now William Grey) has distinguished four general kinds of arguments that tend to be emphasized in arguing for the *preservation* of the nonhuman world on the basis of its instrumental value. He has neatly captured the flavor of these arguments by referring to them as the *silo, laboratory, gymnasium,* and *cathedral arguments.*[5] These arguments claim, respectively, that the nonhuman world ought to be preserved on the basis of its importance:

1. as a stockpile of genetic diversity for agricultural, medical, and other purposes (the silo argument);
2. for scientific study (the laboratory argument);
3. for recreation (the gymnasium argument); and
4. for aesthetic pleasure/spiritual inspiration (the cathedral argument).

I find it helpful to divide Godfrey-Smith's last general kind of argument into two. Although accounts of the beauty associated with some aspect of the nonhuman world do often shade over into the spiritual or religious sphere, it nevertheless seems more informative to distinguish those arguments that tend to emphasize aesthetic qualities (e.g., beauty, richness of texture or color) from those that tend to emphasize spiritual or religious qualities (e.g., the enlivening of one's spirit, intimations of the presence of God). In keeping with Godfrey-Smith's terminology, I therefore refer to arguments of the former kind as instances of the *art gallery argument* and retain the *cathedral* label for arguments of the latter kind.

Another general kind of argument for the preservation of the nonhuman world on the basis of its instrumental value concerns the symbolic instructional value of the nonhuman world. Bryan Norton provides an example of this kind of argument when he argues that "other species, which struggle to survive in living, unmanaged ecosystems" ought to be preserved because they "are our most powerful symbols of human freedom." If we realize this, says Norton, we will then "prefer living symbols to lacquered ones."[6] Although Norton sees unmanaged aspects of nature as "powerful symbols of human *freedom*," it should be noted that this is just one particular example of symbolic instructional value. Other observers might wish to argue that the nonhuman world is valuable on account of quite different kinds of symbolic instructional value; for example, they might argue that unmanaged ecosystems are valuable because they are models of efficiency; they show us that nothing is wasted in nature, or that the vast networks of symbiotic relationships in nature are valuable because they are models of cooperation and harmony; they show us how vastly different kinds of entities can work together to mutual advantage. Again in keeping with Godfrey-Smith's terminology, I classify all these kinds of arguments for the preservation of the nonhuman world on the basis of its symbolic instructional value to humans under the general heading of the *monument argument* since *monument* derives from the Latin *monere*, meaning "to remind" or "advise."

George Sessions has recently drawn on Godfrey-Smith's resource preservation arguments, along with the two additions that I have just suggested, and added five further arguments to this list.[7] However, Sessions's additions seem to represent essentially two general kinds of arguments: the *life support system argument* and the *psychogenetic argument* (*psychogenetic* is used here in the straightforward sense of psychogenesis, or psychological development, rather than in any kind of sense that might be taken to suggest some kind of necessary relationship between one's genetic constitution and one's personality). The life support system argument is the argument that we ought to preserve the nonhuman world because it provides us with all sorts of free "goods and services" that are essential to our healthy physical survival and development (e.g., protection from ultra-violet light, "friendly" temperatures, clean air, clean water, food, fuel, and the materials for clothing and shelter). Sessions actually refers to two arguments in this context (although he notes that they are closely related): the *life support system argument* and the *Gaia hypothesis argument*. However, in my view, the Gaia hypothesis argument is simply a restatement of the life support system argument at the global or ecospherical level—unless, of course, the Gaia hypothesis argument is employed to the effect that the earth itself is a kind of living organism that ought to be valued for its own sake on that account. If the latter applies then the Gaia hypothesis argument is no longer an instrumental value theory argument (and, hence, no longer a *resource* preservation argument) but rather an intrinsic value theory argument. I deal with this form of the Gaia hypothesis argument in the next section under the heading of "Ecosystem Ethics and Ecosphere (or Gaian) Ethics."

It is also possible to add a meta-level argument to the normal "free goods and services" form of the life support system argument. I refer to this meta-level argument as the *early warning system argument*. Both this argument and its meta-level status vis-à-vis the life support system argument can be explained as follows. Whereas the life support system argument states that we ought to preserve the nonhuman world because it provides us with all sorts of free "goods and services" that are essential to our healthy physical survival and development, the early warning system argument states that we ought to preserve certain areas or certain species (often species that exist in the higher levels of food webs) by virtue of the fact that they serve to warn us of more general kinds of deterioration in the quality or quantity of the free "goods and services" that are provided *by* our "life support system." The species and areas that fall within the ambit of this early warning system argument can therefore be thought of as serving a similar function to that of the canaries that coal miners used to take down into the mines with them as a safety measure against poisonous gases: if the canary stopped singing, it was prudent for the miners to proceed with caution; if the canary started to fall off its perch, it was clearly time for the miners to seek a change of environment.

Although I have distinguished the early warning system argument from the life support system argument, the early warning system argument could nevertheless be thought of as just another example of the scientific study/laboratory argument rather than as an argument in its own right. However, the early warning system argument is such a special case that I find it extremely useful to maintain a distinction between it and the laboratory argument. The reason for this becomes clear if we consider the following analogy. If we employ the popular, thoroughly instrumentally oriented image of the earth as a spaceship, then we can think of the life support system argument as an argument for not damaging the spaceship itself—or at least those subsystems that are vital to our survival; the early warning system argument as an argument for not damaging the instrument display, which monitors the "vital signs" of the spaceship; and the laboratory argument as an argument for preserving each and every aspect of the spaceship for what it might be able to tell us about how we came to be in the spaceship, how long the spaceship has been in orbit, what the nature of our relationship to the other passengers might be, what if anything our "mission" or ultimate destination might be, how we might alter the spaceship's functioning to better suit our own ends, how we might repair the spaceship, and so on. Thus, although the scientific argument can be applied just as much to the instrument display—or "vital signs" of the spaceship—as to any other aspect of the spaceship, these "vital signs" are so significant a part of the spaceship that they seem to warrant being argued for on their own account.

In contrast to Sessions's life support system argument, his psychogenetic argument states that we ought to preserve the nonhuman world because it provides us with a range of contexts and experiences that are essential to our healthy *psychological* survival and development. The examples that Sessions provides here (but which he prefers to treat as three arguments) include such things as (1) the psychogenetic importance of *bonding* with wild (i.e., un*man*aged) places and wild animals; (2) the psychogenetic importance of unmanaged places as a *refuge* from the heavily managed aspects of existence (this kind of refuge is known colloquially as "getting away from 'it' all"—a therapeutic practice that common folk psychology often recommends as "the best cure there is" . . . "when 'it' all gets too much"); and (3) since unmanaged places (or wildernesses) represent the opposite of heavily managed, and especially totalitarian, contexts, the importance of unmanaged places as "a *standard* for freedom and autonomous behavior" (emphasis added).[8] This last example, however, seems to be more an example of the monument argument (i.e., the argument that we ought to preserve the nonhuman world on account of its symbolic instructional value) than of the psychogenetic argument.

It is certainly worthwhile to preserve a distinction between the psychogenetic argument and the three experientially based arguments to which I have already referred (i.e., the recreation/gymnasium argument, the aesthetic pleasure/art gallary argument, and the spiritual inspiration/cathedral argument). Although all four arguments may be seen as contributing to general psychological (or character) development, the latter three nevertheless tend to emphasize the importance of the nonhuman world in regard to the satisfaction of particular experiential *preferences,* whereas the psychogenetic argument emphasizes the importance of the nonhuman world in regard to the satisfaction of more fundamental psycho-developmental *needs.* The psychogenetic argument, in other words, emphasizes a deeper or more primitive level of psychological analysis than the other experientially based arguments previously discussed. It emphasizes not simply experiences that we may *like* to have because they enrich our lives, but experiences that we really *ought* to have if we are to maximize our chances of growing and maturing in a sane way. In the light of this understanding, then, we can summarize Sessions's two main resource preservation arguments by saying that whereas the life support system argument emphasizes the importance of the nonhuman world to humans for the development of healthy bodies, the psychogenetic argument emphasizes the importance of the nonhumam world to humans for the development of healthy (sane) minds.

The arguments just summarized provide us with a total of nine general kinds of arguments for the preservation of the nonhuman world on the basis of its instrumental value. I find it convenient to list these arguments in this order:

1. the life support system argument;

2. the early warning system argument;

3. the laboratory argument;

4. the silo argument;

5. the gymnasium argument;

6. the art gallery argument;

7. the cathedral argument;

8. the monument argument; and

9. the psychogenetic argument.

Whereas the unrestrained exploitation and development approach and the resource conservation and development approach can be thought of as emphasizing the *physical transformation value* of the nonhuman world to humans, these nine resource preservation arguments can be thought of as emphasizing other general kinds of instrumental values: the life support system argument emphasizes the *physical nourishment value* of the nonhuman world to humans; the early warning system, laboratory, and silo argu-

ments emphasize the *informational value* of the nonhuman world
to humans (I take the silo argument to be essentially concerned
with the genetic information that is encoded in the nonhuman
world); the gymnasium, art gallery, and cathedral arguments
emphasize the *experiential value* of the nonhuman world to humans; the monument argument emphasizes the *symbolic instructional value* of the nonhuman world to humans; and the psychogenetic argument emphasizes the *psychological nourishment value* of
the nonhuman world to humans (where psychological nourishment value emphasizes a deeper or more primitive level of
psychological analysis than the other experientially based arguments).

We have already noted that one can attempt to argue for,
justify, or legitimate the unrestrained exploitation and expansionism approach, the resource conservation and development
approach, or the resource preservation approach on the basis of
any view that restricts intrinsic value to humans (or that consistently bestows far greater intrinsic value upon humans than upon
the nonhuman world). However, there are also many grounds
upon which one can attempt to reject these instrumental value
theory approaches. These may be divided into negative (or
critical) grounds and positive (or constructive) grounds. Negative
grounds for rejecting instrumental value theory approaches consist of the general kinds of arguments *against* anthropocentric
theorizing outlined in chapter 1 ("A Closer Look at the Issue of
Anthropocentrism"). Positive grounds for rejecting instrumental
value theory approaches, on the other hand, are found in the
variety of specific arguments *for* the attribution of (more than
nominal) intrinsic value to members or aspects of the nonhuman
world. The next section is concerned with presenting and clari-
fying these intrinsic value theory arguments.

INTRINSIC VALUE THEORY

The vast majority of ecophilosophers reject approaches that adopt
an exclusively instrumentalist approach to the nonhuman world

and attempt instead to develop approaches that recognize the intrinsic value of at least some members or aspects of the nonhuman world. Thus, leading environmental ethicists such as J. Baird Callicott and Tom Regan write (respectively) that "the *central* and most recalcitrant problem for environmental ethics is the problem of constructing an adequate theory of intrinsic value for nonhuman natural entities and for nature as a whole," and that "the development of what can properly be called an environmental ethic *requires* that we postulate inherent value [or intrinsic value] in nature" (emphases added).[9]

We will discuss the main kinds of approaches to intrinsic value theory under the following headings:

1. *ethical sentientism* (often referred to, somewhat misleadingly, as *ethical hedonism;* less technically, referred to as *awareness-based ethics*);

2. *biological ethics* and *autopoietic ethics* (often referred to—again, misleadingly—as *ethical conativism;* less technically, referred to as *life-based ethics*);

3. *ecosystem ethics* and *ecosphere* (or *Gaian*) *ethics* (often referred to—more imprecisely than misleadingly—as *ethical holism*); and

4. *cosmic purpose ethics*.

By considering each of these intrinsic value theory approaches in turn, I hope to show in some detail (albeit within the limits of a relatively brief overview) that it is a fairly straightforward matter to argue not only for the intrinsic value of the nonhuman world in a limited sense (e.g., for the ethical sentientism or *animal liberation* approach) but even for approaches that are profoundly nonanthropocentric.

ETHICAL SENTIENTISM (AWARENESS-BASED ETHICS)

Advocates of ethical sentientism reject the validity of the kinds of criteria that have been held to confer intrinsic value exclusively upon humans—or upon humans by an overwhelming margin (i.e., they reject criteria such as a special relationship with God, the possession of a soul, rationality, self-awareness, free will, the capacity for symbolic communication, the capacity to enter into arrangements involving reciprocal duties and obligations, and the capacity to anticipate and symbolically represent the future and thereby to have knowledge of one's own mortality). Following the lead of Jeremy Bentham (1748–1832), the founding father of modern utilitarianism, these advocates point out that if such criteria were accepted then many humans would themselves be excluded from the domain of moral considerability (e.g., "heathens," "primitive savages," imbeciles, infants, the senile, human "vegetables," and people who are temporarily or irreversibly comatose). [10] These excluded humans would then be deemed to be valuable only insofar as they were of instrumental value to those humans who were deemed to be intrinsically valuable. Thus, the logic of anthropocentric moral theorists' own argument can be used to show that it would be morally permissible for those humans who possess intrinsic-value-bestowing characteristics to use those humans who do not possess these characteristics in whatever way they see fit (e.g., it would be morally permissible to throw "heathens" to the lions for one's own amusement, to use "primitive savages" as objects for target practice, and to torture, experiment upon, and in other ways abuse imbeciles, infants, the senile, human "vegetables," and the comatose).

This argument forces anthropocentric moral theorists to "lower their entry standards" for admission to the realm of moral considerability if all humans are to be included. But where should the line be drawn? Following Bentham again, advocates of ethical sentientism propose that the most appropriate criterion of moral considerability is that of sentience, that is, the capacity for sense perception, at however rudimentary a level (*sentient* derives from the Latin *sentire*, meaning "to feel" or "to perceive"). If an entity is sentient, they argue, then it may be said to have interests; in particular, it seeks pleasurable states of being and seeks to avoid unpleasurable states of being. And since interests are interests irrespective of the species to which they attach, it is arbitrary to respect human interests simply *because* it is humans that are the bearers of these interests. Rather, beings that have interests ought to have their interests taken into account in the context of actions regarding them irrespective of the species to which they belong. If an entity is not sentient, on the other hand, then it is incapable of having any interests of its own and thus is not owed any consideration in and of itself in the context of actions regarding it. After all, what does it matter how we treat an entity if that entity cannot matter to itself? Peter Singer, the most prominent exponent of this approach, summarizes this line of argument as follows:

> A stone does not have interests because it cannot suffer. Nothing that we can do to it could possibly make any difference to its welfare. A mouse, on the other hand, does have an interest in not being kicked along the road, because it will suffer if it is.
> If a being suffers there can be no moral justification for refusing to take that suffering into consideration. No matter what the nature of the being, the principle of equality requires that its suffering be counted equally with the like suffering—in so far as rough comparisons can be made—of any other being. If a being is not capable of suffering, or of experiencing enjoyment or happiness, there is nothing to be taken into account. So the limit of sentience . . . is the *only* defensible boundary of concern for the interests of others (emphasis added).[11]

But if, as Singer claims, "the problem of drawing the line [in regard to moral considerability] is the problem of deciding when we are justified in assuming that a being is incapable of suffering," the question arises as to what this means in practical terms. Following a discussion of the grounds we have for thinking that various kinds of animals are capable of experiencing pain, Singer concludes that "somewhere between a shrimp [which is an arthropod] and an oyster [which is a mollusk] seems as good a place to draw the line as any, and better than most."[12]

This sentience-based approach is often referred to as *ethical hedonism* (from the Greek *hedone*, meaning "pleasure"), because its central idea (i.e., the criterion of sentience in regard to the question of moral considerability) is derived from utilitarianism, which is classically associated with the idea of "the greatest happiness of the greatest number," where happiness is defined as pleasure as opposed to pain. However, since the role that the criterion of sentience plays in ecophilosophy is more one of arguing for a massive reduction in the pain that we inflict upon nonhuman animals than one of arguing that we should actively seek to increase the pleasure of nonhuman animals, it is more appropriate in this context to refer to this approach by reference to the criterion of sentience itself, rather than by reference to the aim of increasing pleasure. If the term *ethical sentientism* sounds somewhat formidable, this approach may also be referred to, less technically, as *awareness-based ethics*. It is also known, even more colloquially, as the *animal liberation* or *animal rights* approach.

It is worth pointing out, however, that some writers on ecophilosophy may wish to preserve a distinction between the terms *animal liberation* and *animal rights* in order to take into account certain differences between Singer's approach and that of his influential colleague Tom Regan. In particular, Regan is considerably more restrictive than Singer with respect to the question of where to draw the line in regard to moral considerability. In his book *The Case for Animal Rights,* Regan links the possession of rights primarily to the satisfaction of what he refers to as *the subject-of-a-life criterion*—a criterion that is only satisfied by entities that have "beliefs and desires; perception, memory, and a sense of the future, including their own future; an emotional life; . . . a psychophysical identity over time," and so on. This means that Regan is primarily concerned with arguing the case for the rights of "mentally normal mammals of a year or more."[13] In view of this, some writers associate the animal liberation approach primarily with Singer and the more restrictive animal rights approach primarily with Regan.

Biological Ethics and Autopoietic Ethics (Differing Versions of Life-Based Ethics)

Advocates of life-based approaches to ethics say, in effect:

> Why should an entity have to be *aware* of its interests (i.e., be sentient; be able to feel or to perceive—in at least some rudimentary

sense) for these interests to be taken into account in the context of actions regarding it? Surely interests are interests irrespective of whether or not the bearer of these interests may be said to be aware of them. Plants, animals that are constitutionally nonsentient (e.g., sponges, corals, jellyfish, worms, and mollusks—assuming we accept the boundary that Singer suggests), and animals that are functionally nonsentient (e.g., people in a coma) clearly have certain interests that must be fulfilled if they are to survive—let alone function optimally.[14] These interests are expressed continuously by all biological organisms both in terms of their internal behavior, as can be seen from the multitude of complex biochemical processes that are concerned with homeostatic regulation, and in terms of their externally oriented behavior, as can be seen from such things as positive and negative taxic behavior (in the case of animals) and tropic behavior (in the case of plants). All biological organisms, in other words, are actively *concerned* with seeking some states of affairs rather than others regardless of whether or not they are sentient (and it should be noted in this context that the word *interest* actually derives from the Latin for "it concerns"). To equate having interests (concerns) with *awareness* of interests, as in ethical sentientism, is to bias our understanding of what it means to have interests in a mentalistic and, hence, biologically parochial way. If interests are worthy of moral consideration qua interests then to add the *additional* stipulation that an entity has to be *aware* of its interests before these interests warrant moral consideration simply amounts to the replacement of human chauvinism by sentience chauvinism.

This view does not deny the moral *relevance* of sentience; it simply denies that sentience is an appropriate *criterion* of moral considerability. The fact that an organism is sentient will obviously be relevant to questions regarding the *kinds* of consideration that it should be given since one will need to take both mentally and physically expressed interests into account in the case of sentient organisms but will only need to take physically expressed interests into account in the case of nonsentient organisms. Thus, for example, if one compares a person who is dehydrated with a plant that is dehydrated one can see that it is in the immediate interests of both to be given water. In addition, however, it may also be in the immediate interests of the person to be given, say, an aspirin or a sedative for a headache or anxiety caused by their dehydrated state whereas, by definition, this is not a relevant consideration for nonsentient organisms.

While the dehydrated plant/person comparison can be used to illustrate the obvious moral *relevance of sentience*, it can also be used to illustrate the inappropriateness of sentience as a *criterion* of moral considerability. Specifically, if interests are equated with sentience, as in ethical sentientism, then this raises the question: What is wrong with simply sedating the dehydrated person to the point of unconsciousness (i.e., rendering them functionally nonsentient) and doing nothing else? Or, more pointedly, if the person is *already* unconscious (i.e., functionally nonsentient) then why not just leave them as they are? The answer is obvious: Because they will die without water, that's why! But the point here, of course, is that it is exactly the same with the nonsentient plant. Both the plant and the person have nonsentient interests in maintaining their life even if the person *also* has sentient (or potentially sentient) interests in maintaining their life. As Kenneth Goodpaster argues, "In the face of their obvious tendencies to maintain and heal themselves, it is very difficult to reject the idea of interests on the part of trees (and plants generally) in remaining alive."[15]

It should be clear, then, that sentience cannot be considered to be synonymous with having interests per se. Rather, sentience simply introduces a new class of interests—mentally expressed interests—into the domain of moral considerability. Moreover, as the dehydration example also illustrates, having mentally expressed interests (i.e., being functionally sentient) is in fact *conditional* upon the satisfaction of basic physical interests— interests that the bodies of sentient animals attend to for the most part beneath the threshold of awareness (i.e., in a nonsentient way; for example, in addition to homeostatic processes relating to the body's water balance, consider also the "constant vigilance" of the immune system or the processes of respiration and the operations of the circulatory system). If we consider these basic physical interests to be worthy of moral consideration in sentient animals—and in sentient animals that are functionally nonsentient—then we must also consider them to be morally considerable in nonsentient organisms.

Advocates of this life-based approach to ethics find it just as convincing as Singer finds ethical sentientism. Thus, just as Singer claims that "the limit of sentience . . . is the *only* defensible boundary of concern for the interests of others" (emphasis added), so Goodpaster claims that "neither rationality nor the capacity to experience pleasure and pain seem to me necessary (even though they may be sufficient) conditions on moral considerability. . . . Nothing short of the condition of *being alive* seems to me to be a plausible and nonarbitrary criterion."[16]

Moreover, advocates of this approach can claim that they squarely address issues that Singer tends to avoid. For example, recall that in the passage in which Singer claims that "the limit of sentience . . . is the only defensible boundary of concern for the interests of others"—a pivotal passage that occurs early on in his argument—Singer illustrates his point by employing a comparison between a mouse and a stone. In the light of the general line of argument that I have outlined for advocating a life-based ethics, it can readily be seen that Singer's comparison is all too convenient for his own sentience-based purposes. In comparing an entity that is alive *and* sentient (i.e., a mouse) with an entity that is neither alive nor sentient (i.e., a stone), Singer simply overlooks all those entities that are alive (and, hence, that clearly have certain interests that must be fulfilled if they are to survive—let alone function optimally) but *not* sentient. Singer's convenient comparison thus conflates having interests with being sentient. The upshot is that he effectively assimilates all of the nonsentient biological world to the same irrelevant moral status that he assigns to a stone.

Life-based approaches to ethics are often referred to as ethical *conativism* (from the Latin *conari,* meaning "to try," "attempt," "strive," or "struggle"). This description suggests that what characterizes life (and hence the realm of moral considerability) is the fact that living things strive for certain ends—whatever these ends might be. However, the fact that we live in a cybernetic age means that there is an obvious objection to characterizing living things (and hence moral considerability) in a conative way. Specifically, we are surrounded by many kinds of purely mechanical devices that rely on negative feedback mechanisms in such a way as to exhibit apparently purposive or goal-oriented behavior (e.g., a thermostat tries/attempts/strives to regulate the air temperature of a room, and a ground-to-air heat-seeking missile tries/attempts/strives to home in upon a rapidly moving target). This means that critics of the ethical conativism approach can object, as Edward Johnson does, that if living entities deserve moral consideration on the basis of the fact that they strive for certain ends then goal-oriented machines should also deserve moral consideration. Conversely, if we accept Johnson's view that "there seems to be nothing wrong with interrupting a mechanism because, despite the 'striving' of the machine, there is no frustration; the machine doesn't care if its 'purposes' are thwarted" then, in Johnson's view, this must raise the question: "Why should we be concerned about trees, or other environmental objects that, because they lack consciousness of any kind, don't care what happens to them?"[17]

However, the problem with this objection is that it fails to take into account more recent thinking regarding the nature of living systems. This thinking emphasizes the fact that living systems can be distinguished from nonliving systems by the particular *kinds* of ends for which they strive. Specifically, living systems are seen as being characterized by the property of *autopoiesis* (from the Greek for "self-production"—*autos*, "self," and *poiein*, "to produce"). This term was coined by, and is primarily associated with the work of, the Chilean biologists Humberto Maturana and Francisco Varela.[18] The term *autopoiesis* refers to the fact that living systems continuously strive to produce and sustain their own organizational activity and structure. In other words, the primary product of the operations of living systems is themselves, not something external to themselves. A more technical way of expressing this is to say that the networks of processes that constitute the organizational activity and structure of living systems are continuously engaged in the recursive (or circular) process of regenerating (renewing) themselves. Living systems, then, are not merely self-*organizing* systems, they are self-*regenerating* or self-*renewing* systems. (Maturana and Varela make this distinction because the term *self-organizing* may be taken to refer to unidirectional forms of spontaneous organization, such as the formation of a crystal, rather than to the specifically circular processes of self-organization that characterize living systems.) In contrast, mechanical devices, including those that incorporate principles of negative feedback such as thermostats and ground-to-air heat-seeking missiles, are incapable of regenerating their own organizational activity and structure. The ends for which they strive, such as temperature regulation or hitting an airplane, are external to the production of their own organizational activity and structure. The most obvious way of illustrating this difference between living systems and mechanical systems is simply to compare what happens if you cut yourself (or violate the integrity of any other kind of living system) with what happens if you cut into the parts of any mechanistic device.

Fritjof Capra, in "The Systems View of Life" in *The Turning Point,* provides a vivid illustration of the difference between living systems and mechanical systems:

> Whereas a machine is constructed to produce a specific product or to carry out a specific task intended by its designer, an organism is primarily engaged in renewing itself; cells are breaking down and building up structures, tissues and organs are replacing their cells in continual cycles. Thus the pancreas replaces most of its cells every twenty-four hours, the stomach lining every three days; our white blood cells are renewed in ten days and 98 percent of the protein in the brain is turned over in less than one month. All these processes are regulated in such a way that the overall pattern of the organism is preserved, and this remarkable ability of self-maintenance persists under a variety of circumstances, including changing environmental conditions and many kinds of interference.[19]

Three points should be noted in regard to the characterization of living systems as autopoietic systems. First, this characterization is not meant to be a complete characterization of all that living systems strive to do. It is simply intended to characterize what it is that distinguishes all living systems from all nonliving systems. Second, this dynamic characterization of living systems as systems that continuously strive to produce and sustain their own organizational activity and structure should not be taken to imply that these processes produce a static result, that is, a system that does not change at all. Rather, these dynamic processes account for the relative stability of living systems *despite* the fact that they change over time. And third, it is of particular interest to note that, as Varela, Maturana, and Uribe point out, characterizing living systems in terms of autopoiesis means that "reproduction does *not* enter as a requisite feature for the living organization. In fact for reproduction to take place there must be a unity to be reproduced: the establishment of the unity is logically and operationally antecedent to its reproduction" (emphasis added).[20]

These relatively recent ideas in theoretical biology enable us to distinguish between conative activity in general and conative activity of the kind that may be described as autopoietic. They enable us to see that there is a world of difference between entities that only strive to accomplish tasks that are external to the regeneration of their own organizational activity and structure (i.e., mechanical entities that incorporate principles of negative feedback) and entities that are primarily and continuously concerned with the regeneration of their own organizational activity and structure (i.e., living entities). Moreover, it is easy to see why advocates of life-based ethics consider this difference to be morally relevant. The fact that mechanical entities are not concerned with the regeneration of their own organizational activity and structure means that they cannot be thought of as mattering to themselves. Thus, there is no reason to extend moral consideration to mechanical entities since, to paraphrase Singer in regard to stones, nothing that we can do to them could possibly make any difference to *their* welfare. It is equally clear, on the other hand, that living entities do matter to themselves (although not necessarily in a sentience-based or cognitively oriented sense of "matter to themselves"). They are primarily and continuously concerned with the regeneration of their own organizational activity and structure. What clearer definition of an entity mattering to itself could one possibly want? The fact that living entities matter to themselves means that what we do to them *can* make a difference to their welfare. They must therefore be regarded as morally considerable.

This argument can be expressed in a more formal way. The fact that autopoietic processes are primarily and continuously engaged in the recursive (or circular) process of regenerating (renewing) themselves means that they are not merely means to ends that are external to themselves but rather that they are *ends in themselves*. This amounts to the classical formulation of intrinsic value: by definition, any entity or process that is merely a means to an end has only an instrumental value whereas any entity or process that is an end in itself has an intrinsic value, and is therefore deserving of moral consideration.

Although the criterion of autopoiesis resolves some problems pertaining to life-based approaches to ethics, it does so at the expense of enlarging the domain of moral considerability well beyond the limits that most advocates of life-based approaches to ethics would seem to have in mind. This is because the criterion of autopoiesis does more than simply include all biological organisms in the class of living systems (in the sense in which we ordinarily understand the term *biological organisms,* i.e., entities whose basic subunits are biological cells) and exclude all mechanistic devices (again, in the sense in which we ordinarily understand that term). Specifically, the criterion of autopoiesis suggests that *all* process-structures that continuously strive to regenerate their own organizational activity and structure should be included in the class of living systems. Thus, this criterion definitely opens the door for the inclusion of ecosystems and the ecosphere (Gaia), presumably opens the door for the inclusion of more abstract kinds of entities such as species (or at least gene pools) and social systems (human and nonhuman), and perhaps opens the door for the inclusion of many other, quite different kinds of entities as well (e.g., cognitive processes considered in their own right). The reason for my varying degrees of confidence with respect to the examples in this list is simply that, at present, one quickly reaches uncharted waters in attempting to set precise limits on what kinds of systems may and may not be considered to be members of the class of autopoietic systems. As Fritjof Capra notes in regard to this same question: "This question of the boundaries or parameters of a living system is extremely important, but it has not been thoroughly studied and is therefore not well understood."[21]

Goodpaster acknowledges the existence of some of these possibilities in his defense of "being alive" as the appropriate criterion of moral considerability. He recognizes that precise as opposed to conventional understandings of life lead in the direction of thinking of life in terms of "self-sustaining organization and integration in the face of pressures toward high entropy," and that this in turn means that "it is possible that larger systems besides our ordinarily understood 'linear' extrapolations from human beings (e.g., animals, plants, etc.) might satisfy the conditions [of life], such as the biosystem as a whole."[22] To his credit, Goodpaster then accepts the nonanthropocentric implications that follow from this understanding of living systems:

> But it seems to me that such (perhaps surprising) implications, if true, should be taken seriously. There is some evidence that the biosystem as a whole exhibits behavior approximating to the definition sketched above [i.e., self-sustaining organization and integration in the face of pressures toward high entropy], and I see no reason to deny it moral considerability on that account. Why should the universe of moral considerability map neatly onto our medium-sized framework of organisms?[23]

In the light of these considerations, it is tempting to suggest that life-based ethics should be referred to not as *ethical conativism* but by the more technically precise (if also more formidable) *autopoietic ethics*. But this would be to move too hastily. The fact that most people think of living systems (or living "things") in terms of individual biological organisms means that it is important—if only for descriptive and communicative purposes—to distinguish this conventional, individual biological organisms sense of life-based ethics from the more technical, expanded sense that is entailed by the term *autopoietic ethics*. Such a distinction is also necessary in view of the fact that, Goodpaster's views notwithstanding, many—if not most—life-based ethicists also share this conventional, individual biological organisms understanding of living systems. A significant example is Paul Taylor whose book *Respect for Nature* represents the major recent extended development of a life-based approach to ethics. Taylor characterizes individual organisms in a conative way as "teleological [or goal-oriented] centers of life."[24] (Defining a living organism as any kind of "center of *life*" involves a tautology; Taylor is clearer when he speaks of living organisms as "center[s] of goal-oriented *activity*" [my emphasis].) Like most other ecophilosophers, Taylor writes (or so it would appear) in the absence of any particular knowledge of, or references to, the recent developments in theoretical biology that we have been discussing in regard to the characterization of living systems. As a result he has considerable difficulty in providing any kind of formal characterization of what it is that distinguishes individual biological organisms from mechanical systems on the one hand and from other kinds of autopoietic systems, such as ecosystems and the ecosphere, on the other hand.[25] Thus, on the one hand, Taylor accepts that "the distinction [that he draws] between living things and inanimate machines may break down . . . [in the face of] those complex electronic devices now being developed under the name of artificial intelligence" and, on the other hand, he seems to accept that it may well be the case that the ecosphere is itself a "supraorganism or quasi-organism." Yet, despite this, Taylor nevertheless insists that it is only "individual organisms (not supraorganisms or quasi-organisms [such as ecosystems and the ecosphere]) that . . . are seen to be organisms having a good of their own [and, hence, to be worthy of moral consideration]."[26]

One wonders, then, what Taylor would make of examples of organisms whose individual members he would accept as having "a good of their own" but that, like cellular slime molds, ants, bees, wasps, and termites, also constitute colonies that exhibit distinctly holistic properties, that is, organisms whose *collective* behavior itself resembles that of a single organism. Would he deny that these "supraorganisms," to employ his term, are themselves goal-oriented in a way that is not reducible to—or that transcends—the goal-oriented behavior of their individual members? If he accepts that these supraorganisms themselves represent "center[s] of goal-oriented activity" then he must accept, on the basis of his own criterion of moral considerability, that they have "a good of their own." But if these kinds of supraorganisms can have "a good of their own," what about other possible kinds of supraorganisms such as ecosystems and the ecosphere?

Since it is clearly important to recognize our strong predilection for defining living systems (or at least living systems that are deemed to be worthy of moral consideration) in an atomistic, middle-range (in universal terms), and human-analogic way, I refer to the conventional, individual biological organisms understanding of life-based ethics by the straightforward term *biological ethics* and to the more technical, expanded understanding of life-based ethics by the term *autopoietic ethics*. In making this distinction, however, I hasten to emphasize that I am bowing to convention in speaking about biological *ethics* since it is difficult to see how one can justify such an approach on ethical grounds. The reason for this is as follows. The most obvious way of attempting to demarcate individual biological organisms from other kinds of autopoietic entities is by employing the criterion of reproduction (i.e., asking whether the entities in question are members of a kind whose members, in general, are capable of reproduction). But, from an ethical standpoint, the problem with this criterion is that the question of whether or not an entity is of a kind whose members, in general, are capable of reproduction is *irrelevant* to the question of whether or not it has interests. And, as we have seen, it is the question of whether or not an entity has interests that is central to the issue of whether or not it should be regarded as worthy of moral consideration. Thus, although the criterion of reproduction may perhaps represent a useful way of dividing the class of entities that continuously strive to maintain their own integrity (i.e., autopoietic systems) into biological entities (those entities that are more like us) and nonbiological entities (those entities that are less like us), it is nevertheless a criterion of no moral consequence.

ECOSYSTEM ETHICS AND
ECOSPHERE (OR GAIAN) ETHICS

The argument for ecosystem ethics and ecosphere (or Gaian) ethics has already been given since these approaches simply represent a particular subset of the class of autopoietic ethics— albeit a subset that is of particular ecological interest. The most widely known statement of ecosystem ethics was presented by Aldo Leopold (1887–1948) in his environmental classic A Sand County Almanac. Leopold's pithiest formulation of this approach, which he referred to as the *land ethic,* states that "a thing is right when it tends to preserve the integrity, stability, and beauty of the biotic community. It is wrong when it tends otherwise."[27] James Heffernan has reformulated this maxim in terms that are more ecologically explicit and less dependent upon subjective judgments: "A thing is right when it tends to preserve the characteristic diversity and stability of an ecosystem (or the biosphere). It is wrong when it tends otherwise."[28]

Although Leopold's pithy formulation of his land ethic is a maxim rather than an argument, and although Leopold obviously wrote in the absence of our present knowledge regarding the characterization of living systems (i.e., ideas such as those of *autopoiesis* and *dissipative structures*), it is clear that his land ethic was nevertheless based on his own intuitive grasp of the organismic nature of ecosystems and the ecosphere as a whole.[29] More recent ecosystem ethicists have built on Leopold's intuition by explicitly drawing on some of these more recent ideas regarding the characterization of living systems. Thus, Heffernan writes: "Against those philosophers who contend that the stability of an ecosystem is not an intrinsic value, since it is not possible to harm or benefit anything not at least potentially sentient, I have argued, following Goodpaster, that it is possible to harm or benefit anything that exhibits 'self-sustaining organization and integration in the face of pressures toward high entropy.' "[30]

Ecosystem ethics and ecosphere ethics differ only in emphasis. Thus, the local, ecosystem-based nature of Leopold's observations in *A Sand County Almanac* and his use of terms like *land* and *community* give his ethic an ecosystemic emphasis despite the fact that it can easily be understood in ecospheric terms—and despite the fact that Leopold himself had an organismic conception not only of ecosystems but also of the earth as a whole.[31] In contrast, ethical emphasis on the ecosphere has derived its main inspiration from the more recent work of James Lovelock on the self-regulating, self-regenerating, and hence, organismic or (what I have referred to as) autopoietic nature of the ecosphere considered as a whole. Lovelock refers to this autopoietic entity—the ecosphere of Earth—as *Gaia,* after the Greek goddess of the earth.[32]

Ecosystem ethics and ecosphere (or Gaian) ethics are often referred to under the name of *ethical holism* since they are seen as emphasizing the value of entities that are generally perceived as *wholes* (i.e., the ecosystem and the ecosphere), rather than the value of entities that, like biological organisms, are generally perceived as *individuals.* However, referring to these approaches as *ecosystem ethics* and *ecosphere* (or *Gaian*) *ethics* is more accurate and informative since these terms distinguish the particular kinds of "wholes" that are being considered from the vast array of other possible kinds of "wholes." Having said this, however, it should also be pointed out that there is good reason to believe that what many of the proponents of ecosystem ethics and ecosphere ethics *intend* by these approaches would be better captured simply by employing the previously introduced term *autopoietic ethics.* This follows from the fact that a number of critics of ecosystem ethics and ecosphere ethics see these approaches as suggesting that individual biological organisms are valuable *only* insofar as they contribute to the integrity (read: self-regenerating capacities) of their ecosystem or the ecosphere. These critics therefore consider that ecosystem ethics and ecosphere ethics suggest that it is ethically permissible to sacrifice individual entities for the "good of the whole." In consequence, one prominent ecophilosopher has characterized these approaches as *environmental fascism*.[33]

But this interpretation represents a complete misunderstanding of ecosystem ethics and ecosphere ethics. This is because the thinking that lies behind proposals for ecosystem ethics and ecosphere ethics is essentially the same as the thinking that lies behind proposals regarding the moral considerability of individual biological organisms—that is, both approaches turn on the question of the possession of interests. If "wholes" such as ecosystems and the ecosphere are considered to be worthy of moral consideration by virtue of the fact that they have interests of an intrinsic kind (namely, autopoietic interests or interests in their own self-regeneration) then the moral considerability of individual biological organisms is *guaranteed* since the fact that these kinds of entities have interests of this kind is even easier to establish. Thus, whatever their emphasis might appear to be, proponents of ecosystem ethics and ecosphere ethics are essentially engaged in making the general point that it is not *only* individual biological organisms that have interests and so are worthy of moral consideration. It therefore follows that advocates of ecosystem ethics and ecosphere ethics would convey their approach more clearly by describing it as *autopoietic ethics* rather than as *ecosystem ethics* or *ecosphere ethics* (or *ethical holism*). This is because the former term makes it clear that *all* autopoietic systems are considered to be worthy of moral consideration (from individual organisms to ecosystems and the ecosphere) whereas the latter terms can be, and have been, taken to suggest that only ecosystems or the ecosphere are worthy of moral consideration.

When one understands the reasoning that underpins ecosystem ethics and ecosphere ethics it can be seen that the charge of "environmental fascism" is facile. The practical upshot of ecosystem ethics and ecosphere ethics is not that considerations regarding the good of the ecosystem or the ecosphere should rigidly dictate the lives of individual biological organisms but only that these considerations should set certain limits on the otherwise *diverse* behavior of such organisms. In other words, individual biological organisms should be free to follow their diverse individual and evolutionary paths to the extent that this does not involve seriously damaging the autopoietic (i.e., self-regenerating) functioning of their ecosystem or the ecosphere. If one must look to human socio-political concepts to describe this nonanthropocentric view—a practice that is fraught with difficulties, even dangers, and not one that I would wish to encourage—then this understanding suggests that it would be more informative to look in the direction of democracy than that of fascism. In an ideal democracy, people are free to follow diverse ways of life within limits that must be respected if the democratic social system that enables and encourages these freedoms is to keep renewing itself. Similarly, on the basis of ecosystem ethics and ecosphere ethics, members of an ecosystem or the ecosphere are free to follow diverse ways of life within limits that must be respected if the ecological systems that enable and encourage these freedoms are to keep renewing themselves. In an ideal democracy, we do not think of people as being *downtrodden* by the limits (codified in laws) to which I have referred. Rather, we say instead that "no-one is *above* the law." It is precisely when some people place themselves above the law—replacing democratically elected parliaments with military dictatorships, for example—that fascism begins. Similarly, on the basis of ecosystem ethics and ecosphere ethics, members of an ecosystem or the ecosphere are free within limits that may be encapsulated in the phrase "no entity is *above* the ecology." It is scarcely necessary to add that this message has a profound relevance for our species.

Cosmic Purpose Ethics

Cosmic purpose ethics is a very general category referring to a variety of approaches that have in common the fact that, in addition to humans, some or all nonhuman entities are considered to be morally considerable by virtue of the fact that they in some sense embody or are expressive of some kind of *cosmic* interest. These approaches generally rely upon views about the ultimate ends of evolution or the nature of God or God's purposes. They are therefore often referred to as *evolutionary ethics* or *ethical theism* respectively. However, because these approaches also often rely upon some *combination* of views about the ultimate ends of evolution and views about the nature of God or God's purposes they cannot be adequately characterized simply as "evolutionary ethics" on the one hand or "ethical theism" on the other hand. Moreover, even where these categorizations are appropriate (i.e., even where the approach concerned relies upon views concerning the ultimate ends of evolution but proceeds without particular reference to theological concerns, or vice versa) the similarities between these approaches are generally more impressive than their differences.

For these reasons, then, I find it convenient to speak of cosmic purpose ethics in general, and to characterize the variety of approaches that fall within this general category by a combination of evolutionary and theological labels. For example, approaches that fall within this category can be characterized as adopting an evolutionary stance, an anti-evolutionary stance, or, if they proceed without particular reference to evolutionary concerns, a nonevolutionary stance. In addition, they can also be characterized as adopting a nontheistic stance (i.e., as proceeding without particular reference to theological concerns), a pantheistic stance (i.e., as proceeding on the basis that God and Nature are identical), a panentheistic stance (i.e., as proceeding on the basis that God is immanent in Nature but also transcends Nature; this can be expressed in terms of set theory by saying that Nature is a proper subset of God), and a transcendent theistic stance (i.e., as proceeding on the basis that God, or the Creator, stands outside Nature, or Creation, intervening only in the case of miracles). This diversity of possible theological views means that all or part of the nonhuman world may be considered to be morally considerable for any of a wide variety of theologically related reasons. For example, all or part of the nonhuman world may be considered to be morally considerable by virtue of the fact that private intuitions *or* scriptural dictates reveal it to be identical with, expressive of, part of, created by, valued by, or simply decreed to be so by God.

Given this way of distinguishing different kinds of approaches to cosmic purpose ethics, it is possible to describe some of these approaches more specifically. For example, Murray Bookchin adopts an *evolutionary nontheistic approach* in arguing that evolutionary processes actively strive toward the realization of ever greater degrees of individuation, freedom, and selfhood.[34] Henryk Skolimowski adopts an *evolutionary pantheistic approach* (possibly even an *evolutionary panentheistic approach*) in arguing that the products of evolution (or at least humans) represent "fragments of God in the process of becoming" (Skolimowski is not particularly clear on whether his conception of God is one in which God is simply immanent in nature—pantheism—or one in which God also transcends nature—panentheism).[35] Whiteheadian influenced ecophilosophers such as Charles Birch, John Cobb, and David Griffin quite clearly adopt an *evolutionary panentheistic approach* in arguing that God's persuasive (as opposed to absolute or coercive) power lures all aspects of the universe toward the realization of instances of ever greater richness of experience or intensity of feeling.[36] Finally, for the sake of an anti-evolutionary example, one could say that at least some environmentally oriented fundamentalist Christians would adopt an *anti-evolutionary transcendent theistic approach* in arguing that the nonhuman world is valuable in and of itself. This conclusion could be argued on the basis that the first chapter of Genesis states that God created the world (which many fundamentalist Christians take to justify belief in a transcendent God); that He did so in six days (which many fundamentalist Christians take to deny the existence of evolution); and that God surveyed His work and "saw that it was good" at *each* stage of creation (which fundamentalist Christians can take to justify the view that "goodness" is intrinsic to all aspects of creation, not just humans).

There are at least three general points that should be noted in regard to cosmic purpose ethics. First, cosmic purpose ethics generally have in common the fact that entities are seen as being intrinsically valuable to the extent that they are considered to embody or to be expressive of the ends (or values) that are under discussion (e.g., individuation, freedom, selfhood, richness of experience). This typically means that these approaches issue—either implicitly or explicitly—in a hierarchy of intrinsic value with humans beings seen as (at least currently) occupying the top position. That said, it should be noted that in subscribing either implicitly or explicitly to a hierarchical conception of intrinsic value, none of the authors to whom I have referred means to imply that entities possessing greater intrinsic value have any general right to *dominate* entities possessing lesser intrinsic value. However, their hierarchical conceptions of intrinsic value do, of course, provide a guide to action in situations where values come into genuine conflict.

Second, whatever *theoretical* differences may exist between cosmic purpose ethics and the other intrinsic value theory approaches discussed in this chapter, cosmic purpose ethics need not necessarily differ much in *practice* from these other approaches. For example, notwithstanding the Whiteheadian view that God's persuasive power lures *all* aspects of the universe toward the realization of instances of ever greater richness of experience (and, hence, that all aspects of the universe are sentient in at least some rudimentary sense), Birch and Cobb argue that the capacity for richness of experience that exists at the sub-atomic, atomic, molecular, cellular, and plant levels is such that the primary value of the entities that exist at these levels is generally instrumental rather than intrinsic and, therefore, that these entities can generally be treated primarily as means rather than as ends in themselves. In contrast, the capacity for richness of experience that exists at the level of animals—"especially those with highly developed nervous systems"—is such that they "cannot rightly be treated as mere means. They are entities which we must repect as ends [in themselves] as well."[37] For all *practical* purposes, then, Birch and Cobb's approach approximates that of animal liberation.

Notwithstanding this, however, it does unduly simplify Birch and Cobb's approach to subsume it under the heading of ethical sentientism or animal liberation. This is because the latter approach, as normally understood, makes *no* particular claims about the ultimate ends of evolution or the nature of God or

God's purposes. The same goes for the other intrinsic value theory approaches previously discussed. To assimilate cosmic purpose ethics to these other approaches would therefore be to gloss over the important theoretical differences that exist between them. In particular, such assimilation would ignore the fact that cosmic purpose ethics incorporate far more metaphysical assumptions than the other approaches that we have considered. Drawing attention to the metaphysical aspects of cosmic purpose ethics is important because it raises a question that threatens to render cosmic purpose ethics superfluous. Specifically, why should anyone who wants to argue for the welfare of animals, for example, carry the extra "metaphysical baggage" that comes with Bookchin's, Skolimowski's, Birch and Cobb's, or fundamentalist Christianity's views when they can get the same *practical* result with Singer's argument for animal liberation, which, as I have said, makes no particular claims about the ultimate ends of evolution or the nature of God or God's purposes? Advocates of cosmic purpose ethics are bound to answer, I think, that cosmic purpose ethics offer not only an accurate but also a more complete account of the universe within which moral decisions are made. This is a good answer if it can be substantiated, but therein lies the rub. The very metaphysical richness of cosmic purpose ethics means that these approaches are far less parsimonious than other approaches and, hence, far more contentious.

This brings us to our third and final general point in regard to cosmic purpose ethics, which is that most ecophilosophers do indeed consider ethics that rely on beliefs about the ultimate ends of evolution or the nature of God or God's purposes to be far more contentious than the other, thoroughly naturalistic approaches previously discussed (i.e., ethical sentientism, biological ethics, and autopoietic ethics—which, as I have argued, includes ecosystem ethics and ecosphere ethics).[38] For most ecophilosophers, the unfalsifiable nature of many of the assumptions upon which cosmic purpose ethics rely means that these approaches are considered to be far less open to modification in the light of discussion and criticism than other intrinsic value theory approaches. And for many ecophilosophers, this represents a disqualifying weakness in an ethical theory, just as it does for scientists in a scientific theory.

OBJECTIONS TO INTRINSIC VALUE THEORY APPROACHES

Having presented the major intrinsic value theory approaches and attempted to clarify a number of them, I will conclude this overview by noting a number of possible objections to these approaches.

Mainstream ecophilosophers seem to recognize four main kinds of objections to intrinsic value theory. These lines of objection seek to reject intrinsic value theory approaches, either in particular or in general, on the basis of their (1) possibility, (2) necessity, (3) argumentative logic, or (4) practical consequences.

OBJECTIONS BASED ON POSSIBILITY

The claim that it is not *possible* to establish nonhuman intrinsic value is the first line of defense that is employed by anthropocentric thinkers against those who argue for the intrinsic value of the nonhuman world. These anthropocentric thinkers attempt to argue, for example, that entities can only be worthy of moral consideration in their own right if they are themselves capable of extending moral consideration to others. These thinkers then argue that since only humans can enter into such reciprocal agreements, only humans can be members of the moral community, and, further, that this somehow means that only humans can be intrinsically valuable. But there are at least two fundamental problems with this argument. First, this contractual view of moral considerability does not address the arguments that intrinsic value theorists give *for* the intrinsic value of members or aspects of the nonhuman world. That is, it simply ignores the issue of the moral considerability of interests. Second, it is easy to show that anthropocentric moral theorists themselves recognize all sorts of moral obligations toward other humans that are incapable of entering into reciprocal agreements (e.g., infants and people who are brain damaged). This clearly destroys their argument for not recognizing moral obligations toward nonhumans on the grounds that nonhumans are incapable of entering into reciprocal agreements. Similar kinds of objections attend other arguments of this kind that attempt to show that it is not possible to establish nonhuman intrinsic value.

This *possibility argument* can also be used by nonanthropocentric ecophilosophers, although they use it not to object to intrinsic value approaches in general but rather to object to particular kinds of intrinsic value approaches. Thus, for example, an ethical sentientist might define what it means to have an interest in such a way that they can then claim that it is not *possible* to extend intrinsic value beyond the class of sentient animals. One then gets into the kind of discussion I pursued in the previous section regarding what it means to have an interest.

OBJECTIONS BASED ON NECESSITY

If one accepts that it is *possible* to argue for nonhuman intrinsic value, the next line of defense against intrinsic value approaches in general is to argue that these approaches are not *necessary*. Advocates of this approach can say to intrinsic value theorists:

> Okay, we accept that some members or aspects of the nonhuman world are worthy of moral consideration, but you can get the same result you are after (e.g., preservation of a certain area or a certain species) just as effectively—perhaps even more effectively—by arguing in more familiar and more acceptable human-centered terms (e.g., arguing in terms of the recreational and aesthetic qualities of the area or in terms of the scientific and symbolic value of the species). Thus, it isn't *necessary*—perhaps not even advisable—to argue for the intrinsic value of the nonhuman world.

However, intrinsic value theorists can reject this kind of objection to intrinsic value theory on several grounds. In the first place, this argument is often put forward in bad faith, that is, the real motives for the argument often represent a last-ditch attempt to stop the advance of nonanthropocentric modes of thinking. In these circumstances, the argument deserves to be dismissed out of hand since its avowed acceptance of the view that it is possible to establish nonhuman intrinsic value contradicts its actual subscription to the view that the nonhuman world is not intrinsically valuable. Second, where it is the case that the motives for this argument are genuinely nonanthropocentric (and, thus, where the argument is being put forward on purely pragmatic grounds), intrinsic value theorists can reply that accepting the argument amounts to intellectual cowardice. Why not use intrinsic value arguments *in addition to* all the instrumental value arguments one can muster? Why treat the issue as if it represents some kind of either/or choice? Third, intrinsic value theorists can reject this argument on the grounds that, whatever its short-term advantages might be, it has adverse long-term practical consequences. This is because accepting this argument does not mean that one simply fails to adopt a nonanthropocentric approach; it means that one actively reinforces the anthropocentric view that the nonhuman world is valuable only insofar as it is valuable to humans. The upshot of this is that even if one wins the battle in regard to preserving this area or that species, one is contributing to losing the ecological war by reinforcing the cultural perception that what is valuable in the nonhuman world is what is useful to humans. If the next battle in which one is engaged concerns an area or a species that is relatively "useless" to humans then this battle becomes that much harder to win precisely because of the anthropocentric views that have been reinforced by the way in which the last battle was won—not to mention the battle before that, and so on.

The *necessity argument* can also be used by intrinsic value theorists against intrinsic value theory approaches that extend beyond the limits to which these theorists think it is necessary or advisable (as distinct from possible) to subscribe. In turn, one can then offer modifications of the above comments in reply.

OBJECTIONS BASED ON ARGUMENTATIVE LOGIC

The third general way of objecting to intrinsic value theory approaches is to object to the *argumentative logic* that is employed in these approaches. There are two kinds of objections that should be mentioned here. The first centers on unintended theoretical consequences of the usual kinds of arguments for the intrinsic value of the nonhuman world. The second centers on the issue of *the naturalistic fallacy,* a form of objection to the usual kinds of arguments for the intrinsic value of the nonhuman world that derives from mainstream meta-ethical discussion and that, despite its dubious merits, has occupied a significant place in the history of twentieth-century ethical theorizing. The most significant examples of these two kinds of objections come from ecophilosophers who argue for nonanthropocentric approaches but who are nevertheless dissatisfied with the usual kinds of intrinsic value theory approaches—or with intrinsic value theory approaches in general—and seek to find a way of going beyond these approaches.

John Rodman's inspired and appropriately titled paper "The Liberation of Nature?" contains the best example of an objection to unintended theoretical consequences of the usual kinds of arguments for the intrinsic value of the nonhuman world. Rodman points out that these kinds of arguments actually degrade nonhuman entities in the very process of seeking to establish their moral considerability. This is because, in pressing their case for granting moral considerability to nonhuman entities while not expecting these entities to fulfill any duties, moral philosophers from Bentham on have generally sought to do so on the basis of an analogy with people who are likewise considered to be morally considerable but who cannot fulfill any duties (e.g., imbeciles, infants, the senile, human "vegetables," and people who are comatose). Thus, to put it bluntly, moral philosophers have effectively been arguing that whereas nonhuman entities were previously failed outright in their moral examinations, at least some of these entities should now be awarded conceded passes. Rodman offers this challenge:

> Is this, then, the new enlightenment, to see nonhuman animals as imbeciles, wilderness as a human vegetable? As a general characterization of nonhuman nature it seems patronizing and perverse. . . .

Assimilating [members or aspects of the nonhuman world] to the status of inferior human beings . . . is perhaps analogous to regarding women as defective men who lack penises, or humans as defective sea mammals who lack sonar capability and have to be rescued by dolphins.[39]

Rodman's own solution to this problem is to attempt to move beyond what he sees as the *moral extensionism* approach of intrinsic value theory and in the direction of the cultivation of an *ecological sensibility*—a move that foreshadows the approach we will be considering in the next chapter.[40]

This brings us to the other main kind of objection that has been raised in regard to the argumentative logic of intrinsic value theory approaches of the kind that I have discussed (i.e., objectivist, empirically based intrinsic value theory approaches, which is to say, approaches that claim that there is an objective distribution of value in nature that can be empirically ascertained). This objection relies on G. E. Moore's confused and confusing idea of the naturalistic fallacy. Essentially, Moore claimed, in his influential book *Principia Ethica,* that it is impossible to define what we mean by the term *good*.[41] Moore therefore considered that any ethical approach that attempts to equate goodness with a specific property or characteristic (e.g., pleasure) committed what he (erroneously) termed *the naturalistic fallacy*.[42] For Moore, goodness had to be conceived, like the color yellow, as a simple, unanalyzable quality that could only be directly intuited—a "solution" that would seem to rule out the possibility of rational ethical discussion.

Some thinkers claim that advocates of intrinsic value theory approaches of the kind that I have discussed are guilty of committing Moore's so-called fallacy by virtue of the fact that they attempt to define goodness in terms of the possession of some particular characteristic (e.g., sentience, biological—i.e., cell-based—life, autopoiesis, the capacity of richness of experience, being decreed to be good by God, and so on). For these thinkers, then, it is not possible to establish the existence of intrinsic value on the basis of the major intrinsic value approaches that I have discussed (the only exception here would be any kind of cosmic purpose ethics that is held to be justified solely on the basis of intuition).

Baird Callicott is the most prominent ecophilosopher who rejects objectivist, empirically based intrinsic value theory approaches on the basis that they commit Moore's naturalistic fallacy. Callicott does not mince words. For him, Moore's "fallacy" represents "the nemesis of any naturalistic [read: objectivist, empirically based] theory of inherent value or intrinsic value."[43] (This assessment leads Callicott, a thoroughly nonanthropocentric ecophilosopher, to attempt to develop a subjectivist account of nonhuman intrinsic value.) But it is surprising to see any ethical theorist make a claim like this—let alone with this degree of confidence—in view of the numerous criticisms that have been made of Moore's argument.[44] In contradistinction to Callicott's claim, Moore's naturalistic fallacy is, to say the least, entirely controversial: some ethicists consider it to be significant while many others consider it to be fatally flawed. It is therefore common for the authors of contemporary overviews of ethics to note that Moore's naturalistic fallacy has "given rise to endless controversy."[45] Moreover, the vast majority of ethicists consider that the two obvious kinds of ways around Moore's "fallacy" are of no help at all in providing a constructive way of addressing the practical problems with which ethics must deal. One of these approaches—Moore's own approach—is to claim that there is an objective distribution of value in the world but that these values can only be known through intuition. The other approach, which Callicott adopts, is to retreat to subjectivism; that is, to say that there is no objective distribution of value in the world, that values are purely in the eye of the beholder. Most ethicists consider both of these approaches to lead, at least for all practical purposes, into the abyss of value relativism.

It is not my intention here to embark upon the kind of extended and tedious detour into meta-ethics that would be necessary in order to rehearse the criticisms that others have made of Moore's argument. Here I simply want to do two things. First, given that Callicott is the most prominent ecophilosopher to reject objectivist intrinsic value theory approaches on the basis that they commit the so-called naturalistic fallacy, and given that Callicott is also a sophisticated ethical theorist who is well aware of the problems of value relativism that *other* ethicists often consider to be the nemesis of any *subjectivist* approach to intrinsic value, it seems important to point out that Callicott's own subjectivist approach to ethics nevertheless has serious problems of its own. Second, there is one criticism of the so-called naturalistic fallacy that I want to *add* to those that have already been put forward by other writers since it arises specifically out of a consideration of the difference between the context of Moore's discussion (and that of most of his critics) and the context of ecophilosophical discussion. This criticism shows that the "naturalistic fallacy" charge is out of place in the context of ecophilosophical discussion.

To the first concern then. Callicott attempts to play down the relativistic implications of his own subjectivist approach to intrinsic value theory (i.e., that values are purely in the eye of the beholder) by adopting a sociobiological perspective. For example, he argues that "human feelings like human fingers, human ears, and human teeth, though both individually variable and open to information by cultural manipulation, have been *standardized* by natural selection" (emphasis added).[46] But there would seem to be a gaping hole in this analogy. If this statement is simply referring to the *range* or *structure* of human feelings then it is reasonable or otherwise depending on the meaning that one gives to the word *standardized,* but it says nothing about the question of the specific *content* of human feelings. Thus, it does not address the question of relativism in regard to the specific *kinds* of things that humans consider to be intrinsically valuable. However, if, as the context seems to suggest, this statement is referring not to the range or structure of human feelings but to their specific content (including the question of what *kinds* of things humans consider to be intrinsically valuable) then the appropriate comparison is clearly not with *structures* like fingers, ears, and teeth but rather with what *kinds* of things these structures do, hear, and eat. Yet the variation in the kinds of things that human fingers, ears, and teeth do, hear, and eat is enormous, just as it is with respect to the specific kinds of things that humans consider to be intrinsically valuable. Thus, even though Callicott's sociobiological approach can be used to overcome the extreme case that he refers to as *radical relativism* (e.g., there *are* good biological reasons for the fact that there are some things that virtually no humans value "for themselves," e.g., cancer, life-threatening viruses, the experience of severe and unrelenting pain), there is still plenty of room left for the common, everyday kinds of relativism that have typically been held to render subjectivist approaches impotent (e.g., it is a fact—an evolutionary fact, if you like—that some people will tend to value a tree "for itself" while others will tend to value it only for its economic value; a subjectivist approach to ethics offers no way of adjudicating such value disputes).

Even if Callicott *could* convincingly show that natural selection has led to very little variability in the specific kinds of things that humans consider to be intrinsically valuable (the moral equivalent of human teeth equipping us to eat only a few kinds of closely related plants, for example), it is difficult to see how this would overcome the charge of relativism that attaches to subjectivist approaches to ethics. The fact that advocates of subjectivist approaches to ethics—including sociobiological advocates—cannot, by definition, claim that the specific kinds of things that humans consider to be intrinsically valuable are intrinsically valuable in any objective sense means that one can easily think of scenarios that reveal the relative nature of the kinds of things that humans happen to have evolved to value "for themselves." For example, it is possible that we could make contact with some other intelligent species (dolphins or intergalactic visitors, for example) that has evolved to consider quite different kinds of things to be intrinsically valuable. Again, however, a subjectivist approach to ethics offers no way of adjudicating the value disputes that are likely to arise in these circumstances.

The second concern relates to the charge that objectivist intrinsic value theory approaches commit the "naturalistic fallacy." The main point I want to make here is that Moore was concerned with a different kind of question to the question that concerns ecophilosophical intrinsic value theorists. Specifically, Moore was concerned with the question of whether we can define what we mean by the term *good*. He was not concerned with the question that interests ecophilosophical intrinsic value theorists of whether this or that entity can be said to have "a good of its own." The difference between these two questions can be illustrated as follows. If ecophilosophical intrinsic value theorists are asked what they mean by the term "good," they might reflect on the fact that, like other people, they use this term in a wide variety of contexts, for example, they speak of "a good knife," "a good movie," "a good person," or "a good experience." This might then lead them to agree with Moore that it is impossible to give a precise definition of what is meant by the term *good*. However, if ecophilosophical intrinsic value theorists are asked what they mean when they say that an entity has "a good of its own," they can answer quite precisely:

> To say that an entity has "a good of its own" is to say that it has interests in sustaining itself. We don't know what else "having a good of its own" *could* mean. To us, saying that an entity has interests in sustaining itself and saying that an entity has "a good of its own" are one and the same thing. We might disagree among ourselves about what kinds of entities have interests and how these interests should be weighted but we do not disagree that an entity must be accepted as having a good of its own if it can be established that it has interests in sustaining itself.

In response to this, an advocate of Moore's views might then move in a Humean direction and invoke the "is-ought" fallacy by saying:

> Okay, you don't have any problem in defining what you mean by an entity having "a good of its own," but your definition just refers to a certain state of affairs, namely, the fact that an entity has interests in sustaining itself. What I want to know is why should the fact that an entity has a-good-of-its-own/interests-in-sustaining-itself

lead us to value it (i.e., how do you get from the establishment of a fact to the establishment of a value—or from an *is* to an *ought*)?

But, to this, ecophilosophical intrinsic value theorists—and ethicists in general—can reply:

We are not attempting to *derive* a value from a fact here. Rather, we simply regard it as *axiomatic* that any entity that has "a good of its own" is morally considerable. Every formal system of reasoning (the exemplar being logic) adopts certain axioms at the outset. These axioms are propositions that are assumed to be so obvious as not to stand in need of proof; moreover, these propositions cannot themselves be proved or disproved within the system to which they attach. No formal system of reasoning can get started without adopting at least some fundamental assumptions. Thus, to deny the fundamental assumptions of logic, for example, is to deny the possibility of logical reasoning. Similarly, to deny that an entity is morally considerable if it has "a good of its own" is to deny the possibility of ethics. That is, rational ethical discussion ceases if someone accepts that an entity has "a good of its own" but simultaneously claims that it is not morally considerable. You can't prove that an entity is morally considerable if it has "a good of its own." One either accepts this as obvious—or, at the very least, as a reasonable starting point for ethics—or one doesn't.

The conclusion to be drawn from this discussion, then, is that *whatever* force Moore's argument might have within the context of his own framework of discourse, it does not tell against the question that is of concern to ecophilosophical intrinsic value theorists. These theorists can agree with Moore that it is impossible to define the term *good* (considered as an isolated or contextless term) but have no problem at all in defining what they mean when they say that an entity has "a good of its own." Moreover, to suggest that these theorists commit Hume's "is-ought" fallacy in *assuming* that any entity that has "a good of its own" is morally considerable is to miss the point that this *is* an assumption (and a necessary one if ethics is to be possible), not a logical inference.

OBJECTIONS BASED ON PRACTICAL CONSEQUENCES

The final standard way of objecting to intrinsic value theory approaches is on the grounds of their practical consequences. For example, some ecophilosophers would want to reject evolution-ary-based approaches to ethics on the grounds that, even though these approaches argue for the intrinsic value of at least some members or aspects of the nonhuman world, their practical consequences can be thoroughly undesirable from an ecocentric point of view. Specifically, as we have already seen in the previous chapter, such approaches can be used to legitimate and even recommend human interference in the biology of all organisms to a degree and on a scale that exceeds most environmentalists' worst nightmares. After all, if we think that there is a kind of cosmic interest and that we know what it is, and if we also have the technology to advance whatever we perceive this cosmic interest to be (e.g., by creating organisms that, in our judgment, have the capacity for such things as greater richness of experience or greater degrees of individuation and freedom), then are we not morally *obliged* to do so? Yet to take on this "cosmic responsibil-ity"—which might be thought of as a kind of "intelligent species' burden"—is to underwrite the use of all genetic engi-neering techniques that might conceivably be held to further the evolutionary "project." Although many cosmic purpose oriented ethicists might *personally* wish to resile from the conclusion that we are morally obliged to give evolution a "helping hand" insofar as it is within our power to do so, there generally seems to be nothing in the *theoretical* views of these ethicists that embodies any inherent and unambiguous logical barrier to this conclusion. In contrast, ecocentric critics consider it supremely arrogant for humans to dictate the mode, tempo, and destiny of the evolution of other species.

There are many other possible kinds of objections to intrinsic value theory approaches on the grounds of their practical conse-quences. For example, we have already seen that ethical sentien-tists and biological ethicists can object (although mistakenly in my view) to ecosystem ethics and ecosphere ethics on the grounds that, if followed in practice, these approaches would represent an ecological equivalent of fascism. However, what has not been pointed out is that ecosystem ethicists and ecosphere ethicists (or, more accurately, autopoietic ethicists) can object, in turn, to the practical consequences of approaches like ethical sentientism and biological ethics—and do so in a way that would seem to have considerable force. A vivid illustration of this kind of objection can be gained by imagining what would happen if the ethical sentientists' argument for vegetarianism were pursued with missionary zeal. In the name of minimizing the moral evil of suffering, one could conceive of humans attempting to enforce a shift from carnivorous to herbivorous trophic levels upon other species that, after all, "do not know any better" than to eat other sentient creatures. If predators could not survive on a vegetarian diet, this approach would at least advocate killing their food in a "humane" way and then feeding it to them. Either way, however, this approach would seek to fence lions off from wildebeest, and so on. Yet, from an ecosystem/ecosphere perspective, this represents ecological lunacy. This "progress" in moral thinking would serve, in effect, to endorse the modern project of totally domesticating the nonhuman world. Moreover, it would also condemn as immoral those "primitive" cultures in which hunting is an important aspect of existence. Thus, for ecosystem/ecosphere ethicists, ethical sentientism should be rejected on the grounds that its practical consequences are, in the final analysis, ecologically disruptive, anthropocentric, and ethnocentric.

At the level of practice, there are also many perplexing difficulties involved in knowing how to weight the intrinsic value of the different kinds of entities that one considers to be morally considerable. Things are relatively simple when one is dealing, as the vast majority of ethicists do, with one kind of entity only, namely, humans. However, when one is attempting to take into account many different kinds of entities (as in autopoietic ethics, for example) things become vastly more complicated. But this is not itself an objection to the practical *consequences* of intrinsic value theory approaches. It is simply an expression of the difficulties involved in putting such approaches *into* practice. As

Heffernan notes in regard to the question of calculating conflicting kinds of moral considerability: " 'Weighing the alternatives' has always seemed to me a metaphor for hard thinking rather than something we can do precisely."[47] Against those who would prefer not to have to engage in such hard thinking (e.g., by attempting to dismiss intrinsic value theory approaches as "unworkable"), intrinsic value theorists can point out that it is better to follow the right trail even if it is difficult to find one's way than to follow a misleading trail simply because it is more clearly marked.

In the previous chapter, I concluded that it is necessary to suggest a name other than *deep ecology* for Naess's philosophical sense of deep ecology since this sense does not refer to what Naess intended by the term *deep ecology* and what Naess did intend by this term is, in any case, untenable. In this chapter, I have provided an overview of the most widely recognized approaches to ecophilosophy and the main kinds of objections that can be made in regard to these approaches. This means that we are now in a position to consider both the question of an appropriate name for Naess's philosophical sense of deep ecology and the question of the distinctiveness of Naess's philosophical sense of deep ecology vis-à-vis the most widely recognized approaches to ecophilosophy. Chapter 7 is devoted to these matters.

7

Transpersonal Ecology as a
Distinctive Approach to Ecophilosophy

TRANSPERSONAL ECOLOGY AND
TRANSPERSONAL PSYCHOLOGY

As WE SAW in chapter 4, Naess's philosophical sense of deep ecology refers to the this-worldly realization of as expansive a sense of self as possible in a world in which selves and things-in-the-world are conceived as processes. Since this approach is one that involves the realization of a sense of self that extends beyond (or that is *trans-*) one's egoic, biographical, or personal sense of self, the clearest, most accurate, and most informative term for this sense of deep ecology is, in my view, *transpersonal ecology.*

The fact that the term *transpersonal* derives from recent work in psychology is appropriate since Naess's philosophical sense of deep ecology obviously refers to a psychologically based approach to the question of our relationship with the rest of nature as opposed to an axiologically based (i.e., a value theory based) approach I provide a brief overview of the emergence of transpersonal psychology in appendix B, and knowledge of this background will be assumed in what follows.

There are two main points that should immediately be noted in connection with my introduction of the term *transpersonal.* First, there is one point that I want to make absolutely clear (if it isn't already) in regard to the use of the prefix *trans-.* It is possible that some people who hear the term *transpersonal ecology* for the first time but who are aware neither of the context (and, hence, the intended meaning) of this term as discussed herein nor of the emerging field of transpersonal *psychology* might interpret the prefix *trans-* in *transpersonal* to mean "across," as in *transcontinental*. Thus, *transpersonal* might be taken to suggest something like "across persons," and this in turn could suggest that *transpersonal ecology* refers in some way to an *anthropocentric* approach to ecology! However, the prefix *trans-* also means, *inter alia*, "beyond," as in *transcend;* "changing thoroughly," as in *transfigure, transform,* or *transliterate;* and "transcending," as in *transubstantiation.*[1] And it is these meanings of extending "beyond," "changing thoroughly," and "transcending" one's egoic, biographical, or personal sense of self that the originators of the term *transpersonal* (i.e., Stanislav Grof, Abraham Maslow, and Anthony Sutich), and others influenced by them, have always intended by this term. In general, the most convenient way of capturing these senses of *trans-* is simply to employ the word *beyond.* Thus, Maslow employs this word when he speaks of transpersonal as meaning "beyond individuality, beyond the development of the individual person into something which is more inclusive than the individual person"; Roger Walsh and Frances Vaughan use it in the two-word definition of "transpersonal" that constitutes the main title of their excellent collection of readings in transpersonal psychology: *Beyond Ego: Transpersonal Dimensions in Psychology;* and I use this word when I employ the term *transpersonal* (as in the opening paragraph of this chapter) to describe "a sense of self that extends beyond one's egoic, biographical, or personal sense of self."[2]

A transpersonal approach to ecology is, then, precisely *not* an anthropocentric approach to ecology (and remember here that, as always, I am using the term *anthropocentrism* in its significant sense rather than its trivial sense—see "A Closer Look at the Issue of Anthropocentrism," in chapter 1). Rather, a transpersonal approach to ecology is concerned precisely with *opening* to ecological awareness; with realizing one's ecological, wider, or big Self; or, as I have already expressed it, with the this-worldly realization of as expansive a sense of self as possible.

Having said that, however, it is important to add that a transpersonal approach to ecology does not *deny* the existence of the egoic, biographical, or personal sense of self. This can be seen if we consider transpersonal psychologists' use of the word *beyond*. Although this word can mean either *to* the far side of something or *at* the far side of something, it is axiomatic in transpersonal uses of this word that it is intended in the first sense of *extending beyond* the limits of one's egoic, biographical, or personal sense of self, rather than in the second sense of *lying beyond*, that is, existing wholly *outside* those limits. Thus, when transpersonal psychologists employ the word *beyond* in a transpersonal sense, they mean to *include* the egoic, biographical, or personal sense of self while also pointing, as Maslow says, to "something which is *more inclusive* than the individual person" (emphasis added).

The second main point to be noted in this introduction of the term *transpersonal ecology* is this: the fact that this term implies the existence of a relationship with those recent developments in psychology that go under the heading of transpersonal psychology is in no way intended to suggest that theorizing in transpersonal ecology should be subordinated to theorizing in transpersonal psychology. Rather, transpersonal ecology has as much to do with "ecologizing" transpersonal psychology (which is by *no means* free from anthropocentric theorizing) as it has to do with "psychologizing" our ways of approaching ecophilosophical issues and of arguing for the views advocated by the ecocentric ecology movement. It is important to understand this point, and the rest of the comments in this opening section of the present chapter will therefore expand upon it.

Many people who are attracted to spiritual views (including transpersonal theorists) see God, the Absolute, or the Ultimate as "pure consciousness," or something similar, and see humans as participating more in this ideal than other beings and, consequently, as superior to them. (As I noted in chapter 5, this gnosticized Darwinism—"we are God-in-the-process-of-becoming"—sort of view is associated with many New Age/traditional wisdom adherents.) Thus, one will find transpersonal theorists as respected as Ken Wilber saying things that are radically anthropocentric (not to mention scientifically bankrupt) like "cosmic evolution . . . is completed in and as human evolution, which itself reaches ultimate unity consciousness and so completes that absolute gestalt toward which all manifestation moves," and referring to "the very lowest levels of being" as "the levels that are *sub*human, such as matter, plant, reptile, and mammal" (emphasis added).[3] Transpersonal ecologists reject such views outright. They point out that it shows a total lack of evolutionary (and, hence, ecological) understanding to think of viruses, eucalyptus trees, flies, salmon, frogs, eagles, dolphins, and humans as members of a series that can meaningfully be compared along some linear scale (or Great Chain of Being) of developmental perfection. Rather, evolution has to be thought of as a luxuriously branching bush, not as a linear scale that is filled in by greater and lesser examples of some ideal end point. The fact that all life forms are the products of *distinct* evolutionary pathways and ecological relationships means that, at any given point in time, they should be thought of as more or less perfect (complete) examples *of their own kind.* In evolutionary terms, it simply makes no sense to say that evolution is "completed in and as human evolution" or to refer to other entities or life forms as "subhuman"—never mind Wilber's suggestion that humans are not mammals!

As with a considerable number of other theorists in transpersonal psychology, anthropocentric assumptions are built into Wilber's approach at the theoretical level by virtue of his subscription to a hierarchical ontology of a kind that is generally associated, in the West, with the Renaissance and medieval idea of the Great Chain of Being and with Gnosticism. In contrast, a number of other theorists in transpersonal psychology have avoided anthropocentrism at the theoretical level but then failed to draw out the nonanthropocentric implications of their own theorizing. Thus, Abraham Maslow, for example, seems explicitly to have precluded anthropocentric theorizing in transpersonal psychology when he wrote in regard to this emerging "fourth force" in psychology that it was to be "transpersonal, transhuman, centered in the cosmos rather than in human needs and interest, going beyond humanness, identity, self-actualization, and the like," and that the reason we need such a psychology is because "without the transcendent and the transpersonal, we get sick, violent, and nihilistic, or else hopeless and apathetic. We need something 'bigger than we are' to be awed by and to commit ourselves to in a new, naturalistic, empirical, non-churchly sense, perhaps as Thoreau and Whitman, William James and John Dewey did."[4]

Maslow's endorsement of a "naturalistic, empirical, non-churchly" (or what we might call a thoroughly "this-worldly") approach to the question of our ultimate concerns is consistent with other basic features of his work. For example, Maslow was always concerned to point out that his theorizing was grounded in empirical reality and that his proposals were open to empirical investigation; he had a profound respect for "the *biological* rooting of the value life"; and he continually pointed to Spinozist and Taoist attitudes as characterizing those individuals whom he described as "transcending self-actualizers'[(i.e., he continually pointed to those attitudes that are associated with living "under the aspect of eternity" in this world as opposed to some "next" or "hidden" world that is presumed to be superior to or more real than this world).[5]

Yet despite having originally pointed transpersonal psychology in both a nonanthropocentric and a naturalistic direction (as opposed to the anthropocentric and transcendental direction that has been pursued by Wilber and some other transpersonal theorists), Maslow still proceeded to describe the attributes of transpersonal modes of being in terms like this: "Identification-love . . . means transcendence of the selfish Self. It implies also a wider circle of identifications, i.e., with more and more and more people approaching *the limit of identification with all human beings.* This can also be phrased as the more and more inclusive Self. *The limit here is identification with the human species*" (emphases added).[6]

The general thrust of these comments is, as we will see, "pure Naess"—*except* for the fact that Maslow limits the maximum extent of human identifications (or the limits of "the more and more inclusive Self") to the rest of the human species. Although Maslow does occasionally speak of "behaving and relating, as ends rather than as means, to oneself, to significant others, to human beings in general, to other species, to nature, and to the cosmos,"[7] anthropocentric formulations are the norm in Maslow's writings. For example, the anthropocentric limit that he sets on identification in the "identification-love" quotation above is suggested both implicitly and explicitly at many points in the paper from which the quotation is taken. Yet there is absolutely no theoretical or empirical reason for Maslow to set such anthropocentric limits. Rather, the arbitrariness of Maslow's view regarding the limits of identification/the expansiveness of "the more and more inclusive Self" is simply another illustration of the cultural pervasiveness of anthropocentrism emphasized in chapter 1. One must wonder, did Maslow never identify with a cat, a dog, a wild animal, or a place?

It is instructive to contrast Maslow's views on the limits of transpersonal identification/the expansiveness of "the more and more inclusive Self" with the views of someone like the poet Robinson Jeffers, who has been described as "Spinoza's twentieth-century evangelist."[8] Jeffers explains the meaning of his poem "The Tower Beyond Tragedy":

> Orestes, in the poem, identifies himself with the whole divine nature of things: earth, man, and stars, the mountain forest and the running streams; they are all one existence, one organism. He perceives this, and that himself is included in it, identical with it. This perception is his tower beyond the reach of tragedy; because, whatever may happen, the great organism will remain forever immortal and immortally beautiful. Orestes has "fallen in love outward" not with a human creature, not with a limited cause, but with the universal God. That is the meaning of my poem.[9]

Maslow's own ideas on developing "a wider circle of identifications"/"the more and more inclusive Self" clearly *point* in the nonanthropocentric, naturalistic, ecological-cosmological direction that Jeffers describes so vividly. It is frustrating, therefore, to see a thinker as farsighted as Maslow limited by anthropocentric thought patterns (and caught up in sexist thought patterns as well).[10] On the other hand, it is heartening to see that at least some of the more recent writers on transpersonal psychology *have* been drawing more explicitly upon ecological thinking in their work (even if they have not been especially concerned with drawing out the implications of these ideas for ecological lifestyles and ecodefense). Frances Vaughan, for example, describes the self in a way that is fully compatible with Jeffers's conception in her paper "Discovering Transpersonal Identity":

[In personal growth individuals recognize that development apparently proceeds from dependence, through independence, to interdependence. /Conceptualizing the self as an ecosystem existing within a larger ecosystem can therefore facilitate the shift from thinking of the self as a separate, independent entity to recognizing its complete interdependence in the totality./ . . . [This] view of the self challenges the assumption that we exist only as alienated, isolated individuals in a hostile, or at best, indifferent, environment.[11]]

These observations on the relationship between transpersonal ecology and transpersonal psychology should be enough, then, to suggest two things. First, it should be clear that there is no *inherent* reason why theorizing in transpersonal psychology should be anthropocentric. And second, it should be equally clear that much theorizing in transpersonal psychology nevertheless *is* anthropocentric and, hence, that there is much work to be done in ecologizing transpersonal psychology.

It astonishes me that more serious philosophical work has not already been done in regard to ecologizing transpersonal psychology (the pervasiveness of anthropocentrism hits home again!). Donald Rothberg's critique of the philosophical foundations of transpersonal psychology is one of the few discussions other than the present one to have offered at least a start in this direction. Rothberg wrote his erudite examination of "the centrality of the theory of a 'hierarchical ontology' in transpersonal work" following a 1985 seminar entitled "The Great Chain of Being in World Perspective," which was directed by Huston Smith, another significant perennialist or traditional wisdom theorist who is committed to a radically anthropocentric, hierarchical ontology.[12] Rothberg argues, quite correctly in my view, that it is historically the case that "those exponents of the great metaphysical and religious traditions identified as embodying most closely the core perennialist thesis of a hierarchical ontology (with, to be sure, some significant exceptions) link such an ontology to the devaluation of the body, sexuality, and nature, and to patriarchal and class-based social relations."[13]

But enough for now in regard to the question of transpersonal ecology *ecologizing* transpersonal psychology. What about the more ecophilosophically relevant question of transpersonal ecology *psychologizing* ecophilosophy? The rest of this chapter is concerned with this question. In the process, I will substantiate two claims made in the last section of chapter 3 and reiterated in the concluding sections of chapters 4 and 5: first, that transpersonal ecology (i.e., Naess's philosophical sense of deep ecology) constitutes a distinctive approach to ecophilosophy and, second, that it is a commitment to this approach that distinguishes deep ecologists (whom I would now refer to as transpersonal ecologists) from other ecophilosophers.

PSYCHOLOGIZING ECOPHILOSOPHY

The fact that transpersonal ecology—the idea of the this-worldly realization of as expansive a sense of self as possible—refers to a psychologically based approach to ecophilosophical problems raises the interesting question of how we might conceive of the most widely recognized approaches to ecophilosophy (i.e., instrumental and intrinsic value theory approaches) in psychological rather than axiological (i.e., value theory) terms. It is illuminating to approach this question by considering a well-known and apparently widely accepted way of conceiving of human psychology or the *self*.

There is much theoretical and popular support for a dynamic, tripartite conception of the self. Specifically, most of us recognize a *desiring-impulsive* aspect of the self, a *rationalizing-deciding* aspect, and a *normative-judgmental* aspect. In fact, unless we are exceptionally well integrated, it is often more appropriate to speak not so much of three aspects of *the* self but rather of three selves. Thus, we can speak of a desiring-impulsive self, a rationalizing-deciding self, and a normative-judgmental self. It should of course be noted that these labels simply refer to hypothetical constructs. The validity of these constructs rests upon their usefulness in both describing certain recognizable systems of thought and behavior and illuminating the dynamics between these systems.[14]

The desiring-impulsive self wants much (the desiring aspect) and wants it *now* (the impulsive aspect). This means that it functions without particular regard for others, the future, or the constraints that are imposed by reality in general. The normative-judgmental self sets standards or expectations on our behavior, whether in the moral sphere, where it decrees what *ought* to be and demands conformance with a certain code of conduct, or in other spheres of activity, where it also expects the attainment of certain standards of performance. It judges "us" (the other aspects of our self—or our other selves) critically if we fall short of its standards or expectations. The rationalizing-deciding self sees itself as the decision maker or the locus of control with respect to the three selves. This means that it mediates between the competing demands of the desiring-impulsive self, the normative-judgmental self, and the constraints that are imposed by reality.

This general kind of dynamic, tripartite conception of the self finds popular support in the pre-Darwinian and pre-Freudian distinctions that people commonly used to make (and to some extent still do make) between their *lower*—also called *animal* or *primitive*—nature (i.e., their desiring-impulsive self), their *rational* nature (i.e., their rationalizing-deciding self), and their *higher* nature or conscience (i.e., their normative-judgmental self). This tripartite conception also finds theoretical support in more rigorous, psychological analyses of the self, which (in the West) is to say in Freudian and post-Freudian psychology. For example, the tripartite conception I have outlined has strong parallels with Freud's division of the personality into *id, ego,* and *superego.* Indeed, my characterization of the rationalizing-deciding self as the self that mediates between the competing demands of the desiring-impulsive self, the normative-judgmental self, and the constraints that are imposed by reality represents a more or less textbook definition of the Freudian ego. In terms of more recent psychotherapeutic approaches, this tripartite conception also has strong parallels, for example, with the division that is made in transactional analysis—not to be confused with transpersonal approaches—between childlike, adultlike, and parentlike aspects of the personality (transactional analysts refer to these aspects of the personality simply as *child, adult,* and *parent*).

When we attempt to conceptualize the instrumental and intrinsic value theory approaches discussed in the previous chapter in psychological rather than axiological terms we find a compelling correspondence between these approaches and the well-known and obviously useful tripartite conception of the self that I have just outlined. Specifically, the kind of self that is emphasized *in regard to our relations with the nonhuman world* in the unrestrained exploitation and expansionism approach is the desiring-impulsive, "primitive," id-like, or childlike self, which functions without particular regard for others, the future, or the constraints that are imposed by reality in general; the kind of self that is emphasized *in regard to our relations with the nonhuman world* in the resource conservation and development and resource preservation approaches is the rationalizing-deciding, "rational," (Freudian) ego-like, or adultlike self, which mediates between the competing demands of the desiring-impulsive self, the normative-judgmental self, and the constraints that are imposed by reality; and the kind of self that is emphasized *in regard to our relations with the nonhuman world* in intrinsic value theory approaches in general is the normative-judgmental, "higher," superego-like, or parentlike self, which, *inter alia* decrees what *ought* to be and demands conformance with a certain code of conduct.

The correspondence between the desiring-impulsive self and the unrestrained exploitation and expansionism approach is so obvious as not to stand in need of further comment. However, I will expand in turn upon the correspondence that applies between the rationalizing-deciding self and the resource conservation and development and resource preservation approaches on the one hand and the normative-judgmental self and intrinsic value theory approaches on the other hand.

The rationalizing-deciding self sees itself as the decision maker or the locus of control with respect to the three selves. This means that it sees itself as the essential "I" or "the central core around which all psychic activities revolve,"[15] even though it generally recognizes that it nevertheless has to "live under the same roof" as the other two selves and so must accommodate their competing demands as best it can in order to preserve some degree of (psychic) peace and harmony in the "home." Seeing itself as the essential "I," the rationalizing-deciding self acts as the guardian of the self-image, accepting those psychic and behavioral aspects of the individual's total make-up that are considered to be "really me" and rejecting those that are not. Now, in order for the rationalizing-deciding self to sustain its view that it really is the decision maker—the essential I—it must seek to justify (rationalize) its position in those situations, which may be many, where it would appear *not* to be on top of the situation. Thus, the rationalizing-deciding self is the me that "didn't know what came over me" or that "couldn't help myself" when it succumbs to, say, aggressive or sexual impulses of the id-like, desiring-impulsive self. It protects the self-image by seeking to label such actions as "totally out of character." The rationalizing-deciding self is also the me that (if truth be told) "didn't really want to do it but felt I should" when it goes through the motions in order to accommodate the demands of the superego-like, normative-judgmental self. Finally, the rationalizing-deciding self is the me that "would have done it (or done it better) if only that (event in the external world) hadn't happened"—again protecting the self-image.

These observations explain the psychoanalytical sense in which the rationalizing-deciding self deserves the *rationalizing* part of its label. Specifically, this is because the rationalizing-deciding self is a self that specializes in explanations or justifications (i.e., rationalizations) for those situations where it is likely to be, or has been, unable to satisfactorily accommodate psychic- or reality-imposed demands or where it is likely to be, or has been, able to accommodate these demands but only at the expense of betraying those inclinations that it considers to be most genuine (i.e., inclinations that are experienced as being more central to the essential "I" or self-image). However, there is also another reason why the rationalizing-deciding self deserves the *rationalizing* part of its label, and this reason is the more important of the two in the present context. Specifically, the fact that the rationalizing-deciding self mediates between the competing demands of the desiring-impulsive self, the normative-judgmental self, and the constraints that are imposed by reality means that it is a rationalizing self in the economic, managerial sense that, in order to minimize psychic discomfort, it seeks the most economic or efficient solutions to the competing psychic- and reality-imposed demands and constraints with which it is confronted. This second sense of rationalizing, then, refers not to rationalizing in the sense in which a person is said to rationalize (explain away) their rude behavior or their poor performance in an exam but rather it refers to rationalizing in the sense in which an industry or bureaucracy is said to rationalize (streamline) its operations in order to maximize its productive capacity per unit of cost; in other words, in order to become more efficient.

Like any good business executive, the rationalizing-deciding self seeks the most economic or efficient solutions to the problems with which it is concerned by adopting a *mini-max* strategy (i.e., a strategy that seeks to minimize potential losses while maximizing potential gains) with respect to the competing demands and constraints with which it is confronted. In economics, gambling, game theory, psychology, sociobiology, and other disciplines concerned with decision theory, a mini-max strategy is generally considered to be the most *rational* strategy for an individual to adopt in making decisions. When people adopt such a strategy we also commonly say that they are being "realistic" or have a "realistic appreciation of the situation." Thus, in terms of the way in which we typically define what does and does not constitute *rational* or *realistic* decision-making behavior, the rationalizing-deciding self is considered to represent the rational or realistic aspect of our psyche. In contrast, the desiring-impulsive self and the normative-judgmental self are considered to be *irrational* (or at least *nonrational*) or *unrealistic* in the sense that both, in their different ways, place too much emphasis on their own demands (appetitive demands on the one hand and moralistic and idealistic demands on the other) and thereby fail to take sufficient account not only of the demands associated with other aspects of the psyche but also of the constraints that are imposed by reality (or, in the case of the normative-judgmental self, sometimes of the *opportunities* that are offered by reality, as I shall point out below).

This discussion enables us to see more clearly the correspondence between the resource conservation and development and resource preservation approaches on the one hand and the rationalizing-deciding self on the other hand. Specifically, we can see that these resource-based approaches correspond to the rationalizing-deciding self in that, unlike the unrestrained exploitation and expansionism approach in which the id-like, desiring-impulsive self can clearly be said to predominate, these approaches recognize not only (1) the desire for maximum resource exploitation (whether the resource in question is the physical transformation value, the physical nourishment value, the informational value, the experiential value, the symbolic instructional value, or the psychological nourishment value of the nonhuman world to humans) but also (2) the existence of reality-imposed constraints (i.e., that resources are finite) and (3) certain moral demands (i.e., that the interests of other humans—including both present and future generations of humans—ought to be taken into account when making decisions regarding resource usage). The recognition of these competing demands and constraints means that, from the perspective of these resource-based approaches, it is both irrational (unrealistic) and immoral to endorse an unrestrained exploitation and expansionism approach since to do so ignores both reality-imposed constraints and anthropocentric moral demands. On the other hand, however, it is also considered to be both irrational (unrealistic) and idealistic (as opposed to immoral) to suggest that we ought not to take our "share" of the resources we find (i.e., that we ought to use the resources we find at less than replacement rate—"underutilize" them—in order to leave *more* for others than we inherited) since to do so ignores both reality offered *opportunities* and appetitive demands.

For these resource-based approaches, then, there is only one kind of approach to the nonhuman world that is considered to be *realistic,* as distinct from *idealistic,* in that it recognizes the appetitive demands of the desiring-impulsive self; *realistic,* as distinct from *unduly optimistic* or *complacent,* in that it recognizes the constraints that are imposed by reality; and *realistic,* as distinct from *willful,* in that it recognizes the anthropocentric moral demands of the normative-judgmental self. That approach corresponds to the "rational," mini-max strategy that is represented by the idea of "maximum sustainable yield," the idea of satisfying appetitive demands to the maximum extent that is possible (or, in other words, the idea of not "wasting" reality-offered opportunities) while *also* recognizing both reality imposed constraints and anthropocentric moral demands.

It should be clear that this "realistic," "rational" approach to the nonhuman world, and the dynamics that underlie this approach (i.e., the mini-max trade-offs it makes between appetitive demands, reality-based constraints and opportunities, and moral demands), correspond precisely to the features that characterize, and the dynamics that underlie, the rationalizing-deciding self. Moreover, although it is not my main concern here, it is worth noting that one could develop this correspondence even further by considering the psychoanalytic sense in which the rationalizing-deciding self deserves the *rationalizing* part of its label. That is to say, the elaborate justifications that people have historically produced in order to justify their lack of moral concern for entities that are not considered to be essentially like themselves (i.e., people of different kinds and the nonhuman world in general) could obviously be analyzed in terms of the psychoanalytic concept of rationalization.

Before moving on to consider the correspondence between intrinsic value theory approaches and the normative-judgmental self, there are several other points that arise out of the preceding discussion that ought to be noted and/or clarified. First, whereas I have claimed that the resource conservation and development and resource preservation approaches emphasize the rationalizing-deciding self, it could legitimately be claimed that, as far as our relations with other *humans* are concerned, these approaches emphasize the normative-judgmental self, since they both respect the interests of present and future generations of humans. However, as I emphasized earlier in speaking of these resource-based approaches as emphasizing the rationalizing-deciding self, I have been speaking of the kind of self that they emphasize *in regard to our relations with the nonhuman world*. I also noted that this qualification applies to the other kinds of selves that I claim are emphasized by the other instrumental and intrinsic value theory approaches.

Second, I have been speaking about the resource conservation and development and resource preservation approaches jointly in this discussion because, as I pointed out in the previous chapter, the difference between them is purely one of emphasis. On the one hand, both approaches represent "restrained" (sometimes referred to as "wise use" or "responsible management") resource-based approaches in that they stand opposed to the unrestrained exploitation and expansionism approach. On the other hand, both approaches share with the unrestrained exploitation and expansionism approach the fact that they see the nonhuman world purely in resource (or instrumental value) terms. This means that both generally attempt to argue their case in economic terms since such terms represent the lingua franca of instrumental value theory approaches. Where the resource conservation and development and resource preservation approaches differ is simply in regard to how broadly they construe what counts as a resource. Whereas the resource conservation and development approach construes resources in terms of their physical transformation value (albeit under a regime of sustainable use), the resource preservation approach emphasizes the physical nourishment, informational, experiential, symbolic instructional, and psychological nourishment "yields" that can be gained by preserving certain members or aspects of the nonhuman world. Thus, advocates of the resource preservation approach typically attempt to show that preserving certain members or aspects of the nonhuman world is likely to produce a greater economic yield (e.g., in terms of human health or psychological well-being, in terms of tourism, in terms of helping scientists to develop new kinds of crops or discover cures for certain diseases, in terms of preventing the loss of productive land through erosion and desertification, and so on) than exploiting that resource in a sustainable way for its physical transformation values. Both approaches, in other words, seek mini-max outcomes (i.e., the maximization of sustainable yield), but they differ in regard to the nature of the "yields" that they are concerned to maximize on a sustainable basis and, hence, in regard to the nature of the "variables" that they are concerned to take into account in deriving their "rational," mini-max "solutions."

It should also be noted here that although the nonmaterial kinds of values that are emphasized in the resource preservation approach can usually be assigned some kind of economic value, this is not a necessary condition for the derivation of mini-max solutions. This is because it is quite possible to assign psychological utility to a nonmaterial value without assigning it a corresponding economic value or, alternatively, without agreeing that this psychological utility is adequately reflected in the economic value that others have assigned it.

Finally, although it is useful to distinguish the resource conservation and development and resource preservation approaches for expository purposes, it should of course be noted that many "real world" resource-based approaches represent hybrids of these two "restrained" or "responsible management" resource-based approaches. That is, "real world" resource-based approaches may take both material (i.e., physical transformation) instrumental values and nonmaterial instrumental values into account in seeking mini-max resource management solutions (e.g., they may take into account the income that could be derived from logging as well as the income that could be derived from tourism—or even simply the psychological utility that preservation of a certain area may afford present and future generations of humans). The rationalizing-deciding self is clearly emphasized in these hybrid situations just as it is in the ideal-typical resource conservation and development and resource preservation approaches. Moreover, it should also be obvious from these considerations that some "real world" situations effectively represent uncomfortable mixtures of both "responsible management" and unrestrained resource-based approaches while others represent equally uncomfortable mixtures of both "responsible management" resource-based approaches and intrinsic value theory approaches. It is therefore necessary to speak of the self that is emphasized in these situations as one that fluctuates between, or as one that represents an often psychically uncomfortable mixture of, the rationalizing-deciding self and the desiring-impulsive self on the one hand and the rationalizing-deciding self and the normative-judgmental self on the other hand.

When we move on to consider those approaches that break with our anthropocentric traditions and argue for the moral considerability of the nonhuman world (i.e., intrinsic value theory approaches), we see that, however much these approaches may play upon one's feelings and inspire one to feel a certain way toward certain members or aspects of the nonhuman world, the end that such approaches serve is, finally, that of showing that certain members or aspects of the nonhuman world are morally considerable *irrespective* of how one personally happens to feel about them. Objectivist intrinsic value theory approaches, in other words, are ultimately normative-judgmental in character. They attempt to show that it is morally wrong to do some things to certain members or aspects of the nonhuman world and morally right to do other things; that one's personal likes and dislikes—one's personal prejudices—are neither here nor there with respect to the validity of these judgments; and that, where conflict occurs between intrinsic value based concerns (i.e., moral concerns) and either appetitive, desiring-impulsive concerns or anthropocentric, "responsible management" concerns, it is the intrinsic value based concerns that should be given overriding priority.

214 ∘ TOWARD A TRANSPERSONAL ECOLOGY

These observations clearly suggest that the kind of self that is emphasized in intrinsic value theory approaches is the superego-like, normative-judgmental self, which, *inter alia,* decrees what *ought* to be and demands conformance with a certain code of conduct. This point can be illustrated further by comparing the ways in which the rationalizing-deciding self and the normative-judgmental self deal with particular intrinsic value theory claims. Take the ethical sentientism approach as an example. Ethical sentientists claim that it is always morally wrong to cause unnecessary suffering and that this implies that we should all be vegetarian (in view of this, Singer's already classic statement *Animal Liberation* concludes with an appendix entitled "Cooking for Liberated People," which provides a helpful guide to vegetarian cooking and an annotated list of vegetarian cookbooks). The approach of the rationalizing-deciding self to such normative-judgmental claims is to weigh them against the desiring-impulsive self's desire to eat meat, which may be strong, and to consider these competing demands within the context of the general availability of meat, which, these days, usually means its price. For the rationalizing-deciding self, each of these factors simply represents one factor that must be taken into account among others. Thus, the rationalizing-deciding self's mini-max solution to these competing psychic demands and reality-based constraints or opportunities is, in general, not to stop eating meat altogether but rather to eat somewhat less meat than was eaten prior to registering the normative-judgmental claims of ethical sentientism. In contrast, the normative-judgmental self gives overriding priority to moral claims and so demands that one should stop eating meat altogether. The normative-judgmental self, in other words, is the psychological face of intrinsic value theory approaches since these approaches demand that intrinsic values should, in principle, be accorded overriding priority in deciding how to act as opposed to being regarded as "just another" factor that needs to be taken into account.

The overriding nature of moral claims is most obvious to us in the human realm. Here, for example, claims regarding the intrinsic worth of people mean that, in principle, it is always wrong to torture another person. It is no defense to say that you took their desire not to be tortured "into account" but nevertheless reached a decision that, "on balance," your desire to torture them, along with the likelihood that your crime would not be discovered (i.e., the lack of reality-based constraints), outweighed this "other factor." In respect of interactions between humans, it is *expected* that the interests of the normative-judgmental self should override any contrary decisions that the rationalizing-deciding self may make. Ecophilosophical intrinsic value theorists simply attempt to extend the domain of activities in which this expectation holds.

This overview of the various kinds of self that are emphasized by the most widely recognized approaches to ecophilosophy should now enable us to see more clearly what it is that distinguishes transpersonal ecology from these approaches.

THE DISTINCTIVENESS OF THE TRANSPERSONAL ECOLOGY APPROACH TO ECOPHILOSOPHY

We have thus far concentrated on the differences between the various kinds of self that are emphasized by the most widely recognized approaches to ecophilosophy. However, if we now consider what these selves have in common we can see that transpersonal ecology emphasizes a fundamentally different kind of self to those emphasized in the foregoing tripartite model of the psyche. This is because, whatever their qualitative differences, the desiring-impulsive self, the rationalizing-deciding self, and the normative-judgmental self all refer to a narrow, atomistic, or particle-like conception of self whereas the transpersonal self refers to a wide, expansive, or field-like conception of self. This can be explained as follows. The desiring-impulsive self and the rationalizing-deciding self are both concerned with their own *self*-interest in the sense in which that term is commonly understood, that is, where the self whose interests are being referred to is conceived in a narrow, atomistic, or particle-like sense. The difference between the desiring-impulsive self and the rationalizing-deciding self is essentially that the former is concerned with its own self-interest in an ignorant or unenlightened sense (it wants to eat all the cake today even if that means that it may go hungry tomorrow and even if such heavy consumption serves to make it sick) whereas the latter is concerned with its own self-interest in an informed or enlightened sense (it realizes that there will be no cake left tomorrow if it eats it all today; that it is likely to make itself sick if it consumes the cake too quickly; and that it "pays" to share some of the cake with other entities of the same kind since these entities are likely to value one more if one does this and to reciprocate in the future). The normative-judgmental self has different interests to those of the other two selves in that it is concerned with the satisfaction of idealistic and moralistic standards (or norms) rather than with the satisfaction of unenlightened or enlightened appetitive demands. However, these interests are still related to a self that is conceived in a narrow, atomistic, or particle-like sense. The idealistic and moralistic demands that are issued by the normative-judgmental self are all of the kind that this *particular* self should do better than it has done (or than *other* selves have done), that *other* selves should do better than they have done, that this *particular* self should respect *other* entities, or that *other* selves should respect entities *other* than themselves (including, especially, this *particular* self).

It is important to note that even if the moral demands of the normative-judgmental self are of the (unusual) kind that one *ought* to abandon exclusive identification with a narrow, atomistic, or particle-like sense of self and develop a wide, expansive, or field-like sense of self, the self that is being addressed—the self that "ought" to do this—is still this particular self as distinct from other particular selves. Moral demands, in other words, *proceed* from the assumption of a narrow conception of self even when the *end* they aim for is the realization of an expansive sense of self. There is no way around this; it is inherent in the nature of moral demands. Moral demands necessarily emphasize a self that is capable of choice, a self that is a center of volitional activity, yet our sense of self can be far more expansive than that of being a center of volitional activity. For example, I can experience my volitional self as part of a larger sense of self that includes aspects of my own mind and body over which I do not experience myself as having particularly much control (and toward which it therefore makes no sense to issue *moral* demands). In turn, I can also experience this larger, but still entirely personal, sense of self as part of a still more expansive, transpersonal sense of self that includes my family and friends, other animals, physical objects, the region in which I live, and so on. When this happens, I experience physical or symbolic violations of the integrity of these entities as violations of my self, and I am moved to defend these entities accordingly. However, to attempt to instill the realization of an expansive, transpersonal sense of self through moral demands is counter-productive since moral demands are directed to and thereby reinforce the primary reality of the narrow, atomistic, or particle-like volitional self.

In contrast to the narrow, atomistic, or particle-like conceptions of self that underlie the desiring-impulsive self, the rationalizing-deciding self, and the normative-judgmental self, the transpersonal ecology conception of self is a wide, expansive, or field-like conception from the outset. This has the highly interesting, even startling, consequence that ethics (conceived as being concerned with moral "oughts") is rendered superfluous! The reason for this is that if one has a wide, expansive, or field-like sense of self then (assuming that one is not self-destructive) one will naturally (i.e., spontaneously) protect the natural (spontaneous) unfolding of this expansive self (the ecosphere, the cosmos) in all its aspects. Naess explains this as follows:

> Care flows naturally if the "self" is widened and deepened so that protection of free Nature is felt and conceived as protection of ourselves. . . . Just as we need not morals to make us breathe . . . [so] if your "self" in the wide sense embraces another being, you need no moral exhortation to show care. . . . You care for yourself without feeling any moral pressure to do it—provided you have not succumbed to a neurosis of some kind, developing self-destructive tendencies, or hating yourself.[16]

The idea of self-realization (of one kind or another) rendering morality superfluous is also found in various religious or spiritual traditions. For example, Walt Anderson, in his book *Open Secrets: A Western Guide to Tibetan Buddhism,* distinguishes between *exoteric* religious traditions, which are concerned with outer forms such as "codes of morality . . . rituals . . . [and] a common store of beliefs," and *esoteric* religious traditions, which are "concerned with personal growth and the evolution of the mind."[17] He explains:

> In the esoteric traditions, codes of morality are less important [than in the exoteric traditions] for the simple reason that the ultimate purpose of the spiritual effort is to attain a level of personal development at which morality is natural. It is discovered within oneself, and external authority is no longer necessary or meaningful. This principle is not foreign to Western psychology. . . . The same point is made by Abraham Maslow in his studies of healthy, "self-actualizing" people, who, he says, have relatively little respect for the formal rules and regulations of the society but at the same time a strong sense of concern for others.[18]

Daniel Goleman, in his book *The Varieties of the Meditative Experience,* similarly notes that the emphasis that Zen places upon the "transformation of personality" is such that "there is little emphasis in Zen on moral precepts. Rather than merely imposing precepts from the outside, their observance emerges from within as a by-product of the change in consciousness zazen can bring."[19]

Elaborating this general theme into a strategy for the future development of ecophilosophy, Naess says:

> Academically speaking, what I suggest is the supremacy of environmental ontology and realism over environmental ethics as a means of invigorating the environmental movement in the years to come. If reality is like it is experienced by the ecological self, our behavior *naturally* and beautifully follows norms of strict environmental ethics. We certainly need to hear about our ethical shortcomings from time to time . . . but when people feel they unselfishly give up, even sacrifice, their interest in order to show love for Nature, this is probably in the long run a treacherous basis for conservation. (Through identification [which, as we shall see, is *the* key term in

transpersonal ecology] they may come to see their own interest served by conservation, through genuine self-love, love of a deepened and widened self.[20]

In understanding what it is that is distinctive about the transpersonal ecology approach to ecophilosophy (i.e., Naess's philosophical sense of deep ecology), it is crucial to understand that Naess rejects approaches that issue in moral "oughts" (and, hence, objectivist intrinsic value theory approaches) again and again in his writings. For example, speaking in Australia in 1984, Naess said: "I'm not much interested in ethics or morals. I'm interested in how we experience the world. . . . Ethics follows from how we experience the world. If you experience the world so and so then you don't kill. If you articulate your experience then it can be a philosophy or religion."[21]

In *Ecology, Community and Lifestyle*, Naess draws upon Kant's distinction (put forward in Kant's *Groundwork of the Metaphysic of Morals*) between benevolent actions that are performed out of inclination and benevolent actions that are performed out of duty.[22] Naess endorses actions of the former kind, which he associates with the idea of "Self-realization!," over actions of the latter kind:

Inspired by Kant, one may speak of "beautiful" and of "moral" action. Moral actions are motivated by acceptance of a moral law, and manifest themselves clearly when acting against inclination. A person acts beautifully when acting benevolently from inclination. . . . Assuming that we wish benevolent action to flourish, some of us stress the need for teaching about the moral law, others stress the need for more understanding of the condition under which people get to be benevolent and well-informed through natural inclination. I take this process to be one of maturation as much as of learning. If the conditions for maturation are bad, the process of identification [which, for Naess, is central to the realization of an expansive sense of self] is inhibited and egotisms of various sorts stiffen into permanent traits.

So the norm "Self-realisation!" is a condensed expression of the unity of certain social, psychological, and ontological hypotheses: the most comprehensive and deep maturity of the human personality guarantees *beautiful action*. This is based on traits of human nature. We need not repress ourselves; we need to develop our Self. The beautiful acts are natural and by definition not squeezed forth through respect for a moral law foreign to mature human development.[23]

Although Naess refers to "Self-realization!" as a *norm*, it is obvious from his comments here and below in regard to ethics and moral laws that in using the term *norm* he does not mean to imply any kind of moral "ought" (i.e., an "ought" that is morally binding on others). Rather, when Naess refers to "Self-realization!" as a norm he simply means that it represents the overarching or most generally formulated positive goal or value within his *own* attempt to articulate his views in a logically systematic fashion. Unlike intrinsic value theorists, Naess at no stage attempts to *prove* the correctness of his views in such a way as to make this norm (or any of the norms he derives from it by the addition of hypotheses) morally binding on others. I discuss this point and the reason for it in the section that concludes this chapter, entitled "Proof, Moral Injunctions, and Experiential Invitations."

Naess often draws upon the above Kantian based distinction in rejecting ethical approaches:

> Now, my point is that perhaps we should in environmental affairs primarily try to influence people towards beautiful acts. Work on their inclinations rather than morals. Unhappily, the extensive moralizing within environmentalism has given the public the false impression that we primarily ask them to sacrifice, to show more responsibility, more concern, better morals. . . . All that can be achieved by altruism—the *dutiful, moral* consideration of others— can be achieved—and much more—through widening and deepening ourself. Following Kant we then act beautifully, but neither morally nor immorally.[24]

> I have a somewhat extreme appreciation of what Kant calls beautiful actions (good actions based on inclination), in contrast to dutiful ones. The choice of the formulation "Self-realization!" is in part motivated by the belief that maturity in humans can be measured

along a scale from selfishness to Selfishness, that is, broadening and deepening the self, rather than measures of dutiful altruism.[25]

One learns more from people who are superb in their capacity of acting benevolently by inclination than from people who are masters in acting morally, but against their inclinations. I try to point to the former as sources of inspiration rather than the latter.[26]

The history of cruelty inflicted in the name of morals has convinced me that increase of identification [the process through which the self is broadened and deepened] might achieve what moralizing cannot: beautiful actions.[27]

Commenting on another philosopher's discussion of the relevance of Spinoza's thought to ecophilosophy, Naess says (and note his emphases):

Central to Lloyd's conception of a metaphysics of environmentalism is the *moral* badness of exploiting animals for the sake of humans and, in general, of not treating the non-human realm as an end or value in itself. The term "moral" is used throughout her argumentation. But isn't Spinoza's philosophy [which Naess elsewhere interprets in terms of his concept of "Self-realization!"] one of generosity, fortitude, and love rather than of morals? *Do we need to shift to moralizing in order to find a satisfactory metaphysics of environmentalism?* If so Spinoza cannot be of much help. . . . We need not say that today man's relation to the nonhuman world is *immoral*. It is enough to say that it lacks generosity, fortitude, and love.[28]

In response to another philosopher, Naess writes:

I have the impression that Rollin refers to concepts of intrinsic value which are developed by professional metaphysicians. I do not need them. What Rollin says about the parasitologist suggests that [the parasitologist] appreciates [the value of parasites] independently of any narrow use for humans. He appreciates the meaningfulness of doing things for their own sake. This is all I need for my concept of intrinsic value. The parasitologist has *respect* for life! "Let the worms live!"[29]

It is important to understand what Naess is saying here. On the one hand, Naess does not reject the use of the term *intrinsic value*—indeed, he uses this term in the first point of his and

Sessions's eight-point platform of the deep ecology movement. On the other hand, however, Naess does not intend any formal philosophical meaning by this term and so does not intend a meaning that implies a moral "ought." This should be obvious from Naess's other comments to the effect that he is "not much interested in ethics or morals." Rather, Naess simply wishes to employ the term *intrinsic value* in an expressive, metaphorical, nontechnical, everyday sense. The meaning that Naess gives to this term, in other words, is phenomenological rather than moral: people will say colloquially (i.e., without any reference to formal philosophical views regarding the nature of intrinsic value) that they experience certain entities as being valuable "for their own sake" or "in and of themselves," and others understand them when they say this. Thus, when Naess says "I do not need . . . concepts of intrinsic value which are developed by professional metaphysicians" but then goes on to say that it is meaningful to appreciate the value of entities "independent of any narrow use for humans" and that "this is all I need for my concept of intrinsic value," he is saying that his sense of the term *intrinsic value* is an expressive, metaphorical, nontechnical, everyday one rather than a formal philosophical one. Naess makes this clear when he says elsewhere in the same paper:

> I shall not join a battle of professionals, but speak up in defence of certain ways of thinking and talking among plain people. . . . Among people who are not heavily influenced by certain philosophical or juridical terminology, it is common to be concerned about animals regardless of sentience, and for flowers, patches of landscapes, ecosystems, *for their own sake.* Often people would say they are beautiful, but also they defend their presence because they "belong there," "is part of the whole" etc.[30]

Naess adopts this point of view whenever he employs the term *intrinsic value* or similar terms. Thus, for example, in his 1979 paper on "Self-realization in Mixed Communities of Humans, Bears, Sheep, and Wolves," Naess points out that "the ascription of rights to animals frequently occurs among 'ordinary' people, that is, people without special formal education. It is their use, rather than that of people versed in law or philosophy, that guides my own."[31] Naess also notes in this paper that "it is fairly unimportant whether the term 'rights [of animals]' is or is not used in the fight for human peaceful coexistence with a rich fauna."[32] If we look at Naess's more recent papers, such as his 1986 paper entitled "Intrinsic Value: Will the Defenders of Nature Please Rise?," we continue to find him defending the "everyday use" of expressions like *intrinsic value* and *for its own sake* against the "abstract" (meaning the formal philosophical) uses of such expressions.[33]

Other thinkers who are close to Naess have also made the point that critics misunderstand him if they attempt to read subscription to formal philosophical views that imply moral "oughts" into his use of common terms like *rights* and *intrinsic value*. Not only does this point underpin my 1986 monograph-length response to Richard Sylvan's critique of deep ecology[34] but it was also made some years earlier by George Sessions in response to the same critic. Sessions wrote in his 1981 *Ecophilosophy* newsletter:

> Routley [now Sylvan] mistake[s] what Naess is up to. Naess's position is *not* . . . "an extension of conventional Western ethics" [quoting Routley]. . . . Biocentric egalitarianism is essentially a rejection of human chauvinistic ethical theory and the criteria used to ascribe rights and value; it is a *reductio-ad-absurdum* of conventional ethics. Biocentric egalitarianism is essentially a statement of non-anthropocentrism. Naess's original formulation [by which Sessions means the 1973 *Inquiry* paper in which Naess introduced the shallow/deep distinction] lends itself to misunderstanding in that he speaks of the equal *right* of all things to live and blossom into their own unique forms of self-realization. [However] Naess makes it clear ("Self-realization in Mixed Communities of Humans, Bears, Sheep, and Wolves," *Inquiry*, Vol. 22, 1979) that he is not proposing a "rights" theory in the sense of contemporary ethical theory, but is using the word "right" in a metaphorical or everyday sense.[35]

Writing in response to a paper of my own, Naess confirms Sessions's view that the term *biocentric egalitarianism* is not intended as a formal philosophical position that implies a moral "ought" but rather simply as "a statement of non-anthropocentrism": "The abstract term 'biospherical egalitarianism in principle' and certain similar terms which I have used, do perhaps more harm than good. They suggest a positive *doctrine*, and that is too much. The importance of the intuition is rather its capacity to counteract the perhaps only momentary, but consequential, self-congratulatory and lordly attitude towards what seems less developed, less complex, less miraculous."[36]

Now what most distinguishes the other main writers on deep ecology (and those considered to be closely associated with them) from the mainstream of writers on ecophilosophy (i.e., from philosophical intrinsic value theorists) is that they agree not only with Naess's rejection of formal intrinsic value theory approaches but also with the transpersonal, realization-of-as-expansive-a-sense-of-self-as-possible approach that Naess advocates in preference to these approaches. It is not always easy to disentangle these features in the work of these writers because they often reject approaches that issue in moral "oughts" in much the same breath as they endorse the transpersonal kind of approach that Naess advocates. However, it is useful to attempt to isolate these two features insofar as it is possible to do so in order to show that deep ecologists or, as I would prefer to say, transpersonal ecologists are not simply united in *opposition* to approaches that issue in moral "oughts" but are also united in *subscription* to the approach that I have referred to as transpersonal ecology (i.e., the this-worldly realization of as expansive a sense of self as possible). Thus, before providing an indication of the extent to which the main writers on deep ecology and their close associates endorse Naess's transpersonal approach to ecophilosophy, I want to provide an indication of the extent to which these writers agree with Naess's rejection of approaches that issue in moral "oughts." The best way of doing this is, I think, simply to present examples of what the main writers on deep ecology and their close associates *say*. Although I trust that readers will find them to be highly interesting in their own right, the particular quotations that follow may seem to be repetitive in their general theme. However, the fact that these authors are saying very similar things is *precisely the point.*

GEORGE SESSIONS:

The search for an environmental *ethics,* in the conventional modern sense (which Routley wants to endorse) seems wrong-headed and fruitless. . . . [Routley] thinks "an environmental ethic can be as tough, practical, rational and secular as prevailing Western ethics." I find this neither desirable nor necessary, and perhaps not possible. . . . The search then, as I understand it, is not for environmental ethics but for ecological consciousness.[37]

A logically air-tight formulation of a non-anthropocentric ecological metaphysics or an impeccably formulated "environmental ethics" is not going to solve our problems, even if such things are possible, although they would be of some use and value just as the formulation of paradigms has some value. However, our problems seem to channel down ultimately to human psychology, or states of consciousness, or more generally to the state of being of the whole organism. . . . Those philosophers who see the philosophical environmental problem mainly as one of developing an ethics of the environment fail to understand the major scientific/epistemological/ social paradigm shift which is now underway. Conceptual analysis will be valuable but . . . the attempt to solve these ecophilosophical problems on purely logical or conceptual grounds is to fail to realize that this approach is itself part of the old paradigm which needs to be replaced.[38]

BILL DEVALL:

Cultivating ecological consciousness precedes and pre-empts the search for an "environmental ethic."[39]

While some philosophers see appropriate environmental ethics as the primary task, others understand that the important task is . . . [that of] the psychological development from narrow, egotistical "self" to identification with the whole. . . . This issue of environmental ethics versus ecological consciousness has practical implica-

tions. It is not just a disagreement among some philosophers. . . .
[The former approach] fails to touch the core of the self.[40]

As we discover our ecological self we will joyfully defend and interact
with that with which we identify; and instead of imposing environmental ethics on people, we will naturally respect, love, honor and
protect that which is of our self. . . .

Extending awareness and receptivity with other animals and
mountains and rivers encourages identification and engenders respect
for and solidarity with the field of identification. This does not mean
there will never be conflicts between the vital material needs of
different people or between some humans and some other animals in
specific situations, but it does mean that a basis for "good actions"
or "right livelihood" is not based alone on abstract moralism, self-
denial, or sacrifice. . . .

We need to be reminded of our moral duties occasionally, but we
change our behavior more simply with richer ends through encouragement. Deeper perception of reality and deeper and broader
perception of self is what I call ecological realism. That is, in
philosophical terms, however important environmental ethics are,
ontology is the center of ecosophic concerns.[41]

ANDREW MCLAUGHLIN:

The heart of deep ecology, according to Devall and Sessions, is the
cultivation of "ecological consciousness" [by which they mean the
same as Naess means by "Self-realization"]. . . . This makes deep
ecology a rather more demanding position than contemporary philosophers usually deal with, as it insists on the fundamental importance of the question of what sort of person should I strive to
become?

This concern of deep ecology with the development of the self
harks back to the concerns of Greek philosophy with the development of *character*. As such, this pushes philosophy beyond the
bounds it has usually accepted in the twentieth century. It brings to
the fore the normative question of how should I *be*, rather than
addressing the more abstract and impersonal questions about the
nature of value, the structure of moral argument, and so on. In this

shift of focus, deep ecologists open an old and central question in a new context. . . .

[Yet] this is precisely the question that environmental philosophy *must* address. Disputes over whether or not Nature has or has not "intrinsic value" may not be the central question.[42]

ALAN DRENGSON:

What identifies us in terms of certain cultural patterns does not exhaust the richer possibilities that each of us contains. The conception we have of ourselves as social and human beings comes to constitute an ego self, a self image, which is narrowly boundaried and defined, and which is ultimately based on a rigid array of dualisms that have their basis in a subject/object dichotomy and a human/nature antagonism. . . .

What deep ecology directs us toward, then, is neither an environmental axiology or theory of environmental ethics nor a minor reform of existing practices. It directs us to develop our own sense of self until it becomes Self, that is, until we realize through deepening ecological sensibilities that each of us forms a union with the natural world, and that protection of the natural world is protection of ourselves.[43]

MICHAEL ZIMMERMAN:

In the light of the foregoing analysis, we can say that to determine what kinds of behavior are morally appropriate, we must know what we ourselves and other beings *are*. In other words, ontology precedes ethics. . . . Deep ecologists claim that before knowing what we *ought* to do, we must understand who we really *are*.[44]

NEIL EVERNDEN:

Even the call for an environmental ethic is an admission of this stance [i.e., "our prior action in saying 'It' to the world and to each other" or, in other words, our prior action in conceiving of our self in a narrow, atomistic, or particle-like way such that other entities are likewise seen as "atomistic individuals"], for ethics in Anglo-American philosophy deals with the means of structuring the interactions of atomistic individuals. It is almost another technical fix, a cultural corrective to a congenital deformity. . . . Understanding ourselves is the first task of ethics, and the ethics we derive will depend on our understanding of Being.[45]

Recasting Evernden's "it is almost another technical fix" comment in terms of the tripartite analysis of the self presented earlier, we could say that the moralistic demands of the normative-judgmental self represent an *introjected* "cultural correction" to the "congenital deformity" of what people often refer to as our *animal, lower,* or *primitive* nature (i.e., our desiring-impulsive self).

JOHN LIVINGSTON:

What one is after is not moral guidance but experiential knowing. . . . In nature I can find no place for even the most elegantly contrived rationalization of rights between species. The notion of rights as applied to interspecies affairs is probably a blind alley.

Such also seems to be the unfortunate conclusion, in deep ecology, for most branches of western ethics. . . . So far as I can determine, ethics and morals are unknown in nature. There appears to be no need for them. . . . Ethics and morals were, I believe, invented by one species to meet the particular needs of that species. They have nothing whatever to do with the rest of nature. . . . Conventional moral philosophy and ethics are, I believe prosthetic devices. . . . [What we need instead is an] extended consciousness which transcends mere self. . . . I see this extended sense of belonging as a fundamental biological (and thus human) imperative. I think that the thwarting of such an imperative is in some absolute sense wrong. . . . I cannot however explicate its wrongness by way of any branch of western ethics and moral philosophy of which I am aware.[46]

JOHN RODMAN:

Thanks to this ["the taboo against committing the *naturalistic fallacy*"] the quest for an ethics is reduced to prattle about "values" taken in abstraction from the "facts" of experience; the notion of an ethics as an organic ethos, a way of life, remains lost to us. . . . From the standpoint of an ecology of humanity, it is curious how little appreciation there has been of the limitations of the moral/ legal stage of consciousness. If an existing system of moral and legal coercion does not suffice, our tendency is to assume that the solution lies in more of the same, in "greatly extending the laws and rules which already are beginning to govern our treatment of nature." . . . It is worth asking whether the ceaseless struggle to extend morality and legality may by now be more a part of our problem than its solution.[47]

JOANNA MACY:

Indeed, I consider that this shift [to an emphasis on our "capacity to identify with the larger collective of all beings"] is essential to our survival at this point in history precisely because it can serve in lieu of morality and because moralizing is ineffective. Sermons seldom hinder us from pursuing our self-interest, so we need to be a little more enlightened about what our self-interest is. It would not occur to me, for example, to exhort you to refrain from cutting off your leg. That wouldn't occur to me or to you, because your leg is part of you. Well, so are the trees in the Amazon Basin; they are our external lungs. We are just beginning to wake up to that. We are gradually discovering that we *are* our world.[48]

So much, then, in regard to the question of the extent to which the main writers on deep ecology and their close associates *reject* approaches that issue in moral "oughts." But what about the question of the extent to which these writers *endorse* Naess's transpersonal approach to ecophilosophy? The key to seeing the commonality that exists between these writers in this regard is the concept of *identification*. Thus, Arne Naess writes:

A couple of thousand years of philosophical, psychological and social-psychological thinking has not brought us any stable conception of the I, ego, or the self. In modern psychotherapy these notions play an indispensable role, but, of course, the practical goal of therapy does not necessitate philosophical clarification of the terms.

. . . I shall only offer one single sentence resembling a definition of the ecological self. The ecological self of a person is that with which this person identifies.

This key sentence (rather than definition) about the self shifts the burden of clarification from the term "self" to that of "identification," or rather "process of identification". . . .

Every living being is connected intimately, and from this intimacy follows the capacity of *identification* and as its natural consequences, practice of non-violence. . . . Now is the time *to share* with all life on our maltreated earth through the deepening identification with life forms and the greater units, the ecosystems, and Gaia, the fabulous, old planet of ours.[49]

Throughout his writings, Naess emphasizes identification as the process through which one realizes an expansive sense of self:

How do we develop a wider self? . . . The self is as comprehensive as the totality of our identifications. Or, more succinctly: Our Self is that with which we identify. The question then reads: How do we widen identifications?[50]

Self-realization cannot develop far without sharing joys and sorrows with others, or more fundamentally, without the development of the narrow ego of the small child into the comprehensive structure of a Self that comprises all human beings. The [deep] ecological movement—as many earlier philosophical movements—takes a step further and asks for a development such that there is a deep identification of individuals with all life.[51]

In my outline of a philosophy (Ecosophy T) "Self-realization!" is the logically (derivationally) supreme norm, but it is not an eternal or permanent Self that is postulated. When the formulation is made more precise it is seen that the Self in question is a symbol of identification with an absolute maximum range of beings.[52]

And from *Ecology, Community and Lifestyle:*

The ecosophical outlook is developed through an identification so deep that one's *own self* is no longer adequately delimited by the personal ego or the organism. One experiences oneself to be a genuine part of all life. . . .

We are not outside the rest of nature and therefore cannot do with it as we please without changing ourselves. . . . We are a part of the

ecosphere just as intimately as we are a part of our own society. . . .
Human beings who wish to attain a maximum perspective in the
comprehension of their cosmic condition can scarcely refrain from a
proud feeling of genuine participation in something immensely
greater than their individual and social career. Palaeontology reveals
. . . that the development of life on earth is *an integrated process,*
despite the steadily increasing diversity and complexity. The nature
and limitation of this unity can be debated. Still, this is something
basic. "Life is fundamentally one." . . .

My concern here is the human capability of identification, the
human joy in the identification with [for example] the salmon on its
way to its spawning grounds, and the sorrow felt upon the thought-
less reduction of the access to such important places. . . . When
solidarity and loyalty are solidly anchored in identification, they are
not experienced as moral demands; they come of themselves.[53]

When Naess or other transpersonal ecologists emphasize the
importance of wider and deeper *identification,* it is important in
interpreting them not to get carried away in flights of imaginative
fancy but rather to understand what is being said as far as
possible in a down to earth, ordinary, everyday sense. Identification should be taken to mean what we ordinarily understand by
that term, that is, the experience not simply of a sense of
similarity with an entity but of a sense of *commonality.* To pursue
this further, one can have a sense of certain *similarities* between
oneself and another entity without necessarily identifying with
that entity, that is, without necessarily experiencing a sense of
commonality with that entity. On the other hand, the experience
of commonality with another entity does imply a sense of
similarity with that entity, even if this similarity is not of any
obvious physical, emotional, or mental kind; it may involve
"nothing more" than the deep-seated realization that all entities
are aspects of a single unfolding reality. (The possible bases of
identification will be discussed in chapter 8.) What identification
should not be taken to mean, however, is *identity*—that I literally
am that tree over there, for example. What is being emphasized
is the tremendously *common* experience that through the process
of identification my *sense* of self (my experiential self) can expand

to include the tree even though I and the tree remain physically "separate" (even here, however, the word *separate* must not be taken too literally because ecology tells us that my physical self and the tree are physically *interlinked* in all sorts of ways).

Expressing this point another way, the realization that we and all other entities are aspects of a single unfolding reality—that "life is fundamentally one"—does not mean that all multiplicity and diversity is reduced to homogeneous mush. As Naess says, the idea that we are " 'drops in the stream of life' may be misleading if it implies that individuality of the drops is lost in the stream. Here is a difficult ridge to walk: To the left we have the ocean of organic and mystic views, to the right the abyss of atomic individualism."[54] Thus, for transpersonal ecologists, the fact that we and all other entities are aspects of a single unfolding reality means neither that all entities are fundamentally the same nor that they are absolutely autonomous, but rather simply that they are *relatively* autonomous—a fact that emerges not only from ecological science but also from physics, evolutionary biology, and recent systems-oriented work on autopoietic systems and dissipative structures. (Indeed, in much the same way that a wide variety of recent research on nonlinear dynamical systems is being subsumed under the generic name of *chaos theory,* so the systems-oriented work that I have just referred to on autopoietic systems and dissipative structures could perhaps be referred to as *autonomy theory.* This is because the latter work centers on the question of how certain complex systems manage to organize themselves in such a way as to resist the universal tendency toward increasingly greater disorder, and thereby retain a considerable—but by no means an absolute—degree of autonomy relative to their environment.)

These comments on the relative autonomy of all entities stand in stark contrast to the view expressed by Richard Sylvan, in his monograph *A Critique of Deep Ecology,* that Naess goes "the full metaphysical distance to *extreme* holism, to the shocker that there are no separate things in the world, no wilderness to traverse or for Muir to save[!]."[55] If transpersonal ecologists thought that all entities were fundamentally the same then they would speak in terms of identity rather than identification; if they thought that all entities were absolutely autonomous then they would never have taken up their approach since, for them, identification is a natural (i.e., spontaneous) psychological response to the fact that we *are* intimately bound up with the world around us.

The view that our sense of self can be as expansive as our identifications and that a *realistic* appreciation of the ways in which we are intimately bound up with the world around us inevitably leads to wider and deeper identification (and, thus, to the realization of a more expansive sense of self) pervades not only Naess's work but also the work of the other main writers on deep ecology and their close associates. The only qualification to note here is that Heideggerian and Zen-influenced supporters of deep ecology such as Michael Zimmerman and Robert Aitken are more inclined to speak in terms of the realization of a more *open* sense of self—or the realization of *openness*—than in dimensional terms, that is, in terms of the realization of a *wider, deeper, larger,* or more *expansive* sense of self. The best way of illustrating this claim about what it is that unites the main writers on deep ecology and their close associates in a *positive* sense (as opposed to what it is that unites them in a *negative* sense, namely, their opposition to approaches that issue in moral "oughts") is again to present examples of what the main writers on deep ecology and their close associates *say.* Once again, the repetitive nature of these quotations—the fact that these authors are saying very similar things—is *precisely the point.*

BILL DEVALL:

Exploring ecological self is part of the transforming process required to heal ourselves in the world. Practicing means breathing the air with renewed awareness of the winds. When we drink water we trace it to its sources—a spring or mountain stream in our bioregion— and contemplate the cycles of energy as part of our body. The "living waters" and "living mountains" enter our body. We are part of the evolutionary journey and contain in our bodies connections with our Pleistocene ancestors.

Extending awareness and receptivity with other animals and mountains and rivers encourages identification and engenders respect for and solidarity with the field of identification. . . . Since many people live only with a narrow awareness of self due to their cultural conditioning, it is most important in the deep, long-range movement to encourage the deeper ecological self to contribute to the flourishing of self-realization in the whole biosphere.[56]

GEORGE SESSIONS:

Ecological consciousness is the result of a *psychological* expansion of the narrowly encapsulated sense of self as isolated ego, through identification with all humans (species chauvinism), to finally an awareness of identification and interpenetration of self with ecosystem and biosphere.[57]

DEVALL AND SESSIONS:

In keeping with the spiritual traditions of many of the world's religions, the deep ecology norm of Self-realization goes beyond the modern Western *self* which is defined as an isolated ego striving primarily for hedonistic gratification or for a narrow sense of individual salvation in this life or the next. This socially programmed sense of the narrow self or social self dislocates us, and leaves us prey to whatever fad or fashion is prevalent in our society or social reference group. We are thus robbed of beginning the search for our unique spiritual/biological personhood. Spiritual growth, or unfolding, begins when we cease to understand or see ourselves as isolated and narrow competing egos and begin to identify with other humans from our family and friends to, eventually, our species. But the deep ecology sense of self requires a further maturity and growth, an identification which goes beyond humanity to include the nonhuman world. . . . The "real work" can be summarized symbolically as the realization of "self-in-Self" where "Self" stands for "organic wholeness" [Robinson Jeffers' phrase]. This process of the full unfolding of the self can also be summarized by the phrase, "No one is saved until we are all saved."[58]

The idea that "no one is saved until we are all saved" is of course exemplified by the Buddhist ideal of the Bodhisattva, that is, a person who forgets the egoic self (and, without necessarily intending to, thereby realizes a more expansive sense of self) through working for the realization of others. In regard to this ideal, the Zen roshi and supporter of deep ecology Robert Aitken writes tersely:

> As the world is going, the Bodhisattva ideal holds our only hope for survival or indeed for the survival of any species. The three poisons of greed, hatred and ignorance are destroying our natural and cultural heritage. I believe that unless we as citizens of the world can take the radical Bodhisattva position, we will not even die with integrity.[59]

How then do we save all beings? "We save all beings by including them," says Aitken.[60] The Bodhisattva ideal represents the Buddhist equivalent of Naess's concept of Self-realization—a concept that, as we have seen, was itself deeply inspired by the work and ideas of the modern Bodhisattva Mahatma Gandhi.

ALAN DRENGSON:

> Here is where "Deep Ecology" comes in. When we use the word "Deep Ecology" here, we are referring to the philosophical approach described by George Sessions, Bill Devall, Arne Naess, and others. . . . Using Naess's terminology, we can say that the follower of the Deep Ecology Way practices extended self-identification . . . [which] involves an extension of one's concerns, commitments, and political actions. This sense of extended caring was expressed well in Spinoza's observation that we are as large as our loves.[61]

DAVID ROTHENBERG

> When Arne begins his system with the norm "Self-realisation!" many associations will be raised. [However, Naess makes it clear]

that we are not meant to narrow this realisation to our own limited egos, but to seek an understanding of the widest "Self," one with a capital S that expands from each of us to include all [through the process of identification]. . . . The word ["Self-realisation"] in Norwegian is *Selv-realisering*: Self-realising. It is an active condition, not a place one can reach. No one ever reaches Self-realisation, for complete Self-realisation would require the realisation of all. Just as no one in certain Buddhist traditions ever reaches nirvana, as the rest of the world must be pulled along to get there. It is only a process, a way to live one's life.[62]

ANDREW McLAUGHLIN:

Ecology, understood narrowly as the study of the interrelations between nonhuman organisms and their environments, may not force a fundamental change in our image of nature. However, when this perspective is applied self-referentially, it does require a fundamentally new image of humanity and nature. If, instead of seeing nature as separate from humanity, we see humanity and nature as one matrix, then it is clear that we are a part of nature. Our relations to nature are internal, in the sense that we are as we are because of the larger context within which we exist. . . .

What the ecological image suggests is that the identification of the self with the biological being is a basic error, an undue limiting, and that an expanding identification with larger human and nonhuman communities is continuous with what we can know about our world. Ultimately, what the self in Self-realization refers to is the organic wholeness of which we are but an aspect.[63]

FREYA MATHEWS:

Deep Ecology is concerned with the metaphysics of nature, and of the relation of self to nature. It sets up ecology as a model for the basic metaphysical structure of the world, seeing the identities of all things—whether at the level of elementary particles, organisms, or galaxies—as logically interconnected: all things are constituted by their relations with other things. . . .

Applying this principle of interconnectedness to the human case, it becomes apparent that the individual denoted by "I" is not constituted merely by a body or a personal ego or consciousness. I am, of course, partially constituted by these immediate physical and mental structures, but I am also constituted by my ecological relations with the elements of my environment—relations in the image of which the structures of my body and consciousness are built. I am a holistic element of my native ecosystem, and of any wider wholes under which that ecosystem is subsumed. . . .

From the point of view of deep ecology, what is wrong with our culture is that it offers us an inaccurate conception of the self. It depicts the personal self as existing in competition with and in opposition to nature. . . . [We thereby fail to realize that] if we destroy our environment, we are destroying what is in fact our larger self.[64]

JOHN LIVINGSTON:

Now, my point in reporting all of this is not to apply one more layer of mystery (mysticism) to the wildlife experience, but rather to emphasize that when I say that the fate of the sea turtle or the tiger or the gibbon is mine, I mean it. All that is in my universe is not merely mine; it is me. And I shall defend myself. I shall defend myself not only against overt aggression but also against gratuitous insult. . . .

There is absolutely nothing unusual about this experience. Anyone who has ever loved a nonhuman being knows the extraordinarily encompassing sense of unity that is possible, at least occasionally. . . . All I ask here is that you allow yourself to extend this selfless "identification"—for that, essentially, is what it is—beyond those individuals that you "know" in the conventional sense [i.e., by personal acquaintance].[65]

NEIL EVERNDEN:

For our purposes it is the notion that the self is not necessarily defined by the body surface that is especially interesting. This means that there is some kind of involvement with the realm beyond the skin, and that the self is more a sense of self-potency throughout a region than a purely physical presence. . . .

It has become apparent in the study of ethology that the extension of self into setting is by no means abnormal or unusual. The idea that an organism regards parts of its environment as belonging to its field of self seems strange only when we begin with the assumption that visual boundaries are more real than experiential boundaries. Our own sensation of personal space gives us some insight into the nature of self-extension, but of course the animal territory is not only larger but constitutes a fluctuating field. That is, while the area immediately around the self-center may always be regarded as a part of the individual, the extension of that image to dimensions large enough for us to notice and designate as territory varies with the mood of the organism. What we see in territoriality is the visible manifestation of what each of us goes through in sculpting a self. However, in this case we can see the gap between the boundary of the body and the boundary of the self. We cannot deny what we see in territorial animals, but our own less visible commitment to an extended self is easier to neglect. . . . [If one is open to experiencing this commitment then] one does not really experience the boundary of the self as the epidermis of the body, but rather as a gradient of involvement in the world, . . . [as] a field of concern or care. . . . If we were to regard ourselves as "fields of care" rather than as discrete objects in a neutral environment, our understanding of our relationship to the world might be fundamentally transformed.[66]

MICHAEL ZIMMERMAN:

We are so entrenched in the *contents* of awareness that we fail to notice awareness or openness as such. Awareness itself, of course, is not a thing, but instead constitutes the open realm in which things can be revealed. Within the open realm of awareness, both ego-subject and objects can first reveal themselves and thus "be." This awareness is not the property of my ego; instead, the ego "belongs" to the open awareness. But we must not be misled by the metaphor of ownership. Awareness is not a thing that possesses another thing, "me." The point here is that human existence involves something more fundamental than the ego-subject. Heidegger suggests that a human being becomes "authentic" when released from the compulsive activity of the ego. When it is authentic, human existence functions to serve, not to dominate. In the moment of releasement, enlightenment, or authenticity, things do not dissolve into an undifferentiated mass. Instead, they stand out or reveal themselves in their own unique mode of Being. Aware of the Being of beings, authentic human existence is also profoundly aware of the beings as such. . . . These beings include not only animals, plants, mountains, stars, and other people—but also our own bodies, wishes, feelings, memories, hopes, and thoughts. When we are at home with our mortal openness, we no longer have to be enemies of the events— the pain, loss, and death—that occur within the clearing. If we no longer identify ourselves with the ego that craves security and gratification, we do not have to resist what things are, nor do we feel compelled to manipulate them solely to suit our desires.[67]

ROBERT AITKEN:

Deep ecology . . . requires openness to the black bear, becoming truly intimate with the black bear, so that honey dribbles down your fur as you catch the bus to work.[68]

JOHN SEED:

As the implications of evolution and ecology are internalized and replace the outmoded anthropocentric structures in your mind, there is an identification with all life. . . . [Thus] "I am protecting the rain forest" develops to "I am part of the rain forest protecting myself. I am that part of the rain forest recently emerged into thinking."[69]

The fundamental problem may be who we as a species think we are. Who do we refer to, or mean, when we say "I"? We can't seem to break into the actual realization of our true nature. We can study evolution and appreciate how we evolved over four hundred million years. We can trace in our physical appearance this immense old creature which is manifest in my body in the briefest manifestation. But some people, many people, have difficulty identifying with the whole process. It is only by identification with the whole process

that correct values will emerge. Otherwise we see it as self-sacrifice
or effort. In shallow ecology arguments we're always trying to
balance jobs and environment. If we identify with the immense
process . . . we see immediately our correct self-interest whereas the
self-interest of the narrow ego in modern societies is mistaken self-
interest.[70]

JOANNA MACY:

The ecological perspective, then, as John Seed shows us, offers us a
vaster sense of who and what we are. Systems cyberneticians like
Gregory Bateson and Norbert Weiner remind us that all concepts
setting boundaries to what we term the self are arbitrary. In the
systems view, we consist of and are sustained by interweaving
currents of matter, energy and information that flow through us
interconnecting us with our environment and other beings. Yet, we
are accustomed to identifying ourselves only with that small arc of
the flow-through that is lit, like the narrow beam of a flashlight, by
our individual subjective awareness. But we don't *have* to so limit
our self-perceptions. . . . It is as plausible to align our identity with
[the] larger pattern, interexistent with all beings, as to break off one
segment of the process and build our borders there.[71]

JOHN RODMAN:

Acts of Ecological Resistance are not undertaken primarily in the
spirit of calculated, long-term self-interest (of the individual, the
society, or the species), or in the spirit of obedience to a moral duty,
or in the spirit of preventing profanation. . . . [Rather] Ecological
Resistance . . . assumes a version of the theory of internal relations:
the human personality discovers its structure through interaction
with the nonhuman order. I am what I am at least partly in relation
to my natural environment, and changes in that environment affect
my own identity. If I stand idly by and let it be destroyed, a part of
me is also destroyed or seriously deranged. An act of Ecological
Resistance, then, is an affirmation of the integrity of a naturally
diverse self-and-world. . . . Ecological Resistance thus has something

of the character of a ritual action whereby one aligns the self with the ultimate order of things.[72]

This consideration of the central views of the main writers on deep ecology (and those considered to be closely associated with them) should be enough to show that these writers are distinguished from the mainstream of writers on ecophilosophy (i.e., intrinsic value theorists) by the fact that they agree not only with Naess's rejection of approaches that issue in moral "oughts" but also with the transpersonal, realization-of-as-expansive-a-sense-of-self-as-possible approach that Naess advocates in preference to these approaches. Moreover, these writers generally look to Naess as the thinker who has elaborated these views in the greatest detail—or, at the very least, they align themselves with colleagues of Naess who in turn look to him in this way.

From the discussion here and in chapter 1 it should also be apparent that, of the writers considered in chapter 1 who have proposed typologies of ecology and environmentalism other than the shallow/deep ecology typology, only Rodman has developed his typology in such a way as to have come close to expressing similar ideas to Naess. That is, only in Rodman's work does one find definite moves—rather than perhaps the odd hint—not only in the direction of rejecting approaches that issue in moral "oughts" but also in the direction of emphasizing the view that our sense of self can be as expansive as our identifications and that a realistic appreciation of the ways in which we are intimately bound up with the world around us inevitably leads to wider and deeper identification. However, it is nothing against the brilliance of Rodman's work to say that these particular ideas are elaborated in considerably greater detail in Naess's work. One can find them in Rodman's work if one knows what to look for. In contrast, Naess elaborates these views—and responds to the various questions that are raised by their discussion—over and over in his work.

Finally, in concluding this section, it is important to dispel a thoroughly misguided objection that can arise for some people when they first hear about the emphasis that Naess and his colleagues place upon the psychological process of identification. Specifically, the fact that transpersonal ecologists focus on the *human* capacity for, and experience of, wide and deep identification can lead some people to charge that this approach is anthropocentric. However, the problem here is that this represents a fundamental misunderstanding of the intended, evaluative sense of the term *anthropocentric*—a term to which some discussion was devoted in chapter 1 ("A Closer Look at the Issue of Anthropocentrism"). This can be explained as follows. Just as the terms *sexist, racist,* and *imperialist,* for example, are intended to refer to approaches that promote unwarranted differential treatment of people on the basis of their sex, race, or culture, so the term *anthropocentric* is intended to refer to approaches that promote unwarranted differential treatment of other entities on the basis of the extent to which they are considered to be humanlike. It follows from these understandings that to say that transpersonal ecology is anthropocentric simply because it *focuses* on the human capacity for identification is as perverse a use of this term as it is to say that a group such as Men Overcoming Violent Emotions (MOVE) is sexist simply because it *focuses* on men. Rather, just as MOVE is wholly directed toward *overcoming* domestic violence in particular and sexist behavior in general, so transpersonal ecology is wholly directed toward *overcoming* the various forms of human chauvinism and domination. What is at issue, then, in deciding whether a particular approach is sexist, racist, imperialist, or anthropocentric is not the question of what class of entities the approach focuses on per se, but rather the intention that lies behind this focus of interest as well as its practical upshot. Seen in this light, it should be clear that transpersonal ecology's focus on the human capacity for, and experience of, wide and deep identification is not remotely anthropocentric in the intended, evaluative sense of that term.

PROOF, MORAL INJUNCTIONS, AND EXPERIENTIAL INVITATIONS

As we have seen, deep ecologists—or transpersonal ecologists—sometimes reject approaches that issue in moral "oughts" without offering any explanation; at other times they offer any of a number of different reasons (e.g., they may hold such approaches to constitute a superficial approach to the issues concerned or to be repressive or ineffective). However, my analysis of the kind of self that is emphasized by approaches that issue in moral "oughts" suggests that the most fundamental reason for the fact that transpersonal ecologists reject these approaches is that these thinkers explicitly emphasize a wide, expansive, or field-like conception of self whereas advocates of approaches that issue in moral "oughts" necessarily emphasize a narrow, atomistic, or particle-like conception of self—whether they intend to do this or not. If this view is correct then transpersonal ecologists consider these approaches to be superficial, repressive, or ineffective precisely *because* they emphasize a limited and limiting conception of self.

This rejection of approaches that issue in moral "oughts" explains a peculiar and, for many, a particularly frustrating fact about the transpersonal ecology approach. Specifically, the fact that transpersonal ecologists are not in the business of wanting to claim that their conclusions are *morally binding* on others means that they do not attempt to *prove* the correctness of their approach. They present their approach as a realistic, positive option (i.e., as an approach that one *can* take and that one might *want* to take) rather than as a logically or morally established obligation (i.e., as an approach with which one ought to *comply*). Taking Naess as the exemplar of the transpersonal ecology approach, we see that he continually puts his views forward in a manner that *invites* the reader's interest rather than in a manner that demands the reader's *compliance*. Thus, for example, Naess introduces the lengthy chapter that outlines his ideas on Self-realization and identification in *Ecology, Community and Lifestyle* by saying, "In this chapter a basic positive attitude to nature is articulated in philosophical form. It is not done to win compliance, but to offer some of the many who are at home in such a philosophy new opportunities to express it in words."[73] Again, when discussing the concept of Self-realization in a Spinozist context, Naess begins with this introduction: "In what follows I do not try to prove anything. I invite the reader to consider a set of connections between Spinoza's *Ethics* and the trend in thinking and living inspired in part by ecology and sometimes called *the deep ecological movement*. . . . Most of the connections seem clear to me, but each needs to be carefully scrutinized."[74] And finally, when expressing his views on the purpose of philosophical discussion in a more general context, Naess says: "Concluding this introduction I invite you to try to understand rather than to try to find weakness of exposition and argument. We are, I presume, all of us here as seekers, *zetetics* or 'sceptics' in the good sense of Sextus Empiricus. We do not wish to impose any doctrines upon anybody. . . . We look for helpful cooperation rather than for opportunity to preach."[75]

Naess's writings are characterized by comments of this kind— or comments to the effect that he is only meaning to put his views forward in a "tentative" manner. This stance differs markedly from that of intrinsic value theorists for the following reason. Intrinsic value theorists need to establish the correctness of their arguments for intrinsic value as best they can if their arguments are to have any normative force, that is, if their arguments are to be considered as carrying any moral (i.e., morally obliging) weight. If intrinsic value theorists are unable to establish the correctness of their arguments for intrinsic value successfully then the "oughts" in which these arguments issue are not considered to be morally compelling; their arguments are said to "fail." In contrast, however, there is a *theoretical* reason why transpersonal ecologists do not attempt to prove the correctness of their approach in such a way that their conclusions are morally binding on others. This is because to attempt to do this would be to reinforce the primary reality of the narrow, atomistic, or particle-like volitional self (see the earlier part of "The Distinctiveness of the Transpersonal Ecology Approach to Ecophilosophy" in this chapter). Rather than dealing with moral *injunctions,* transpersonal ecologists are therefore inclined far more to what might be referred to as experiential *invitations*: readers or listeners are invited to experience themselves as intimately bound up with the world around them, bound up to such an extent that it becomes more or less impossible to *refrain* from wider identification (i.e., impossible to refrain from the this-worldly realization of a more expansive sense of self).

From a phenomenological point of view, we could say that moral demands—even moral demands to realize a more expansive sense of self—are experienced (at least in the first instance) as forceful and constricting. They are experienced as forces that *impinge* upon (from the Latin *impingere,* meaning "to drive at," "dash against") us, where *us* refers to our narrow, volitional sense of self. We can therefore depict these moral forces as vectors or arrows that point in toward our narrow, volitional sense of self. In contrast, invitations to experience a more expansive sense of self are experienced from the beginning as nonforceful and potentially liberating. This situation can best be depicted not as arrows or lines of force that point out from "us," since this could also suggest that such invitations are forceful in some normative sense, but rather simply as doors, gates, or barriers (representing the limits of our narrow, atomistic, particle-like sense of self) that have been opened—or even removed. *Can we resist taking a stroll outside?* That is, as our knowledge grows regarding the extent to which we are intimately bound up with the world, can we resist identifying more widely and deeply with the world (i.e., realizing a more expansive sense of self) such that we are naturally inclined to care for all aspects of the world's unfolding?

Some philosophers are bound to feel uneasy about this invitational as opposed to injunctive approach to ecophilosophy. Some are likely to claim that transpersonal ecologists do not deserve to be taken seriously precisely because they do not attempt to prove their arguments in such a way that their conclusions are morally binding on others. On the other hand, others are likely to claim that transpersonal ecologists *do* attempt to smuggle a moral "ought" into their conclusions. For these philosophers, transpersonal ecologists are effectively deriving an *ought* from an *is* when they link the fact of our interconnectedness with the world to the response of wider and deeper identification. In regard to the first objection, one quickly reaches an impasse. Transpersonal ecologists can only reiterate that there is a *theoretical* reason for the fact that they do not attempt to prove their arguments in such a way that their conclusions are morally binding on others and for the fact that they reject approaches that do attempt to do this. This reason turns on the different kinds of self that are emphasized in transpersonal ecology on the one hand and approaches that issue in moral "oughts" on the other. Moreover, this theoretical reason enables transpersonal ecologists to criticize approaches that issue in moral "oughts" (namely, for emphasizing a narrow, atomistic, or particle-like sense of self) just as vigorously as advocates of these approaches may wish to criticize the approach of transpersonal ecology. The nature of the differences between these contrasting points of view is such that they should properly be regarded as alternative ecophilosophical paradigms. This means that the choice between them may not be a function of which is the more "correct" (since they work from different assumptions and incorporate different kinds of facts) so much as a function of other kinds of criteria such as which is the more fruitful to the discussion of ecophilosophical problems, which is the more relevant to our experience, which is the more exciting or appealing to certain kinds of temperaments, which is the more easily communicated, which is the more likely to influence behavior, and so on.

The second objection (i.e., that transpersonal ecologists are effectively deriving an *ought* from an *is* when they link our interconnectedness with the world to the response of wider and deeper identification) is simply wrong. Transpersonal ecologists claim that ecology, and modern science in general, provides a compelling account of our interconnectedness with the world. However, they are not in the business of attempting to claim that this fact *logically* implies that we ought to care about the world. The fact of our interconnectedness with the world does not *logically* imply either that we ought to care about the world of which we are a part or that we ought *not* to care about it. Logic, in other words, is of no help to us either way in proceeding from the fact of our interconnectedness with the world to the practical question of how we should live. Accordingly, transpersonal ecologists are not concerned with the question of the *logical* connection between the fact that we are intimately bound up with the world and the question of how we should behave but rather with the *psychological* connection between this fact and our behavior. Their analysis of the self is such that they consider that if one has a deep understanding of the way things *are* (i.e., if one empathically incorporates the fact that we and all other entities are aspects of a single unfolding reality) then one *will* (as opposed to should) naturally be inclined to care for the unfolding of the world in all its aspects. For transpersonal ecologists, this kind of response to the fact of our interconnectedness with the world represents a natural (i.e., spontaneous) unfolding of human potentialities. Indeed, given a deep enough understanding of this fact, we can scarcely *refrain* from responding in this way. This is why one finds transpersonal ecologists making statements to the effect that they are more concerned with ontology or cosmology (i.e., with the general question of the way the world is) than with ethics.

We have seen, then, that transpersonal ecology constitutes a distinctive approach to ecophilosophy in that it emphasizes a fundamentally different kind of self to the kinds of self that are emphasized by instrumental and intrinsic value theory approaches. Understanding this fact enables us to see why transpersonal ecologists reject approaches that issue in moral "oughts" (and this, of course, includes intrinsic value theory approaches of the kind discussed in the previous chapter) and why they do not attempt to prove the correctness of their views in such a way that their conclusions are morally binding on others. In both cases, the reason is that they are not interested in supporting approaches that serve to reinforce the primary reality of the narrow, atomistic, or particle-like volitional self. For transpersonal ecologists, given a deep enough understanding of the way things are, the response of being inclined to care for the unfolding of the world in all its aspects follows "naturally"—not as a *logical* consequence but as a *psychological* consequence; as an expression of the spontaneous unfolding (development, maturing) of the self.

8

Transpersonal Ecology
and the Varieties of Identification

THREE BASES OF IDENTIFICATION

HOW DOES ONE realize, in a this-worldly sense, as expansive a sense of self as possible? The transpersonal ecology answer is: through the process of identification. As Naess says: "The ecological self of a person is that with which this person identifies. This key sentence (rather than definition) about the self, shifts the burden of clarification from the term 'self' to that of 'identification,' or rather 'process of identification.' "[1] How, then, does one proceed in realizing a way of being that sustains the widest and deepest possible identification? I suggest that there are three general kinds of bases for the experience of commonality that we refer to as identification; three general kinds of ways in which we may come to identify more widely and deeply. I refer to these bases of identification as *personal, ontological,* and *cosmological.*

Personally based identification refers to experiences of commonality with other entities that are brought about through personal involvement with these entities. This is the way in which most of us think of the process of identification most of the time. We generally tend to identify most with those entities with which we are often in contact (assuming our experiences of these entities are of a generally positive kind). This applies not only to concrete entities (e.g., the members of our family, our friends and more distant relations, our pets, our homes, our teddy bear or doll) but also to those more abstract kinds of entities with which we have considerable personal involvement (our football or basketball club, the individual members of which may change from year to year; our country). We experience these entities as part of "us," as part of our identity. An assault upon their integrity is an assault upon our integrity.

In contrast to personally based identification, ontologically and cosmologically based forms of identification are transpersonal in that they are not primarily a function of the personal contacts or relationships of this or that particular person. There is, of course, a sense in which *all* forms of identification beyond one's egoic, biographical, or personal sense of self can be described as *transpersonal*. However, the point here is that personally based identification is, as its name suggests, a far more personal—or, alternatively, a far less *trans*personal—form of identification than either ontologically or cosmologically based identification, since it is a function of the personal contacts or relationships of this or that particular person, whereas, as we shall see below, the latter two forms of identification are not.

Ontologically based identification refers to experiences of commonality with all that is that are brought about through deep-seated realization of the fact *that* things are. (I am using the complex and variously employed term *ontology* in this context to refer to the fact of existence per se rather than to refer to the question of what the basic aspects of existence are or how the world is.) This is not a simple idea to communicate in words! Moreover, I do not intend to say very much about this idea since, in my view, it properly belongs to the realm of the training of consciousness (or perception) that is associated, for example, with Zen Buddhism, and those who engage in such training continually warn about the limits of language in attempting to communicate their experientially based insights. Martin Heidegger is a notable Western philospher who does attempt to convey such insights in words, but then, although deeply rewarding, he is also notorious for the difficulty of his language. It is interesting to note in this connection, however, that upon reading a book by the Zen master D. T. Suzuki, Heidegger is reported to have said, "If I understand this man correctly, this is what I have been trying to say in all my writings."[2]

The basic idea that I am attempting to communicate by

referring to ontologically based identification is that the fact—
the utterly astonishing fact—that things *are* impresses itself upon
some people in such a profound way that all that exists seems to
stand out as foreground from a background of nonexistence,
voidness, or emptiness—a background from which this foreground arises moment by moment. This sense of the specialness
or privileged nature of all that exists means that "the environment" or "the world at large" is experienced not as a mere
backdrop against which our privileged egos and those entities
with which they are most concerned play themselves out, but
rather as just as much an expression of the manifesting of Being
(i.e., of existence per se) as we ourselves are. We have perhaps all
experienced this state of being, this sense of commonality with
all that is simply by virtue of the fact *that* it is, at certain
moments. Things *are!* There is something rather than nothing!
Amazing! If we draw upon this experience we can then gain some
insight into why it is that people who experience the world in
this way on a regular or semi-regular basis (typically as the result
of arduous spiritual discipline) find themselves tending to experience a deep but impartial sense of identification with *all*
existents. We can gain some insight into why such people find
themselves spontaneously inclined "to be open for the Being [the
sheer manifesting] of [particular] beings" and, hence, why, for
them, "the best course of 'action' is to let beings be, to let them
take care of themselves in accord with their own natures."[3]

For those who cannot see any logical connection between deep-
seated realization of the fact that things *are* and the experience of
deep-seated commonality with—and thus respect for—all that
is, I can only reiterate that these remarks cannot and should not
be analyzed through a logical lens. We are here in the realm of
what Wittgenstein referred to as the mystical when he said, "It
is not *how* things are in the world that is mystical, but *that* it
exists."[4] If one seriously wishes to pursue the question of ontologically based identification then one must be prepared to undertake arduous practice of the kind that is associated with certain
kinds of experientially based spiritual disciplines. (Roger Walsh
captures what is of central interest about these disciplines in this

context by referring to them as *consciousness disciplines* in order to distinguish them "from the religious dogma, beliefs, and cosmologies to which most religious devotees adhere, and from the occult popularisms of both East and West."⁵ Those who are not prepared to do this—that is, most of us—are no more in a position to dismiss the fruits of such practice than are people who would dismiss the fruits of scientific research without being prepared to undertake the training that is necessary to become a scientist or at least to understand the general features of scientific procedure.⁶

Cosmologically based identification refers to experiences of commonality with all that is that are brought about through deep-seated realization of the fact that we and all other entities are aspects of a single unfolding reality. This realization can be brought about through the empathic incorporation of *any* cosmology (i.e., any fairly comprehensive account of *how* the world is) that sees the world as a single unfolding process—as a "unity in process," to employ Theodore Roszak's splendid phrase.⁷ This means that this realization can be brought about through the empathic incorporation of mythological, religious, speculative philosophical, or scientific cosmologies.⁸ I am not meaning to assert by this that these various kinds of accounts of how the world is are equal in epistemological status, only that each is *capable* of provoking a deep-seated realization that we and all other entities are aspects of a single unfolding reality. Consider, for example, the world-views of certain indigenous peoples (e.g., of some North American Indians), the philosophy of Taoism, or the philosophy of Spinoza.

For many people in the modern world the most viable—perhaps the only truly viable—source of cosmological ideas is science. Yet, despite this, there are many other people (including many who are formally trained in science or who simply have a general interest in science) who seem unable or unwilling to see science in a cosmological light. For them, science is all about prediction, manipulation, and control ("instrumental rationality") and cosmology is seen as something that belongs to mythology, religion, or speculative philosophy, or else as a highly specialized sub-discipline of physics that deals with the evolution and structure of the physical universe. But the anthropocentrically fueled idea that science is all about prediction, manipulation, and control is only half the story. As George Sessions says, "Modern science . . . [has] turned out to be a two-edged sword."[9] The other side of science is its importance for understanding our place in the larger scheme of things (and it is scarcely necessary to add that this aspect has had profoundly *non*anthropocentric implications). This side of science is its cosmological aspect. Considered from this side, modern science can be seen as providing an account of creation that is the equal of any mythological, religious, or speculative philosophical account in terms of scale, grandeur, and richness of detail. More specifically, modern science is providing an increasingly detailed account of the physical and biological evolution of the universe that compels us to view reality as a single unfolding process.[10]

The most obvious feature of the physical and biological evolution of the universe as revealed by modern science is the fact that it has become increasingly differentiated over time. This applies not just at the level of biological evolution but also at the level of the physical evolution of the cosmos. If we think of this process of increasing differentiation over time diagrammatically then it is natural to depict it as a branching tree. Indeed, this is precisely the way in which evolutionary theorists think of biological evolution.[11] In general terms, ancestral species do not change *into* newer species; rather, newer species radiate out (branch away) from ancestral species, which can continue to exist alongside the newer species. This "budding off" process occurs when populations of a particular kind of organism become in any way reproductively isolated (e.g., through geographical divergence or through divergence in breeding seasons) and then undergo changes in their genetic composition, primarily as a result of natural selection, to the point where members of one population are no longer capable of interbreeding with members of the other population.[12] But it is not only phylogenetic development (the evolution of species) that must be depicted as a continually branching tree. The image of a branching tree is just as relevant to other forms of development that involve increasing differentiation over time, whether it be ontogenetic development (the evolution of individual organisms from a cell to maturity) or the evolution of the universe itself from *nothing* to its present state some fifteen billion years later.[13] As the science writer Stephen Young explains in a brief recent introduction to the importance of the tree metaphor in science generally: "Trees are indispensable to science. From physics to physiology, they serve as metaphors, expressing in a word details that would otherwise occupy a paragraph. . . . The theory of evolution is unthinkable without trees. Elsewhere within science, afforestation continues apace. If trees did not exist, scientists would have to invent them."[14]

Even if our present views on cosmological evolution (including phylogenetic and ontogenetic evolution) turn out to stand in need of modification in crucial respects, we still have every reason to believe that the particular views that supersede these views will be entirely in conformity with the far more general idea that all entities in the universe are aspects of a single unfolding reality that has become increasingly differentiated over time. The justification for such confidence lies not only in the fact that *all* the evidence that bears on this question across *all* scientific disciplines points in this general direction, but also in the fact that even the most radical scientific (i.e., empirically testable) challenges to our present scientific views also point in this general direction. What is at issue in scientifically framed debates about the evolution of the universe or the evolution of life is only the question of the *mechanisms* of evolution (i.e., the mechanisms that underlie the increasing differentiation of the universe over time), not the fact of evolution per se.

A good illustration of this general point is provided by Rupert Sheldrake's *hypothesis of formative causation,* which constitutes a fundamental challenge to our present understanding of the development of form in ontogenetic, phylogenetic, and cosmological evolution.[15] Sheldrake's hypothesis suggests that the form that every entity takes is shaped by, and in turn contributes to the shaping of, a formative field—Sheldrake calls it a *morphic field—* that is associated with that particular kind of entity. Thus, the physical forms of crystals, daisies, and elephants are supposed to be influenced by the morphic fields that have been built up by earlier examples of their own kind. Even the *behavior* of organisms is supposed to be influenced by the morphic fields that have been built up by the behaviors of earlier examples of their own kind. This suggests that people who have never learned Morse code, for example, ought to learn real Morse code faster or more accurately than a comparable group of people who are asked to learn a newly created version of Morse code. In Sheldrake's view this would be expected simply because many people have previously learned the real version of Morse code, and thereby contributed to the creation of a morphic field for the learning of that code, whereas no morphic field exists for the newly created code. As it happens, this experiment has been performed and the results support Sheldrake's hypothesis.[16]

Now if Sheldrake's fascinating but presently highly controversial hypothesis turns out to be supported by a wide range of experimental findings, then this would, I think, cause the biggest revolution in biology, and in the sciences generally, since Darwin's theory of evolution by means of natural selection. But the point in this context is this: even if Sheldrake's ideas were accepted, we would still find ourselves living in an evolutionary, "branching tree" universe because, as Sheldrake explains, the idea of formative causation does not reject Darwinian evolution but rather "greatly extends Darwin's conception of natural selection to include the natural selection of morphic fields."[17] Thus, even when we consider a challenge to mainstream science that is as broad and as profound in its implications as Sheldrake's, we find, as I have already stated, that what is at issue is still only the question of the *mechanisms* that underlie evolutionary processes, not the fact of evolution *per se*. Evolutionary development, in other words, is the great unifying theme of modern science.[18]

If we empathically incorporate (i.e., have a lived sense of) the evolutionary, "branching tree" cosmology offered by modern science then we can think of ourselves and all other presently existing entities as leaves on this tree—a tree that has developed from a single seed of energy and that has been growing for some fifteen billion years, becoming infinitely larger and infinitely more differentiated in the process. A deep-seated realization of this cosmologically based sense of commonality with all that is leads us to identify ourselves more and more with the entire tree rather than just with our leaf (our personal, biographical self), the leaves on our twig (our family), the leaves we are in close proximity to on other twigs (our friends), the leaves on our minor sub-branch (our community), the leaves on our major sub-branch (our cultural or ethnic grouping), the leaves on our branch (our species), and so on. At the limit, cosmologically based identification, like ontologically based identification, therefore leads to impartial identification with *all* particulars (all leaves on the tree).

Having said this, it must immediately be noted that, as with ontologically based identification, the fact that cosmologically based identification tends to be more *impartial* than personally based identification does not mean that it need be any less deeply felt. Consider the Californian poet Robinson Jeffers! For Jeffers, "This whole [the universe] is *in all its parts* so beautiful, and is felt by me to be so intensely in earnest, that I am *compelled* to love it" (emphases added).[19] Although Jeffers may represent a relatively extreme exemplar of cosmologically based identification, it should nevertheless be clear that this form of identification issues at least—perhaps even primarily?—in an orientation of steadfast (as opposed to fair-weather) friendliness. Steadfast friendliness manifests itself in terms of a clear and steady expression of positive interest, liking, warmth, goodwill, and trust; a steady predisposition to help or support; and, in the context of these attributes, a willingness to be firm and to criticize constructively where appropriate. Indeed, if a particular entity or life form imposes itself unduly upon other entities or life forms, an impartially based sense of identification may lead one to feel that one has no real choice but to *oppose*—even, in extreme cases, to terminate the existence of—the destructive or oppressive entity or life form. Even here, however, an impartially based sense of identification leads one to oppose destructive or oppressive entities or life forms in as educative, least disruptive, and least vindictive a way as possible.

Over time, steadfast friendliness often comes to be experienced by the recipient as a deep form of love precisely because it does not cling or cloy but rather gives the recipient "room to move," room to be themselves. In the context of this book, it may be of particular interest to add here that Arne Naess seems to me to be an exemplar of steadfast friendliness—and of course I am not only talking here about his relationship with me over the years, but of his orientation toward the world in general. It is also interesting to note that Naess has himself written a paper on the importance of the concept of friendship in Spinoza's thinking in which he notes that "the intellectual sobriety of Spinoza favours *friendship rather than worship*" and that, for Spinoza, "friendship is the basic social relation" between members of a free society.[20] Naess concludes this paper by explicitly linking the theme of friendship in Spionza's philosophy with "the ecological concept of symbiosis as opposed to cutthroat competition." "Both in Spinoza and in the thinking of the field ecologist," says Naess, "there is respect for an extreme diversity of beings capable of living together in an intricate web of relations."[21]

Notwithstanding the eloquent testimonies to cosmologically based identification that have been offered by Spinoza, Gandhi, Jeffers, Naess, and many others (even Einstein, for example), many people find it difficult to think of identification in anything other than personally based terms. For these people, cosmologically based identification approximates to something like going out, encountering every entity in the universe (or, at least, on the planet) on a one-to-one basis, and coming to identify with each entity on the basis of that contact. But this simply represents an example of personally based identification that has been blown up into universal (or global) proportions. In contrast, cosmologically based identification means having a lived sense of an overall scheme of things such that one comes to feel a sense of commonality with all other entities (whether one happens to encounter them personally or not) in much the same way as, for example, leaves on the same tree would feel a sense of commonality with

258 ○ TOWARD A TRANSPERSONAL ECOLOGY

each and every other leaf if, say, we assumed that these leaves
were all conscious and had a deep-seated realization of the fact
that they all belonged to the same tree. In summary, then,
personally based identification proceeds from the person—and
those entities that are psychologically, and often physically,
closest to the person—and works outward to a sense of commonality with other entities. In contrast, cosmologically based identification proceeds from a sense of the cosmos (such as that
provided by the image of the tree of life) and works inward to
each particular individual's sense of commonality with other
entities. In vectorial terms, this contrast in approaches means
that we can think of personally based identification as an "inside-
out" approach and cosmologically based identification as an
"outside-in" approach.

One may gain or seek to cultivate a cosmologically based sense
of identification in a wide variety of ways. Even if we exclude
mythological, religious, and speculative philosophical cosmologies and restrict ourselves to the cosmology of modern science,
these ways of coming to embody a cosmologically based sense of
identification can range from approaches such as the ritualized
experientially based work being developed by John Seed and
Joanna Macy under the title "Council of All Beings"[22]; to
participation in theoretical scientific work (a number of the very
best scientists have had a profound sense of cosmologically based
identification); to more practically oriented involvement in natural history (many naturalists and field ecologists, for example,
effectively come to experience themselves as leaves on the tree of
life and seek to defend the unfolding of the tree in all its aspects
as best they can); to simply developing a deeper personal interest
in the scientific world model and in natural history along with
one's other interests.

IDENTIFICATION, DELUSION,
AND ENLIGHTENMENT

Having now identified three general forms of identification, it is
important to consider the question of the role that these forms of

identification play in transpersonal ecology. To begin with, it is important to note that transpersonal ecologists often discuss identification in terms of personally based identification. This, of course, is only to be expected: most of us are so familiar with this form of identification and are so used to thinking of the process of identification in this way that it is difficult *not* to discuss identification in terms of personally based identification. But, having said that, the interesting point to note here is that the *theoretical* emphases in transpersonal ecology lie squarely with the two transpersonal forms of identification (i.e., ontologically and cosmologically based identification). More specifically, although some Heideggerian and Zen-influenced transpersonal ecologists have tended to emphasize an ontological basis for wider and deeper identification, most of the main writers on transpersonal ecology have followed Naess in emphasizing a cosmological basis. As we have seen in chapter 7, for Naess, identification has a cosmological basis in that it follows (psychologically) *from* the realization that "life is fundamentally one."[23]

The fact that Naess emphasizes a cosmologically based approach to identification is clear not only from his writings but also from the nature of the sources that inspired his central concept of Self-realization. As we saw in chapter 4, the inspiration for this concept derives from Gandhi and Spinoza, both of whom explicated their views within the context of a monistic metaphysics, that is, within the context of a cosmology that emphasized the fundamental unity of existence. Gandhi was committed to Advaita Vedanta (i.e., monistic or, more literally, nondual Hinduism), to the belief that all life comes from "the one universal source, call it Allah, God or Parmeshwara."[24] He expressed this belief by conceiving of all entities as drops in the ocean of life: "The ocean is composed of drops of water; each drop is an entity and yet it is a part of the whole; 'the one and the many.' In this ocean of life, we are little drops. My doctrine means that I must identify myself with life, with everything that lives, that I must share the majesty of life in the presence of God. The sum-total of this life is God."[25]

Spinoza developed a philosophy that conceived of all entities as *modes* of a single *substance*—or what might today be thought of as expressions of a single energy.[26] As Roger Scruton notes in a recent study of Spinoza: "There is a modern equivalent of Spinoza's monism in the view that all transformations in the world are transformations of a single stuff—matter for the Newtonians, energy for the followers of Planck and Einstein."[27] For Spinoza, the highest end to which humans could aspire consists in "knowledge of the union existing between the mind and the whole of nature."[28] Thus, humans (one particular kind of mode) realize the truth of existence, or attain self-realization, when they realize that they arise out of and so are united with "the whole of nature," the single substance (or energy) that constitutes all modes of existence.

Despite the fact that transpersonal ecologists have generally emphasized cosmologically based identification more than ontologically based identification, I do not think that there is any particular *theoretical* reason for preferring one of these approaches to the other in transpersonal ecology. There may be a *practical* reason for this emphasis, however, in that it would seem to be much easier to communicate and inspire a cosmologically based sense of identification with all that is rather than an ontologically based sense of identification with all that is. This should be apparent from my previous comments to the effect that, beyond a certain point (namely, drawing attention to the fact *that* the world is), one simply cannot *say* very much about ontologically based indentification. One can only direct those who are interested in deep-seated realization of the fact of Being (the fact of existence per se) to the consciousness disciplines—and no-one should doubt that these disciplines *are* disciplines, and arduous ones at that. Anyone who mistakes this pointing *to* the consciousness disciplines for insight into the fact of Being itself is, as the Zenists say, mistaking a finger that is pointing at the moon for the moon itself. In contrast, the fact that cosmologies (i.e., general accounts of *how* the world is) are formulated in both words and images means that cosmologically based identification can readily be inspired through symbolic communication. These forms of symbolic communication may range from the communication of scientific, speculative philosophical, religious, and mythological views to the communication of vivid visual images such as mandalas and the kinds of images that have been presented here in which entities have been conceived of as leaves on a tree (as I have urged), drops in the ocean (Gandhi), or, more abstractly, as modes of a single substance (Spinoza).

One could, of course, also mention various other images at this point, such as ripples on a tremendous ocean of energy (an image employed by the physicist David Bohm) or knots in a cosmological net (which is a cosmological version of Naess's image of "organisms as knots in the biospherical net").[29] However, I prefer conceiving of all entities as leaves on the tree of life rather than in terms of any of these other images for at least two general reasons. First, insofar as an image can "fit the facts," the image of leaves on a tree is preferable because it captures the fact that all that exists has arisen from a single seed that has grown into an infinitely larger and infinitely more differentiated entity over time. In contrast, the images (as distinct from the thinking that may have given rise to these images) of drops in the ocean, modes of a single substance, ripples on a tremendous ocean of energy, and knots in a cosmological net do not readily suggest these attributes (i.e., increasing size, increasing differentiation, and a temporal dimension). Second, the image of leaves on a tree clearly suggests the existence of an entity that must be nurtured in all its aspects if all its aspects are to flourish. Damage a leaf badly enough and it will die; damage a branch (say, the branch of cosmic differentiation that became the earth some 4.6 billion years ago) and all the leaves on that branch will die. In contrast, the images of drops in the ocean, modes of a single substance, ripples on a tremendous ocean of energy, and knots in a cosmo- logical net do not readily suggest the existence of entities that need to be nurtured in any way at all.

The image of leaves on a tree also has more specific advantages. For example, although it clearly suggests that all entities (all leaves) are interconnected (by virtue of the fact that they are all part of the same tree), it also gives due recognition to the relative automony of different entities (different leaves). In contrast, some of the other images (especially that of drops in the ocean) can easily suggest the loss of individuality. Another example is the fact that although the image of leaves on a tree recognizes the relative autonomy or distinctness of different entities, it also clearly and quite correctly suggests that these entities are impermanent. Leaves come and go—and so does the tree itself (the cosmos), but over a much greater time span. In contrast, at least one of the other images (that of knots in a net) can easily suggest a sense of permanence (again, I stress that my concern here is with the images themselves, not with the thinking that lies behind them).

I want to turn now from the emphasis that is placed in transpersonal ecology on ontologically and, especially, cosmologically based forms of identification and consider the relative lack of emphasis that is placed on personally based identification. In contrast to the other two forms of identification, there *is* a fundamental theoretical reason why transpersonal ecologists do not emphasize personally based identification. Specifically, the fact that personally based identification refers to experiences of commonality with other entities that are brought about through personal involvement with these entities means that this form of identification *inevitably* leads one to identify most with those entities with which one is most involved. That is, one tends to identify with *my* self first, followed by *my* family, then *my* friends and more distant relations, *my* cultural or ethnic grouping next, *my* species, and so on—more or less what the sociobiologists say we are genetically predisposed to do. The problem with this is that, while extending love, care, and friendship to one's nearest and dearest is laudable in and of itself, the *other* side of emphasizing a purely personal basis for identification is that its practical upshot (*my* self first, *my* family and friends next, *my* cultural or ethnic grouping next, *my* species next, and so on) would seem to have far more to do with the *cause* of possessiveness, greed, exploitation, war, and ecological destruction than with the solution to these seemingly intractable problems.

I can hardly stress the importance of this last point enough. Personally based identification can slip so easily—and imperceptibly—into attachment and proprietorship. Anybody who doubts that personally based identification is a potentially treacherous basis for identification need only reflect on the way in which romantic love between two people—a paradigmatic example of intense personally based identification—can sometimes collapse into acrimonious divorce; or the truth in the old adage about family fights often being the worst fights; or the fact that we will do things to "others" (or allow things to be done to "them") that we would never do (or allow to happen) to "one of us." Yet again and again ecophilosophical discussants are all too prepared to extol the virtues of what effectively amounts to personally based identification while simply ignoring the possessive, greedy, exploitative, warmongering, and ecologically destructive drawbacks that can also attend this particular basis of identification. In particular, examples of such one-sided interest in personally based identification can be found in some of the ecofeminist literature and in the work of those who adopt a sociobiologically based approach to ecophilosophy. I have elaborated my criticisms of some forms of ecofeminism in this regard in another context and will not repeat them here.[30] However, I have not pursued the link between personally based identification and a sociobiologically based approach to ecophilosophy elsewhere and will do so here. This link is of particular interest in the context of this book because it allows me to explain why I omitted the important ecophilosopher J. Baird Callicott from the list of deep ecologists in chapter 3—in spite of the fact that his work has much in common with the approach that is taken in deep (or, as I would now say, transpersonal) ecology.

It is important to note that Callicott's work does share two obvious features with transpersonal ecology. First, much of his work is informed by a strong cosmological sense.[31] Second, Callicott has occasionally referred to the importance of identification in terms that sound much like any of the other transpersonal ecologists I quoted in the chapter 7. For example: "The injury *to me* of environmental destruction transcends the secondary, indirect injury to the conventional, constricted ego encapsulated in this bag of skin and all the functioning organs it contains. Rather, the injury *to me* of environmental destruction is primarily and directly to my extended self, to the larger body and soul with which 'I' (in the conventional narrow and constricted sense) am continuous."[32]

Why, then, should Callicott be excluded from my list of transpersonal ecologists?[33] The answer lies in the fact that, as pointed out in chapter 3 and again in chapter 6, Callicott's *favored* approach to ecophilosophy is a sociobiologically oriented one.[34] What does it mean to adopt such an approach? The central idea in sociobiology is that of *inclusive fitness*—a concept that sociobiologists use to explain a wide range of behaviors including those that would appear to be altruistic, selfless, or "ethical." Inclusive fitness refers to the "selfish gene" idea that if organisms cannot pass on their own genes directly, their next best strategy is to sacrifice themselves in ways that will help their closest of kin to pass *their* genes on, since these kin will share some portion of the sacrificing organism's genotype. J. B. S. Haldane captured the essence of this idea in memorable style when he (reportedly) said that he "would lay down his life for more than two brothers or sisters, eight cousins, thirty-two second cousins, etc., these numbers corresponding to the proportions of his own genes shared by these relatives."[35] Thus, sociobiology explains—and also serves to legitimate—the fact that we generally tend to favor our "nearest and dearest" over and against those to whom we are not genetically related or those who are not useful to us in the business of transmitting our genes (i.e., those who are not members of whatever we take "our group" to be).

Sociobiologists would claim that the evolutionary advantage (in terms of the continuation of an organism's own genotype) that is conferred by this strategy provides a biological basis for the psychological experience of identification with other entities. Moreover, it is even possible for sociobiologists to claim that this evolutionary strategy is able to accommodate a positive concern for the wider environment, since a habitable environment is necessary for the continuation of an organism's genetic lineage. However, in strict sociobiological terms, such a concern must generally run *last* in terms of any particular organism's immediate personal preferences and priorities for the obvious reason that the idea of inclusive fitness invests primary importance in the survival of the organism itself, the organism's closest kin, the organism's next closest kin, and so on, *in that order.* In terms of the three bases of identification that we have discussed, this means that a sociobiological approach clearly represents (and can *only* reasonably be taken as representing) a biological underpinning for *personally* based identification.

It is, then, Callicott's sociobiologically based emphasis on personally based identification that accounts for his exclusion from the list of deep ecologists in chapter 3. As we have seen, rather than emphasizing a biological-genetical level of analysis— or any other level of analysis for that matter—that serves to underwrite the significance of personally based identification, transpersonal ecologists emphasize a psychological level of analysis that opens us up to the possibility, desirability, and importance of ontologically and, particularly, cosmologically based identification. That is, transpersonal ecologists emphasize forms of identification that tend to promote impartial identification with *all* entities. Robyn Eckersley, in a major study of Green political thought, has appropriately described the political upshot of this orientation as "emancipation writ large."[36]

These considerations regarding the particular kinds of identification that are emphasized in transpersonal ecology allow me to characterize the approach that is adopted in transpersonal ecology more specifically than I have done hitherto. In the previous chapter, I characterized the approach that is adopted in transpersonal ecology simply as a psychologically based approach (as opposed to an axiologically based approach). This characterization was adequate in terms of capturing the emphasis that is placed in transpersonal ecology on the process of identification in general. However, the discussion in this chapter of the particular *kinds* of identification that are emphasized in transpersonal ecology means that we can now characterize the approaches that are adopted in transpersonal ecology more specifically as a psychological-ontological approach and a psychological-cosmological approach. These hyphenated, dual-aspect characterizations are more accurate and informative than simply describing the approach that is adopted in transpersonal ecology as psychological. This is because the latter characterization can suggest that the process of identification *begins and ends* with the subject whereas, for transpersonal ecologists, the psychological process of identification has an ontological or a cosmological basis in that it flows *from* the deep-seated realization that things *are* (ontologically based identification) or that "life is fundamentally one"—that all entities are, as I would say, leaves on the tree of life (cosmologically based identification).

Using these characterizations of transpersonal ecology approaches, we can say that the psychological-ontological approach and the psychological-cosmological approach both stand in contrast to the psychological-personal approach that is adopted, for example, in much ecofeminist theorizing and in sociobiologically based approaches. We can also say that all three identification based approaches stand in contrast to the objectivist axiological approach that predominates in ecophilosophy generally.

It has been important to go beyond transpersonal ecology's concern with identification in general and to consider the particular kinds of identification that are emphasized in transpersonal ecology. However, having done this, it is also important to note that the emphasis that transpersonal ecologists place on ontologically and, particularly, cosmologically based identification is just that—an emphasis, not an outright *opposition*. Thus, for example, when Naess says that "a rich variety of acceptable motives can be formulated for being more reluctant to injure or kill a living being of kind A than a being of kind B," he makes it clear that "felt nearness" (i.e., personally based identification) is an important example of such a motive.[37] I have simply emphasized the negative aspects of personally based identification here in order to show why transpersonal ecologists choose to emphasize transpersonally based forms of identification (and, in the process, as a corrective to the one-sided way in which personally based identification is often presented by other ecophilosophical discussants). But transpersonal ecologists still recognize that personally based identification is an inescapable aspect

THE VARIETIES OF IDENTIFICATION ° 267

of living and that it plays a fundamental role in human development.

The upshot, then, is that transpersonal ecologists simply want to put personally based identification in what they see as its appropriate place. For transpersonal ecologists, this occurs when ontologically and cosmologically based identification are seen as providing a *context* for personally based identification. This context serves as a corrective to the partiality and problems of attachment that are associated with personally based identification. When personally based identification is set within the context of ontologically and cosmologically based forms of identification (i.e., within the context of forms of identification that tend to promote impartial identification with *all* entities) then it is expressed in terms of a person being, as Naess says, more *reluctant* to interfere with the unfolding of A than B in those situations where a choice is unavoidable if the person is to satisfy nontrivial needs of their own. However, considered in the absence of the overarching context provided by ontologically and cosmologically based identification, personally based identification is expressed in terms of a person having no desire to harm A in any way (say, their child) but having few or no qualms about interfering with—or standing by while others interfere with— the unfolding of B (where B is an entity of any kind—plant, animal, river, forest—with which the person has no particular personal involvement). And this, of course, can apply even when the reasons for interfering with B are relatively trivial.

The significance of these considerations should be clear: although the *positive* aspects of personally based identification are praiseworthy and fundamental to human development, the *negative* aspects that go with exclusive or primary reliance upon this form of identification (*my* self first, *my* family and friends next, and so on) are costing us the earth. They underlie the egoisms, attachments, and exclusivities that find personal, corporate, national, and international expression in possessiveness, greed, exploitation, war, and ecocide. As an antidote to these poisons, transpersonal ecologists emphasize the importance of setting personally based identification firmly within the context of onto-

268 ∘ TOWARD A TRANSPERSONAL ECOLOGY

logically and cosmologically based identification—forms of identification that lead to impartial identification with all entities. In terms of politics and lifestyles, the latter, transpersonal forms of identification are expressed in actions that tend to promote the freedom of all entities to unfold in their own ways; in other words, actions that tend to promote symbiosis. (Indeed, Naess says at one point that "if I had to give up the term ['Self-realization!'] fearing its inevitable misunderstanding, I would use the term 'symbiosis.' ")[38] Actions of this kind include not only actions that consist in "treading lightly" upon the earth (i.e., lifestyles of voluntary simplicity) but also actions that respectfully but resolutely attempt to alter the views and behavior of those who persist in the delusion that self-realization lies in the direction of dominating the earth and the myriad entities with which we coexist.

> *That the self advances and confirms the*
> *myriad things is called delusion.*
> *That the myriad things advance and confirm*
> *the self is enlightenment.*[39]

Appendix A: A Guide to the Primary Sources on Deep Ecology Published during the 1980s

THE FOLLOWING is a comprehensive, author-by-author guide to the primary sources on deep ecology published (with a few exceptions) during the 1980s. This guide to sources would be considerably longer if it were also to include unpublished manuscripts. This applies particularly in the case of Arne Naess. Although Naess has published a prodigious amount of material, he has also written many other manuscripts that have been circulated amongst his deep ecology colleagues but that have never seen the published light of day. Part of the reason for Naess's large number of unpublished manuscripts lies in the fact that he produces manuscripts at such an astounding rate. When I spent time with Naess at his isolated cabin in the mountains in Norway; in Olso; in Perth, Western Australia; and in Hobart, Tasmania; he was continually retiring to his room—in between perhaps roughly equal periods of conversation on the one hand and outdoor physical activity on the other—to write further notes for the various papers and replies to other authors that he was working on at any given time. Rather than following all of his manuscripts through into print, Naess is often more interested in moving on to the next thing he wants to write.

The fact remains, however, that unpublished manuscripts are not freely accessible to the wider public. I have therefore refrained from listing such manuscripts (including papers presented to conferences if the conference proceedings have not been published) in the bibliographical guide that follows. I do, however, refer to unpublished manuscripts by deep ecology writers—

especially Naess, of course—elsewhere in this book where it is of particular relevance to my argument.

There is also another reason for overlooking unpublished manuscripts in the already lengthy bibliographical guide that follows. Whereas in chapter 3 I made a point of emphasizing the pivotal role that Devall's and Sessions's unpublished manuscripts played in the emergence of deep ecology up to and including 1980, the role of post-1980 manuscripts cannot be viewed as pivotal in the same way. Rather, once deep ecology "arrived" on the scene, in 1980, the role of unpublished manuscripts became, and has continued to be, simply one of reinforcing what has been happening on the larger stage that is constituted by publically accessible books and journals.

For a comprehensive guide to the primary sources on deep ecology up to and including 1980 (which is effectively to say: for a comprehensive guide to the ecophilosophically relevant work of Devall, Sessions, and Naess up to and including 1980), readers should consult the notes to the sections of chapter 3 entitled "The Advocacy Answer . . ." and "The Substantive Answer." I refer to all of Devall's and Sessions's ecophilosophically relevant work up to and including 1980 in the context of the former section and to all of Naess's ecophilosophically relevant work published in English up to and including 1980 in the context of the latter section. As far as secondary sources are concerned, I provide a comprehensive guide to the main secondary literature that has been published on deep ecology up to the end of the 1980s in chapter 2.

Following references to the work of Devall, Sessions, and Naess, I refer in the bibliographical guide that follows to the work of each writer in the order in which his or her name is listed in "The Advocacy Answer." I also comment, where it seems appropriate, on the personal interests and the elective affinities and informal lines of communication that exist among these writers. I realize that comments of this kind can run the risk of being branded as "intellectual gossip," but I believe that this kind of reaction is unenlightened in several respects. Not only do such comments add some life to (and, thus, hopefully, increase the reader's interest in) the writers to whom one is referring, but, as every sociologist of knowledge knows, these more personal kinds of observations about the members of an intellectual community can add considerably to one's understanding of that community and the ideas that it espouses.

On a very minor point (but in order to avoid confusion), it should be noted that I provide volume and issue numbers for references in *The Trumpeter* up until the end of volume 4 (1987), but only volume numbers for references from volume 5 (1988) on. This is because page numbers in *The Trumpeter* began to be numbered consecutively across issues within a volume from the beginning of volume 5 (1988).

Finally, note that if a reference is included in Further Reading, the facts of publication have been omitted in this appendix.

Bill Devall and George Sessions. Devall and Sessions's joint post-1980 written work includes "The Development of Natural Resources and the Integrity of Nature," *Environmental Ethics* 6 (1984): 293–322; and their 1985 book *Deep Ecology: Living as if Nature Mattered.*

Bill Devall. Devall's other main post-1980 written work includes, in addition to his contributions to *Ecophilosophy III* (1981)–VI (1984): review essay of *John Muir and His Legacy: The American Conservation Movement,* by Stephen Fox, in *Humboldt Journal of Social Relations* 9 (1981/82): 172–96; "John Muir as Deep Ecologist," *Environmental Review* 6 (1982) 63–86; "Ecological Consciousness and Ecological Resisting: Guidelines for Comprehension and Research," *Humboldt Journal of Social Relations* 9 (1982): 177–96; "David Brower," *Environmental Review* 9 (1985): 238–53; "Wilderness," *The Trumpeter* 3(2) (1986): 22–24; "Reply to Skolimowski," *The Trumpeter* 3(4) (1986): 15–16; *Simple in Means, Rich in Ends: Practicing Deep Ecology;* interview, "Simple in Means, Rich in Ends," *The New Settler Interview,* November/December 1988, pp. 18–32; interviewed by Richard Leviton, "World Without End," *East West,* August 1989, pp. 28–33; and "Ecocentric Sangha," in *Dharma Gaia: A Harvest of Essays in Buddhism and Ecology,* ed. Allan Hunt Badiner (Berkeley: Parallax Press, 1990).

In addition to these papers and his book *Simple in Means, Rich in Ends,* Devall has also written many articles, book reviews, and critical discussions of conferences for *Earth First!.* See, for example, "Dave Brower: Muir's Disciple," *Earth First!,* 20 March 1984, pp. 12–13; review of *An Environmental Agenda for the Future,* by "leaders of America's foremost environmental organizations," in *Earth First!,* 1 November 1986, pp. 24–25; "Green Conference Mired in Anthropocentrism" and review of four new books on John Muir, in *Earth First!,* 21 June 1986, p. 17 and pp. 24–25 respectively; "Was it the World Wilderness Conference or the Economic Development Conference?," *Earth First!,* 1 November 1987, pp. 9–10; "Deep Ecology and its Critics," *Earth First!,* 22 December 1987, pp. 18–20 (reprinted in a shortened version in *The Trumpeter* 5 [1988]: 55–60); reviews of *The History of the Sierra Club,* by Michael Cohen, and *The Rights of Nature: A History of Environmental Ethics,* by Roderick Nash, in *Earth First!,* 1 May 1989, pp. 30–31; and review of *Crossroads: Environmental Priorities for the Future,* ed. Peter Borrelli, in *Earth First!,* 1 August 1989, p. 30.

George Sessions. Sessions's other main post-1980 written work includes, in addition to his editing of, and contributions to, *Ecophilosophy III* (1981)–*VI* (1984): review of *The Soul of the World,* by Conrad Bonifazi, in *Environmental Ethics* 3 (1981): 275–81; "Ecophilosophy, Utopias, and Education," *Journal of Environmental Education* 15 (1983): 27–42; with Arne Naess, "Basic Principles of Deep Ecology," *Ecophilosophy VI,* May 1984, pp. 3–7 (I include this particular contribution to the *Ecophilosophy* newsletter because it has been reprinted, in whole or in part, in various places including Devall and Sessions, *Deep Ecology,* pp. 70–73, and *The Trumpeter* 3[4] [1986]: 14); review of *Eco-Philosophy,* by Henryk Skolimowski, in *Environmental Ethics* 6 (1984): 167–74; "Ecological Consciousness and Paradigm Change," in *Deep Ecology,* ed. Michael Tobias (San Diego: Avant Books, 1985), pp. 28–44 (this paper was written for Tobias's collection in 1981 but, as noted in chapter 2, it took several years for this volume to be published); review of *Playing God in Yellowstone,* by Alston Chase, in *Earth First!,* 21 December 1986, pp. 19–21; "The Deep Ecology Movement: A Review"; "Deep Ecology, New Age, and Gaian Consciousness," *Earth First!,* 23 September 1987, pp. 27–30; "Ecocentrism and the Greens: Deep Ecology and the Environmental Task," *The Trumpeter* 5 (1988): 65–69; interview, *Creation,* June 1989 (special issue on wilderness; page numbers unknown); and "Ecocentrism, Wilderness, and Global Ecosystem Protection," in *The Wilderness Condition: Essays on Environment and Civilization,* ed. Max Oelschlaeger (forthcoming, no further publication details; reprinted in part as "Ecocentrism and Global Ecosystem Protection," *Earth First!,* 21 December 1989, pp. 26–28).

Arne Naess. Arne Naess's main ecophilosophically relevant work published in English from 1981 on includes the following.

1981: "The Primacy of the Whole," in *Holism and Ecology,* working paper for the Project on Goals, Processes and Indicators of Development, The United Nations University, 1981, pp. 1–10.

1982: interviewed by Stephan Bodian, "Simple in Means, Rich in Ends: A Conversation with Arne Naess," *The Ten Directions,* Summer/Fall 1982, pp. 7 and 10–12; "Validity of Norms—But Which Norms? Self-Realization?: Reply to Harald Ofstad," in *In Sceptical Wonder: Inquiries into the Philosophy of Arne Naess on the Occasion of his 70th Birthday,* ed. Ingemund Gullvag and Jon Wetlesen (Oslo: Oslo University Press, 1982), pp. 257–69; and "A Comparison of Two System Models: Reply to Siri Naess," ibid., pp. 281–88.

1983: "How my Philosophy Seemed to Develop," in *Philosophers on Their Own Work,* vol. 10, ed. Andre Mercier and Maja Svilar (Bern: Peter Lang, 1983), pp. 209–26; and "Spinoza and Attitudes Towards Nature," in *Spinoza—His Thought and Work* (Jerusalem: The Israel Academy of Sciences and Humanities, 1983), pp. 160–75.

1984: "A Defence of the Deep Ecology Movement," *Environmental Ethics* 6 (1984): 265–70; with George Sessions, "Basic Principles of Deep Ecology," *Ecophilosophy VI*, May 1984, pp. 3–7 (reprinted, in whole or in part, in various places including Devall and Sessions, *Deep Ecology*, pp. 70–73, and *The Trumpeter* 3[4] [1986]: 14); "Deep Ecology and Lifestyle," in *The Paradox of Environmentalism*, ed. Neil Evernden (Downsview, Ontario: Faculty of Environmental Studies, York University, 1984), pp. 57–60; "Intuition, Intrinsic Value and Deep Ecology," *The Ecologist* 14 (1984): 201–3; and "The Arrogance of Antihumanism?," *Ecophilosophy VI*, May 1984, pp. 8–9.

1985: "Identification as a Source of Deep Ecological Attitudes"; and "The World of Concrete Contents," *Inquiry* 28 (1985): 417–28.

1986: "Deep Ecology in Good Conceptual Health," *The Trumpeter* 3(4) (1986): 18–21; "Intrinsic Value: Will the Defenders of Nature Please Rise?," in *Conservation Biology: The Science of Scarcity and Diversity*, ed. Michael Soule (Sunderland, Massachusetts: Sinauer Associates, 1986), pp. 504–15; and "The Deep Ecology Movement: Some Philosophical Aspects."

1987: "For its Own Sake," *The Trumpeter* 4(2) (1987): 28–29; "Notes on the Politics of the Deep Ecology Movement," in *Sustaining Gaia: Contributions to Another World View* (papers from the "Environment, Ethics, and Ecology II" conference, Monash University, 26–28 October 1984), ed. Frank Fisher (Clayton, Victoria: Graduate School of Environmental Science, Monash University, 1987), pp. 178–98; "Experts and Deep Ecology," ibid., pp. 199–202; "Philosophy of Wolf Policies I: General Principles and Preliminary Exploration of Selected Norms," *Conservation Biology* 1 (1987): 396–409; and "Self-Realization: An Ecological Approach to Being in the World" (The Fourth Keith Roby Memorial Lecture in Community Science, Murdoch University, Western Australia, 12 March 1986).

1988: "A European Looks at North American Branches of the Deep Ecology Movement," *The Trumpeter* 5 (1988): 75–76; "Deep

Ecology and Ultimate Premises," *The Ecologist* 18 (1988): 128–31; "Ecosophy, Population, and Free Nature," *The Trumpeter* 5 (1988): 113–19; "Sustainable Development and the Deep Long-Range Ecology Movement," *The Trumpeter* 5 (1988): 138–42; and "The Basics of Deep Ecology," *Resurgence,* January–February 1988, pp. 4–7.

1989: *Ecology, Community and Lifestyle: Outline of an Ecosophy;* "Comments on Edward Goldsmith's 'The Way,' " *The Ecologist* 19 (1989): 196–97; "Ecosophy and Gestalt Ontology," *The Trumpeter* 6 (1989): 134–37; "Finding Common Ground," *Green Synthesis,* March 1989, pp. 9–10; "Metaphysics of the Treeline," *The Trumpeter* 6 (1989): 45–46 (also in *Appalachia,* 15 June 1989, pp. 56–59); and "The Deepness of Deep Ecology," *Earth First!,* 21 December 1989, pp. 32.

Naess's extraordinary productivity (bearing in mind the large number of unpublished manuscripts he has also written) becomes even more obvious when one realizes that his deep ecology related work from 1973 to the present (the above only referring to Naess's deep ecology related work from 1981 on) is a subset of his total philosophical output during that period (albeit a significant subset) and that his English language deep ecology related work is, in turn, a subset of that subset (although, again, a significant subset).

Alan R. Drengson. Alan Drengson's main work on deep ecology includes: "Shifting Paradigms: From the Technocratic to the Person-Planetary," *Environmental Ethics* 2 (1980): 221–40; *Shifting Paradigms: From Technocrat to Planetary Person* (Victoria, B.C.: LightStar Press, 1983); "Developing Concepts of Environmental Relationships," *Philosophical Inquiry* 8 (1986): 50–65; "A Critique of Deep Ecology?: Response to William Grey," *Journal of Applied Philosophy* 4 (1987): 223–27; "Reflections on Ecosophy," *Pan Ecology,* Fall 1987, pp. 1–3 (*Pan Ecology,* "an irregular journal of nature and human nature," is edited by Alan Wittbecker and published by the Marsh Institute, Viola, Idaho); review of *Deep Ecology: Living as if Nature Mattered,* by Bill Devall and George Sessions, in *Environmental Ethics* 10 (1988): 83–89; "Nature,

Community and Self," *Communities Magazine*, Summer 1988, pp. 42–49; *Beyond Environmental Crisis: From Technocrat to Planetary Person* (a thoroughly revised version of Drengson's earlier book *Shifting Paradigms*); and "Protecting the Environment, Protecting Ourselves: Reflections on the Philosophical Dimension," in *Environmental Ethics Vol. II*, ed. R. Bradley and S. Duguio (Vancouver: Humanities Institute, Simon Fraser University, 1989), pp. 35–52.

In addition, Drengson's various contributions to *The Trumpeter*, which he founded and edits, are all written from a deep ecology perspective. Drengson's main explicit discussions of deep ecology in *The Trumpeter* are to be found in the five introductory issues that constitute volume 1 (1984; Drengson wrote all of these issues) as well as his papers "Fundamental Concepts of Environmental Philosophy: A Summary," *The Trumpeter* 2(4) (1985): 23–25; and "Paganism, Nature and Deep Ecology," *The Trumpeter* 5 (1988): 20–22. Other papers in *The Trumpeter* by Drengson include several articles on both agriculture and wilderness for volumes 2 and 3 respectively. Drengson has also written many papers for other journals on a variety of themes such as wise political rule, the philosophy of technology, ecoagriculture, experientially based learning, wilderness travel, mastery (as in mastery of an art or craft), aikido, compassion, and religion.

It is of more than passing interest to note that Drengson shares with Devall a strong interest in the Japanese martial art of aikido. My own limited acquaintance with this art, which exemplifies many of the principles associated with Taoism, suggests that it embodies a philosophy that is most congenial to a deep ecology view of the world.

Michael Zimmerman. Michael Zimmerman's main work on or relating to deep ecology includes: "Toward a Heideggerean *Ethos* for Radical Environmentalism," *Environmental Ethics* 5 (1983): 99–131; "The Critique of Natural Rights and the Search for a Non-Anthropocentric Basis for Moral Behavior," *Journal of Value Inquiry* 19 (1985): 43–53; "Implications of Heidegger's Thought for Deep Ecology"; "Philosophical Reflections on Reform versus

Deep Environmentalism," *The Trumpeter* 3(4) (1986): 12–13; "Feminism, Deep Ecology, and Environmental Ethics"; "Quantum Theory, Intrinsic Value, and Panentheism," *Environmental Ethics*, 10 (1988): 3–30; interviewed by Alan Atkisson, "Introduction to Deep Ecology," *In Context*, no. 22 (1989), pp. 24–28; and "Applying Heidegger to Radical Environmentalism," in *Applied Heidegger*, ed. Hubert L. Dreyfus and Michael E. Zimmerman (Bloomington, Indiana: Indiana University Press, forthcoming, 1991). Zimmerman's "Marx and Heidegger on the Technological Domination of Nature" (*Philosophy Today*, 23 [1979]: 99–112) is also of particular relevance to the "red vs. green" (or socialist vs. ecologically oriented) debate in ecopolitics.

As with virtually all the other supporters of deep ecology that I have referred to and will be referring to, Zimmerman has a strong interest in spiritual traditions. See, for example, in addition to some of the above papers (those on Heidegger and panentheism), Zimmerman's *Eclipse of the Self: The Development of Heidegger's Concept of Authenticity* (Athens: Ohio University Press, 1981), which explores the relationship between Heidegger's thought and Zen Buddhism in its final section (pp. 255–76), as well as his papers "Heidegger and Heraclitus on Spiritual Practice," *Philosophy Today* 27 (1983): 87–103; and "The Role of Spiritual Discipline in Learning to Dwell on Earth," in *Dwelling, Place and Environment*, ed. David Seamon and Robert Mugerauer (Boston: Martinus Nijoff, 1985), pp. 247–56.

Zimmerman has written much more on the difficult but rewarding philosophy of Martin Heidegger than the few papers and the book that I have cited (the present guide being limited to works on or relating to deep ecology). Those interested in Zimmerman's work on Heidegger in particular should also see his book *Heidegger's Confrontation with Modernity: Technology, Politics, and Art* (Bloomington, Indiana: Indiana University Press, 1990).

Sessions first met Zimmerman in the context of Zimmerman's work on Heidegger. The occasion was Zimmerman's delivery of a paper entitled "Technological Culture and the End of Philosophy" (subsequently published under that title in *Research in Philosophy and Technology*, vol. 2, ed. Paul T. Durbin and Carl Mitcham [Greenwich, Conn.: Jai Press, 1979]) to a March 1976 American Philosophical Association meeting in Berkeley. Sessions drew attention to this paper in his *Ecophilosophy I* newsletter (April 1976), drew heavily upon it in his "Spinoza and Jeffers" paper, and based the Heidegger section of his review of the philosophical literature for *Ecological Consciousness* largely upon this and other work by Zimmerman. Sessions and Zimmerman have stayed in touch ever since that 1976 meeting. They also served together on a panel at the conference on "Ecofeminist Perspectives," University of Southern California, 27–29 March 1987.

Warwick Fox. My own work on deep ecology includes: review of *The Liberation of Life: From the Cell to the Community*, by Charles Birch and John Cobb, in *The Ecologist* 14 (1984): 178–82; "Deep Ecology: A New Philosophy of our Time?," *The Ecologist* 14 (1984): 194–200 (my title for this paper was "The Intuition of Deep Ecology"; the published title represents an editorial decision by *The Ecologist*); "On Guiding Stars to Deep Ecology," *The Ecologist* 14 (1984): 203–4 (this is a response to Arne Naess, "Intuition, Intrinsic Value and Deep Ecology," *The Ecologist* 14 [1984]: 201–3, which, in turn, is a response to my "A New Philosophy?" paper); "Towards a Deeper Ecology?," *Habitat Australia*, August 1985, pp. 26–28; "An Overview of My Response to Richard Sylvan's Critique of Deep Ecology," *The Trumpeter* 2(4) (1985): 17–20; "A Postscript on Deep Ecology and Intrinsic Value," *The Trumpeter* 2(4) (1985): 20–23; review of *Deep Ecology: Living as if Nature Mattered*, by Bill Devall and George Sessions, in *Resurgence*, January-February 1986, pp. 41–42 (reprinted in *Holistic Human Concern for World Welfare*, ed. A. Kannan [Adyar, Madras: The Theosophical Society, 1987], pp. 39–40); *Approaching Deep Ecology: A Response to Richard Sylvan's Critique of Deep Ecology*, Environmental Studies Occasional Paper no. 20 (Hobart, Tasmania: Centre for Environmental Studies, University of Tasmania, 1986); "Post-Skolimowski Reflections on Deep Ecology,"

The Trumpeter 3(4) (1986): 16–18; "Ways of Thinking Environmentally (and Some Brief Comments on their Implications for Acting Educationally)," *Thinking Environmentally . . . Acting Educationally: Proceedings of the Fourth National Conference of the Australian Association for Environmental Education*, ed. J. Wilson, G. Di Chiro, and I. Robottom (Melbourne: Victorian Association for Environmental Education, 1986); contributing author to *The Green Alternative* (see ch. 11: "The Green Philosophy"), ed. Peter Bunyard and Fern Morgan-Grenville (London: Methuen, 1987); "Further Notes in Response to Skolimowski," *The Trumpeter* 4(4) (1987): 32–34; "The Deep Ecology–Ecofeminism Debate and its Parallels"; "The Meanings of Deep Ecology," *Island Magazine*, no. 38 (Autumn 1989), pp. 32–35 (reprinted in *The Trumpeter* 7 [1990]: 48–50); and "On the Interpretation of Naess's Central Term 'Self-Realization!,' " *The Trumpeter* 7 (1990): 98–101.

Dolores LaChapelle. Dolores LaChapelle's main work on or relating to deep ecology includes: "Systemic Thinking and Deep Ecology," in *Ecological Consciousness: Essays from the Earthday X Colloquium*, ed. Robert C. Schultz and J. Donald Hughes (Washington DC: University Press of America, 1981), pp. 295–323; and *Sacred Land, Sacred Sex: Rapture of the Deep* (Silverton, Colorado: Way of the Mountain Learning Center, 1988). LaChapelle's earlier book *Earth Wisdom* (Los Angeles: The Guild of Tutors Press, 1978) contains brief discussions of Arne Naess and his work and is also written from a deep ecology perspective. Unlike *Sacred Land, Sacred Sex*, however, it does not contain any discussion of deep ecology under that name. In view of the debate between those who advocate deep ecology and ecofeminist approaches, some readers will also be interested to read LaChapelle's brief essay "No, I'm Not an Eco-Feminist: A Few Words in Defense of Men," *Earth First!*, 21 March 1989, p. 31. In terms of helping to locate where LaChapelle is coming from—and where a number of other deep ecology oriented writers who also happen to be women are coming from—it may be of particular interest to read LaChapelle's essay in the context of my discussion of ecofeminism—and my positive references to LaChapelle's work—in my paper "The Deep Ecology–Ecofeminism Debate and its Parallels," see esp. pp. 9–13 and footnote 20.

LaChapelle is an experienced skier and t'ai chi teacher who sees in these practices much the same thing that Devall and Drengson see in aikido: a way of achieving and maintaining harmony and balance both within ourselves (mind, body, and feeling) and between ourselves and our wider environment (see *Earth Wisdom*, chapter 19).

LaChapelle organized a "Heidegger in the Mountains Symposium," which was held in the San Juan Mountain location of Silverton, Colorado (an altitude of more than 9,000 feet), over twelve days in August 1981 and was attended by Devall, LaChapelle, Sessions, Zimmerman, and a few others. LaChapelle, Sessions, and Zimmerman got together again in Silverton in August 1985. For an overview of the "Heidegger in the Mountains Symposium," see Dolores LaChapelle, "The Blue Mountains are Constantly Walking," *Ecophilosophy IV*, 1982, pp. 22–32; reprinted in *The Trumpeter* 3(4) (1986): 24–30. See also LaChapelle's insightful discussion of the ecophilosophical implications of Heidegger's philosophy in *Earth Wisdom*.

Robert Aitken. Robert Aitken is *roshi* ("venerable teacher") at the Diamond Sangha in Hawaii. He is included here on the basis of his brief but striking essay "Gandhi, Dogen and Deep Ecology," appendix C in Devall and Sessions, *Deep Ecology*. Similar views (albeit without explicit reference to deep ecology) are expressed in his *Taking the Path of Zen* (San Francisco: North Point Press, 1982).

Gary Snyder. Gary Snyder's ecological vision is presented in *Earth Household* (New York: New Directions, 1969); *Turtle Island* (New York: New Directions, 1974; see esp. his essay entitled "Four Changes," pp. 91–102); *The Old Ways* (San Francisco: City Lights Books, 1977); *The Real Work: Interviews and Talks, 1964–1979* (New York: New Directions, 1980); and "Buddhism and the Possibilities of a Planetary Culture," appendix G in Devall and Sessions, *Deep Ecology*.

As is the case with other supporters of deep ecology who have been attracted to Buddhism, Snyder's Buddhism is entirely compatible with—indeed, *demands*—ecological/social activism. Thus, "the real work," says Snyder, is "to check the destruction of the interesting and necessary diversity of life on the planet so that the dance can go on a little better for a little longer" and "to take the struggle on without the least hope of doing any good" (*The Real Work*, p. 82). Devall and Sessions's book on deep ecology is dedicated to both Snyder and Arne Naess.

The Zen Buddhist Michael Soule (an internationally respected biologist working in the field of conservation biology), with support from fellow Zen Buddhists Robert Aitken and Gary Snyder, organized a gathering at the Zen Center of Los Angeles in April 1982 which was attended by Naess, Devall, and Sessions as well as Aitken, Soule, and several other Buddhist scholars. (Gary Snyder was prevented from attending at the last minute because of heavy snow around his home in the Sierra foothills.) It was here that Devall met Naess for the first time and that Naess did the interview with Stephan Bodian that was published in the ZCLA's journal ("Simple in Means, Rich in Ends: A Conversation with Arne Naess," *The Ten Directions*, Summer/Fall 1982, pp. 7 and 10–12) and that was reprinted, in part, in chapter 5 of Devall and Sessions's book on deep ecology.

John Seed. John Seed is an ecological activist (also with what might be loosely described as Buddhist affinities) who has been at the forefront of grassroots-based efforts to protect rainforests worldwide. He is also primarily responsible for introducing the ideas of deep ecology to Australia in the early 1980s—along with distributing papers by Devall, Naess, and Sessions to interested people like myself. As someone who has been strongly influenced by these ideas, I am profoundly indebted to Seed's initial stimulus and encouragement. Seed is also responsible, together with Joanna Macy, for developing the Council of All Beings workshop/ritual. See John Seed, "Plumbing Deep Ecology," *Habitat Australia*, June 1982, pp. 27–28; John Seed, "Anthropocentrism," appendix E in Devall and Sessions, *Deep Ecology;* John Seed, Joanna Macy, Pat Fleming, and Arne Naess, *Thinking*

Like a Mountain: Towards a Council of All Beings (Philadelphia/ Santa Cruz: New Society Publishers, 1988); and the interviews with John Seed carried in the May/June 1989 issue of *Mother Earth News*, the June 1989 issue of *Green Line*, and the November/ December 1989 issue of *Yoga Journal*.

Seed organized an informal conference on deep ecology that was held on the coast of northern New South Wales at Ballina in September 1983. This was attended by Devall, John Martin (founding editor of the Australian-based newsletter *The Deep Ecologist*), myself, and others. Devall, Seed, and I first met two weeks before this conference at the more formal "Ethics, Ecology, and Environment I" conference held at the Australian National University in Canberra. We spent the intervening time discussing deep ecology at Bodhi Farm, the loosely Buddhist oriented community in the rainforest near Lismore (northern New South Wales) where John Seed was then living.

Joanna Macy. Joanna Macy's main essays on or relating to deep ecology include "Deep Ecology and the Council of All Beings" and "Gaia Meditations (Adapated From John Seed)," both in *Awakening in the Nuclear Age*, Summer/Fall 1986, pp. 6–10 (and both reprinted in *Revision*, Winter/Spring 1987, pp. 53–57); "Faith and Ecology," *Resurgence*, July–August 1987, pp. 18–21; and "Awakening to the Ecological Self," in *Healing the Wounds: The Promise of Ecofeminism*, ed. Judith Plant (Philadelphia/Santa Cruz: New Society Publishers, 1989), pp. 201–11. See also Joanna Macy, interviewed by Charlene Spretnak, "The Eroticism of Deep Ecology," *Creation*, May/June 1987, pp. 29–31; and Seed, Macy, Fleming, and Naess, *Thinking Like a Mountain: Towards a Council of All Beings* (full details given under Seed's publications). Macy has also written two books on the general theme of personal and community empowerment: *Dharma and Development: Religion as Resource in the Sarvodaya Self-Help Movement* (Hartford, Connecticut: Kumarian Press, 1983); and *Despair and Personal Power in the Nuclear Age* (Philadelphia/Santa Cruz: New Society Publishers, 1983).

Jeremy Hayward. Jeremy Hayward's essays on or relating to deep ecology are "Deep Ecology and the Perception of the Sacredness of our World," *Zen Buddhism Today: Annual Report of the Kyoto Zen Symposium,* no. 7 (1989): 94–110; "Ecology and the Experience of Sacredness," *Dharma Gaia: A Harvest of Essays in Buddhism and Ecology,* ed. Allan Hunt Badiner (Berkeley: Parallax Press, 1990); and "Transpersonal Ecology," *The Vajradhatu Sun* 12 (3) (1990): 13–14. Hayward has also written two books focusing on the mutual questioning of science and spirituality: *Perceiving Ordinary Magic: Science and Intuitive Wisdom* (Boston: Shambhala Publications, 1984) and *Shifting Worlds, Changing Minds: Where the Sciences and Buddhism Meet* (Boston: Shambhala Publications, 1987). As science editor at Shambhala Publications, Hayward is dedicated to publishing books that bring a spiritual or transpersonal perspective to global issues.

Hayward is a founding trustee of the Naropa Institute in Boulder, Colorado. As this book was going to press, Hayward was organizing a conference, for spring of 1991 at the Institute, entitled "Human in Nature." The conference will examine how the biological and cognitive sciences as well as the science of complexity and chaos are changing our fundamental views of our selves as living and mentating beings and of our relationships with our environment. For the first time a considerable number of the main writers on deep ecology will be brought together. It will also provide the first significant meeting of these writers with cognitive scientists to explore the cognitive/perceptual issues in the concept and practice of Self-realization. Hayward tells me that his acquaintance with several of the deep ecology writers invited to the conference began with his editing the manuscript for this book.

Neil Evernden and John Livingston. For deep ecology oriented work by Neil Evernden and John Livingston, both in the Faculty of Environmental Studies at York University, Ontario, see Neil Evernden, "Beyond Ecology: Self, Place, and the Pathetic Fallacy," *North American Review,* Winter 1978, pp. 16–20; Neil Evernden, *The Natural Alien: Humankind and Environment;* John A. Livingston, *One Cosmic Instant: Man's Fleeting Supremacy* (Boston: Houghton Mifflin, 1973); John A. Livingston, *The Fallacy of Wildlife Conservation;* John A. Livingston, "Rightness or Rights?," *Osgoode Hall Law Journal* 22 (1984): 309–21; and John A. Livingston, "Moral Concern and the Ecosphere," *Alternatives,* Winter 1985, pp. 3–9.

Arne Naess joined Evernden and Livingston in a small symposium held at York University in May 1983. The proceedings were published as Neil Evernden, ed., *The Paradox of Environmentalism* (Downsview, Ontario: Faculty of Environmental Studies, York University, 1984). See the following essays therein: Neil Evernden, "The Environmentalist's Dilemma," pp. 7–17 (reprinted in *The Trumpeter* 5 [1988]: 2–5); John Livingston, "The Dilemma of the Deep Ecologist," pp. 61–72; and Arne Naess, "Deep Ecology and Lifestyle," pp. 57–60.

It is interesting to note that Neil Evernden originally trained as a zoologist and that John Livingston is a respected naturalist.

Andrew McLaughlin. Andrew McLaughlin's main work on or relating to deep ecology includes: "Images and Ethics of Nature"; "Ecology and Philosophy: By Way of Introduction," *Philosophical Inquiry* 8 (1986): 1–9; and "The Critique of Humanity and Nature: Three Recent Philosophical Reflections," *The Trumpeter* 4(4) (1987): 1–6. Other relevant papers by McLaughlin include "Is Science Successful?: An Ecological View," *Philosophical Inquiry* 6 (1984): 39–46; and "Homo Faber or Homo Sapiens?," *The Trumpeter* 6 (1989): 21–24.

McLaughlin is yet another supporter of deep ecology with strong interests in Buddhism; in fact, he lived in a Zen community at one stage. (See his "Images and Ethics" paper for a discussion of a Buddhist view of nature.) He has been active in (successfully) defending the valley in which he lives against nuclear dumping. McLaughlin joined Devall in attending the 1986 "Round River Rendezvous" (the name given to the annual summer gathering of the Earth First! "tribe"), which was held in the mountains of central Idaho.

Freya Mathews. Freya Mathews's main work on or relating to deep ecology includes: "Plumbing Deep Ecology," *Habitat Australia,* April 1986, p. 15; "Deep Ecology: Where All Things are

Connected," *Habitat Australia,* October 1988, pp. 9–12; "Conservation and Self-Realization: A Deep Ecology Perspective," *Environmental Ethics* 10 (1988): 347–55; and *The Ecological Self* (London: Routledge, forthcoming, 1990). Mathews initiated and organized the conference on "Environmental Activism and Deep Ecology," Museum of Victoria, Melbourne, 17–18 May 1986; she also founded the Deep Ecology Collective in Melbourne.

John Rodman. Although John Rodman is not concerned in his papers with the elaboration of deep ecology under that name, he is clearly (and correctly) perceived by other ecophilosphers as sharing a similar sensibility to the main writers on deep ecology. In particular, see his papers "The Liberation of Nature?"; "Theory and Practice in the Environmental Movement: Notes Towards an Ecology of Experience," in *The Search for Absolute Values in a Changing World,* vol. 1 (New York: The International Cultural Foundation, 1978), pp. 45–56; and "Four Forms of Ecological Consciousness Reconsidered."

David Rothenberg. As a lover of mountains, David Rothenberg first came across Naess's work when he read Naess's brief article "Modesty and the Conquest of Mountains," in *The Mountain Spirit,* ed. Michael Charles Tobias and Harold Drasdo (London: Victor Gollancz, 1980), pp. 12–16. Following this, says Rothenberg, "I wrote to [Naess] for more—he sent a large pile, and commented 'we will climb together if you come to Norway' " (personal correspondence with the author, 25 July 1986). Rothenberg visited Naess in Norway in 1983 and returned to Norway in 1985 following his graduation from Harvard (where he had taken "a bachelor's degree in a made-up subject, 'music and communication' " [ibid.]). Rothenberg then worked as Naess's personal assistant from 1985 to 1987, before returning to the U.S. to take up doctoral studies in philosophy at Boston University.

Rothenberg has been instrumental in getting Naess to update and publish his major Norwegian publication on ecophilosophy entitled *Okologi, samfunn og livsstil* [Ecology, Community and Lifestyle], 5th ed. (Oslo: University of Oslo Press, 1976). This

286 ∘ APPENDIX A

has now been published as Arne Naess, *Ecology, Community and Lifestyle: Outline of an Ecosophy*. Together with Peter Reed, another young American member of the Ecophilosophy Group at the University of Oslo, Rothenberg has also edited a collection of Norwegian ecophilosophical writings: Peter Reed and David Rothenberg, eds., *Wisdom and the Open Air: Selections from Norwegian Ecophilosophy* (Oslo: Council for Environmental Studies, University of Oslo, 1987). (Peter Reed died in an avalanche in Norway on 27 March 1987. Naess's *Ecology, Community and Lifestyle* is dedicated to Peter with these words from Kevork Emin: "and you, my mountain, will you/never walk towards me?" At the time of his death, Peter was engaged in a dialogue with Naess and myself with a view to developing his own distinctive approach to ecophilosophy. This approach is elaborated in his paper "Man Apart: An Alternative to the 'Self-Realization' Approach as a Basis for an Environmental Ethic," *Environmental Ethics* 11 (1989): 53–69—a paper that offers ample testimony to the power of the developing mind that is now lost to us.) Rothenberg's main published paper on deep ecology is "A Platform of Deep Ecology," *The Environmentalist* 7 (1987): 185–90. On the subject of mountains, see Rothenberg's essay "Ways Toward Mountains," *The Trumpeter* 6 (1989): 71–75.

Alan Wittbecker. Alan Wittbecker defends deep ecology against the criticisms of Salleh, Skolimowski, and Watson in his paper "Deep Anthropology: Ecology and Human Order," *Environmental Ethics* 8 (1986): 261–70. See also Wittbecker's paper "Nature as Self," *The Trumpeter* 6 (1989): 77–81. Like Rothenberg, Reed, and myself, Wittbecker has also visited Naess in Norway (Wittbecker in April 1987).

Other Recent Contributors. New writers are also emerging to articulate and defend deep ecology ideas in the face of the various critiques that these ideas have been attracting. In the past year or two, one thinks in particular of people such as R. Wills Flowers and Bill McCormick. See, for example, R. Wills Flowers, "Of Old Wine in New Bottles: Taking up Bookchin's Challenge," *Earth First!*, 1 November 1987, pp. 18–19; R. Wills

Flowers, "Earth First?," letter to the editor, *The Ecologist* 19
(1989): 163–64; Bill McCormick, letter to the editor, *Green
Synthesis*, no. 28 (1988), p. 3; Bill McCormick, "How Deep is
Social Ecology?," *Kick it Over*, November 1988; and Bill McCormick, letter to the editor, *Alternatives* 16 (1989): 52–53.

Appendix B: The Emergence of Transpersonal Psychology

THIS APPENDIX provides background information that is relevant to the discussion of transpersonal *ecology* in chapter 7. It aims to provide a basic introduction to the related questions of how and why transpersonal psychology arose and what its main concerns are. It also serves as an introduction to the rather scattered references that bear on these questions.

The two main people involved in establishing transpersonal psychology as an institutionalized force in psychology were the same two people who, a decade earlier, had been the prime movers in establishing humanistic psychology as an institutionalized force in psychology: Abraham H. Maslow (1908–1970) and Anthony J. Sutich (1907–1976). In order to understand something of the inspirations and frustrations that led Maslow and Sutich to the development of ideas associated with the transpersonal orientation to psychology it is therefore first necessary to understand something of the inspirations and frustrations that led them to the development of ideas associated with the humanistic orientation to psychology.

In terms of broad approaches to psychology, humanistic psychology occupies the historical and theoretical middle ground between behaviorist and Freudian theory on the one hand (despite *their* immense differences) and transpersonal psychology on the other hand. At the theoretical level, humanistic psychology emerged in response to a critique of the mechanistic, deterministic, and, to many, limited and limiting—if not outrightly pessimistic—view of human nature presented by behaviorist and Freudian theory. Behaviorist theory simply ignored the interior life of organisms and regarded them basically as machines. In contrast, Freud accepted the importance of the interior life, yet he nevertheless thought that the best that could be hoped for from his "psychotherapeutic operations" was the transformation of "hysterical misery into common unhappiness."[1] Consistent with this, there are some four hundred references to neurosis in the index to Freud's collected papers, but none to health.[2]

Against this background, Abraham Maslow asserted in his influential 1954 book *Motivation and Personality:* "The science of psychology has been far more successful on the negative than on the positive side; it has revealed to us much about man's shortcomings, his illnesses, his sins, but little about his potentialities, his virtues, his achievable aspirations, or his full psychological height. It is as if psychology had voluntarily restricted itself to only half its rightful jurisdiction, and that the darker, meaner half."[3]

In regard to Freudian theory in particular, Maslow wrote that "Freud supplied to us the sick half of psychology," and urged that psychologists work to fill out the "healthy half."[4] For Maslow, moving from a "low-ceiling or cripple or jungle psychology" to a "*general* psychology" meant developing a "positive psychology," a psychology that could also provide for "the full height to which the human being can attain."[5] Such a psychology would eschew the behaviorist emphasis on adjustment in favor of an emphasis on creativity and would eschew the Freudian emphasis on the amelioration of neurotic misery in favor of an emphasis on psychological well-being and self-fulfilment.

Maslow's influential theory of human motivation, presented in *Motivation and Personality* and developed further in papers that were subsequently published together as *Toward a Psychology of Being* (1962) and *The Farther Reaches of Human Nature* (1971), played a significant role in the theoretical development of this emerging "third force" psychology (so named because it emerged after both positivistic behaviorist theory and classical psychoanalytic theory). Maslow's theory proposed that human needs were ordered in a hierarchy of five levels such that the emergence of needs at higher levels was conditional upon some reasonable degree of gratification of the needs at lower levels. Maslow divided this hierarchy into *basic, deficiency,* or *lower* needs on the one hand and *meta-, Being,* or *higher* needs on the other. The basic needs, in order of their demand for immediate gratification, were those of a physiological nature, such as hunger and thirst, followed by needs for safety, needs for love and belonging, and needs for self-esteem. Beyond these lay the individual's meta-needs, which Maslow referred to collectively as the need for *self-actualization* (i.e., the actualization of the individual's positive or creative potentials—or what is commonly referred to as *personal growth*). In Maslow's view, which came to be widely accepted, it was the exploration of these metaneeds that constituted the domain of interest of humanistic psychology. Reviewing the development of humanistic and transpersonal psychology, Anthony Sutich writes that "by 1966 it was commonly understood that the basic goal in Humanistic Psychology was 'self-actualization' or some such equivalent."[6]

With this optimistic agenda, humanistic psychology emerged as an organized force in psychology in the early 1960s with the establishment by Anthony Sutich, in close collaboration with Maslow, of the *Journal of Humanistic Psychology* in 1961 and the American Association for Humanistic Psychology (now the Association for Humanistic Psychology) over the period 1961–63.[7] However, as humanistic psychology became institutionalized and as the potentialities of the countercultural sixties "actualized," it became increasingly obvious that another broad approach to psychology was emerging from within humanistic psychology. While humanistic psychology had greatly expanded the boundaries and relevance of formal Western psychology, there were those (including Maslow and Sutich themselves) who felt, or came to feel, that its concerns, as they had emerged in practice at least, were still unable to accommodate significant aspects of human experience. One way of explaining the reason for these reservations is to say that the self that most humanistic psychologists were seeking to actualize was in important respects not all that different from the self of depth psychology (as for behaviorism, the self was simply an irrelevant concept). Specifically, the self with which most humanistic psychologists were concerned still tended to be conceived as a skin-encapsulated ego, as a separate "I"-sense, or, borrowing an analogy from physics, as particle-like rather than field-like.

This general point has been well developed in a recent paper by Maureen O'Hara, who has herself been a vigorous supporter of humanistic psychology and currently serves as an associate editor for the *Journal of Humanistic Psychology*. Reflecting on the nature of humanistic psychology, O'Hara says that although there was a time when she would have argued that "humanistic psychologies in their varied forms . . . [represented] an unqualified positive development, . . . in the last few years . . . I have come to believe that because of their profound epistemological contradictions and their overemphasis on the individual self, instead of leading to new coherence in existential understanding, widespread resort to humanistic psychologies can lead to still *more* fragmentation and alienation" (emphasis added).[8]

To emphasize her point, O'Hara goes on to refer to a widely adopted textbook on humanistic psychology and notes that "the seven themes [that the author of this textbook] identifies as major elements of a humanistic psychological view, when considered together, reveal a radically individualistic or egocentric view of human existence." Thus, in O'Hara's view:

[Humanistic psychology] sets an idealized "unencumbered self" *against* the world that gives it life, breath and, especially, meaning. . . . [L]ike the rest of modern American culture, [it] fails to acknowledge that our sense of personal autonomy, our sense of identity, our sense of stable personality, our sense of personhood . . . is *given to us by our culture*. . . . [Yet as many people have argued] we pay a high price for our illusion of autonomy—in the form of loneliness, unsatisfying relations with mates and families, longing for a sense of community, a pervading sense of isolation in an indifferent universe, and other modern angsts. To the extent that humanistic psychological theory gives scientific-sounding or religious-sounding credibility and support for this illusion, it may itself become a *source* of alienation and suffering (final emphasis added).[9]

Part of the reason for the perpetuation of an autonomous, particle-like conception of the self into the development of humanistic psychology is that many of those who were initially attracted to this orientation (whether as therapists or "clients") had been deeply influenced by the secular, postwar existential philosophy that had informed the cultural mood of the 1950s. Existentialism had highlighted the confrontation between self (conceived very much as an isolated particle rather than as an embracing field) and other (whether that other be another person, society in general, or nonhuman nature). The self stood over and against an often wholly different and indifferent—if not openly hostile—other; the self was "alienated" from the other; there was an "existential gulf" between the two. In response, humanistic psychology, in practice, focused especially on dealing with the common "human condition" as it applied to this sense of self (i.e., such existential concerns as authentic self-disclosure, intimacy, the need for meaning, and death). However, it seemed unable to comfortably accommodate experiences that went beyond (i.e., that were *trans-*) this narrow, atomistic, particle-like sense of self. Yet such transpersonal experiences were informing the cultural mood of the 1960s—by way of disciplined meditative and yogic approaches to altered states of consciousness and exceptional levels of well-being as well as by way of "chemical yoga"—just as surely as existentialism had informed the 1950s.

In a personal account of the emergence of the transpersonal orientation published in 1976, Sutich explains how by 1966 he had begun to feel that "something was lacking in the [humanistic] orientation"—and this notwithstanding the fact that he was still the editor of the *Journal of Humanistic Psychology*.[10] Among other things, Sutich had begun to feel that humanistic psychology did not "give sufficient attention to the place of man in the universe or cosmos" (and here he is talking about our sense of involvement in, rather than alienation from, a larger scheme of things). Sutich adds:

A special problem was my growing realization that the concept of self-actualization was no longer comprehensive enough. This was something of a surprise to me because I had thought that it was a very large conceptual "umbrella" and that it would be several generations before a larger one would be necessary. I frequently discussed with Maslow various problems and limitations in his theories, and my longstanding interest in the psychological aspects of mystical experience continued to provoke disturbing questions about basic humanistic theory. . . .

The transition that I was experiencing began to accelerate. I thought from time to time about how this development was going to affect my responsibilities as the editor of JHP and my association with the AAHP (American Association for Humanistic Psychology). I must say that as time went on I momentarily experienced guilt, disloyalty, irresponsibility, etc., toward my humanistic commitments. On the other hand, repeated events and incidents kept steering me toward a basic re-orientation.[11]

At the same time (and thus in conjunction with the developments I referred to that informed the cultural mood of the 1960s), Maslow was finding that his own studies of self-actualizing people were suggesting the theoretical importance of distinguishing between humanistic and transpersonal orientations. Toward the end of the 1960s—and the end of his life—Maslow concluded that the particularly psychologically healthy people he had previously been grouping together in the single catch-all category of *self-actualizers* were better thought of as constituting two groups: *"merely healthy"* self-actualizers and *individuals who have transcended self-actualization* (this latter classification implicitly adding a sixth level to his previously developed hierarchy of human motivation).[12]

"Merely healthy" self-actualizers, according to Maslow, adopt an essentially pragmatic approach to the world in that they assess people and other entities in terms of their usefulness for satisfying not only the self-actualizer's basic or deficiency needs (such as they are, since, by definition, these needs are already reasonably well satisfied in self-actualizers) but also the self-actualizer's Being (i.e., self-actualization) needs. These "merely healthy" self-actualizers can be described "*primarily* as strong identities, people who know who they are, where they are going, what they are good for, in a word, as strong Selves." They are vital, successful (in their own terms), and popular/lovable egoists (which is not to suggest that they need be egotistical since, to reiterate, in Maslow's scheme, self-actualizers are people who already feel reasonably well gratified in their basic needs— including those concerned with self-esteem).[13]

[In contrast to "merely healthy" self-actualizers, transcenders are those individuals who "find it easier to transcend the ego, the self, the identity, to go beyond self-actualization." (Note that Maslow's equation here of transcending the ego with going beyond self-actualization underscores my previous comments regarding the kind of self that tends to be emphasized in humanistic psychology.) [Maslow repeatedly describes transcendence and transcenders in terms of both the Spinozist ideal of living "under the aspect of eternity" and the Taoist ideal of living in harmony with the nature of things by allowing them to develop or unfold in their own way.[14] [Transcenders live in a Kingdom of Ends (i.e., they see people and other entities in the world as ends in themselves rather than in terms of their use value), and they identify their own good with the good of greater wholes (humankind, the cosmos) such that they must be thought of as "transcend[ing] the dichotomy between selfishness and unselfishness and includ[ing] them both in a single superordinate concept." Another way of expressing this, of course, is to say that transcenders have a more expansive sense of self than the narrow, egoic sense of self that typifies "merely healthy" self-actualizers. [Furthermore, while transcenders can be "more ecstatic, more rapturous, and experience greater heights of 'happiness' (too weak a word) than the ('merely') happy and healthy ones," Maslow also considers that they can be "*as* prone and maybe more prone to a kind of cosmic-sadness . . . over the stupidity of people, their self-defeat, their blindness, their cruelty to each other, their shortsightedness." [Finally, and significantly, it is, in Maslow's experience, these individuals who have transcended (not repressed, but moved beyond exclusive identification with) their own egoic self-actualization needs that are most likely to seem saintly, to inspire awe, and to provoke that rare but profound feeling that one is in the presence of a great human being.]

In the light of these studies, and informed by the cultural developments of the 1960s, Maslow felt it necessary to extend even further his optimistic, pace-setting agenda for psychology. Thus, in the preface to the *second* (1968) edition of his *Toward a Psychology of Being* (first published in 1962) he wrote: "I consider Humanistic, Third Force Psychology to be transitional, a preparation for a still 'higher' Fourth Psychology, transpersonal, transhuman, centered in the cosmos rather than in human needs and interest, going beyond humanness, identity, self-actualization, and the like."[15]

As I have indicated, Sutich had also been working toward much the same conclusion. As a result, he resolved his growing sense of a conflict of interest with his humanistic psychology commitments by resigning his editorship of the *Journal of Humanistic Psychology* in 1968 in order to establish, again in close collaboration with Maslow, *The Journal for Transpersonal Psychology*, which was first published the following year. Sutich then went on to form the Association for Transpersonal Psychology in 1971.

The term *transpersonal psychology* itself was hard won. Sutich's personal account of the emergence of the transpersonal orientation suggests something of the many hours that he and Maslow spent wrestling with potential names for the approach to psychology that now bears this name. Sutich describes how he and Maslow had discussed suggestions like *transhumanistic psychology, transhuman psychology, meta-personal psychology,* and *meta-psychology* between themselves and with others and how the name *transpersonal psychology* was finally settled upon following a February 1968 letter from Maslow in which Maslow referred to a meeting with Stanislav Grof (now a leading theorist in transpersonal psychology): "The main reason I am writing is that in the course of our conversations we thought of using the word 'transpersonal' instead of the clumsier word 'transhumanistic' or 'transhuman.' The more I think of it, the more this word says what we are all trying to say, that is, beyond individuality, beyond the development of the individual person into something which is more inclusive than the individual person. . . . What do you think?"[16]

Although Grof, Maslow, and Sutich had each employed the term *transpersonal* prior to this, there had been no sense of collective agreement upon it. However, Maslow's February 1968 formulation of the term "clicked" with Sutich immediately, and by June 1969 Sutich had edited and published the first issue of *The Journal of Transpersonal Psychology*.

On a personal note, it may be of interest to add here that my own progress toward the adoption of the term *transpersonal ecology* parallels that of Maslow and Sutich toward the adoption of the term *transpersonal psychology*. That is to say, behind my own adoption of *transpersonal ecology* lie reams of pages carrying notes on alternative suggestions and many hours spent wrestling with these alternatives. The point here, however, is not to highlight any of my own intellectual struggles simply for the sake of doing so, but rather to convey what I hope is a more significant observation, namely, that *transpersonal ecology* is the term to which I have found myself *returning* again and again in my own thinking about Naess's philosophical sense of deep ecology. *Transpersonal ecology* therefore represents what might be thought of (drawing a rather loose analogy with chaos theory) as the *attractor* toward which my own thought processes have gravitated.

Both the term *transpersonal psychology* and the ideas associated with that term have clearly survived Maslow (who died in 1970) and Sutich (who died in 1976).[17] New thinkers have emerged to develop the empirical and theoretical bases of transpersonal psychology to a surprisingly high degree of sophistication in a relatively short time. Notable among these thinkers are Daniel Goleman, Stanislav Grof, Charles Tart, Frances Vaughan, Roger Walsh, John Welwood, and, especially, Ken Wilber, a prolific and brilliant—albeit highly anthropocentric—writer who began publishing major work in the latter part of the 1970s, when still only in his twenties (he was born in 1949), and who is now generally regarded as the leading theorist in transpersonal psychology.[18]

Consistent with my previous remarks concerning the conceptions of self that are subscribed to in humanistic (and earlier) approaches to psychology on the one hand and transpersonal approaches on the other hand, these writers would all agree with the following assessment by Roger Walsh:

> Western psychotherapy [and he is here including humanistic approaches] usually has as its final goal a strong ego capable of living with and adapting to the existentially inevitable realities, such as continuous ego-superego conflict. For transpersonal theorists, however, more is possible. They agree with the premise that a strong ego is better than a weak, ineffective one, but they suggest that the relinquishing of exclusive identification with ego many be essential to higher development. As Needleman states in *A Sense of the Cosmos:* "The self that psychology [i.e., pre-transpersonal psychology] talks about is too small, too egotistical and too introverted."[19]

Moreover, like Maslow, these more recent transpersonal writers have been concerned not just with the transpersonal realm per se (i.e., with states of being that lie beyond an exclusive identification with one's ego, personality, or self-image), but, more generally, with the development of a broader theoretical framework for psychology that comprehends both (what have traditionally been thought of as) the "lower" and the "higher" realms of psychological well-being. To develop such a framework, these writers have had to look to the psychologies that have been developed in both the West *and* the East. This is because they consider that while Western psychology has developed the most comprehensive account to date of the subconscious, pre-egoic, or prepersonal realm of being, in the form of Freudian theory and its derivatives, and of the self-conscious, egoic, or personal realm of being, in the form of humanistic-existential psychology and related therapies, it is in the psychologies associated with a number of the Eastern spiritual traditions that one finds the most comprehensive account developed to date of the superconscious, trans-egoic, or transpersonal realm of being. This is not to say, of course, that transpersonal writers do not also recognize the existence of various minority traditions in the West that, like Spinoza and some Christian mystics, have been concerned with attaining the highest possible spiritual contentment in this world (as opposed to considering such states to be reserved for some heavenly hereafter). Nor is it to say that these writers do not recognize the existence of a limited number of earlier Western psychologists who have also been concerned with the "higher" realms of psychological well-being (the main names here include William James [1842–1910], Carl Jung [1875–1961], and Roberto Assagioli [1888–1974]). However, it is to say that transpersonal writers have found these concerns to be more typical of, more continuous through, and, consequently, more comprehensively developed in, Eastern spiritual traditions (including Middle Eastern traditions) such as Sufism, Vedanta Hinduism (nondual Hinduism), Theravada Buddhism (the earlier, south and southeast Asian development of Buddhism), Mahayana Buddhism (the later, northern development of Buddhism), Taoism, Zen Buddhism (the Japanese development of Ch'an—a Taoist-infused Chinese variety of Mahayana Buddhism), and Vajrayana Buddhism (Tibetan Buddhism). Thus, thinkers with interests in transpersonal states of being have generally felt it necessary to look to Eastern thought as a source of conceptual language, theoretical models, and practical guidance.[20]

It is appropriate to conclude this brief overview of the emergence of transpersonal psychology with Roger Walsh's comments on the affinity between Eastern thought and transpersonal psychology:

Western psychologists usually assume that our normal, natural, and optimal identity is egoic. However, Eastern and transpersonal psychologies suggest that our sense of self potentially may be considerably more plastic than we usually recognize.

They suggest that our sense of self can expand to include aspects of both the mind and the world that we usually regard as "other" or "not me." . . . [They suggest that] the individual can also identify with aspects of the world and humanity beyond the body, transcending the condition of separateness and isolation in recognition of the interrelated unity of existence.[21]

The obvious relevance of these remarks to an ecophilosophical context leads us back to the discussion of transpersonal ecology in chapter 7 and on to the discussion, in chapter 8, of ontologically and cosmologically based forms of identification.

Notes

If a reference is included in "Further Reading," the facts of publication have been omitted from the notes.

CHAPTER 1. MOVING AWAY FROM HUMAN-CENTEREDNESS

1. For readable but quite comprehensive overviews of these sorts of environmental issues there is probably no better source than the annual *State of the World* reports (New York: W. W. Norton) prepared by Lester R. Brown and his colleagues at the Worldwatch Institute, Washington, D.C., since 1984. The weekly British-based science journal *New Scientist* likewise keeps watch on these developments and generally communicates them in a way that is clear to nonspecialist audiences. See also the September 1989 special issue of *Scientific American,* which was devoted to an examination of, and appropriate responses to, our global ecological predicament.

   A large number of relatively popularly aimed presentations of the sorts of issues I have referred to are now available. Some excellent introductions include Michael Allaby, *Green Facts: The Greenhouse Effect and Other Key Issues;* Anne H. Ehrlich and Paul R. Ehrlich, *Earth;* Edward Goldsmith and Nicholas Hildyard, gen. eds., *Battle for the Earth: Today's Key Environmental Issues;* and Norman Myers, gen. ed., *The Gaia Atlas of Planet Management.*

   Significant reports on our global ecological predicament that have been published during the 1980s and that have been aimed directly at affecting government opinion and/or have been fairly technical in presentation include the *World Conservation Strategy: Living Resource Conservation for Sustainable Development,* prepared and published by the International Union for Conservation of Nature and Natural Resources in collaboration primarily with the United Nations Environment Programme and the World Wildlife Fund

(Gland: Switzerland, 1980); Gerald O. Barney, study director, *The Global 2000 Report to the President: Entering the Twenty-First Century* (Harmondsworth, Middlesex: Penguin, 1982); Essam El-Hinnawi and Manzur-Ul-Haque Hashmi, eds., *Global Environmental Issues: United Nations Environment Programme* (Dublin: Tycooly International for the UNEP, 1982); Martin W. Holdgate, Mohammed Kassas, and Gilbert F. White, eds., *The World Environment 1972– 1982: A Report by the United Nations Environment Programme* (Dublin: Tycooly International for the UNEP, 1982); Robert Repetto, ed., *The Global Possible: Resources, Development, and the New Century* (New Haven: Yale University Press, 1985; this report represents the outcome of a conference organized by the World Resources Institute); and Gro Harlem Brundtland, chairperson, *Our Common Future: The Report of the World Commission on Environment and Development* (see also Don Hinrichsen, *Our Common Future: A Reader's Guide* {London: Earthscan, 1987}).

2. Rachel Carson, *Silent Spring* (New York: Fawcett Crest Books, 1962). For histories of this movement, its leading figures, and the main ideas that have informed it, see Donald Fleming, "Roots of the New Conservation Movement," *Perspectives in American History* 6 (1972): 7–91; Stephen R. Fox, *John Muir and his Legacy: The American Conservation Movement;* Donald Worster, *Nature's Economy: A History of Ecological Ideas,* 2nd ed.; and John McCormick, *The Global Environmental Movement: Reclaiming Paradise.*

3. Fox, *John Muir and his Legacy,* p. 292.

4. Robert B. Downs, *Books That Changed the World,* rev. ed. (New York: Mentor, 1983), p. 333. Also see Neil Evernden, *The Natural Alien: Humankind and Environment* (Toronto: University of Toronto Press, 1985), pp. 7–8. Evernden notes that the original *Time* magazine review of Carson's book assured readers that "while some pesticides may be dangerous, many 'are roughly as harmless as DDT,' " which, as Evernden adds, "is now banned in most industrial countries."

5. Lynn White, Jr., "The Historical Roots of Our Ecologic Crisis," *Science* 155 (1967): 1203–7.

6. White, "The Historical Roots of Our Ecologic Crisis," reprinted in *Western Man and Environmental Ethics: Attitudes Toward Nature and Technology,* pp. 25 and 27. Barbour's book is of particular value in studying White's views because it also includes a specially com-

missioned reply by White ("Continuing the Conversation," pp. 55–64) to critics of his "Historical Roots" paper.

7. Ibid., pp. 28–30.

8. Ibid.

9. White, "Continuing the Conversation," pp. 56 and 62.

10. For discussions of this tradition and the tradition to which it has been opposed, see George Sessions, "Anthropocentrism and the Environmental Crisis"; George Sessions, "Spinoza and Jeffers on Man in Nature"; and Bill Devall and George Sessions, *Deep Ecology: Living as if Nature Mattered.* For those readers interested in my particular reference to "the *later* Heidegger," I would recommend J. Glenn Gray's very clear commentary on Heidegger's work, "Heidegger's Course: From Human Existence to Nature," *The Journal of Philosophy* 54 (1957): 197–207.

11. *Environmental Ethics* was founded by, and continues to be edited by, Eugene Hargrove. The journal's editorial address is: Department of Philosophy, University of North Texas, P.O. Box 13496, Denton, TX 76203–3496.

12. Donella H. Meadows and others, *The Limits to Growth: A Report for The Club of Rome's Project on the Predicament of Mankind* (New York: Universe Books, 1972); and Edward Goldsmith and others, *A Blueprint for Survival* (Harmondsworth, Middlesex: Penguin Books, 1972).

13. Bertrand Russell, *History of Western Philosophy* (London: Unwin Paperbacks, 1979), p. 90. Note, however, that Russell's other writings clearly suggest that he would see Spinoza as an exception to this generalization. (I briefly refer to Russell's attraction to Spinoza in chapter 4.) With respect to the major periods of Greek philosophy, Nicholas A. Horvath's overview of Western philosophy (*Essentials of Philosophy: Hellenes to Heidegger* [Woodbury, N.Y.: Barron's Educational Series, 1974], see pp. 17–46) concurs with Russell's assessment in describing Early Greek philosophy as "the Cosmocentric Period or the Period of Naturalism" in contrast to "the Anthropocentric Period" of Classical Greek philosophy. For excellent discussions of the anthropocentric nature of Western philosophy since the time of the pre-Socratics, see Sessions's previously cited essays "Anthropocentrism and the Environmental Crisis" and "Spinoza and Jeffers on Man in Nature."

14. Both quotations are from Brian Easlea's erudite and inspiring book *Liberation and the Aims of Science: An Essay on Obstacles to the Building of a Beautiful World* (London: Chatto and Windus, 1973), p. 253.

15. John Seed, "Anthropocentrism," appendix E in Devall and Sessions, *Deep Ecology*, p. 243. Within this *general* dominant assumption of human self-importance in the larger scheme of things, it is of course also true that certain classes of humans have typically adjudged themselves to be *more* human than others in order to legitimate their domination over these others. For a discussion of these "higher-order" aspects of anthropocentrism, see my paper "The Deep Ecology–Ecofeminism Debate and its Parallels."

16. Rene Descartes, "Meditations on First Philosophy," in *The Philosophical Writings of Descartes*, vol. 2, trans. John Cottingham, Robert Stoothoff, and Dugald Murdoch (Cambridge: Cambridge University Press, 1984), pp. 12–13.

17. William Barret, *The Illusion of Technique: A Search for Meaning in a Technological Civilization* (Garden City, N.Y.: Anchor Books, 1979), pp. 365–66. Recall here that Descartes, philosophizing in just such a situation, came to the conclusion that animals were nothing more than complex machines. Karl Popper makes a point that is closely related to Barrett's in the quotation at the beginning of part 1 in this book. Barrett implies a distinction here that Wallace Matson makes explicitly in his *A History of Philosophy* (New York: American Book Company, 1968) between two general approaches to philosophy. One of these approaches (typified by Descartes) begins with an account of the data of consciousness and then proceeds to work outward from that account to provide an account of the world. The other approach (typified by Spinoza) proceeds in reverse; it "begins with an account of the world, and at the end, or near the end, explains the human mind and its knowledge in the terms developed in that account" (ibid., p. 287). Matson refers to these contrasting approaches as the "inside-out" and the "outside-in" approach respectively. From an ecophilosophical viewpoint, this is a particularly interesting way of dividing philosophers. As Matson notes, it cuts across traditional forms of categorizing philosophers (such as the empiricism/rationalism distinction, which lumps Descartes and Spinoza *together* in the category of Continental Rationalists), and, as George Sessions points out, it reveals the major "outside-in" philosophers as essentially constitut-

ing the philosophical side of the Western minority tradition that has stood opposed to anthropocentrism. Sessions takes up and develops Matson's distinction in his previously cited essays "Anthropocentrism and the Environmental Crisis" and "Spinoza and Jeffers on Man in Nature." In the latter essay, incidentally, Sessions rates Matson's book as "the most insightful and valuable short history of Western philosophy which has been done" (p. 514).

18. Eugene C. Hargrove, "Problems and Prospects," editorial, *Environmental Ethics* 9 (1987): 195–96, p. 195. I am pleased to be able to report that Hargrove was *finally* granted tenure at the University of Georgia in May 1988 (Eugene Hargrove, personal correspondence with the author, 13 May 1988). Hargrove and *Environment Ethics* have since moved on to the University of North Texas. Hargrove's published work includes "The Role of Rules in Ethical Decision Making," *Inquiry* 28 (1985): 3–42; "Foundations of Wildlife Protection Attitudes," *Inquiry* 30 (1987): 3–31; and *Foundations of Environmental Ethics*.

19. Peter Farb, *Humankind* (St. Albans, Herts: Triad/Panther Books, 1978), pp. 12–13.

20. John Rodman, "The Liberation of Nature?" *Inquiry* 20 (1977): 83–131, p. 94.

21. John Earman, "The SAP Also Rises: A Critical Examination of the Anthropic Principle," *American Journal of Philosophy* 24 (1987): 307–17, p. 315.

22. George Santayana quoted in Sessions, "Spinoza and Jeffers on Man in Nature," p. 521. As Sessions shows, Spinoza and the Californian poet Robinson Jeffers are two other significant figures who found that their experience of the world did not accord with anthropocentrism. (Although Spinoza claimed to deduce all his conclusions in the *Ethics* from first principles, his arguments against anthropocentrism at times rely heavily on reflection upon his experience of the world; see, for example, Spinoza's appendix to part 1 of the *Ethics*.)

23. Barrett, *The Illusion of Technique*, p. 373.

24. Alan Watts, *Nature, Man, and Woman* (New York: Vintage Books, 1970), p. 123.

25. I discuss examples of critics who commit this fallacy in my paper "The Deep Ecology–Ecofeminism Debate and its Parallels"; see pp. 19–21.

26. See my "Further Notes in Response to Skolimowski," *The Trumpeter* 4(4) (1987): 32–34. This was a response to the then most recent edition of Henryk Skolimowski's ongoing critique of the deep ecology perspective ("To Continue the Dialogue With Deep Ecology," *The Trumpeter* 4[4] [1987]: 31–32) wherein Skolimowski (p. 31) attempted to turn the notion of anthropocentrism into an "ambiguous and indeed a double edged sword" on account of the fact that "it cuts deeply into *every* contention of deep ecology for each of these contentions is a *human* contention." As I have shown, however, this kind of claim simply reflects a failure to distinguish between the trivial and significant senses of anthropocentrism. (Skolimowski's earlier critiques of deep ecology, along with critiques by other writers, are referenced in chapter 2.)

27. Walter H. O'Briant, "Man, Nature, and the History of Philosophy," in *Philosophy and the Environmental Crisis*, ed. William T. Blackstone (Athens, Ga.: University of Georgia Press, 1974), pp. 79–89; Ian G. Barbour, *Technology, Environment, and Human Values* (New York: Praeger, 1980); and John Passmore, *Man's Responsibility for Nature: Ecological Problems and Western Traditions*.

Note that I object to the use of the term *nature* when, as is all too often the case in the studies listed in this note, the intended referent of the term is actually the nonhuman world rather than nature in the round, i.e., inclusive of humans. As should be obvious, the reason for my objection is that this kind of usage implies that humans are somehow outside the natural order, that their life history is not part and parcel of the single history of the physical and biological evolution of the universe. (Tom Colwell makes a similar point in regard to our usage of the term *nature* in the final section of his paper "The Ethics of Being Part of Nature," *Environmental Ethics* 9 [1987]: 99–113.) In employing the phrase *attitudes toward nature* in this note, then, I am simply bowing to the conventional description that is given to the studies to which I am referring rather than wishing to endorse this description.

For further general discussions of attitudes toward nature, see Clarence J. Glacken, *Traces on the Rhodian Shore: Nature and Culture in Western Thought from Ancient Times to the End of the Eighteenth Century* (Berkeley: University of California Press, 1967); Clarence J. Glacken, "Man Against Nature: An Outmoded Concept," in *The Environmental Crisis: Man's Struggle to Live with Himself*, ed.

Harold W. Helfrich, Jr. (New Haven: Yale University Press, 1970), pp. 127–42; Morris Berman, *The Reenchantment of the World* (Ithaca: Cornell University Press, 1981); Brian Morris, "Changing Views of Nature," *The Ecologist* 11 (1981): 130–37; Carolyn Merchant, *The Death of Nature: Women, Ecology, and the Scientific Revolution* (London: Wildwood House, 1982); Robin Attfield, *The Ethics of Environmental Concern;* Keith Thomas, *Man and the Natural World: Changing Attitudes in England 1500–1800* (London: Allen Lane, 1983); and James Serpell, *In the Company of Animals: A Study of Human-Animal Relationships* (Oxford: Basil Blackwell, 1986).

28. For reasonably exhaustive overviews of these positions, see William K. Frankena, "Ethics and the Environment"; John A. Livingston, *The Fallacy of Wildlife Conservation;* J. Baird Callicott, "Non-anthropocentric Value Theory and Environmental Ethics"; Edward Johnson, "Treating the Dirt: Environmental Ethics and Moral Theory"; J. Baird Callicott, "The Search For an Environmental Ethic"; and my own overview in chapter 6.

29. Henryk Skolimowski, *Eco-Philosophy: Designing New Tactics for Living;* William R. Catton, Jr., and Riley E. Dunlap, "Environmental Sociology: A New Paradigm," *The American Sociologist* 13 (1978): 41–49; and William R. Catton, Jr., and Riley E. Dunlap, "A New Ecological Paradigm for Post-Exuberant Sociology," *American Behavioral Scientist* 24 (1980): 15–47 (this issue of *American Behavioral Scientist* is dedicated to discussions of the implications of ecological thinking for the social sciences). Note that although Catton and Dunlap choose to capitalize the initial letters of such terms as *Human Exceptionalism Paradigm* in their own work, for sake of consistency of style, I have not retained this practice.

30. *Encyclopaedia Britannica* 1970 ed., s.v. "Ecology, Human," by Otis Duncan.

31. Grant McConnell, "The Environmental Movement: Ambiguities and Meanings," *Natural Resources Journal* 11 (1971): 427–35; Frederick H. Buttell and Oscar Larson III, "Whither Environmentalism?: The Future Political Path of the Environmental Movement," *Natural Resources Journal* 20 (1980): 323–44; and Stephen Cotgrove, *Catastrophe or Cornucopia: The Environment, Politics and the Future* (Chichester: John Wiley and Sons, 1982).

32. Riley E. Dunlap and Kent D. Van Liere, "The 'New Environmen-

tal Paradigm,' " *The Journal of Environmental Education* 9 (1978): 10–19.

33. Cotgrove, *Catastrophe or Cornucopia*, p. 31. On the matter of Cotgrove misreporting Dunlap and Van Liere's data, Cotgrove (p. 31) claims that he is quoting the environmentalists' agreement or disagreement percentages for various items on Dunlap and Van Liere's "New Environmentalism Paradigm (NEP) Scale"—which includes items like "mankind was created to rule over the rest of nature" and "plants and animals exist primarily to be used by humans"—when in fact he is reporting the general public's significantly lower percentages.

It is important to make some further comments on Cotgrove's research not only because it represents the main quantitatively based research on environmentalism to have come out of England but also because it makes a claim to methodological superiority that I think ought (in this instance at least) to be vigorously resisted. Although Cotgrove collects data on "environmental concern" (which he measures in terms of agreement/disagreement percentages on a scale containing items such as "global weather patterns are being upset"), his failure to include "questions on *relations* with the natural environment" (i.e., the sorts of questions asked by Dunlap and Van Liere in their new environmentalism paradigm scale, examples of which were given above) means that he pays no attention to the extent to which the "environmental concern" he measures is motivated by anthropocentric or nonanthropocentric concerns among his sample populations. This represents a remarkable omission for any major piece of empirical research on environmentalism. Moreover, such an omission gives the lie to Cotgrove's earlier methodological assertion that "the existence of any coherent environmentalist ideology or ideologies within the minds of identifiable groups of environmentalists can *only* be discovered by empirical research among the membership" (pp. 10–11, my emphasis). Rather than vindicating the power of quantitative social research, Cotgrove's work serves to demonstrate its limitations: you can only find what you are able to measure or allow yourself to measure. Cotgrove looks for differences between environmentalists and the general public in terms of attitudes toward industrialism, science, material values, and economic values (all quite respectable sociological variables) and finds them. He does not look for differences between various kinds of environmentalists or between environmentalists and the general public with respect to the hitherto nonsociological variable of anthropocentrism and, consequently, does not find them.

It should also be added here that if Cotgrove's assertion regarding the power of empirical research is interpreted, as seems to be intended, along positivist lines as endorsing quantitative research over other forms of research, then it overlooks the fact that the close, qualitative analysis of what representative environmentalists say or write—such as is undertaken by historians, philosophers, and social commentators—is also an empirically *based* form of research even though it does not employ *quantitative* techniques.

For an example of quantitative social research that does take the issue of anthropocentrism into account, see Lester W. Milbrath, *Environmentalists: Vanguard for a New Society* (Albany: State University of New York Press, 1984), who reports that "previous studies conducted at the Environmental Studies Center at SUNY Buffalo disclosed that one of the outstanding characteristics of ['vanguard'] environmentalists is their high valuation of nature . . . for its own sake; many of them have an almost worshipful love for it. . . . Environmentalists, much more than non-environmentalists, [were found in these studies to] have a generalized sense of compassion that extends to other species, to people in remote communities and countries, and to future generations" (pp. 26 and 28).

Having introduced the topic of quantitatively based social research on environmentalism, it is important to make one last point in conclusion. A considerable amount of this research (e.g., Dunlap and Van Liere, "The 'New Environmental Paradigm' "; Cotgrove, *Catastrophe;* Milbrath, *Environmentalists;* Arne Naess, private research, unpublished, personal discussions 1984 and 1986) demonstrates not only that environmentalists score significantly higher on environmental concern scales than other groups, including the general public, but also that there is quite a strong degree of support for environmentalist attitudes among the general public itself as well as among business, media, and political leaders. These findings have surprised some investigators, yet the kinds of comments that have been employed in order to gauge the opinion of these groups in regard to environmental concern have often been of the "motherhood is a good thing" variety, with respondents being asked to state the degree to which they agree or disagree (e.g., Dunlap and Van Liere: "The balance of nature is very delicate and easily upset"; Cotgrove: "Some animals and plants are being threatened with extinction"). In view of this, it would be surprising if the general public were *not* found to exhibit some considerable degree of environmental concern. Thus, when considering quantitative empirical research on support for environmental concern, it is important to bear in mind Lynn White's shrewd observation that he has "not discovered anyone who publicly advocates pollution. Everybody says that [they are] against it. . . . [It is just that] according to our structure of values, so many other things have *priority* over achieving a viable ecology" ("Continuing the Conversation," in *Western Man and Environmental Ethics: Attitudes Toward Nature and Technology*, at p. 56, emphasis added).

White's point is underscored by Riley Dunlap's review of American public opinion polls on environmental issues over the period from the early 1970s to 1986 ("Polls, Pollution, and Politics Revisited: Public Opinion on the Environment in the Reagan Era," *Environment*, July/August 1987, pp. 6–11 and 32–37). Dunlap's review concludes (p. 36) that while public opinion polls record widespread support for environmental issues, this support represents a "permissive consensus" (i.e., "widespread but not terribly intense public support") that does "not translate directly into pro-environment votes and political action." In other words: "public concern over basic economic conditions will typically outweigh concern about environmental quality in the ballot booth—survey responses to environment-economy tradeoffs notwithstanding!" (ibid.)

34. Leo Marx, "American Institutions and Ecological Ideals," *Science* 170 (1970): 945–52, pp. 945–46.

35. Donald Worster, *Nature's Economy: The Roots of Ecology* (1977), pp. 378 and 257.

36. Theodore Roszak, *Where the Wasteland Ends: Politics and Transcendence in Postindustrial Society* (London: Faber and Faber, 1973; originally pub., New York: Doubleday, 1972), pp. 403–4.

37. Jeremy Rifkin, in collaboration with Nicanor Perlas, *Algeny: A New Word—A New World* (Harmondsworth: Penguin, 1984; originally pub., New York: The Viking Press, 1983), p. 252.

38. Ibid., p. 251.

39. Timothy O'Riordan, *Environmentalism*, p. 1.

40. Alan R. Drengson, "Shifting Paradigms: From the Technocratic to the Person-Planetary," *Environmental Ethics* 2 (1980): 221–40; and Alan R. Drengson, *Shifting Paradigms: From Technocrat to Planetary Person* (Victoria, B.C.: LightStar Press, 1983; a thoroughly revised version has been published as *Beyond Environmental Crisis: From Technocrat to Planetary Person*). Roszak's book is *Person/Planet: The Creative Disintegration of Industrial Society*.

41. Drengson, "Shifting Paradigms," p. 237.

42. Joseph W. Meeker, "Toward a New Natural Philosophy," in *Ecological Consciousness: Essays from the Earthday X Colloquium*, ed. Robert C. Schultz and J. Donald Hughes (Washington, DC: University Press of America, 1981), pp. 251–64, at pp. 254–55.

43. Ibid., pp. 254–55.

44. Ibid.

45. This distinction can be found, for example, in Bookchin's 1974 essay "Toward an Ecological Society," published in his book of the same name, pp. 57–71; in his 1980 essay "An Open Letter to the Ecology Movement" (ibid., pp. 75–83); in his major statement of social ecology *The Ecology of Freedom: The Emergence and Dissolution of Hierarchy* (Palo Alto: Cheshire Books, 1982); and in his paper "Toward a Philosophy of Nature—The Bases for an Ecological Ethics," in *Deep Ecology*, ed. Michael Tobias (San Diego: Avant Books, 1985), pp. 213–39. In this last paper (p. 236), Bookchin notes that his "distinction between 'environmentalism' and ecology—more precisely, social ecology" was initially put forward in a lecture delivered at the University of Michigan, Ann Arbor, in the spring of 1973.

46. Bookchin, *Toward an Ecological Society*, p. 76.

47. Bookchin, *The Ecology of Freedom*, p. 21.

48. Bookchin, *Toward an Ecological Society*, p. 59.

49. Murray Bookchin, interview, "What is Social Ecology?" *Alternatives* 12(3/4) (1985): 62–65, p. 62. Although Bookchin is referring to *social ecology* in the interview from which this quotation is taken, he makes essentially identical points in regard to his understanding of *ecology* (as opposed to *environmentalism*) in his essay "Toward an Ecological Society."

50. Worster, *Nature's Economy*, p. 192.

51. Stephen Toulmin, *The Return to Cosmology: Postmodern Science and the*

Theology of Nature (Berkeley: University of California Press, 1982), p. 272.

52. Ibid., p. 271.

53. Joseph Grange, "On the Way Towards Foundational Ecology," *Soundings* 60 (1977): 135–49, p. 136.

54. Ibid., pp. 146–48.

55. John Rodman, "Four Forms of Ecological Consciousness Reconsidered." For an earlier presentation of this typology, see John Rodman, "Theory and Practice in the Environmental Movement: Notes Towards an Ecology of Experience," in *The Search for Absolute Values in a Changing World: Proceedings of the Sixth International Conference on the Unity of the Sciences* (San Francisco: The International Cultural Foundation, 1978), pp. 45–56. In this earlier presentation, Rodman referred to the latter two currents of thought as *nature moralism* and *ecological resistance* respectively. Note that although Rodman departs from the practice of the other authors whose typologies I have presented in capitalizing the descriptive labels he gives to his distinctions, for the sake of consistency within the present work, I have not retained this practice.

56. Rodman, "Four Forms of Ecological Consciousness," pp. 87–88.

57. Ibid., p. 88. In referring to Rodman's earlier work, I particularly have in mind his brilliant paper "The Liberation of Nature?" *Inquiry* 20 (1977): 83–131.

58. Rodman, "Four Forms of Ecological Consciousness," p. 88.

59. David Pepper, *The Roots of Modern Environmentalism*; David Seamon, "The Phenomenological Contribution to Environmental Psychology," *Journal of Environmental Psychology* 2 (1982): 119–40, see p. 135. Seamon also mentions Grange's distinction in some of his other work, e.g., see his review of Edward Relph's *Rational Landscapes and Humanistic Geography* in *Environmental Ethics* 5 (1983): 181–83. Neil Evernden, *The Natural Alien: Humankind and Environment*, see pp. 68–69. George Sessions, *Ecophilosophy* II, May 1979, see pp. 37–41; and George Sessions, "Shallow and Deep Ecology: A Review of the Philosophical Literature," see pp. 400–402 and 440–41.

60. For examples of writers who have taken up Bookchin's term *social ecology*, see back issues of *Harbinger: The Journal of Social Ecology* (which is the journal of Bookchin's Institute for Social Ecology in

Plainfield, Vermont); John Clark: *The Anarchist Moment: Reflections on Culture, Nature and Power* (Montreal: Black Rose Books, 1984), especially his essay "The Social Ecology of Murray Bookchin" (ch. 9); and John Clark, ed., *Renewing the Earth: Writings on Social Ecology in Honor of Murray Bookchin* (Basingstoke, Hampshire: Green Print, forthcoming), especially Clark's introductory essay (a preview of this essay has been published under the title "What is Social Ecology?," in *The Trumpeter* 5 [1988]: 72–75).

61. Robyn Eckersley, "Divining Evolution: The Ecological Ethics of Murray Bookchin," *Environmental Ethics* 11 (1989): 99–116. For other attempts to pin down the central elements in Bookchin's views and subject them to critical scrutiny, see R. Wills Flowers, "Of Old Wine in New Bottles: Taking Up Bookchin's Challenge," *Earth First!* 1 November 1987, pp. 18–19; and the brief comments on Bookchin's approach in my paper "The Deep Ecology-Ecofeminism Debate and its Parallels," see esp. pp. 15–16.

62. Murray Bookchin, "Social Ecology Versus 'Deep Ecology': A Challenge for the Ecology Movement," *Green Perspectives: Newsletter of the Green Program Project,* Summer 1987, pp. 1–23. I convey some of the flavor of Bookchin's attack on deep ecology in chapter 2.

63. "The Shallow and the Deep, Long-Range Ecology Movement: A Summary." This paper is a summary of an introductory lecture delivered at the "3rd World Future Research Conference" held in Bucharest, Rumania, 3–10 September 1972. In a note to his *Inquiry* summary, Naess stated (p. 95) that "the lecture itself will be published as part of the Proceedings of the meeting." However, Naess has since informed me that "political turmoil resulted in no proceedings as far as I know. I had only one copy of the lecture, which I left with my unfortunate friends in Bucharest. One of them planned to make a book on my philosophy, but gave up" (personal correspondence, 6 December 1985). Thus, for all practical purposes, Naess's summary of his original paper in *Inquiry* can be taken as representing the introduction of his shallow/deep distinction.

CHAPTER 2: DEEP ECOLOGY

1. I will be referring to many papers either on or related to deep ecology from *Environmental Ethics* and other academic philosophical

journals in the course of this and subsequent chapters. For now, however, a good example of the influence of deep ecology on ecophilosophical contributions to "other academic philosophical journals" (i.e., other than *Environmental Ethics*) is provided by the Winter-Spring 1986 (vol. 8) issue of the general philosophical journal *Philosophical Inquiry*, since that is a special issue devoted to ecology and philosophy. In that issue alone, the papers by Robin Attfield, Andrew Brennan, Alan Drengson, Hwa Jol Jung, and Arne Naess all either develop their arguments in dialogue with ideas that they explicitly associate with deep ecology or else are themselves primarily devoted to the explication of deep ecology.

In regard to the influence of deep ecology on recent ecophilosophical books, the following books, in addition to this one, are explicitly devoted to the presentation and development of the ideas associated with deep ecology: Alan R. Drengson, *Beyond Environmental Crisis: From Technocrat to Planetary Person;* Bill Devall and George Sessions, *Deep Ecology: Living as if Nature Mattered;* Bill Devall, *Simple in Means, Rich in Ends: Practicing Deep Ecology;* Dolores LaChapelle, *Sacred Land, Sacred Sex: Rapture of the Deep* (Silverton, Colorado: Way of the Mountain Learning Center, 1988); John Seed, Joanna Macy, Pat Fleming, and Arne Naess, *Thinking Like a Mountain: Towards a Council of All Beings* (Philadelphia/Santa Cruz: New Society Publishers, 1988); and Arne Naess, *Ecology, Community and Lifestyle: Outline of an Ecosophy.*

Deep ecology is also discussed in a number of other notable book-length contributions to ecophilosophy. See, for example, Robin Attfield, *The Ethics of Environmental Concern;* Neil Evernden, *The Natural Alien: Humankind and Environment:* and Andrew Brennan, *Thinking About Nature: An Investigation of Nature, Value, and Ecology.*

Deep ecology also features in the introductions and contributions to edited ecophilosophical collections such as Robert C. Schultz and J. Donald Hughes's *Ecological Consciousness: Essays from the Earthday X Colloquium* (Washington, DC: University Press of America, 1981; see the essay by Dolores LaChapelle and the substantial, shallow/deep ecology based review of the ecophilosophical literature by George Sessions); Tom Regan's *All That Dwell Therein: Animal Rights and Environmental Ethics* (Berkeley: University of California Press, 1982; see the essay by Regan that dwells at ch. 10 therein); Neil Evernden's *The Paradox of Environmentalism*

(Downsview, Ont.: Faculty of Environmental Studies, York University, 1984; see the contributions by Evernden, Naess, and John Livingston); and Michael Tobias's *Deep Ecology* (San Diego: Avant Books, 1985; see the contributions by Naess and Sessions). Since Tobias's book bears the same title as the book by Devall and Sessions, who are two of the main writers on deep ecology, it is important to note that the title of Tobias's collection is misleading since only a few of the contributors to it are specifically associated with the deep ecology approach to ecophilosophy—indeed, one of its contributors is Murray Bookchin, who has recently made his contempt for deep ecology quite clear. Tobias originally intended to call his collection "Humanity and Radical Will"; however, over the course of the several years that it took for this volume to be published that title was dropped in favor of *Deep Ecology* (LaChapelle has some very critical things to say about the genesis of Tobias's anthology in *Sacred Land, Sacred Sex,* see pp. 14–15).

Finally, as one might expect, deep ecology is also given considerable attention in the three major recent overviews of the ecophilosophical literature: Donald E. Davis, *Ecophilosophy: A Field Guide to the Literature*; Eric Katz, "Environmental Ethics: A Select Annotated Bibliography, 1983–87"; and Roderick F. Nash, *The Rights of Nature: A History of Environmental Ethics.*

2. George Sessions (Philosophy Department, Sierra College, Rocklin, CA, U.S.A. 95677) issued editions I–VI of *Ecophilosophy* in April 1976, 14 pp.; May 1979, 48 pp.; April 1981, 20 pp.; May 1982, 34 pp.; May 1983, 24 pp.; and May 1984, 20 pp. These newsletters were privately distributed within the ecophilosophy community.

3. John Passmore, *Man's Responsibility for Nature: Ecological Problems and Western Traditions*, p. 220.

4. Information on *The Trumpeter* can be obtained by writing to its editor, Alan Drengson, a professor of philosophy at the University of Victoria, British Columbia, at this address: *The Trumpeter,* P.O. Box 5853 Stn. B, Victoria, B.C., Canada V8R 6S8. Although I refer in the course of this book to virtually all the major articles specifically devoted to deep ecology that have appeared in *The Trumpeter,* readers who consult back issues of this journal will still find a number of miscellaneous articles on deep ecology that are not referred to herein.

5. The following papers criticize deep ecology from ecofeminist points of view: Ariel Kay Salleh, "Deeper than Deep Ecology: The Eco-Feminist Connection," *Environmental Ethics* 6 (1984): 339–45; Janet Biehl, "It's Deep, But is it Broad? An Eco-Feminist Looks at Deep Ecology," *Kick it Over*, Winter 1987, pp. 2a–4a (reprinted as "Deep Ignorance," *Green Line*, February 1988, pp. 12–14, and March 1988, pp. 15–16); Jim Cheney, "Eco-Feminism and Deep Ecology," *Environmental Ethics* 9 (1987): 115–45; Marti Kheel, "Ecofeminism and Deep Ecology: Reflections on Identity and Difference," paper presented to the conference on "Ecofeminist Perspectives: Culture, Nature, and Theory," University of Southern California, 27–29 March 1987; and Jennifer Sells, "An Eco-Feminist Critique of Deep Ecology: A Question of Social Ethics," 1988, ms.

For critical discussions of these and other ecofeminist critiques of deep ecology, see Michael E. Zimmerman, "Feminism, Deep Ecology, and Environmental Ethics"; and Warwick Fox, "The Deep Ecology–Ecofeminism Debate and its Parallels."

Other writers informed by both ecological and feminist perspectives find it useful to make at least passing reference to deep ecology in the elaboration of their views. See, for example, Fritjof Capra, *The Turning Point: Science, Society, and the Rising Culture* (New York: Bantam Books, 1983), ch. 12; Don E. Marietta, "Environmentalism, Feminism, and the Future of American Society," *The Humanist,* May-June 1984, pp. 15–18 and 30; Don Davis, "Ecosophy: The Seduction of Sophia?" *Environmental Ethics* 8 (1986): 151–62; Charlene Spretnak, "The Spiritual Dimension of Green Politics," appendix C in Charlene Spretnak and Fritjof Capra, *Green Politics: The Global Promise*; and Patsy Hallen, "Making Peace with Nature: Why Ecology Needs Feminism," *The Trumpeter* 4(3) (1987): 3–14.

The point of the preceding list of references is simply to establish the influence that deep ecology has had on ecofeminist thinking, not to provide a comprehensive guide to the ecofeminist literature. Even so, the works just cited collectively reference most of the ecologically oriented feminist literature and thus can be referred to for a fairly comprehensive guide to that literature. It would also be helpful to place the following on this "initial consultation" list: Marti Kheel, "The Liberation of Nature: A Circular Affair," *Environmental Ethics* 7 (1985): 135–49; Karen J. Warren, "Feminism and Ecology: Making Connections"; and Judith Plant, ed., *Healing the Wounds: The Promise of Ecofeminism* (Philadelphia/Santa Cruz: New Society Publishers, 1989).

6. See the prefaces to the second editions of John Passmore's *Man's Responsibility for Nature: Ecological Problems and Western Traditions* and Donald Worster's *Nature's Economy: The Roots of Ecology*.

7. I have already referred to various ecofeminist critiques of deep ecology, and have myself responded to these critiques at some length in *Environmental Ethics*. In the survey that follows, then, I will, for the sake of illustration, confine my attention to a range of other critiques of deep ecology.

8. William Grey, "A Critique of Deep Ecology," *Journal of Applied Philosophy* 3 (1986): 211–16. Alan Drengson has responded to Grey's critique in "A Critique of Deep Ecology?: Response to William Grey," *Journal of Applied Philosophy* 4 (1987): 223–27.

9. Grey, "A Critique of Deep Ecology," p. 215.

10. Richard Watson, "A Critique of Anti-Anthropocentric Biocentrism," *Environmental Ethics* 5 (1983): 245–56, p. 251. Arne Naess has responded to Watson's critique in "A Defence of the Deep Ecology Movement," *Environmental Ethics* 6 (1984): 265–70.

11. Richard Watson, "A Note on Deep Ecology," *Environmental Ethics* 6 (1984): 377–79.

12. Richard Watson, "Eco-Ethics: Challenging the Underlying Dogmas of Environmentalism," *Whole Earth Review*, March 1985, pp. 5–13, at pp. 10 and 13.

13. Isaac Asimov, *Asimov's New Guide to Science* rev. ed. (Harmondsworth, Middlesex: Penguin Books, 1987), p. 743. A good example of a woman's view that fully supports Asimov's view (or at least my modification of Asimov's view) is Leslie Lyon, "Love Your Mother—Don't Become One," *Earth First!*, 1 August 1989, p. 28.

14. Alston Chase, *Playing God in Yellowstone: The Destruction of America's First National Park* (Boston: The Atlantic Monthly Press, 1986), pp. 372–73.

15. Dave Foreman, Doug Peacock, and George Sessions have each responded to Chase's critique in "Who's 'Playing God in Yellowstone?': A Tripartite Review of the Alston Chase/Yellowstone National Park Controversy," *Earth First!*, 21 December 1986, pp.

18−21. The quotation from Peacock is from p. 18. For a corrective to Chase's distorted view of deep ecology in regard to the question of "hands-on" versus "hands-off" wildlife management, see Sessions's *Earth First!* response, and Bill Devall and George Sessions, "The Development of Natural Resources and the Integrity of Nature," *Environmental Ethics* 6 (1984): 293−322.

16. Barry S. Allen, review of *Playing God in Yellowstone* in *Environmental Review* 11 (1987): 76−78, at p. 78.

17. Sessions, "Who's 'Playing God in Yellowstone?,' " p. 20.

18. Henryk Skolimowski, "The Dogma of Anti-Anthropocentrism and Ecophilosophy," *Environmental Ethics* 6 (1984): 283−88, pp. 283 and 288. This critique was written in response to a review by George Sessions of Skolimowski's *Eco-Philosophy: Designing New Tactics for Living.* In that review (*Environmental Ethics* 6 [1984]: 167−74), Sessions took Skolimowski to task for the anthropocentrism inherent in Skolimowski's approach to ecophilosophy. Skolimowski has since become a regular critic of deep ecology. His subsequent critiques include: "In Defense of Ecophilosophy and of Intrinsic Value: A Call for Conceptual Clarity," *The Trumpeter* 3(4) (1986): 9−12; "To Continue the Dialogue with Deep Ecology," *The Trumpeter* 4(4) (1987): 31−32; and "Eco-Philosophy and Deep Ecology," *The Ecologist* 18 (1988): 124−27.

For responses to Skolimowski's "In Defense of Ecophilosophy," see the following in *The Trumpeter* 3(4) (1986): Bill Devall, "Reply to Skolimowski," pp. 15−16; Warwick Fox, "Post-Skolimowski Reflections on Deep Ecology," pp. 16−18; and Arne Naess, "Deep Ecology in Good Conceptual Health," pp. 18−21. For a response to Skolimowski's "To Continue the Dialogue," see my "Further Notes in Response to Skolimowski," *The Trumpeter* 4(4) (1987): 32−34, in which, among other things, I defend Sessions's reading of Skolimowski; see also my critical remarks in "The Deep Ecology−Ecofeminism Debate and its Parallels" concerning Skolimowski's suggestion in this paper that deep ecologists are misanthropic. Finally, for a response to Skolimowski's "Eco-Philosophy and Deep Ecology," see Arne Naess, "Deep Ecology and Ultimate Premises," *The Ecologist* 18 (1988): 128−31.

19. Murray Bookchin, "Social Ecology Versus 'Deep Ecology': A Challenge for the Ecology Movement," *Green Perspectives: Newsletter of*

the Green Program Project, Summer 1987, pp. 1–23, pp. 11 and 23. Available from P.O. Box 111, Burlington, VT, U.S.A. 05402.

20. Ibid., pp. 3–5, 10, and 13–14. For direct responses to Bookchin's critique, see R. Wills Flowers, "Of Old Wine in New Bottles: Taking up Bookchin's Challenge," *Earth First!,* 1 November 1987, pp. 18–19; Chim Blea "Why the Venom?" ibid., p. 19; Bill Devall, "Deep Ecology and its Critics," *Earth First!,* 22 December 1987, pp. 18–20 (a shortened version of this response is reprinted under the same title in *The Trumpeter* 5[2] [1988]: 55–60); Kirkpatrick Sale, "Deep Ecology and Its Critics," *The Nation,* 14 May 1988, pp. 670–75; and George Sessions, "Ecocentrism and the Greens: Deep Ecology and the Environmental Task," *The Trumpeter* 5(2) (1988): 65–69. I criticize the basic structure of Bookchin's argument for what he terms *social ecology* in "The Deep Ecology–Ecofeminism Debate and its Parallels." Robyn Eckersley criticizes fundamental features of Bookchin's general views at greater length in her paper "Divining Evolution: The Ecological Ethics of Murray Bookchin," *Environmental Ethics* 11 (1989): 99–116.

21. Richard Sylvan, *A Critique of Deep Ecology,* Discussion Papers in Environmental Philosophy no. 12 (Canberra: Depts. of Philosophy, Australian National University, 1985), pp. 1, 2, 12, and 29. Sylvan's monograph has also been published in two parts in the British journal *Radical Philosophy* 40 (1985): 2–12 and 41 (1985): 10–22. The most comprehensive response to Sylvan's critique is my monograph *Approaching Deep Ecology: A Response to Richard Sylvan's Critique of Deep Ecology,* Environmental Studies Occasional Paper no. 20 (Hobart: Centre for Environmental Studies, University of Tasmania, 1986). Arne Naess has also written two brief responses—one to the final version of Sylvan's critique ("Notes on Professor Sylvan's *Critique of the Deep Ecology Movement,*" 1985, ms.) and one to an earlier, privately distributed version of Sylvan's critique ("Deep Ecology Disentangled?" 1984, ms.).

Robin Attfield has written a critical review of the debate between Sylvan and myself ("Deep Ecology: A View from the Continental Shelf," paper presented to the British Society for Applied Philosophy, 24 May 1986) in which he accepts (p. 8), despite his own disagreements with deep ecology, that "Fox's remarks tally with my own, admittedly less exhaustive, reading of the literature" and that "Sylvan has," as I claim in my *Approaching Deep Ecology,* "mistaken the main emphases of deep ecology." For other, less detailed comments on Sylvan's critique and my reply, see Donald E. Davis, *Ecophilosophy: A Field Guide to the Literature* (San Pedro: R. and E. Miles, 1989), p. 43; and Eric Katz, "Environmental Ethics: A Select Annotated Bibliography, 1983–87," *Research in Philosophy and Technology* 9 (1989): 251–85, pp. 268–69 and 273–74.

I defend my endorsement of the view referred to in the last quotation from Sylvan, which concerns the implications of quantum theory for our vision of reality, in the fourth part of my *Approaching Deep Ecology*.

22. For yet other critical discussions of deep ecology, see P. S. Elder, "Legal Rights for Nature—The Wrong Answer to the Right(s) Question," *Osgoode Hall Law Journal* 22 (1984): 285–95; George Bradford, "How Deep is Deep Ecology: A Challenge to Radical Environmentalism," *Fifth Estate,* Fall 1987, pp. 5–30; Tim Luke, "The Dreams of Deep Ecology," *Telos,* no. 76 (1988): 65–92; Brian Tokar, "Exploring the New Ecologies: Social Ecology, Deep Ecology and the Future of Green Political Thought," *Alternatives* 15(4) (1988): 30–43 (see the letters section of *Alternatives* 16[2] and 16[3] [1989] for responses to Tokar's article); Brian Tokar, "Ecological Radicalism," *Z,* December 1988, pp. 84–91; the papers by various authors in the "special 'deep ecology' issue" of *The Ecologist* 18 (1988), no. 4/5; George Bradford, "Return of the Son of Deep Ecology: The Ethics of Permanent Crisis and the Permanent Crisis in Ethics," *Fifth Estate,* Spring 1989, pp. 5–32; Andrew Dobson, "Deep Ecology," *Cogito,* Spring 1989, pp. 41–46; Ramachandra Guha, "Radical American Environmentalism and Wilderness Preservation: A Third World Critique," *Environmental Ethics* 11 (1989): 71–83; Lewis P. Hinchman and Sandra K. Hinchman, "Deep Ecology' and the Revival of Natural Right," *Western Political Quarterly* 42 (1989) 201–28; and Jim Cheney, "The Neo-Stoicism of Radical Environmentalism," *Environmental Ethics* 11 (1989): 293–325. (I responded to a prepublication version of Cheney's "Neo-Stoicism" paper in my paper "The Deep Ecology–Ecofeminism Debate and its Parallels.")

23. Paul R. Ehrlich, *The Machinery of Nature: The Living World Around Us—and How it Works,* pp. 17–18.

In regard to the influence of deep ecology upon other professional ecologists, see, for example, Frank B. Golley, "Deep Ecology from the Perspective of Ecological Science," *Environmental Ethics* 9 (1987): 45–55 (reprinted in *The Trumpeter* 6 [1989]: 24–29); and articles by ecologists (such as Reed Noss) that appear from time to time in the deep ecology influenced, activist oriented journal *Earth First!* Something of the growing significance in scientific ecology circles of the ideas associated with deep ecology is also indicated by the fact that the keynote address delivered to the "Second International Conference on Conservation Biology," held at the University of Michigan in May 1985, was delivered not by a biologist or ecologist but by the deep ecology ecophilosopher Arne Naess: see Arne Naess, "Intrinsic Value: Will the Defenders of Nature Please Rise?" in *Conservation Biology: The Science of Scarcity and Diversity*, ed. Michael, E. Soule (Sunderland, Massachusetts: Sinauer Associates, 1986), pp. 504–15.

It should also be noted that other ecologists have put forward views that have much in common with the spirit of deep ecology even if they do not necessarily refer to deep ecology explicitly. See, for example, the following by the naturalist John A. Livingston: *One Cosmic Instant: Man's Fleeting Supremacy* (Boston: Houghton Mifflin, 1973); and *The Fallacy of Wildlife Conservation* (Toronto: McClelland and Stewart, 1981), which refers in passing to the "useful distinction" that has been drawn between shallow and deep ecology (p. 60); and the following by the human ecologist Paul S. Shepard: "Introduction: Ecology and Man—A Viewpoint," in *The Subversive Science: Essays Toward an Ecology of Man*, ed. Paul Shepard and Daniel McKinley (Boston: Houghton Mifflin, 1969), pp. 1–10; *The Tender Carnivore and the Sacred Game* (New York: Scribner's, 1973); *Thinking Animals: Animals and the Development of Human Intelligence* (New York: The Viking Press, 1978); and *Nature and Madness* (San Francisco: Sierra Club Books, 1982). In addition, particular mention should be made here of a significant work by the ecologist Charles Birch and the philosopher/theologian John B. Cobb, Jr., both of whom share a Whiteheadian, process philosophy orientation. Their book *The Liberation of Life: From the Cell to the Community* develops what is probably the most comprehensive ecologically based world-view in the literature (i.e., their book actually lives up to the promise of its subtitle, which, in this instance, is saying a lot). Supporters of deep ecology would endorse much in the metaphysical and sociopolitical aspects of Birch and

Cobb's world-view but would regard the quite specific hierarchical theory of value that Birch and Cobb derive from their metaphysics as an unnecessary and, ultimately, unhelpful burden upon the human task of making peace with nonhuman nature. For a critical overview of this book by an impressed and indebted reader see my book review article "The Liberation of Life," *The Ecologist* 14 (1984): 178–82. (Like many other Australians, I am also indebted to Birch's earlier, popular work *Confronting the Future: Australia and the World: The Next Hundred Years* [Harmondsworth, Middlesex: Penguin, 1976]. See also Charles Birch, *On Purpose* [Kensington, New South Wales: New South Wales University Press, 1990].)

24. Ehrlich, *The Machinery of Nature*, p. 18.

25. Theodore Roszak, *Where the Wasteland Ends: Politics and Transcendence in Postindustrial Society* (London: Faber and Faber, 1973; see especially the section on "Ecology and the Uses of Mysticism" in ch. 11); Theodore Roszak, *Person/Planet: The Creative Disintegration of Industrial Society;* Morris Berman, *The Reenchantment of the World* (Ithaca: Cornell University Press, 1981); and Fritjof Capra, *The Turning Point: Science, Society, and the Rising Culture* (New York: Bantam Books, 1982). Roszak does not explicitly refer to deep ecology, Berman references papers by some of the main writers on deep ecology (Naess and Devall), while Capra discusses deep ecology explicitly. For a briefer and more sociologically oriented analysis than the preceeding, see Alwyn Jones, "The Violence of Materialism in Advanced Industrial Society: An Eco-Sociological Approach," *The Sociological Review* 35 (1987): 19–47. Like Capra, Jones also concludes by explicitly endorsing deep ecology.

Other analysts of our modern, global, urban-industrial-informational culture who draw upon the shallow/deep ecology distinction in passing in their discussions include Langdon Winner, *The Whale and the Reactor: A Search for Limits in an Age of High Technology* (Chicago: The University of Chicago Press, 1986); and Patrick Rivers, *The Stolen Future: How to Rescue the Earth for Our Children* (Basingstoke, Hants: Green Print/Marshall Pickering, 1988).

26. Capra, *The Turning Point*, pp. 411–12.

27. Lynn White, Jr., "The Historical Roots of Our Ecologic Crisis," p. 30.

28. See Charlene Spretnak and Fritjof Capra, *Green Politics: The Global Promise* and Fritjof Capra and Charlene Spretnak, "Who are the

Greens?" *New Age Journal,* April 1984, pp. 34–41 and following. See also Charlene Spretnak, *The Spiritual Dimension of Green Politics* (Santa Fe: Bear and Company, 1986). (Capra has also founded The Elmwood Institute [P.O. Box 5805, Berkeley, CA, U.S.A. 94705] whose purpose is "to nurture new ecological visions." The institute has been organizing some exciting symposia and publishes a quarterly newsletter.)

Deep ecology is also either endorsed (even if sometimes only in passing) or at least discussed with considerable positive interest in other recent book-length contributions to Green politics; see, for example, Jonathon Porritt, *Seeing Green: The Politics of Ecology Explained*; Brian Tokar, *The Green Alternative: Creating an Ecological Future*; Walter and Dorothy Schwarz, *Breaking Through: Theory and Practice of Wholistic Living* (Hartland, Devon: Green Books, 1987), which devotes a chapter to deep ecology; the chapter on "The Green philosophy," which is based on contributions from Edward Goldsmith and Peter Bunyard of *The Ecologist,* David Rothenberg (a former assistant to Arne Naess), myself, and others, in *The Green Alternative: Guide to Good Living*; Jonathon Porritt and David Winner, *The Coming of the Greens*; and John Young, *Post Environmentalism.*

29. The address for *Earth First!* is P.O. Box 5871, Tucson, AZ, U.S.A. 85703; the address for *The Deep Ecologist* is c/o P.O. Birdwood, South Australia, Australia 5234.

For articles on deep ecology in the publications to which I have referred, see, for example, Joanna Macy, "Deep Ecology and the Council of All Beings," and John Seed, "Anthropocentrism," in *Awakening in the Nuclear Age Journal,* Summer/Fall 1986, pp. 6–9 and 11–13 respectively (Macy's article and accompanying "Gaia Meditations," adapted from Seed, are reprinted in *Revision,* Winter/Spring 1987, pp. 53–57); Peter Borrelli, "The Ecophilosophers," *The Amicus Journal,* Spring 1988, pp. 30–39; and Arne Naess, interviewed by Stephan Bodian, "Simple in Means, Rich in Ends: A Conversation with Arne Naess," *The Ten Directions,* Summer/Fall 1982, pp. 7 and 10–12.

From *Resurgence* (and *Holistic Human Concern for World Welfare*), see Bill Devall and George Sessions, "Deep Ecology" (extracts from their book of the same name), November/December 1985, pp. 18–21; Warwick Fox, "Living as if Nature Mattered" (a review of

Devall and Sessions's book), January/February 1986, pp. 41–42 (reprinted in *Holistic Human Concern for World Welfare*, ed. A. Kannan [Adyar, Madras: The Theosophical Society, 1987], pp. 39–40); Arne Naess, "Deep Ecology" (extracts from his *Ten Directions* interview), July/August 1987, p. 13; Joanna Macy, "Faith and Ecology," July/August 1987, pp. 18–21; and Arne Naess, "The Basics of Deep Ecology" (Naess's 1987 Schumacher Lecture), January/February 1988, pp. 4–7.

From *The Ecologist*, see Warwick Fox, "Deep Ecology: A New Philosophy of our Time?," *The Ecologist* 14 (1984): 194–200; Arne Naess, "Intuition, Intrinsic Value and Deep Ecology," *The Ecologist* 14 (1984): 201–3; Warwick Fox, "On Guiding Stars to Deep Ecology," *The Ecologist* 14 (1984): 203–4; and *The Ecologist* 18 (1988), no. 4/5, which is a special issue devoted to discussion of deep ecology (see especially Arne Naess's article "Deep Ecology and Ultimate Premises," pp. 128–31).

From *Habitat Australia*, see William Godfrey-Smith, "Environmental Philosophy," June 1980, pp. 24–25; John Seed, "Plumbing Deep Ecology," June 1982, pp. 27–28; Penny van Oosterzee, "More About Deep Ecology," December 1982, pp. 11–12; John Martin, "Making a Start in Deep Ecology," February 1983, pp. 10–12; Warwick Fox, "Towards a Deeper Ecology," August 1985, pp. 26–28; Freya Mathews, "Plumbing Deep Ecology," April 1986, p. 25; and Freya Mathews, "Deep Ecology: Where All Things are Connected," October 1988, pp. 9–12.

30. See Capra and Spretnak, "Who are the Greens?" *New Age Journal*, April 1984, pp. 34–41 and following; Richard Watson, "Eco-Ethics: Challenging the Underlying Dogmas of Environmentalism" *Whole Earth Review*, March 1985, pp. 5–13; Tanya Kucak, "Deep Ecology," *Yoga Journal*, September/October 1986, pp. 32–37 and 49; interview with John Seed, *Yoga Journal*, November/December 1989 (no further details at the time of revising); Kirkpatrick Sale, "The Forest for the Trees: Can Today's Environmentalists Tell the Difference?" *Mother Jones*, November 1986, pp. 25–33 and 58; Dave Foreman, interviewed by Bill Devall, "A Spanner in the Woods," *Simply Living*, vol. 2, no. 12, n.d., pp. 40–43; Kirkpatrick Sale, "Deep Ecology and Its Critics," *The Nation*, 14 May 1988, pp. 670–75; John Seed, interviewed by Pat Stone, "John Seed and the Council of All Beings," *Mother Earth News*, May/June

1989, pp. 58–63; Richard Hill, "Ecology Wars," *Omni*, August 1989, p. 25; Melanie Stephens, "The Green Party," *Arete*, September/October 1989, pp. 14–15; and Alston Chase, "The Great, Green Deep-Ecology Revolution," *Rolling Stone*, 23 April 1987, pp. 61–64 and following. (It is interesting to note that Chase is considerably less critical of deep ecologists in his *Rolling Stone* article than in his earlier book *Playing God in Yellowstone*.)

31. See Daniel J. Kevles, "Paradise Lost" (review of *The End of Nature*, by Bill McKibben, and *Global Warming: Are We Entering the Greenhouse Century?*, by Stephen H. Schneider), *The New York Review of Books*, 21 December 1989, pp. 32–38.

32. R. Wills Flowers, "Of Old Wine in New Bottles: Taking up Bookchin's Challenge," *Earth First!*, 1 November 1987, pp. 18–19, at p. 18. The 1985 publication of Devall and Sessions's *Deep Ecology*, written for a general audience, has no doubt contributed much to the recent popular notice that deep ecology has received.

33. John Passmore, "Political Ecology: Responsibility and Environmental Power," *The Age Monthly Review*, February 1983, pp. 15–16, at p. 15. (Passmore is especially well-known for his overview of modern philosophy entitled *A Hundred Years of Philosophy* [Harmondsworth, Middlesex: Penguin, 1968].)

CHAPTER 3: WHY SO INFLUENTIAL?

1. Recall that Lynn White's controversial paper "The Historical Roots of Our Ecologic Crisis" was published in *Science* (155: 1203–7) in 1967. Other well-known and likewise controversial ecophilosophically relevant papers published in *Science* in the period under consideration include Garrett Hardin, "The Tragedy of the Commons," *Science* 162 (1968): 1243–48; and Martin H. Krieger, "What's Wrong with Plastic Trees?," *Science* 179 (1973): 446–55. Somewhat less well-known (but still subsequently anthologized) ecophilosophically relevant papers published in *Science* during this general period include Daniel Callahan, "Ethics and Population Limitation," *Science* 175 (1972): 487–94; and W. H. Murdy, "Anthropocentrism: A Modern Version," *Science* 187 (1975): 1168–72.

2. Theodore Roszak, *Where the Wasteland Ends: Politics and Transcendence in Postindustrial Society* (New York: Doubleday, 1972).

3. In regard to the cited list of distinctions, the dates I have given both here and in chapter 1 refer, with one exception, to the earliest known dates of publication in books or journals that are available (at least in theory) to ecophilosophers internationally through university libraries or personal subscription. The one exception is Meeker's distinction, which I have dated here to 1980 rather than to its publication in 1981, since it was originally presented in April 1980 to one of the major ecophilosophy conferences to have been held in the United States to that time—the Earthday X Colloquium. I do not, of course, intend to suggest that the writers referred to in this list may not have developed their distinctions and discussed them informally, presented them in lectures, or published them in formats that the international ecophilosophy community could not be expected to have heard about (such as local magazines) some time before the dates that I have given for each distinction. The other side of this, however, is that writers who claim to have developed their distinctions some time before the dates I have listed can hardly complain that the international ecophilosophy community has done them an injustice if they failed to see to the publication of their typology in a format that was available to this community. Moreover, to cry foul on this basis (i.e., that it is *unfair* that their typology wasn't widely adopted instead of Naess's since their typology was the earlier of the two) would in any case be to subscribe to the myth that the widespread acceptance of Naess's shallow/deep ecology typology *is* a function of historical precedence.

4. Alan Drengson, "Shifting Paradigms: From the Technocratic to the Person-Planetary," *Environmental Ethics* 2 (1980): 221–40; and Alan Drengson, *Shifting Paradigms: From Technocrat to Planetary Person* (Victoria, B.C.: LightStar Press, 1983; see also the thoroughly revised version, *Beyond Environmental Crisis: From Technocrat to Planetary Person*).

5. George Sessions, *Ecophilosophy I,* 1976, see pp. 3–4 and 10.

6. Around the end of 1985, I asked Devall and Sessions if they could each furnish me with an informal, intellectual history of the paths they had followed to the present stage of their work on deep ecology. I am extremely grateful to them for their generous

NOTES TO PAGES 62–63 ∘ 327

responses (Devall, personal correspondence with the author, 2 February 1986; Sessions, personal correspondence with the author, 21 January 1986). What follows is based on this correspondence as well as other sources acknowledged below; quotations that are not referenced are taken from this correspondence.

The only other account of the background to Devall's and Sessions's successful advocacy of Naess's work of which I am aware is contained in Dolores LaChapelle's *Sacred Land, Sacred Sex: Rapture of the Deep* (Silverton, Colo.: Finn Hill Arts, 1988); see pp. 10–15. Neither LaChapelle nor I were aware of each other's accounts at the time we wrote them. Some of the parallels between our accounts are due to the fact that LaChapelle has also had access to the informal, intellectual history by Sessions to which I have referred.

7. George Sessions, "Anthropocentrism and the Environmental Crisis."

8. George Sessions, "Panpsychism versus Modern Materialism: Some Implications for an Ecological Ethics," revised and expanded version of a paper presented to the conference on "The Rights of Nonhuman Nature," Pitzer College, Claremont, Calif., 18–20 April 1974.

9. For the proceedings of this conference, see Jon Wetlesen, ed., *Spinoza's Philosophy of Man: Proceedings of the Scandinavian Spinoza Symposium 1977* (Oslo: Oslo University Press, 1978).

10. George Sessions, "Spinoza and Jeffers on Man in Nature." Sessions's interest in the Californian poet Robinson Jeffers should come as no surprise for at least two reasons. First, as Sessions notes in his paper, Jeffers has been described as "Spinoza's twentieth century evangelist." Sessions notes that this phrase comes from Arthur B. Coffin, *Robinson Jeffers: Poet of Inhumanism* (Madison, Wisconsin: University of Wisconsin Press, 1971), p. 255, and comments that it was this claim that "initially drew my attention to the possibilities of parallels between Spinoza and Jeffers" (p. 527). *Inhumanism* was Jeffers's term for his scientifically informed pantheistic philosophy. The term is misleading, however, if it suggests that Jeffers's approach was an *anti*-human one; rather, his approach was a nonanthropocentric, cosmological one. Jeffers makes this point clearly in the preface to his collection *The Double Axe and Other Poems* [New York: Liveright, 1977], p. xxi.)

A second reason for Sessions's interest in Jeffers must also be that Jeffers's poetry had served as a great inspiration to David Brower, who, remember, had himself served as a great inspiration to Sessions. Not only had Brower edited a beautiful book entitled *Not Man Apart: Lines From Robinson Jeffers* (San Francisco: Sierra Club, 1965), which placed Jeffers's poetry alongside photographs of the Big Sur coast by Ansel Adams and others, but Brower's new group, Friends of the Earth, had also adopted Jeffers's phrase "not man apart" as its motto and the name of its journal.

11. As previously noted, however, Sessions had also referenced this paper in his 1976 *Ecophilosophy* newsletter. Sessions also pointed out in that newsletter that Naess's paper had been reprinted in P. Struhl and K. Struhl, *Philosophy Now,* 2nd ed. (New York: Random House, 1975), pp. 599–604.

12. Sessions, "Spinoza and Jeffers on Man in Nature," p. 526.

13. George Sessions, *Ecophilosophy II*, 1979, p. 29.

14. See, for example, W. B. Devall, "Conservation: An Upper-Middle Class Social Movement: A Replication," *Journal of Leisure Research* 2 (1970): 123–26; Bill Devall, "Redwood National Park: The Clearcutting of a Dream," *Humboldt Journal of Social Relations* 2 (1974): 82–91; and William B. Devall, "The Forest Service and its Clients: Input to Forest Service Decision-Making," *Environmental Affairs* 3 (1975): 732–57.

15. Sessions, *Ecophilosophy II*, p. 4.

16. Bill Devall, "Currents in the River of Environmentalism," *Econews,* April 1977, p. 9.

17. Sessions, *Ecophilosophy II*, p. 2.

18. William B. Devall, "Reformist Environmentalism," *Humboldt Journal of Social Relations* 6 (1979): 129–58; and Bill Devall, "The Deep Ecology Movement."

19. George Sessions, "Spinoza, Perennial Philosophy and Deep Ecology," paper presented to the "Reminding" national conference, Dominican College, San Raphael, Calif., 29 June–4 July 1979. In the opening paragraph of this paper, Sessions describes this conference as "the first national conference to invite academic philosophy back into our lives as spiritual and practical guidance."

20. Sessions had been strongly influenced by both Needleman's *A Sense of the Cosmos: The Encounter of Modern Science and Ancient Truth* (New

York: Doubleday, 1975) and Roszak's *Where the Wasteland Ends*. The respected physicist David Bohm subsequently set out his ideas of explicate and implicate orders of reality (using holography as one kind of model for these ideas), in *Wholeness and the Implicate Order* (London: Routledge and Kegan Paul, 1980). For a critique of Bohm's (and related) ideas from the kind of perspective that Sessions has in mind, see Morris Berman, "The Cybernetic Dream of the Twenty-First Century," *Journal of Humanistic Psychology* 26 (1986): 24–51.

21. George Sessions, "Shallow and Deep Ecology: A Review of the Philosophical Literature."

22. See Drengson, "Shifting Paradigms"; and Dolores LaChapelle, "Systemic Thinking and Deep Ecology," in *Ecological Consciousness*, ed. Schultz and Hughes, pp. 295–323.

23. John Passmore, "Political Ecology: Responsibility and Environmental Power," *The Age Monthly Review*, February 1983, pp. 15–16, at p. 15.

24. Alston Chase, "The Great, Green Deep-Ecology Revolution," *Rolling Stone*, 23 April 1987, pp. 61–64 and following, at p. 62.

25. As with any list that simplifies and fixes what is in fact a complex and changing scene, this list of contributors to the positive articulation of deep ecology ideas is bound to meet with objections, in terms of both who is included and who is excluded. The compilation of such a list necessarily means that complex, genuinely multidimensional questions of family resemblance are reduced to a unidimensional, in-group/out-group level; shades of grey are transformed into black and white. Even so, providing such a list is still far preferable to referring to just a few of the main writers on deep ecology when one wants to be specific but always referring nebulously—as ecophilosophers often tend to do—to the deep ecologists when one wants to speak more generally. A list of this kind gives a specific substance and texture to the otherwise nebulous label *deep ecologist*.

To raise an important reservation of my own about my list of deep ecology thinkers (or, at least, thinkers that can be thought of as particularly close relatives to the main writers on deep ecology), I am well aware, for example, that the work of J. Baird Callicott— one of the most important contributors to the development of ecophilosophy in general—has a considerable amount in common

with what I take to be the essence of the deep ecology approach to
ecophilosophy. (I discuss this approach to ecophilosophy in relation
to other ecophilosophical approaches in part 4.) This similarity
means that Callicott could perhaps be included in the list for much
the same reason that Rodman is, that is, as someone who is
primarily dedicated to the elaboration of an ecophilosophical
approach that is similar to the deep ecology approach in essential
ways but who does not elaborate their approach under the name of
deep ecology (see my listing of Rodman's work in appendix A).
However, there are also some significant differences between Callicott's *favored* approach to ecophilosophy and what I have just
referred to as the essence of the deep ecology approach to ecophilosophy that lead me, at least at present, to exclude Callicott but
include Rodman. Callicott favors a sociobiologically oriented approach to ecophilosophy that draws upon the thought of Hume,
Darwin, and, especially, Aldo Leopold (author of the conservationist classic *A Sand County Alamanc* [Oxford: Oxford University Press,
1949]). For various developments of this approach (often in the
context of excellent overviews of other ecophilosophical approaches), see Callicott's papers "Non-Anthropocentric Value Theory and Environmental Ethics"; "Intrinsic Value, Quantum Theory, and Environmental Ethics," *Environmental Ethics* 7 (1985):
257–75; "On the Intrinsic Value of Nonhuman Species," in *The
Preservation of Species,* ed. Bryan G. Norton (Princeton, N.J.: Princeton University Press, 1986), pp. 138–172; "The Search for an
Environmental Ethic"; and "The Conceptual Foundations of the
Land Ethic," in *Companion to A Sand County Almanac: Interpretive
and Critical Essays,* ed. J. Baird Callicott (Madison, Wisconsin:
University of Wisconsin Press, 1987), pp. 186–217.

For critical discussions of Callicott's approach, see Warwick Fox,
"A Postscript on Deep Ecology and Intrinsic Value," *The Trumpeter*
2(4) (1985): 20–23; Michael E. Zimmerman, "Quantum Theory,
Intrinsic Value, and Pantheism," *Environmental Ethics* 10 (1988):
3–30; and the sections entitled "Objections to Intrinsic Value
Theory Approaches" and "Identification, Delusion, and Enlightenment" in chapters 6 and 8 respectively herein.

My reasons for including Rodman will become obvious in
chapter 7. However, my reason for excluding Callicott can only be
explained properly in the context of the argument that I advance
in part 4 concerning the distinctive nature of the deep ecology

approach to ecophilosophy. I therefore discuss my reasons for excluding Callicott in chapter 8. I want to reiterate, however, that, at this level, we are dealing with shades of grey. The classification of philosophers of any kind has always been an inexact science.

26. Devall and Sessions list these norms as "Self-realization"—spelled with a capital *S* for reasons we shall come to in chapter 4—and "biocentric equality." It should be noted, however, that, as we will see in chapter 4, Naess actually proposes only *one* ultimate norm for his system—the norm of "Self-realization." For Naess, the attitude of biocentric egalitarianism follows *from* this norm.

27. These two quotations are from Alston Chase, *Playing God in Yellowstone: The Destruction of America's First National Park* (Boston: Atlantic Monthly Press), p. 373, and Murray Bookchin, "Social Ecology Versus 'Deep Ecology': A Challenge for the Ecology Movement," *Green Perspectives: Newsletter of the Green Program Project,* Summer 1987, p. 3, respectively.

28. Peter R. Hay and Marcus G. Haward, "Comparative Green Politics: Beyond the European Context?," *Political Studies* 36 (1988): 433–48, p. 447.

29. Chase, "The Great, Green Deep-Ecology Revolution," p. 166.

30. Naess explicitly develops his understanding of the term *Self-realization* in the following works prior to and including 1980: "The Place of Joy in a World of Fact," *North American Review,* Summer 1973, pp. 53–57; *Gandhi and Group Conflict: An Exploration of Satyagraha: Theoretical Background* (Oslo: University of Oslo Press, 1974); *Freedom, Emotion and Self-Subsistence: The Structure of a Central Part of Spinoza's Ethics* (Oslo: University of Oslo Press, 1975); *Okologi, samfunn og livsstil* [Ecology, Community and Lifestyle], 5th ed. (Oslo: University of Oslo Press, 1976; parts of this work, including the lengthy seventh chapter in which Naess discusses his concept of Self-realization in some detail, were made available by Naess to close colleagues in an English translation); "Notes on the Methodology of Normative Systems," *Methodology and Science* 10 (1977): 64–79; "Spinoza and Ecology," which appeared in two places in 1977: *Philosophia* 7 (1977): 45–54; and *Speculum Spinozanum 1677–1977,* ed. Siegfried Hessing (London: Routledge and Kegan Paul, 1977), pp. 418–25; and "Self-realization in Mixed Communities of Humans, Bears, Sheep, and Wolves," *Inquiry* 22 (1979): 231–41. Naess also discusses ideas

that are central to his understanding of the term *Self-realization*—although without employing that precise term—in "Through Spinoza to Mahayana Buddhism or Through Mahayana Buddhism to Spinoza?," in *Spinoza's Philosophy of Man: Proceedings of the Scandinavian Spinoza Symposium 1977*, ed. Jon Wetlesen (Oslo: Oslo University Press, 1978), pp. 136–58; and "Environmental Ethics and Spinoza's Ethics: Comments on Genevieve Lloyd's Article," *Inquiry* 23 (1980): 313–25.

Naess was also giving lectures that presented his understanding of the term *Self-realization* from the early 1970s on. For example, Naess has given me a fifty-four-page typescript of lectures he delivered on "Philosophy and the Ecological Movement" to students in Hong Kong in 1972. These lecture notes present Self-realization as the starting point for his own approach to ecosophy/ecophilosophy.

For the sake of completeness, and also as an indication of the extent to which the idea of Self-realization featured in most of Naess's ecophilosophically relevant 1973–80 work, Naess's only ecophilosophically relevant publications between 1973 and 1980 that did *not* discuss ideas that are central to his understanding of the term *Self-realization* were (aside from his introductory 1973 *Inquiry* paper) two fairly minor publications: "The Ecopolitical Frontier: A Case Study," *Intecol Bulletin* (1974, no. 5): 18–26 (this paper reiterates some of the points that were contained in Naess's 1973 *Inquiry* paper, but is virtually unknown by virtue of its place of publication); and "Group Chairman's Introductory Remarks," in *The Search for Absolute Values in a Changing World*, vol. 1 (New York: The International Cultural Foundation, 1978), pp. 27–30 (even in this paper, however, Naess emphasizes that the deep ecology movement has a religious or philosophical basis, and anyone who is familiar with his work would know that the term that Naess uses to describe the philosophical basis of his own approach to ecophilosophy is *Self-realization*). Naess, incidentally, has checked this *particular* note and confirms that it represents a complete listing—in his terms, an "embarassingly complete" listing—of his ecophilosophically relevant 1973–80 work (personal correspondence with the author, 27 July 1988).

31. Devall describes deep ecology as resting on a "metaphysical-spiritual" basis in "Streams of Environmentalism," 1979, ms., pp.

17 and 38. All of Devall's and Sessions's subsequent work attests to this understanding. In regard to Devall's and Sessions's cognizance and referencing of Naess's Self-realization oriented work (as well as their employment of Naess's term *Self-realization*) from the time of their earliest work on deep ecology, see Devall, "Streams of Environmentalism," esp. notes 76 and 142; Devall, "The Deep Ecology Movement," esp. note 96; Sessions, "Spinoza, Perennial Philosophy and Deep Ecology," 1979, ms., esp. note. 67; Sessions, *Ecophilosophy II*, p. 29; and Sessions, "Shallow and Deep Ecology: A Review of the Philosophical Literature," esp. notes 13 and 39.

CHAPTER 4. ARNE NAESS AND THE MEANINGS OF *DEEP ECOLOGY*

1. Naess discusses these and other experiences, including his fascination with and love for the nonhuman world since very early childhood, his psychologically painful early years and adolescence, and his teenage thoughts on the most worthwhile thing to do in life, in a candid but rarely cited autobiographical article entitled "How My Philosophy Seemed to Develop," in *Philosophers on Their Own Work*, vol. 10, ed. Andre Mercier and Maja Svilar (Bern: Peter Lang, 1983), pp. 209–26. The quotation regarding Naess's reception by the Vienna Circle is from p. 222 of this article.

2. *The Encyclopedia of Philosophy*, s.v. "Scandinavian Philosophy," by Justus Hartnack.

3. Naess's major elaboration of his approach to semantics is *Interpretation and Preciseness: A Contribution to the Theory of Communication* (Oslo: Oslo University Press, 1953). A simpler, more popularly aimed presentation is Naess's *Communication and Argument: Elements of Applied Semantics* (Oslo: Oslo University Press, 1966, reprinted 1981). For briefer overviews of Naess's approach to semantics, see Arne Naess, "Toward a Theory of Interpretation and Preciseness," in *Semantics and the Philosophy of Language*, ed. Leonard Linsky (Urbana, Ill.: The University of Illinois Press, 1952), pp. 248–69; and Ingemund Gullvag, "Depth of Intention," *Inquiry* 26 (1983): 31–83.

4. Ingemund Gullvag, "Philosophy in Norway since 1936," *Ruch*

Filozoficzny 40 (1982–83): 143–81, pp. 143–44 and 171. As Gullvag's comments here suggest, his overview of contemporary Norwegian philosophy, while comprehensive, is nevertheless dominated by discussion of Naess's work. A briefer, less detailed overview of postwar Norwegian philosophy is provided in Arne Naess and Jon Hellesnes, "Norway," in *Handbook of World Philosophy: Contemporary Developments Since 1945*, ed. John R. Burr (Westport, Conn.: Greenwood Press, 1980), pp. 159–71.

5. Mercier and Svilar, eds., *Philosophers on Their Own Work*, vol. 10, see pp. 247–68.

6. The "lecturing in many places" quotation is taken from Naess's autobiographical notes at the conclusion of *Sustaining Gaia: Contributions to Another World View* (Papers from the Environment, Ethics and Ecology II Conference, October 1984), ed. Frank Fisher (Clayton, Victoria: Graduate School of Environmental Science, Monash University, 1987), p. 218. Naess has also given lectures at many other places in Europe, the U.S., and Australia in addition to those mentioned in this list.

   Naess's debate with Ayer is published as "The Glass is on the Table: An Empiricist versus a Total View," in *Reflexive Water: The Basic Concerns of Mankind*, ed. Fons Elders (London: Souvenir Press, 1974), pp. 13–68. Naess's interview for the journal of the Zen Center of Los Angeles is published as "Simple in Means, Rich in Ends: A Conversation with Arne Naess," *The Ten Directions*, Summer/Fall 1982, pp. 7 and 10–12; and Naess's 1987 Schumacher Lecture is published as "The Basics of Deep Ecology," *Resurgence*, January/February 1988, pp. 4–7.

7. Ingemund Gullvag and Jon Wetlesen, preface to *In Sceptical Wonder: Inquiries into the Philosophy of Arne Naess on the Occasion of his 70th Birthday*, ed. Gullvag and Wetlesen (Oslo: University of Oslo Press, 1982).

8. Elders, ed., *Reflexive Water*, pp. 274–75.

9. Ibid., pp. 276–78.

10. Fons Elders, "Norwegian Perspective No. 27011230992 or the TAO of Arne Naess," in *In Sceptical Wonder*, ed. Gullvag and Wetlesen, pp. 11–21, at p. 13.

11. Geir Hestmark, "Possible Monsters in Loch Naess?," in *In Sceptical Wonder*, pp. 301–14, at p. 301.

12. Arne Naess, "The Deep Ecological Movement: Some Philosophical Aspects," *Philosophical Inquiry* 8 (1986): 10–31, pp. 22–23.

13. Arne Naess, interviewed by David Rothenberg, "Is it Painful to Think?: A Discussion with Arne Naess," 1986, ms., pp. 7–9.

14. Erik Dammann, *Revolution in the Affluent Society* (London: Heretic Books, 1984), p. 151.

15. Ron Eyerman, "Intellectuals and Popular Movements: The Alta Confrontation in Norway," *New Praxis* 3 (1983): 185–98, at p. 185.

16. From Naess's autobiographical notes in *Sustaining Gaia*, p. 218. Naess's reputation for ecologically oriented nonviolent direct action seems to have reached almost legendary status. For example, Dolores LaChapelle recounts a story of "one of Arne Naess's outstanding non-violent protests" in her book *Earth Wisdom* (Los Angeles: The Guild of Tutors Press, 1978, see p. 154) that Naess tells me is totally without foundation (personal discussions, March 1986).

17. Naess cites this paper as "under publication" under the title "Depth of Questions" in a collection to be entitled *Papers in Honour of H. Tennessen* (no further details) in a note to his paper "Validity of Norms—But Which Norms? Self-Realization?: Reply to Harald Ofstad," in *In Sceptical Wonder*, pp. 257–69. However, this collection has never been published and Naess's "Deepness of Questions" (16 pp., double-spaced) has not been published elsewhere. I am not aware of any reference to this paper in the ecophilosophy literature other than Naess's reference to it in *In Sceptical Wonder*. The quotations that follow are from sections 1, 2, and 5 of "Deepness of Questions."

18. Arne Naess, "Notes on the Methodology of Normative Systems," *Methodology and Science* 10 (1977): 64–79, p. 65.

19. Naess has told me that my teaching hand-out on normative systems is the first of which he is aware (personal correspondence, 18 April 1988). To my mind, this is a terrible state of affairs: the basic ideas involved are simple, easily communicated, and easily remembered, yet they also serve as a significant aid to clear thinking and communication as well as serving as a stimulus to deeper thinking. In my view, *every* student would benefit from being aware of these

336 ° NOTES TO PAGES 102–104

ideas and periodically attempting to construct his or her own normative systems.

20. Bill Devall, "Streams of Environmentalism," 1979, ms., p. 38 (I do not know the reason for Devall's reference to a 1980 letter in a 1979 paper; perhaps my version of Devall's paper is an updated, post-1979 version).

21. Arne Naess, interviewed by Stephan Bodian, "Simple in Means, Rich in Ends: A Conversation with Arne Naess," *The Ten Directions*, Summer/Fall 1982, pp. 7 and 10–12, at p. 10. This section of the interview is also reprinted in Bill Devall and George Sessions, *Deep Ecology: Living as if Nature Mattered*.

22. Arne Naess, "Spinoza and the Deep Ecology Movement," 1982, ms., p. 1. This paper is a revised version of "Spinoza and Ecology," which appeared in two places in 1977: *Philosophia* 7 (1977): 45–54; and *Speculum Spinozanum 1677–1977*, ed. Siegfried Hessing (London: Routledge and Kegan Paul, 1977), pp. 418–25.

23. Arne Naess, "Deep Ecology Disentangled?" 1984, ms., p. 3.

24. Arne Naess, "Identification as a Source of Deep Ecological Attitudes," p. 256.

25. Arne Naess, "The Deep Ecological Movement: Some Philosophical Aspects," pp. 17 and 21–22.

26. Ibid., pp. 26–27.

27. This version of Ecosophy T is taken from Arne Naess, *Ecology, Community and Lifestyle*, see pp. 196–209.

28. In introducing his most recent version of Ecosophy T (i.e., the one that I have presented here), Naess notes that "what follows is only one particular exposition of Ecosophy T. Other versions may be cognitively equivalent, expressing the same concrete content but a different abstract structure" (ibid., p. 197). For slightly differently expressed versions of Ecosophy T, see Arne Naess, *Økologi, samfunn og livsstil*, [Ecology, Community, and Lifestyle], 5th ed. (Oslo: Oslo University Press, 1976); and Arne Naess, "Notes on the Methodology of Normative Systems" (this version is reproduced in both Arne Naess, "A Comparison of Two System Models: Reply to Siri Naess," in *In Sceptical Wonder*, pp. 281–86; and Devall and Sessions, *Deep Ecology*, see appendix A: "Ecosophy T: Arne Naess").

29. Devall and Sessions's presentation of Ecosophy T in appendix A of their book *Deep Ecology* is entirely consistent with this statement.

However, they suggest in chapter 5 of their book (p. 66) that "Naess has developed *two* ultimate norms or intuitions which are themselves not derivable from other principles or intuitions," i.e., "Self-realization!" and "Biocentric Equality!" (emphasis added). But this is not so. Naess's normative systematization of his own approach to ecophilosophy has always proceeded from the *single* fundamental norm of "Self-realization!" Naess has then always *derived* a norm of the kind that Devall and Sessions refer to as "Biocentric Equality!" from this norm (e.g., see H1, H2, H3, and N2 in the version of Ecosophy T quoted above).

30. Personal correspondence with the author, 18 April 1988.

31. Personal correspondence with the author, 6 October 1986.

32. See Baruch Spinoza, *The Ethics,* in *The Ethics and Selected Letters,* trans. Samuel Shirley and ed. Seymour Feldman (Indianapolis: Hackett Publishing Company, 1982), part III, proposition 6, and following.

33. Bertrand Russell, *History of Western Philosophy* (London: Unwin Paperbacks, 1979), p. 555. For Russell, "Spinoza (1632–77) is the noblest and most lovable of the great philosophers. Intellectually, some others have surpassed him, but ethically he is supreme" (ibid., p. 552).

    On the subject of Spinoza's monistic metaphysics, Spinoza scholars in general would agree with Seymour Feldman's comment in his introduction to Spinoza's *Ethics and Selected Letters* (p. 9) that "unity is the dominant and pervasive theme in Spinoza's philosophy. [Indeed, Spinoza is] almost obsessed with the perception of the oneness of things. . . ."

34. Arne Naess, *Freedom, Emotion and Self-Subsistence: The Structure of a Central Part of Spinoza's Ethics* (Oslo: University of Oslo Press, 1975), p. 97.

35. Ibid., p. 99.

36. Ibid., p. 98.

37. See the version of Ecosophy T found in Naess, *Økologi, samfunn og livsstil,* 5th ed. (Oslo: Oslo University Press, 1976), and the normative systematization of Gandhi's views found in Arne Naess, "A Systematization of Gandhian Ethics of Conflict Resolution," *Conflict Resolution* 2 (1958): 140–55. The latter systematization is reproduced as Systematization *E in Arne Naess, *Gandhi and Group*

Conflict: An Exploration of Satyagraha: Theoretical Background (Oslo: University of Oslo Press, 1974), pp. 52–86. I am grateful to Naess for providing me with an English translation of the relevant, lengthy final chapter of *Økologi, samfunn og livsstil* a few years ago. (For that matter, I am grateful to Naess for providing me with all the works cited in this note as well as many others that I would not otherwise have been able to obtain very easily. As a non–Norwegian speaker, however, my thanks are doubly great in regard to the translation of the main philosophical chapter of *Økologi, samfunn og livsstil*. This translation has enabled me to trace the development of Naess's formulations of Ecosophy T prior to his English language presentations, which I have referred to in note 28.)

38. Arne Naess, "Through Spinoza to Mahayana Buddhism or Through Mahayana Buddhism to Spinoza?," in *Spinoza's Philosophy of Man: Proceedings of the Scandinavian Spinoza Symposium 1977,* ed. Jon Wetlesen (Oslo: University of Oslo Press, 1978), pp. 136–58, at pp. 138 and 141.

39. Arne Naess, "Self-realization: An Ecological Approach to Being in the World," *The Trumpeter* 4(3) (1987): 35–42, pp. 38–39. 1930 was the year of Gandhi's famous "salt march" from his home near Ahmedabad to the sea. This was Gandhi's largest civil disobedience campaign and was followed closely by the world's major newspapers.

40. Naess, *Freedom, Emotion and Self-Subsistence,* p. 98; and Mahatma Gandhi, *The Writings of Gandhi: A Selection,* ed. Ronald Duncan (London: Fontana/Collins, 1983), pp. 34–35.

41. Naess, *Gandhi and Group Conflict,* p. 34.

42. See W. L. Reese, *Dictionary of Philosophy and Religion: Eastern and Western Thought* (New Jersey: Humanities Press, 1980), s.v. "Shankara."

43. Agehananda Bharati, "The Self in Hindu Thought and Action," in *Culture and Self: Asian and Western Perspectives,* ed. Anthony J. Marsella, George DeVos, and Francis L. K. Hsu (New York: Tavistock Publications, 1985), pp. 185–230, at pp. 198–99.

44. Quoted in Ramashray Roy, *Self and Society: A Study in Gandhian Thought* (New Delhi: Sage Publications, 1984), p. 74.

45. Ibid., p. 58. It might seem contradictory that Gandhi viewed

attachment to the senses as the worst kind of prison and sensual gratification as a sin. However, this view can also be taken as a reflection upon the self—specifically, upon how easily the self allows its spiritual quest to be side-tracked—rather than as a reflection upon the empirical world as being *inherently* defiled, contaminated, or in some sense second-rate.

46. See Arne Naess, "The World of Concrete Contents," *Inquiry* 28 (1985): 417–28.

47. Arne Naess, *Gandhi and Group Conflict: An Exploration of Satyagraha: Theoretical Background* (Oslo: University of Oslo Press, 1974), pp. 163, 162, and 12 respectively. It should be noted that the notion that Buddhism is "reformed Hinduism" or that reformed Hinduism embraced the teachings of Buddhism in anything like their Buddhist form is a particularly Hindu viewpoint. This viewpoint is rejected both by early and modern indigenous Buddhist scholars as well as by Western scholars of Buddhism. I am grateful to Jeremy Hayward for emphasizing this point to me.

48. Robert Aitken, *Taking the Path of Zen* (San Francisco: North Point Press, 1982), p. 61. Not all readers will be familiar with the name of A. T. Ariyaratne, the founder of the Sarvodaya Movement in Sri Lanka. For further details, see A. T. Ariyaratne, interviewed by David Beatty, "Awakening of Sri Lanka," *Resurgence*, July/August 1983, pp. 13–15; A. T. Ariyaratne, "No Poverty Society," *Resurgence*, January/February 1985, pp. 4–8; Joanna Macy, *Dharma and Development: Religion as Resource in the Sarvodaya Self-Help Movement* (Hartford, Conn.: Kumarian Press, 1983); and Joanna Macy, "Return to the Spirit," *Resurgence*, July/August 1983, pp. 10–13.

49. Roy, *Self and Society*, p. 58.

50. Robert Aitken, "Gandhi, Dogen and Deep Ecology," appendix C in Devall and Sessions, *Deep Ecology*, p. 232.

51. Arne Naess, "Gestalt Thinking and Buddhism," 1983, ms., pp. 12–13 and 16–17.

52. See Naess, *Okologi, samfunn og livsstil*. The seven-point characterization of the deep ecology movement contained in Naess's introductory paper on deep ecology in English ("The Shallow and the Deep, Long-Range Ecology Movement: A Summary," *Inquiry* 16 [1973]: 95–100) effectively represented an incomplete condensa-

tion of the eighteen-point list contained in *Okologi, samfunn og livsstil.*

53. Since its formulation in April 1984, this list has been published in various places including George Sessions, *Ecophilosophy VI,* 1984, p. 5; Devall and Sessions, *Deep Ecology* (1985), p. 70; Naess, "The Deep Ecological Movement: Some Philosophical Aspects," p. 14; *The Trumpeter* 3(4) (1986): 14; and Arne Naess, "The Basics of Deep Ecology," *Resurgence,* January/February 1988, p. 7. I will concentrate on this list here since it is clear from Naess's recent presentations of deep ecology that he not only favors this list over earlier formulations but also accepts that certain aspects of these earlier formulations were too prone to misinterpretation (e.g., writing in reply to an early paper of my own, Naess has said: "The abstract term 'biospherical egalitarianism in principle' and certain similar terms which I have used, do perhaps more harm than good" ["Intuition, Intrinsic Value and Deep Ecology," *The Ecologist* 14 (1984): 201–203, p. 202]).

54. Arne Naess, "Sustainable Development and the Deep Long-Range Ecology Movement," *The Trumpeter* 5 (1988): 138–42, p. 139.

55. Naess, "Intuition, Intrinsic Value, and Deep Ecology," p. 202. Naess fully accepts that "any realistic praxis necessitates some killing, exploitation, and suppression" ("The Shallow and the Deep, Long-Range Ecology Movement: A Summary," [1973]: 95–100, p. 95). For more on the relevance of tradition and culture, see Naess's paper "Self-realization in Mixed Communities of Humans, Bears, Sheep, and Wolves," *Inquiry* 22 (1979): 231–41.

56. This qualification appears in the set of comments that generally accompany Naess and Sessions's eight-point list of "basic principles," sources for which were given in a previous note.

57. *Biocentric* and *ecocentric* are equally useful in connoting the biosphere and the ecosphere respectively, and these latter terms are themselves generally used interchangeably. See, for example, G. Tyler Miller, Jr., *Living in the Environment,* 2nd ed. (Belmont, Calif.: Wadsworth, 1979) and R. J. Lincoln, G. A. Boxshall and P. F. Clark, *A Dictionary of Ecology, Evolution and Systematics* (Cambridge: Cambridge University Press, 1982). However, where a distinction *is* made between the terms *biosphere* and *ecosphere,* it is the latter term that is taken as the more inclusive (see Michael Allaby, *A Dictionary of the Environment,* 2nd ed. [New York: New York

University Press, 1983]). Naess illustrates this himself when he writes: "The deep ecology movement is of course concerned about the Earth as a whole, including landscapes which are valued independently of the life forms which happen at some time to live there. We are seriously concerned about the *ecosphere* in its widest sense, not only the *biosphere*" ("Population Reduction: An Ecosophical View," 1987, ms.; emphases added).

I have so far found the ecosphere/biosphere distinction to be too vaguely defined to constitute a particularly strong argument for preferring *ecocentric* to *biocentric* on account of the former term's allegedly broader ecological connotations. Nevertheless, if this distinction could be sustained then it would provide yet another reason for describing the kind of egalitarianism advocated by deep ecologists as ecocentric rather than biocentric.

CHAPTER 5. THE PROBLEM WITH THE LABEL
DEEP ECOLOGY

1. Gary D. Suttle, "Deep Ecology by Any Other Name," *Earth First!*, 23 September 1986, p. 26.

2. John Passmore, "Political Ecology: Responsibility and Environmental Power," *The Age Monthly Review*, February 1983, pp. 15–16, at p. 15.

3. John Passmore, *Man's Responsibility for Nature: Ecological Problems and Western Traditions*, p. x.

4. Hwa Yol Jung, "The Harmony of Man and Nature: A Philosophic Manifesto," *Philosophical Inquiry* 8 (1986): 32–49, p. 46.

5. William Godfrey-Smith, "Environmental Philosophy," *Habitat Australia*, June 1980, pp. 24–25.

6. Tom Regan, *All That Dwell Therein: Animal Rights and Environmental Ethics* (Berkeley: University of California Press, 1982), p. 210.

7. See, for example, Devall and Sessions's book *Deep Ecology: Living as if Nature Mattered*.

8. Bill Devall, "The Deep Ecology Movement," p. 299.

9. Ibid.

10. Arne Naess, "Deep Ecology Disentangled?," 1984, ms., p. 8.

11. Suttle, "Deep Ecology by Any Other Name," p. 26.

12. Ibid.

13. Quoted in Bill Devall, "Streams of Environmentalism," 1979, ms., p. 38.

14. Arne Naess, "Deepness of Questions," 1982, ms., p. 14.

15. Arne Naess, interviewed by Stephan Bodian, "Simple in Means, Rich in Ends: A Conversation with Arne Naess," *The Ten Directions,* Summer/Fall 1982, pp. 7 and 10–12, at p. 10. This section of the interview is also reprinted in Devall and Sessions, *Deep Ecology,* p. 74.

16. Arne Naess, "Spinoza and the Deep Ecology Movement," 1982, ms., p. 1. This paper is a revised version of "Spinoza and Ecology," which appeared in two places in 1977: *Philosophia* 7 (1977): 45–54; and *Speculum Spinozanum 1677–1977,* ed. Siegfried Hessing (London: Routledge and Kegan Paul, 1977), pp. 418–25.

17. Naess, "Deep Ecology Disentangled?," p. 3.

18. Arne Naess, "Identification as a Source of Deep Ecological Attitudes," p. 256.

19. Arne Naess, "The Deep Ecological Movement: Some Philosophical Aspects," pp. 17 and 21–22.

20. Devall and Sessions, *Deep Ecology,* p. 65.

21. Naess, "The Deep Ecological Movement," p. 27.

22. Arne Naess, interviewed by David Rothenberg, "Is it Painful to Think?: A Discussion with Arne Naess," 1986, ms., p. 8.

23. Naess, "The Deep Ecological Movement;" p. 26.

24. There is a huge literature on the subject of how the Bible should be interpreted in respect to our attitudes toward the nonhuman world. For discussions of alternative interpretations to the one that, for the sake of example, I have developed here, one could begin with Robin Attfield, *The Ethics of Environmental Concern;* Ian G. Barbour, *Technology, Environment, and Human Values* (New York: Praeger, 1980); Susan Power Bratton, "The Ecotheology of James Watt," *Environmental Ethics* 5 (1983): 225–236; Susan Power Bratton, "Christian Ecotheology and the Old Testament," *Environmental Ethics* 6 (1984): 195–209; and Philip N. Joranson and Ken Butigan, eds., *Cry of the Environment: Rebuilding the Christian Creation Tradition* (Santa Fe: Bear and Company, 1984).

25. Steven S. Schwarzschild, "The Unnatural Jew," *Environmental Ethics* 6 (1984): 347–62, p. 347.

26. For a counter to Schwarzschild's interpretation of Judaism, see David Ehrenfeld and Joan G. Ehrenfeld, "Some Thoughts on Nature and Judaism," *Environmental Ethics* 7 (1985): 93–95.

27. Henryk Skolimowski, *Eco-Philosophy: Designing New Tactics for Living*, p. 115. George Sessions has taken Skolimowski to task for the anthropocentrism that is inherent in this kind of view: see his review of Skolimowski's *Eco-Philosophy* in *Environmental Ethics* 6 (1984): 167–74. For Skolimowski's reply, see his paper "The Dogma of Anti-Anthropocentrism and Ecophilosphy," *Environmental Ethics* 6 (1984): 283–88. I defend Sessions's reading of Skolimowski in my "Further Notes in Response to Skolimoski," *The Trumpeter* 4(4) (1987): 32–34.

28. Both quotations from Arne Naess, "How My Philosophy Seemed to Develop," in *Philosophers on Their Own Work*, vol. 10, ed. Andre Mercier and Maja Svilar (Bern: Peter Lang, 1983), pp. 209–26, at p. 211.

29. Naess, "Deepness of Questions," p. 15.

CHAPTER 6. THE MOST WIDELY RECOGNIZED
APPROACHES TO ECOPHILOSOPHY

1. The *Collins English Dictionary*, for example, lists this common, anthropocentric sense of *environment* before the more precise, ecological (nonanthropocentric) sense of the word: "environment n. 1. external conditions or surroundings, *esp. those in which people live or work*. 2. Ecology. the external surroundings in which a plant or animal lives, which tend to influence its development and behaviour" (emphasis added).

2. For a discussion, see K. S. Shrader-Frechette, " 'Frontier or Cowboy Ethics' and 'Lifeboat Ethics,' " in *Environmental Ethics*, ed. K. S. Shrader-Frechette (Pacific Grove, Calif.: The Boxwood Press, 1981), pp. 31–44. Shrader-Frechette takes the phrase "the myth of superabundance" from Stewart L. Udall, *The Quiet Crisis* (New York: Avon, 1963), pp. 66–67.

3. Udall (ibid., p. 190) refers to this attitude as "the myth of scientific supremacy."

4. John Rodman, "Theory and Practice in the Environmental Movement: Notes Towards an Ecology of Experience," in *The Search for Absolute Values in a Changing World: Proceedings of the Sixth International Conference on the Unity of the Sciences,* vol. 1 (New York: The International Cultural Foundation, 1978), pp. 45-56.

5. William Godfrey-Smith, "The Value of Wilderness," *Environmental Ethics* 1 (1979): 309-319.

6. Bryan G. Norton, "Sand Dollar Psychology," *The Washington Post Magazine,* 1 June 1986, pp. 11-14. The quotations are from pp. 13 and 14 respectively.

7. George Sessions, "Ecocentrism, Wilderness, and Global Ecosystem Protection," paper presented to the conference "The Wilderness Condition," Estes Park, Colo. 17-23 August 1989. Forthcoming in Max Oelschlaeger, ed., *The Wilderness Condition: Essays on Environment and Civilization* (no further publication details).

8. Ibid., p. 9. Two of the three arguments that Sessions presents in connection with the examples noted in this list relate to the first example (i.e., the psychogenetic importance of bonding with wild places and wild animals). Sessions refers to these two arguments as the *minding animals argument* and the *natural human ontogeny argument.* Both rely heavily upon the work of Paul Shepard. See especially Paul Shepard, *Thinking Animals: Animals and the Development of Human Intelligence* (New York: The Viking Press, 1978) and Paul Shepard, *Nature and Madness* (San Francisco: Sierra Club Books, 1982).

9. J. Baird Callicott, "Intrinsic Value, Quantum Theory, and Environmental Ethics," *Environmental Ethics* 7 (1985): 257-75, at p. 257; and Tom Regan, "The Nature and Possibility of an Environmental Ethic," *Environmental Ethics* 3 (1981): 19-34, at p. 34.

10. Bentham argued in his *Introduction to the Principles of Morals and Legislation* (1789) that "a full-grown horse or dog is beyond comparison a more rational, as well as a more conversable animal, than an infant of a day or a week, or even a month, old." This passage is regularly quoted in the main introductions to a sentience based approach to ethics: see, for example, Peter Singer, *Animal Liberation: A New Ethics for our Treatment of Animals,* p. 8; Peter Singer, *Practical Ethics* (Cambridge: Cambridge University Press, 1979), p. 50; Tom Regan, *The Case for Animal Rights,* p. 95; and

Peter Singer, ed., *In Defence of Animals* (Oxford: Basil Blackwell, 1985), p. 5.

11. Singer, *Animal Liberation*, pp. 8–9.

12. Ibid., pp. 176 and 179. Note that *arthropod* and *mollusk* refer to the phylum (a level of biological classification) to which each of these life forms belong.

13. Regan, *The Case for Animal Rights*, pp. 243 and 78. For a much shorter exposition of Regan's views, see his paper "The Case for Animal Rights," in *In Defence of Animals*, pp. 13–26. For an excellent critical review of Regan's approach, see J. Baird Callicott, review of *The Case for Animal Rights*.

14. I refer to two *kingdoms* here: the plant kingdom and the animal kingdom. However, following Robert H. Whittaker ("New Concepts of Kingdoms of Organisms," *Science* 163 [1969]: 150–60), modern biologists tend to divide life forms into five kingdoms: plants, animals, fungi (which includes true fungi as well as slime molds), and two kingdoms of microorganisms: Protista and Monera. The Protista kingdom includes those organisms that are eukaryotes (i.e., organisms whose cells have a true nucleus) but that are not plants, animals, or fungi. In contrast, the Monera kingdom includes those organisms that are prokaryotes (i.e., organisms whose cells do not have a true nucleus—specifically, bacteria, blue-green algae, and mycoplasmas). Other theorists have suggested taxonomic systems based on ten, thirteen, seventeen, and even twenty kingdoms. Given the extraordinary diversity of life forms, however, it is hardly necessary to add that each of these systems has its own particular problems. For gentle introductions to these matters, see Isaac Asimov, *Asimov's New Guide to Science* rev. ed. (Harmondsworth, Middlesex: Penguin, 1987), ch. 16; and Linda Gamlin and Gail Vines, eds., *The Evolution of Life* (London: Collins, 1986), p. 159. For a more detailed discussion, see William T. Keeton, James L. Gould, and Carol Grant Gould, *Biological Science*, 4th ed. (New York: W. W. Norton, 1986), chs. 6 and 37 in particular and part 5 in general.

   For the sake of simplicity of exposition here, I think I can be forgiven for retaining the common practice of referring to the variety of life forms simply in terms of plants and animals. Purists who object can read in however many other kingdoms they subscribe to!

15. Kenneth E. Goodpaster, "On Being Morally Considerable," p. 319.

16. Singer, *Animal Liberation,* p. 9; and Goodpaster, "On Being Morally Considerable," p. 310.

17. Edward Johnson, "Treating the Dirt: Environmental Ethics and Moral Theory," pp. 350–51.

18. For a technical, early paper, see Francisco J. Varela, Humberto R. Maturana, and Ricardo Uribe, "Autopoiesis: The Organization of Living Systems, Its Characterization and a Model," *Biosystems* 5 (1974): 187–96. For a recent, general-audience oriented presentation of Maturana and Varela's ideas, see Humberto R. Maturana and Francisco J. Varela, *The Tree of Knowledge: The Biological Roots of Human Understanding* (Boston: Shambhala, 1988), esp. chap. 2: "The Organization of Living Things." For other relatively non-technical discussions of Maturana and Varela's ideas, see John P. Briggs and F. David Peat, *Looking Glass Universe: The Emerging Science of Wholeness* (New York: Cornerstone Library, 1984), esp. chap. 10: "Founding a Science of Spontaneous Order"; Jeremy W. Hayward, *Perceiving Ordinary Magic: Science and Intuitive Wisdom* (Boulder: Shambhala, 1984), esp. chap. 8: "Self-Organization and the Pattern of Life"; and Jeremy W. Hayward, *Shifting Worlds, Changing Minds: Where the Sciences and Buddhism Meet* (Boston: Shambhala, 1987), esp. chap. 9: "Self-Organization." For a somewhat more technical discussion of ideas of this general kind, see Erich Jantsch, *The Self-Organizing Universe: Scientific and Human Implications of the Emerging Paradigm of Evolution* (Oxford: Pergamon Press, 1980), esp. chap. 10: "The Circular Processes of Life." Ilya Prigogine and Isabelle Stengers's *Order Out of Chaos: Man's New Dialogue with Nature* (New York: Bantam, 1984) is also highly relevant, although these authors talk in terms of *dissipative structures* rather than *autopoietic structures*. Prigogine and Stengers use the name *dissipative structure* to capture the fact that self-regenerating (and, hence, highly organized or "far from equilibrium") structures retain their order only through the constant intake of energy from, and dissipation of waste products (or disorder) into, their environments.

Fritjof Capra draws on Prigogine's ideas on dissipative structures in *The Turning Point: Science, Society, and the Rising Culture* (New York: Bantam, 1983), see chap. 9: "The Systems View of Life."

More recently, Capra has also been drawing directly on the work of Maturana and Varela: see Fritjof Capra, "The Santiago Theory of Life and Cognition," *Revision,* Summer/Fall 1986 (special issue on "Critical Questions about New Paradigm Thinking"), pp. 59–61.

19. Capra, *The Turning Point,* pp. 271–72.

20. Varela, Maturana, and Uribe, "Autopoiesis," p. 189.

21. Capra, "The Santiago Theory of Life and Cognition," p. 60.

22. Goodpaster, "On Being Morally Considerable," p. 323.

23. Ibid.

24. Paul W. Taylor, *Respect for Nature: A Theory of Environmental Ethics;* see esp. the section entitled "Individual Organisms as Teleological Centers of Life," pp. 119–29.

25. For Taylor's attempt to distinguish biological organisms from mechanical systems, see ibid., pp. 123–25; for his attempt to distinguish biological organisms from ecosystems and the ecosphere, see ibid., pp. 118–19.

26. Ibid., pp. 124–125 and 119 respectively.

27. Aldo Leopold, *A Sand County Almanac,* pp. 224–25.

28. James D. Heffernan, "The Land Ethic: A Critical Appraisal," p. 247.

29. See Aldo Leopold, "Some Fundamentals of Conservation in the Southwest," *Environmental Ethics* 1 (1979): 131–41, esp. pp. 139–40. See also J. Baird Callicott, "The Conceptual Foundations of the Land Ethic," in *Companion to A Sand County Almanac: Interpretive and Critical Essays,* ed. J. Baird Callicott (Madison: The University of Wisconsin Press, 1987), pp. 186–217, see esp. pp. 201–2; Susan L. Flader, "Leopold's 'Some Fundamentals of Conservation': A Commentary," *Environmental Ethics* 1 (1979): 143–48; Heffernan, "The Land Ethic"; and Roderick Nash, "Aldo Leopold's Intellectual Heritage," in *Companion to A Sand County Almanac,* pp. 63–88, see esp. pp. 77–78.

30. Heffernan, "The Land Ethic," p. 247.

31. See Leopold, "Some Fundamentals of Conservation in the Southwest."

32. See James E. Lovelock, *Gaia: A New Look at Life on Earth* (Oxford: Oxford University Press, 1979) and James E. Lovelock, *The Ages of Gaia: A Biography of Our Living Earth.* See also James E. Lovelock

and Sidney Epton, "The Quest for Gaia," *New Scientist,* 6 February 1975, pp. 304–6; James E. Lovelock, "Gaia: The World as Living Organism," *New Scientist,* 18 December 1986, pp. 25–28; and James E. Lovelock, "Man and Gaia," in *Battle for the Earth: Today's Key Environmental Issues,* ed. Edward Goldsmith and Nicholas Hildyard (Brookvale, New South Wales: Child and Associates, 1988), pp. 51–64. For discussions, see David Abram, "The Perceptual Implications of Gaia," *The Ecologist* 15 (1985): 96–103; Peter Bunyard, "Gaia: The Implications for Industrialized Societies," *The Ecologist* 18 (1988): 196–206; Edward Goldsmith, "Gaia: Some Implications for Theoretical Ecology," *The Ecologist* 18 (1988): 64–74; Edward Goldsmith, "Gaia and Evolution," *The Ecologist* 19 (1989): 147–53; Charles J. Hughes, "Gaia: A Natural Scientist's Ethic for the Future," *The Ecologist* 15 (1985): 92–95; Lynn Margulis, in discussion with Fritjof Capra, "Gaia: The Living Earth," *The Elmwood Newsletter,* Summer 1989, pp. 1 and 8–9 (reprinted in *Resurgence,* September/October 1989, pp. 22–25; in this interview, Margulis discusses the Gaia hypothesis with specific reference to Maturana and Varela's concept of autopoiesis); Patrick D. Murphy, "Sex-Typing the Planet: Gaia Imagery and the Problem of Subverting Patriarchy," *Environmental Ethics* 10 (1988): 155–68; Fred Pearce, "Gaia: A Revolution Comes of Age," *New Scientist,* 17 March 1988, pp. 32–33; Dorion Sagan and Lynn Margulis, "The Gaian Perspective of Ecology," *The Ecologist* 13 (1983): 160–67; Dorion Sagan and Lynn Margulis, "Gaia and Philosophy," in *On Nature,* ed. Leroy S. Rouner (Notre Dame, Ind.: University of Notre Dame Press, 1984), pp. 60–75; Rafal Serafin, "Noosphere, Gaia, and the Science of the Biosphere," *Environmental Ethics* 10 (1988): 121–37; and Anthony Weston, "Forms of Gaian Ethics," *Environmental Ethics* 9 (1987): 217–30. See also the proceedings of the annual symposium on the Gaia hypothesis organized by *The Ecologist* and begun in 1988 (available from *The Ecologist*).

33. Tom Regan, "Ethical Vegetarianism and Commercial Animal Farming," in *Contemporary Moral Problems,* ed. James E. White (St. Paul, Minn.: West Publishing Co., 1985), pp. 279–94.

34. See Murray Bookchin, *The Ecology of Freedom: The Emergence and Dissolution of Hierarchy* (Palo Alto: Cheshire Books, 1982). For a critical discussion of Bookchin's views, see Robyn Eckersley,

"Divining Evolution: The Ecological Ethics of Murray Bookchin," *Environmental Ethics* 11 (1989): 99–116.

35. Henryk Skolimowski, *Eco-Philosophy: Designing New Tactics for Living*, p. 117. For a critical discussion of Skolimowski's views, see George Sessions, review of *Eco-Philosophy: Designing New Tactics for Living*, by Henryk Skolimowski, in *Environmental Ethics* 6 (1984): 167–74.

36. See Charles Birch and John B. Cobb, Jr., *The Liberation of Life: From the Cell to the Community;* Charles Birch, *On Purpose* (Kensington, New South Wales: New South Wales University Press, 1990); and David Griffin, "Whitehead's Contributions to a Theology of Nature," *Bucknell Review* 20 (1972): 3–24. For an extended review of Birch and Cobb's ideas, see Warwick Fox, review of *The Liberation of Life: From the Cell to the Community*, by Charles Birch and John B. Cobb, Jr., in *The Ecologist* 14 (1984): 178–82.

37. Birch and Cobb, *The Liberation of Life*, p. 153.

38. For critiques by prominent evolutionary theorists of the view that evolutionary processes are purposive or that we can or need to infer the existence of cosmic interests from the products of these processes, see Richard Dawkins, *The Blind Watchmaker* (London: Penguin, 1988); and Ernst Mayr, *Toward a New Philosophy of Biology: Observations of an Evolutionist* (Cambridge, Mass.: Belknap Press, 1988), chap. 3: "The Multiple Meanings of Teleological."

39. John Rodman, "The Liberation of Nature?," p. 94.

40. See John Rodman, "Four Forms of Ecological Consciousness Reconsidered."

41. George Edward Moore, *Principia Ethica* (Cambridge: Cambridge University Press, 1903).

42. On the erroneous nature of this term, see W. K. Frankena, "The Naturalistic Fallacy," *Mind* 192 (1939): 464–77; and Bernard Williams, *Ethics and the Limits of Philosophy* (London: Fontana Press/Collins, 1985), p. 121.

43. Callicott, "Intrinsic Value, Quantum Theory, and Environmental Ethics," p. 258.

44. See, for example, H. Gene Blocker and William Hannaford, *Introduction to Philosophy* (New York: D. Van Nostrand, 1974), pp. 220–22; *The Encyclopedia of Philosophy*, 1967, s.v. "Ethical Naturalism," by Jonathan Harrison; ibid., s.v. "Ethics, History of," by

Raziel Abelson and Kai Nielsen; Frankena, "The Naturalistic Fallacy"; Alasdair MacIntyre, *A Short History of Ethics* (London: Routledge and Kegan Paul, 1967), pp. 249–53; John Hospers, *An Introduction to Philosophical Analysis,* 2nd ed. (London: Routledge and Kegan Paul, 1967), pp. 573–75; J. L. Mackie, *Ethics: Inventing Right and Wrong* (Harmondsworth: Penguin, 1977), chap. 2; Mary Midgley, "The Flight from Blame," *Philosophy* 62 (1987): 271–91; Mary Midgley, *Wisdom, Information, and Wonder: What is Knowledge For?* (Routledge: London, 1989), chs. 14–16; and Bernard Williams, *Ethics and the Limits of Philosophy,* p. 16 and pp. 121–22.

45. This particular quotation is taken from Bernard Mayo, *The Philosophy of Right and Wrong: An Introduction to Ethical Theory* (London: Routledge and Kegan Paul, 1986), p. 42.

46. Callicott, "Intrinsic Value, Quantum Theory, and Environmental Ethics," p. 265.

47. Heffernan, "The Land Ethic," p. 247.

CHAPTER 7. TRANSPERSONAL ECOLOGY AS A
DISTINCTIVE APPROACH TO ECOPHILOSOPHY

1. *Collins English Dictionary.*

2. Abraham Maslow, quoted in Anthony J. Sutich, "The Emergence of the Transpersonal Orientation: A Personal Account," *The Journal of Transpersonal Psychology* 8 (1976): 5–19, p. 16; Roger N. Walsh and Frances Vaughan, eds., *Beyond Ego: Transpersonal Dimensions in Psychology* (Los Angeles: J. P. Tarcher, 1980).

3. Ken Wilber, *Eye to Eye: The Quest for the New Paradigm* (Garden City, N.Y.: Anchor Books, 1983), p. 100; and Ken Wilber, "Odyssey: A Personal Inquiry into Humanistic and Transpersonal Psychology," *Journal of Humanistic Psychology* 22(1) (1982): 57–90, p. 72. See also Ken Wilber, *Up from Eden: A Transpersonal View of Human Evolution* (New York: Doubleday, 1981).

4. Abraham H. Maslow, *Toward a Psychology of Being,* 2nd ed. (Princeton: D. Van Nostrand, 1968), p. iv.

5. The phrase "the biological rooting of the value life" is taken from the title of Maslow's paper "A Theory of Metamotivation: The

Biological Rooting of the Value-Life," contained in his book *The Farther Reaches of Human Nature* (New York: The Viking Press, 1971), pp. 299–342; reprinted in part in Walsh and Vaughan, eds., *Beyond Ego: Transpersonal Dimensions in Psychology*, pp. 122–31. On the Spinozist/Taoist point see, for example, the chapters entitled "Various Meanings of Transcendence" and "Theory Z" in *The Farther Reaches of Human Nature*, pp. 269–79 and 280–95 respectively.

6. Maslow, *The Farther Reaches of Human Nature*, p. 272.

7. Ibid., p. 279.

8. Arthur B. Coffin, *Robinson Jeffers: Poet of Inhumanism* (Madison: University of Wisconsin Press, 1971), p. 255; cited in George Sessions, "Spinoza and Jeffers on Man in Nature," p. 527.

9. Quoted in Bill Devall and George Sessions, *Deep Ecology: Living as if Nature Mattered*, p. 102.

10. For example, Maslow says that identification with the human species "can also be expressed intrapsychically, phenomenologically, as experiencing one's self to be one of the band of brothers, to belong to the human species. . . . One is identified with the whole human species and therefore . . . one's brothers on the other side of the earth are part of oneself" (*The Farther Reaches of Human Nature*, pp. 272 and 276). But whatever happened to my sisters? Although Maslow does occasionally speak in terms of brothers *and* sisters, as with anthropocentric formulations, masculine formulations are the norm in his writings.

11. Frances Vaughan, "Discovering Transpersonal Identity," *Journal of Humanistic Psychology* 25 (1985): 13–38, p . 20.

12. Donald Rothberg, "Philosophical Foundations of Transpersonal Psychology: An Introduction to Some Basic Issues," *The Journal of Transpersonal Psychology* 18 (1986): 1–34, p. 1.

13. Ibid., pp. 23–24.

14. In regard to this general point, see John Rowan, "The Self: One or Many," *The Psychologist*, July 1989, pp. 279–81.

15. Arthur S. Reber, *The Penguin Dictionary of Psychology* (Harmondsworth, Middlesex: Penguin, 1985), s.v. "ego."

16. Arne Naess, "Self-realization: An Ecological Approach to Being in the World," (The Fourth Keith Roby Memorial Lecture in Com-

munity Science, Murdoch University, Western Australia, 12 March 1986), pp. 39−40.

17. Walt Anderson, *Open Secrets: A Western Guide to Tibetan Buddhism* (Harmondsworth, Middlesex: Penguin, 1980), p. 17.

18. Ibid., p. 19. For more on Maslow's observations on self-actualizing people, see appendix B herein.

19. Daniel Goleman, *The Varieties of the Meditative Experience* (London: Rider, 1978), p. 95.

20. Naess, "Self-realization: An Ecological Approach," pp. 40 and 36.

21. Quoted in Bill Devall, "Greenies: Observations on the Deep, Long-Range Ecology Movement in Australia," 1984, ms., p. 17.

22. Arne Naess, *Ecology, Community and Lifestyle: Outline of an Ecosophy;* Immanuel Kant, *Groundwork of the Metaphysic of Morals* (1785), in *The Moral Law: Kant's Groundwork of the Metaphysic of Morals,* trans. H. J. Paton (London: Hutchinson and Company, 1972).

23. Naess, *Ecology, Community and Lifestyle,* pp. 85−86.

24. Naess, "Self-realization: An Ecological Approach," pp. 40 and 35 respectively.

25. Arne Naess, "The Deep Ecological Movement: Some Philosophical Aspects," p. 29.

26. Arne Naess, "Validity of Norms—But Which Norms? Self-realization?: Reply to Harald Ofstad," in *In Sceptical Wonder: Inquiries into the Philosophy of Arne Naess on the Occasion of his 70th Birthday,* ed. Ingemund Gullvag and Jon Wetlesen (Oslo: Oslo University Press, 1982), pp. 257−69, at p. 264.

27. Arne Naess, "Identification as a Source of Deep Ecological Attitudes," p. 264.

28. Arne Naess, "Environmental Ethics and Spinoza's Ethics: Comments on Genevieve Lloyd's Article," *Inquiry* 23 (1980): 313−25, pp. 314−15 and 323.

29. Arne Naess, "Environmental Ethics and International Justice," 1987, ms., p. 10.

30. Ibid., pp. 3 and 8.

31. Arne Naess, "Self-realization in Mixed Communities of Humans, Bears, Sheep, and Wolves," *Inquiry* 22 (1979): 231−41, p. 238.

32. Ibid., p. 231.

33. Arne Naess, "Intrinsic Value: Will the Defenders of Nature Please

Rise?," in *Conservation Biology: The Science of Scarcity and Diversity,* ed. Michael Soule (Sunderland, Mass.: Sinauer Associates, 1986), pp. 504–15, at p. 505.

34. See Warwick Fox, *Approaching Deep Ecology: A Response to Richard Sylvan's Critique of Deep Ecology,* Environmental Studies Occasional Paper no. 20 (Hobart, Tasmania: Centre for Environmental Studies, University of Tasmania, 1986).

35. George Sessions, *Ecophilosophy III,* 1981, pp. 5–5a.

36. Arne Naess, "Intuition, Intrinsic Value, and Deep Ecology," *The Ecologist* 14 (1984): 201–3, p. 202. This paper was a response to my earliest paper on deep ecology: "Deep Ecology: A New Philosophy of Our Time?," *The Ecologist* 14 (1984): 194–200. See my *Approaching Deep Ecology* for further discussion of the meaning of the term *biospherical egalitarianism in principle.*

37. Sessions, *Ecophilosophy III,* p. 5a.

38. George Sessions, *Ecophilosophy V,* 1983, p. 4.

39. Bill Devall, "Ecological Realism," 1981, ms., p. 6.

40. Bill Devall, "Issues in Contemporary Ecophilosophy," paper presented to the "Ecology and Society Conference," University of Wisconsin at Waukesha, 7 April 1984, p. 8.

41. Bill Devall, *Simple in Means, Rich in Ends: Practicing Deep Ecology,* pp. 42–44.

42. Andrew McLaughlin, "The Critique of Humanity and Nature: Three Recent Philosophical Reflections," *The Trumpeter* 4(4) (1987): 1–6, p. 2

43. Alan Drengson, review of *Deep Ecology: Living as if Nature Mattered,* by Bill Devall and George Sessions, in *Environmental Ethics* 10 (1988): 83–89, at pp. 86–87. For an earlier discussion of issues that are relevant to these ideas (albeit written without specific reference to deep ecology), see Alan Drengson, "Compassion and Transcendence of Duty and Inclination," *Philosophy Today* 25 (1981): 34–45.

44. Michael Zimmerman, "Implications of Heidegger's Thought for Deep Ecology," pp. 22–23.

45. Neil Evernden, *The Natural Alien: Humankind and Environment,* pp. 69 and 137.

46. John Livingston, "The Dilemma of the Deep Ecologist," in *The*

Paradox of Environmentalism, ed. Neil Evernden (Downsview, Ontario: Faculty of Environmental Studies, York University, 1984), pp. 61–72, at pp. 61, 63–64, and 70–71.

47. John Rodman, "The Liberation of Nature?," pp. 96 and 103–4.

48. Joanna Macy, "Faith and Ecology," *Resurgence*, July/August 1987, pp. 18–21, at p. 20.

49. Naess, "Self-realization: An Ecological Approach," pp. 35 and 39–40.

50. Naess, "Identification as a Source of Deep Ecological Attitudes," p. 261.

51. Arne Naess, "Notes on the Methodology of Normative Systems," *Methodology and Science* 10 (1977): 64–79, p. 71.

52. Arne Naess, "Gestalt Thinking and Buddhism," 1983, ms., p. 13.

53. Naess, *Ecology, Community and Lifestyle*, pp. 174, 165–66, 170, and 172 respectively.

54. Ibid., p. 165.

55. Richard Sylvan, *A Critique of Deep Ecology*, Discussion Papers in Environmental Philosophy no. 12 (Canberra: Depts. of Philosophy, Australian National University, 1985), p. 27. I discuss the centrality of the concept of relative autonomy to deep (or, as I would now say, transpersonal) ecological views in the third section of my mongraph *Approaching Deep Ecology: A Response to Richard Sylvan's Critique of Deep Ecology*, Environmental Studies Occasional Paper no. 20 (Hobart, Tasmania: Centre for Enviromental Studies, University of Tasmania, 1986). I also discuss some of the implications of modern science for an ecological view of the world in the fourth section of that monograph.

56. Devall, *Simple in Means, Rich in Ends*, pp. 42 and 70.

57. Sessions, *Ecophilosophy III*, p. 5a.

58. Devall and Sessions, *Deep Ecology*, pp. 66–67.

59. Robert Aitken, *Taking the Path of Zen* (San Francisco: North Point Press, 1982), p. 62.

60. Ibid., p. 73.

61. Alan Drengson, "Paganism, Nature and Deep Ecology," *The Trumpeter* 5 (1988): 20–22, at p. 22.

62. David Rothenberg, "Introduction: Ecosophy T: From Intuition to

System," translator's introduction to Naess, *Ecology, Community and Lifestyle*, pp. 6 and 9.

63. Andrew McLaughlin, "Images and Ethics of Nature," pp. 312–314.

64. Freya Mathews, "Conservation and Self-Realization: A Deep Ecology Perspective," *Environmental Ethics* 10 (1988): 347–55, pp. 349–50 and 354.

65. John Livingston, *The Fallacy of Wildlife Conservation*, pp. 113–14.

66. Evernden, *The Natural Alien*, pp. 43, 45, 64, and 47 respectively.

67. Michael Zimmerman, "The Role of Spiritual Discipline in Learning to Dwell on Earth," in *Dwelling, Place and Environment*, ed. David Seamon and Robert Mugerauer (Boston: Martinus Nijoff, 1985), pp. 247–56, at pp. 252 and 254.

68. Robert Aitken, "Gandhi, Dogen, and Deep Ecology," *Zero* 4 (1980): 52–58, p. 57. This essay is reprinted as appendix C in Devall and Sessions, *Deep Ecology*. Unfortunately, however, the startling image of "honey dribbl[ing] down your fur as you catch the bus to work" (very much the product of a Zen mind) has been omitted from the rest of this quotation in the *Deep Ecology* version.

69. John Seed, "Anthropocentrism," appendix E in Devall and Sessions, *Deep Ecology*, p. 243.

70. Quoted in Devall, "Greenies," p. 6.

71. Macy, "Faith and Ecology," p. 20.

72. John Rodman, "Theory and Practice in the Environmental Movement: Notes Towards an Ecology of Experience," in *The Search for Absolute Values in a Changing World*, vol. 1 (New York: The International Cultural Foundation, 1978), pp. 45–56, at p. 54.

73. Naess, *Ecology, Community and Lifestyle*, p. 164.

74. Arne Naess, "Spinoza and the Deep Ecology Movement," 1982, ms., p. 1. This paper is a revised version of "Spinoza and Ecology," which appeared in two places in 1977: *Philosophia* 7 (1977): 45–54; and *Speculum Spinozanum 1677–1977*, ed. Siegfried Hessing (London: Routledge and Kegan Paul, 1977), pp. 418–25.

75. Arne Naess, "Group Chairman's Introductory Remarks," in *The Search for Absolute Values in a Changing World*, vol. 1 (New York: The International Cultural Foundation, 1978), pp. 27–30, p. 30.

CHAPTER 8. TRANSPERSONAL ECOLOGY AND THE
VARIETIES OF IDENTIFICATION

1. Arne Naess, "Self-realization: An Ecological Approach to Being in the World," p. 35.

2. Quoted in William Barrett, "Zen for the West," in *Zen Buddhism: Selected Writings of D. T. Suzuki,* ed. William Barrett (Garden City, N.Y.: Doubleday/Anchor Books, 1956), p. xi. There is a whole literature on the similarities between Heidegger's thought and Eastern thought, especially Zen. For a guide to much of this literature, see the papers and books listed at note 3 in Michael Zimmerman, "Heidegger and Heraclitus on Spiritual Practice," *Philosophy Today* 27 (1983): 87–103. Special mention should be made here of Zimmerman's own book on Heidegger entitled *Eclipse of the Self: The Development of Heidegger's Concept of Authenticity* (Athens: Ohio University Press, 1981), which explores the relationship between Heidegger's thought and Zen in its final section (pp. 255–76). In addition to the papers and books cited by Zimmerman in "Heidegger and Heraclitus," see the following inspirational papers by Hwa Jol Jung: "The Ecological Crisis: A Philosophic Perspective, East and West," *Bucknell Review* 20 (1972): 25–44; and "The Paradox of Man and Nature: Reflections on Man's Ecological Predicament," *The Centennial Review* 18 (1974): 1–28.

3. Michael Zimmerman, "Toward a Heideggerean Ethos for Radical Environmentalism," *Environmental Ethics* 5 (1983): 99–131, pp. 102 and 115.

4. Ludwig Wittgenstein, *Tractatus Logico-Philosophicus,* trans. D. F. Pears and B. F. McGuiness (London: Routledge and Kegan Paul, 1961), proposition 6.44.

5. Roger Walsh, "The Consciousness Disciplines and the Behavioral Sciences: Questions of Comparison and Assessment," *American Journal of Psychiatry* 137 (1980): 663–73, p. 663.

6. On this general point, see Ken Wilber's insightful essays "Eye to Eye" and "The Problem of Proof," which constitute the first two chapters of his book *Eye to Eye: The Quest for the New Paradigm* (Garden City, N.Y.: Anchor Books, 1983).

7. Theodore Roszak, *Where the Wasteland Ends: Politics and Transcendence in Postindustrial Society* (London: Faber and Faber, 1973), p. 400.

NOTES TO PAGES 252–254 ∘ 357

8. On the general question of the empathic incorporation of cosmologies or "world models," see Alex Comfort, *Reality and Empathy: Physics, Mind, and Science in the 21st Century* (Albany: State University of New York Press, 1984). By *empathy*, Comfort means an "incorporation going beyond intellectual assent" (p. xviii). See also Stephen Toulmin, *The Return to Cosmology: Postmodern Science and the Theology of Nature* (Berkeley: University of California Press, 1982), esp. the final chapter in which Toulmin explicitly links the cultivation of a cosmological sense of things—or what I am referring to as cosmologically based identification—with the development of "a genuine piety . . . toward creatures of other kinds: a piety that goes beyond the consideration of their usefulness to Humanity as instruments for the fulfillment of human ends" (p. 272).

9. George Sessions, "Ecocentrism and the Greens: Deep Ecology and the Environmental Task," *The Trumpeter* 5 (1988): 65–69, p. 67.

10. One could drown in the number of semi-popular and more technical books that could be cited at this point! A gentle approach might be more effective; thus, for a highly readable, comprehensive, *single* volume overview of the scientific view of the world, see Isaac Asimov's exemplary guide *Asimov's New Guide to Science*, rev. ed. (Harmondsworth, Middlesex: Penguin Books, 1987). For an excellent systems-oriented overview of the scientific view of the world, see Ervin Laszlo, *Evolution: The Grand Synthesis* (Boston: Shambhala, 1987).

11. See, for example, Richard Dawkins, *The Blind Watchmaker* (London: Penguin Books, 1988), esp. ch. 10: "The One True Tree of Life."

12. See Mark Ridley, *The Problems of Evolution* (Oxford: Oxford University Press, 1985), ch. 8: "How Can One Species Split into Two?"

13. For overviews of recent work on the origins of the physical cosmos, see Paul Davies, *God and the New Physics* (Harmondsworth, Middlesex: Penguin Books, 1984); Paul Davies, *Superforce: The Search for a Grand Unified Theory of Nature* (London: Unwin Paperbacks, 1985); John Gribbin, *In Search of the Big Bang: Quantum Physics and Cosmology* (London: Corgi Books, 1987); Alan H. Guth and Paul J. Steinhardt, "The Inflationary Universe," *Scientific American*, May 1984, pp. 90–102; Stephen W. Hawking, *A Brief History of Time: From The Big Bang to Black Holes* (New York: Bantam Books, 1988);

and Heinz R. Pagels, *Perfect Symmetry: The Search for the Beginning of Time* (New York: Bantam Books, 1986).

14. Stephen Young, "Root and Branch in the Groves of Academe," *New Scientist,* 23/30 December 1989, pp. 58–61, at pp. 58 and 61.

15. Rupert Sheldrake, *A New Science of Life: The Hypothesis of Formative Causation,* 2nd ed. (London: Paladin/Grafton Books, 1987); and Rupert Sheldrake, *The Presence of the Past: Morphic Resonance and the Habits of Nature* (New York: Vintage Books, 1989).

16. Arden Mahlberg, "Evidence of Collective Memory: A Test of Sheldrake's Theory," *Journal of Analytical Psychology* 32 (1987): 23–34. Sheldrake's two books provide overviews of the experimental work that has been performed to test his hypothesis thus far. The appendix in the second edition of *A New Science of Life* also contains an overview of the controversy that greeted the original publication of his hypothesis.

17. Sheldrake, *The Presence of the Past,* p. 294.

18. See Ervin Laszlo, *Evolution: The Grand Synthesis* (Boston: Shambhala, 1987).

19. Quoted in Bill Devall and George Sessions, *Deep Ecology: Living as if Nature Mattered,* p. 101.

20. Arne Naess, "Friendship, Strength of Emotion, and Freedom," in *Spinoza Herdacht 1677–1977* (no further details), pp. 11–19, at p. 13.

21. Ibid., p. 19.

22. See John Seed, Joanna Macy, Pat Fleming, and Arne Naess, *Thinking Like a Mountain: Towards a Council of All Beings* (Santa Cruz: New Society Publishers, 1988).

23. See, for example, Arne Naess, *Ecology, Community and Lifestyle: Outline of an Ecosophy,* ch. 7: "Ecosophy T: Unity and Diversity of Life" (the "Life is fundamentally one" quotation is from p. 166 of this chapter).

24. Quoted in Ramashray Roy's illuminating study in Gandhian thought: *Self and Society: A Study in Gandhian Thought* (New Delhi: Sage Publications, 1984), p. 73. Having met Gandhi as well as studied his thought, Ronald Duncan observes that "Gandhi's whole philosophy was based on the oneness or the wholeness of

life" (Mahatma Gandhi, *The Writings of Gandhi: A Selection,* ed. Ronand Duncan [London: Fontana/Collins, 1983] p. 29).

25. Quoted in Roy, *Self and Society,* p. 103. The chapter of Roy's book from which this quotation is taken is entitled "The Drop and the Ocean" and represents an extended discussion of the point that Gandhi makes in this quotation. It is interesting to note that Roy explicates Gandhi's metaphysics in this chapter in an extremely Naessian way (despite the fact that he does not appear to be familiar with Naess's work). Thus, Roy explains that, for Gandhi, "self-realization . . . is manifested in an endeavour to identify with the surging sea of life without—life that, in sum-total, is God. In seeking such an identity the self extends beyond its physical boundaries . . . [so that] society is not conceived as something out there but as an extended self" (p. 106).

26. Baruch Spinoza, *The Ethics and Selected Letters,* trans. Samuel Shirley and ed. Seymour Feldman (Indianapolis: Hackett Publishing Company, 1982).

27. Roger Scruton, *Spinoza,* Past Masters series (Oxford: Oxford University Press, 1986), p. 51.

28. From Spinoza's *On the Improvement of the Understanding* in *The Chief Works of Benedict de Spinoza,* trans. R. H. M. Elwes (New York: Dover, 1955), p. 6.

29. See David Bohm, interviewed by Renee Weber, "The Enfolding-Unfolding Universe: A Conversation with David Bohm," in *The Holographic Paradigm and Other Paradoxes: Exploring the Leading Edge of Science,* ed. Ken Wilber (Boulder: Shambhala, 1982), pp. 44–104, esp. pp. 56–57; and Arne Naess, "The Shallow and the Deep, Long-Range Ecology Movement: A Summary," p. 95.

30. See Warwick Fox, "The Deep Ecology–Ecofeminism Debate and its Parallels," esp. pp. 9–13.

31. See, for example, the following papers by J. Baird Callicott: "Traditional American Indian and Western European Attitudes Toward Nature: An Overview," *Environmental Ethics* 4 (1982): 293–318; "Intrinsic Value, Quantum Theory, and Environmental Ethics," *Environmental Ethics* 7 (1985): 257–75; "The Metaphysical Implications of Ecology"; and "Conceptual Resources for Environmental Ethics in Asian Traditions of Thought: A Propaedeutic," *Philosophy East and West* 37 (1987): 115–130.

32. Callicott, "Intrinsic Value, Quantum Theory, and Environmental Ethics," p. 275.

33. It is interesting to note that in a recent paper Callicott has also seen fit to distinguish his approach from that of deep ecology (Callicott, "The Case against Moral Pluralism," *Environmental Ethics* 12 [1990]: 99–124).

34. For various developments of this approach (often in the context of excellent overviews of other ecophilosophical approaches), see Callicott's papers "Non-Anthropocentric Value Theory and Environmental Ethics"; "Intrinsic Value, Quantum Theory, and Environmental Ethics"; "On the Intrinsic Value of Nonhuman Species," in *The Preservation of Species*, ed. Bryan G. Norton (Princeton, N.J.: Princeton University Press, 1986), pp. 138–172; "The Search for an Environmental Ethic"; and "The Conceptual Foundations of the Land Ethic," in *Companion to A Sand County Almanac: Interpretive and Critical Essays*, ed. J. Baird Callicott (Madison: The University of Wisconsin Press, 1987), pp. 186–217.

35. Michael Allaby, *The Oxford Dictionary of Natural History* (Oxford: Oxford University Press, 1985), s.v. "inclusive fitness."

36. Robyn Eckersley, *Emancipation Writ Large: Toward an Ecocentric Green Political Theory*, Ph.D. dissertation, University of Tasmania, 1990. Eckersley provides the most sustained application of an ecocentric perspective to political theory of which I am aware. (I assume that her study will be forthcoming in book form.) The general theme of what Eckersley refers to as "emancipation writ large" is also pursued in my paper "The Deep Ecology–Ecofeminism Debate and its Parallels."

37. Arne Naess, "Intuition, Intrinsic Value, and Deep Ecology," *The Ecologist* 14 (1984): 201–3, p. 202. Naess fully accepts that "any realistic praxis necessitates some killing, exploitation, and suppression" ("The Shallow and the Deep, Long-Range Ecology Movement: A Summary," p. 95).

38. Arne Naess, "The Deep Ecological Movement: Some Philosophical Aspects," p. 28.

39. Dogen Zenji (1200–1253), quoted in Robert Aitken, "Gandhi, Dogen and Deep Ecology," appendix C in Devall and Sessions, *Deep Ecology*, p. 232; from *The Way of Everyday Life: Zen Master*

Dogen's Genjokoan with Commentary, trans. Hakuyu Taizan Maezumi (Los Angeles: Center Publications, 1978), n.p.

APPENDIX B. THE EMERGENCE OF TRANSPERSONAL
PSYCHOLOGY

1. Josef Breuer and Sigmund Freud, *Studies on Hysteria,* trans. and ed. by James and Alix Strachey, ed. assist. by Angela Richards, The Pelican Freud Library, vol. 3 (Harmondsworth, Middlesex: Penguin Books, 1974), pp. 392–93.

2. *The Encyclopedia of Psychology,* ed. Raymond J. Corsini (New York: John Wiley, 1984), s.v. "Psychological Health," by D. H. Shapiro.

3. Abraham H. Maslow, *Motivation and Personality* (New York: Harper and Brothers, 1954), p. 354.

4. Abraham H. Maslow, *Toward a Psychology of Being* (Princeton: D. Van Nostrand, 1962), p. 5.

5. Maslow, *Motivation and Personality,* pp. 359 and 353.

6. Anthony J. Sutich, "Transpersonal Therapy," *The Journal of Transpersonal Psychology* 5 (1973): 1–6, p. 1.

7. Anthony J. Sutich, "Some Considerations Regarding Transpersonal Psychology," *The Journal of Transpersonal Psychology* 1 (1969): 11–20.

8. Maureen O'Hara, "When I Use the Term *Humanistic Psychology . . . ,*" *Journal of Humanistic Psychology* 29 (1989): 263–73, p. 270. This issue of the *Journal of Humanistic Psychology* (Spring 1989) contains a running discussion on the nature of humanistic psychology (and, by implication, on the nature of transpersonal psychology) by some of the leading contributors to humanistic psychology.

9. Ibid., pp. 270–72.

10. Anthony J. Sutich, "The Emergence of the Transpersonal Orientation: A Personal Account," *The Journal of Transpersonal Psychology* 8 (1976): 5–19, p. 7. For similar comments from someone who followed Sutich in editing both the *Journal of Humanistic Psychology* and *The Journal of Transpersonal Psychology* respectively, see Miles A. Vich, "The Origins and Growth of Transpersonal Psychology," *Journal of Humanistic Psychology* 30(2) (1990): 47–50.

11. Sutich, "The Emergence of the Transpersonal Orientation," pp. 7–8.

12. Abraham H. Maslow, *The Farther Reaches of Human Nature* (New York: The Viking Press, 1971), p. 282.

13. The quotations from Maslow in this and the following paragraph are from ibid., pp. 287–88 and 292. On the distinction between *egoism* and *egotism:* "Egoistic refers to those who view themselves as at the center of things and who have great concern for their own self-interest; egotistic refers to those who tend to have, in addition, an unrealistic and obnoxious sense of self-importance. One can be very egoistic and have little in the way of egotism and egotistic behavior." Arthur S. Reber, *The Penguin Dictionary of Psychology,* (Harmondsworth, Middlesex: Penguin, 1985), s.v. "egotistic(al)."

14. See especially the chapters entitled "Various Meanings of Transcendence" and "Theory Z" in *The Farther Reaches of Human Nature,* pp. 269–79 and 280–95 respectively.

15. Abraham H. Maslow, *Toward a Psychology of Being,* 2nd ed. (Princeton: D. Van Nostrand, 1968), pp. iii–iv.

16. Sutich, "The Emergence of the Transpersonal Orientation," p. 16. See also Miles A. Vich, "Some Historical Sources of the Term 'Transpersonal,' " *The Journal of Transpersonal Psychology* 20 (1989): 107–10.

17. Sutich's contributions to the institutional development of both humanistic psychology and transpersonal psychology (including the establishment of the two leading journals in these fields) is all the more remarkable for the fact that, as a result of progressive physical deterioration following a baseball accident at the age of twelve, his formal education ceased at ninth grade, and he was totally physically disabled, unable even to use his hands, from the age of eighteen on (i.e., since 1925). See the eulogies for Sutich in the *Journal of Humanistic Psychology* 16(3) (1976).

18. For an excellent introduction to the work of these and other authors, and for a guide to further reading, see Roger N. Walsh and Frances Vaughan, eds., *Beyond Ego: Transpersonal Dimensions in Psychology* (Los Angeles: J. P. Tarcher, 1980). For shorter introductions to transpersonal psychology, see *The Encyclopedia of Psychology,* s.v. "Transpersonal Psychology (I)," by N. Sunberg and C. Keutzer, and "Transpersonal Psychology (II)," by Roger Walsh.

NOTES TO PAGES 298-299 ○ 363

The three main journals that carry contributions on transpersonal psychology are the *Journal of Humanistic Psychology, ReVision,* and *The Journal of Transpersonal Psychology.* The Fall 1989 issue of the *Journal of Humanistic Psychology* contains a running debate on transpersonal psychology of the Wilberian variety.

A few of the most significant contributions to transpersonal psychology that have appeared since the publication of Walsh and Vaughan's *Beyond Ego* include Ken Wilber, *Eye to Eye: The Quest for the New Paradigm* (Garden City, N.Y.: Anchor Books, 1983); and Stanislav Grof, *Beyond the Brain: Birth, Death, and Transcendence in Psychotherapy* (Albany: State University of New York Press, 1985). One should also mention in this context a significant book by John H. Crook entitled *The Evolution of Human Consciousness* (Oxford: Clarendon Press, 1980), which does not seem to have been noticed by transpersonal theorists. Fritjof Capra provides a clear overview of the emergence of humanistic and transpersonal psychology and briefly reviews the work of Grof and Wilber in a chapter entitled "Journeys Beyond Space and Time" in his book *The Turning Point: Science, Society, and the Rising Culture* (New York: Bantam Books, 1983), pp. 359-88. For a stimulating intellectual autobiography by Ken Wilber, see his paper "Odyssey: A Personal Inquiry into Humanistic and Transpersonal Psychology," *Journal of Humanistic Psychology* 22(1) (1982): 57-90.

19. William N. Thetford and Roger Walsh, "Theories of Personality and Psychopathology: Schools Derived from Psychology and Philosophy," in *Comprehensive Textbook of Psychiatry,* 4th ed., ed. H. I. Kaplan and B. J. Sadock (Baltimore: Williams and Wilkins, 1985), pp. 459-81, p. 481.

20. For an introduction to Eastern psychologies from a transpersonal perspective, see *The Encyclopedia of Psychology,* s.v. "Asian Psychologies," by Roger Walsh.

21. *The Encyclopedia of Psychology,* s.v. "Transpersonal Psychology (II)," by Roger Walsh.

Further Reading

Ecology and the Ecological Crisis

Allaby, Michael. *Green Facts: The Greenhouse Effect and Other Key Issues.* London: Hamlyn, 1989.

Brown, Lester R., project director. *State of the World 1984: A Worldwatch Institute Report on Progress Toward a Sustainable Society.* New York: W. W. Norton, 1984, and annually thereafter.

Brundtland, Gro Harlem, chairperson. *Our Common Future: World Commission on Environment and Development.* Oxford: Oxford University Press, 1987.

Ehrlich, Paul R. *The Machinery of Nature: The Living World Around Us—and How it Works.* New York: Simon and Schuster, 1986.

Ehrlich, Paul R., and Ehrlich, Anne H. *Extinction: The Causes and Consequences of the Disappearance of Species.* New York: Ballantine, 1983.

Ehrlich, Paul R., and Ehrlich, Anne H. *Earth.* New York: Franklin Watts, 1987.

Goldsmith, Edward, and Hildyard, Nicholas, gen. eds. *Battle for the Earth: Today's Key Environmental Issues.* London: Mitchell Beazley, 1988; Brookvale, New South Wales: Child and Associates, 1988.

Lovelock, James. *The Ages of Gaia: A Biography of Our Living Earth.* Oxford: Oxford University Press, 1988.

Myers, Norman, gen. ed. *The Gaia Atlas of Planet Management.* London: Pan Books, 1985.

Scientific American, September 1989 (Special issue: "Managing Planet Earth").

Time, 2 January 1989 ("Planet of the Year: Endangered Earth" issue).

Environmentalism and Ecopolitics

Bookchin, Murray. *Toward an Ecological Society.* Montreal: Black Rose Books, 1980.

366 ∘ FURTHER READING

Bunyard, Peter, and Morgan-Grenville, Fern, eds. *The Green Alternative: Guide to Good Living.* London: Methuen, 1987.

Fox, Stephen R. *John Muir and his Legacy: The American Conservation Movement.* Boston: Little, Brown and Co., 1981.

Irvine, Sandy, and Ponton, Alec. *A Green Manifesto: Policies for a Green Future.* London: Optima, 1988.

McCormick, John. *The Global Environmental Movement: Reclaiming Paradise.* London: Belhaven Press, 1989.

Milbrath, Lester W. *Envisioning a Sustainable Society: Learning Our Way Out.* Albany: State University of New York Press, 1989.

Nash, Roderick. *Wilderness and the American Mind.* 3rd ed. New Haven, Conn.: Yale University Press, 1982.

O'Riordan, Timothy. *Environmentalism.* 2nd ed. London: Pion, 1981. Originally published, London: Pion, 1976.

Paehlke, Robert. *Environmentalism and the Future of Progressive Politics.* New Haven, Conn.: Yale University Press, 1989.

Parkin, Sara. *Green Parties: An International Guide.* London: Heretic Books, 1989.

Pepper, David. *The Roots of Modern Environmentalism.* London: Croom Helm, 1984.

Porritt, Jonathon. *Seeing Green: The Politics of Ecology Explained.* Oxford: Basil Blackwell, 1984.

Porritt, Jonathon, and Winner, David. *The Coming of the Greens.* London: Fontana/Collins, 1988.

Rodman, John. "Paradigm Change in Political Science: An Ecological Perspective." *American Behavioral Scientist* 24 (1980): 49–78.

Roszak, Theodore. *Person/Planet: The Creative Disintegration of Industrial Society.* London: Victor Gollancz, 1979.

Spretnak, Charlene, and Capra, Fritjof. *Green Politics: The Global Promise.* London: Paladin/Grafton Books, 1985.

Tokar, Brian. *The Green Alternative: Creating an Ecological Future.* San Pedro, Calif.: R. and E. Miles, 1987.

Worster, Donald. *Nature's Economy: The Roots of Ecology.* San Francisco: Sierra Club Books, 1977. New edition: *Nature's Economy: A History of Ecological Ideas.* Cambridge: Cambridge University Press, 1985.

Young, John. *Post Environmentalism.* London: Belhaven Press, 1990.

Ecophilosophy in General

Attfield, Robin. *The Ethics of Environmental Concern*. Oxford: Basil Blackwell, 1983.

Birch, Charles, and Cobb, John B., Jr. *The Liberation of Life: From the Cell to the Community*. Cambridge: Cambridge University Press, 1981.

Borrelli, Peter. "The Ecophilosophers." *The Amicus Journal*, Spring 1988, pp. 30–39.

Brennan, Andrew. *Thinking About Nature: An Investigation of Nature, Value, and Ecology*. London: Routledge, 1988.

Callicott, J. Baird. "Animal Liberation: A Triangular Affair," *Environmental Ethics* 2 (1980): 311–38.

Callicott, J. Baird. "Non-Anthropocentric Value Theory and Environmental Ethics." *American Philosophical Quarterly* 21 (1984): 299–309.

Callicott, J. Baird. Review of *The Case for Animal Rights*, by Tom Regan. *Environmental Ethics* 7 (1985): 365–72.

Callicott, J. Baird. "The Metaphysical Implications of Ecology." *Environmental Ethics* 8 (1986): 301–16. Reprinted in *Nature in Asian Traditions of Thought: Essays in Environmental Philosophy*. Edited by J. Baird Callicott and Roger T. Ames. Albany: State University of New York Press, 1989.

Callicott, J. Baird. "The Search For an Environmental Ethic." In *Matters of Life and Death*, pp. 381–424. 2nd ed. Edited by Tom Regan. New York: Random House, 1986.

Davis, Donald E. *Ecophilosophy: A Field Guide to the Literature*. San Pedro, California: R. and E. Miles, 1989.

Evernden, Neil. *The Natural Alien: Humankind and Environment*. Toronto: University of Toronto Press, 1985.

Frankena, William K. "Ethics and the Environment." In *Ethics and Problems of the 21st Century*, pp. 3–20. Edited by Kenneth E. Goodpaster and Kenneth M. Sayre. Notre Dame, Ind.: University of Notre Dame Press, 1979.

Godfrey-Smith, William. "The Value of Wilderness." *Environmental Ethics* 1 (1979): 309–319.

Goodpaster, Kenneth E. "On Being Morally Considerable." *The Journal of Philosophy* 75 (1978): 308–25.

Hargrove, Eugene C. *Foundations of Environmental Ethics.* Englewood Cliffs, N.J.: Prentice Hall, 1989.

Heffernan, James D. "The Land Ethic: A Critical Appraisal." *Environmental Ethics* 4 (1982): 235–47.

Johnson, Edward. "Treating the Dirt: Environmental Ethics and Moral Theory." In *Earthbound: New Introductory Essays in Environmental Ethics,* pp. 336–65. Edited by Tom Regan. New York: Random House, 1984.

Katz, Eric. "Environmental Ethics: A Select Annotated Bibliography, 1983–87." *Research in Philosophy and Technology* 9 (1989): 251–85.

Leopold, Aldo. *A Sand County Almanac.* Oxford: Oxford University Press, 1949; reprint ed., Oxford: Oxford University Press, 1981.

Livingston, John A. *The Fallacy of Wildlife Conservation.* Toronto: McClelland and Stewart, 1981.

McLaughlin, Andrew. "Images and Ethics of Nature." *Environmental Ethics* 7 (1985): 293–319.

Nash, Roderick F. *The Rights of Nature: A History of Environmental Ethics.* Madison: The University of Wisconsin Press, 1989.

Passmore, John. *Man's Responsibility for Nature: Ecological Problems and Western Traditions.* 2nd ed. London: Duckworth, 1980.

Regan, Tom. *The Case for Animal Rights.* Berkeley: University of California Press, 1983.

Rodman, John. "The Liberation of Nature?" *Inquiry* 20 (1977): 83–131.

Rodman, John. "Four Forms of Ecological Consciousness Reconsidered." In *Ethics and the Environment,* pp. 82–92. Edited by Donald Scherer and Thomas Attig. Englewood Cliffs, N.J.: Prentice-Hall, 1983.

Rolston, Holmes, III. *Environmental Ethics: Duties to and Values in the Natural World.* Philadelphia: Temple University Press, 1988.

Singer, Peter. *Animal Liberation: A New Ethics for Our Treatment of Animals.* New York: Avon Books, 1977.

Skolimowski, Henryk. *Eco-Philosophy: Designing New Tactics for Living.* London: Marion Boyars, 1981.

Stone, Christopher D. *Earth and Other Ethics: The Case for Moral Pluralism.* New York: Harper and Row, 1987.

FURTHER READING ∘ 369

Taylor, Paul W. *Respect for Nature: A Theory of Environmental Ethics.* Princeton: Princeton University Press, 1986.

Warren, Karen J. "Feminism and Ecology: Making Connections." *Environmental Ethics* 9 (1987): 3–20.

White, Lynn, Jr. "The Historical Roots of Our Ecologic Crisis" and "Continuing the Conversation." In *Western Man and Environmental Ethics: Attitudes Toward Nature and Technology,* pp. 18–30 and 55–64 respectively. Edited by Ian G. Barbour. Reading, Mass.: Addison-Wesley, 1973.

Deep Ecology in Particular

Devall, Bill. "The Deep Ecology Movement." *Natural Resources Journal* 20 (1980): 299–322.

Devall, Bill. *Simple in Means, Rich in Ends: Practicing Deep Ecology.* Salt Lake City: Peregrine Smith Books, 1988.

Devall, Bill, and Sessions, George. *Deep Ecology: Living as if Nature Mattered.* Salt Lake City: Peregrine Smith Books, 1985.

Drengson, Alan R. *Beyond Environmental Crisis: From Technocratic to Planetary Person.* New York: Peter Lang, 1989.

Fox, Warwick. "The Deep Ecology–Ecofeminism Debate and its Parallels." *Environmental Ethics* 11 (1989): 5–25.

Naess, Arne. "The Shallow and the Deep, Long-Range Ecology Movement: A Summary." *Inquiry* 16 (1973): 95–100.

Naess, Arne. "Identification as a Source of Deep Ecological Attitudes." In *Deep Ecology,* pp. 256–70. Edited by Michael Tobias. San Diego: Avant Books, 1985.

Naess, Arne. "The Deep Ecological Movement: Some Philosophical Aspects." *Philosophical Inquiry* 8 (1986): 10–31.

Naess, Arne. "Self-Realization: An Ecological Approach to Being in the World." *The Trumpeter* 4(3) (1987): 35–42.

Naess, Arne. *Ecology, Community and Lifestyle: Outline of an Ecosophy.* Translated and revised by David Rothenberg. Cambridge: Cambridge University Press, 1989.

Sessions, George. "Anthropocentrism and the Environmental Crisis." *Humboldt Journal of Social Relations* 2 (1974): 71–81.

Sessions, George. "Spinoza and Jeffers on Man in Nature." *Inquiry* 20 (1977): 481–528.

Sessions, George. "Shallow and Deep Ecology: A Review of the Philosophical Literature." In *Ecological Consciousness: Essays from the Earthday X Colloquium,* pp. 391–462. Edited by Robert C. Schultz and J. Donald Hughes. Washington, DC: University Press of America, 1981.

Sessions, George. "The Deep Ecology Movement: A Review." *Environmental Review* 11 (1987): 105–25.

Zimmerman, Michael E. "Implications of Heidegger's Thought for Deep Ecology." *The Modern Schoolman* 64 (1986): 19–43.

Zimmerman, Michael E. "Feminism, Deep Ecology, and Environmental Ethics." *Environmental Ethics* 9 (1987): 21–44.

(For a more complete listing of sources on deep ecology see appendix A.)

Index

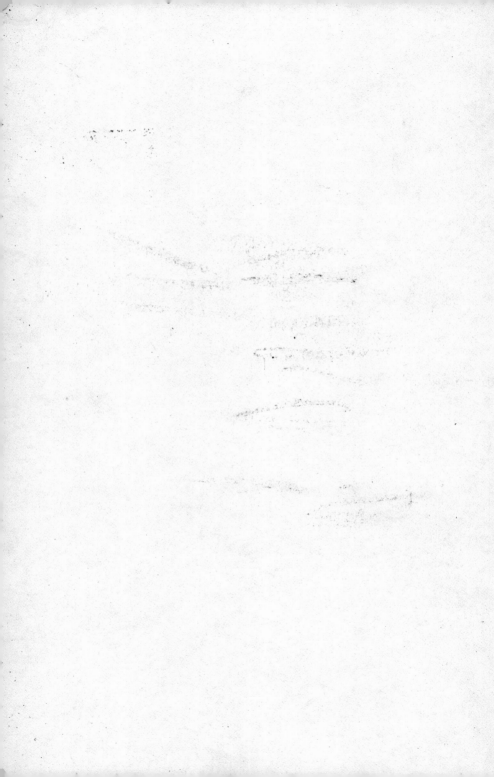